Beginning MySQL Database Design and Optimization:

From Novice to Professional

JON STEPHENS AND CHAD RUSSELL

Apress®

Beginning MySQL Database Design and Optimization: From Novice to Professional
Copyright © 2004 by Jon Stephens and Chad Russell

ISBN (pbk): 1-59059-332-4

Printed and bound in the United States of America 9 8 7 6 5 4 3 2

Lead Editors: Dominic Shakeshaft and Jason Gilmore
Technical Reviewer: Mike Hillyer
Editorial Board: Steve Anglin, Dan Appleman, Ewan Buckingham, Gary Cornell, Tony Davis,
    Jason Gilmore, Chris Mills, Dominic Shakeshaft, Jim Sumser
Project Manager: Tracy Brown Collins
Copy Edit Manager: Nicole LeClerc
Copy Editors: Ami Knox and Marilyn Smith
Production Manager: Kari Brooks-Copony
Production Editor: Katie Stence
Compositor: Dina Quan
Proofreader: Christy Wagner
Indexer: Kevin Broccoli
Artist: Kinetic Publishing Services, LLC
Cover Designer: Kurt Krames
Manufacturing Manager: Tom Debolski

Distributed to the book trade in the United States by Springer-Verlag New York, Inc., 233 Spring Street, 6th Floor, New York, NY 10013, and outside the United States by Springer-Verlag GmbH & Co. KG, Tiergartenstr. 17, 69112 Heidelberg, Germany.

In the United States: phone 1-800-SPRINGER, fax 201-348-4505, e-mail orders@springer-ny.com, or visit http://www.springer-ny.com. Outside the United States: fax +49 6221 345229, e-mail orders@springer.de, or visit http://www.springer.de.

For information on translations, please contact Apress directly at 2560 Ninth Street, Suite 219, Berkeley, CA 94710. Phone 510-549-5930, fax 510-549-5939, e-mail info@apress.com, or visit http://www.apress.com.

The source code for this book is available to readers at http://www.apress.com in the Downloads section. You will need to answer questions pertaining to this book in order to successfully download the code.

Contents at a Glance

Contents

About the Authors

Jon Stephens has contributed as an author to seven previous books on Web development and related technologies, including *Usable Shopping Carts, Professional PHP Web Services, Professional JavaScript (Second Edition)*, and *Professional PHP 4 Web Development Solutions*, and has served as a technical reviewer of a dozen or so more on a number of development topics, including PHP, MySQL, XML, JavaScript, and Visual Basic. He was also one of the original developers of phpUDDI, a PHP Web Services library  that has since been incorporated into PEAR as PEAR::UDDI. His articles on MySQL, DOM programming, and other topics have appeared in *International PHP* magazine. Jon studied mathematics in university and started his professional programming career in the early 1990s teaching computers how to operate radio stations. Originally from the USA, Jon now resides in Brisbane, Australia, where he works as a PHP developer for Snapsoft Pty Ltd. and lives with his wife, their daughter, and numerous computers and cats. His chief vices are coffee, cigarettes, and cheap paperback novels.

Chad Russell is currently a contract software developer for staffing industry software leader LiquidMedium, LLC and founder of Russell Information Technologies, Inc. (RIT), an enterprise software startup. Chad has worked on numerous enterprise-level projects over the past 5 years, primarily developing and integrating PHP and MySQL-based applications. He is currently busy with RIT developing enterprise-level, cross-platform software solutions and providing IT consulting. Chad, who resides in Jacksonville,  Florida, is very active in his church where he has been a member for 23 years. His hobbies include music (playing bass guitar), writing, fishing, hunting, and programming.

About the
Technical Reviewer

Mike Hillyer has been using MySQL for more than three years. In that time, he has received both the MySQL Core and MySQL Professional certifications and has spoken at the 2003 and 2004 MySQL User Conferences. Mike is the webmaster of VB/MYSQL.com (`http://www.vbmysql.com`), a site dedicated to helping Visual Basic developers use MySQL, and volunteers as the resident MySQL expert in the Ask the Experts section of SearchDatabase.com (`http://www.searchdatabase.com`). Mike is also the top-ranked MySQL expert at Experts Exchange (`http://www.experts-exchange.com`). In April 2004, Mike joined MySQL AB as a member of the documentation team and now spends his days writing in his basement and trying to take over the world. So far Mike has taken over the basement and is currently battling for the main floor of his house, but his wife seems to be winning.

Acknowledgments

A GREAT MANY PEOPLE HAVE HELPED as MySQL and this book have grown and evolved over the last 10 months, and some of them have labored very hard indeed to bring you a quality addition to your development library.

Dominic Shakeshaft and Jason Gilmore both did an excellent job of technical editing. Dom encouraged me not only to provide good information, but to produce a good narrative as well. Jason worked extensively on Chapters 7 and 8; his close attention to technical matters undoubtedly improved these chapters greatly over the original drafts. Marilyn Smith and Ami Knox, our copy editors, each contributed by exercising a fine eye for detail. Our project manager, Tracy Brown Collins, deserves special mention for keeping it all hanging together, even in the face of widely divergent schedules and time zones. I have grown to admire and respect all of these people for their competence, dedication, and Just Being Good Folks To Work With. Also at Apress: Chris Mills, Katie Stence, Tina Nielsen, Doris Wong, and Gary Cornell.

Thanks to Chad Russell for being a good co-author and a great friend and collaborator.

Mike Hillyer served as our technical reviewer and was outstanding in that role. (He went to work for MySQL AB about halfway through the piece—this should tell you something about his caliber.) I would also like to thank the following individuals at MySQL AB for taking the time to respond to my questions and to point me in the direction of the right answers: Zak Greant, Peter Gulutzman, and Oleksandr Byelkin. In addition, Sasha Pachev at MySQL AB reviewed some material for an earlier writing project that Chad and I worked on but which was never published; some of this later found its way into the present book.

I'm also grateful to Scott, Nathanael, Kenny, Mark, and Cyril at Snapsoft, for putting up with my absences from the office (and the fact I sometimes forgot to announce these ahead of time).

I'd also like to mention some people who've provided me with a great deal of moral and other support over these last few months: Gordy in Edinburgh, Luciana Maria in São Paulo, Sam in Indianapolis, Rachel in New Haven, Jody in Phoenix, JMike in Dallas, Carl in Ljusdal, Dawn in Denver, Dilip in Bangalore, Beatriz in Knoxville, Ana in Ciudad Obregón, Arvind in Buffalo, and Irishka in Moscow; everyone at Hiveminds.Info; people who asked good questions or gave good answers at Experts Exchange; the Thomas family; and my mother and father.

Portions of Chapters 7 and 8 appeared in a somewhat different form in Issues 05.04, 06.04, and 01.05 of *International PHP* magazine, copyright © 2004 Software & Support Verlag GmbH, Frankfurt/Main, and are reused in this book with the kind permission of the publisher. Our thanks go to Editor-in-Chief Indu Britto for helping to make this possible.

Jon Stephens

Brisbane, 16 September 2004

Many thanks to the following—without their help, this opportunity would not have been possible for me: God, who makes all things possible; and Jon Stephens, for being the greatest co-author to work with and for all his hard work on this project! Special thanks to my darling Kim for putting up with me while I worked to meet deadlines. Thanks to everyone at Apress for such a wonderful opportunity! My key to success—Matthew 6:33.

Chad Russell

Introduction

THE NEED TO ACCESS DATA through an application is a constant, rather than a variable, in programming. It's probably safe to say that nearly any nontrivial application requires some form of storage and retrieval of data, and for any application of significant size and scope, this means using a relational database. MySQL is a very popular choice because it is

- Available free of charge; anyone can download MySQL from http://www.mysql.com for the price of the Internet connection.

- Fast, robust, and scalable; while MySQL is optimized for speed, it still can be (and is) used for datastores containing hundreds and even thousands of tables holding millions of records.

- Easy to install on the most common computing platforms, with executable binaries available for Windows, Linux, Solaris, Mac OS, and others. Since the source code is freely available, MySQL can be compiled for platforms for which executables don't exist, as needed.

- Extremely portable between platforms; it's not difficult to move MySQL databases between machines, and MySQL itself behaves very nearly identically on all supported platforms.

However, all too many developers—even seasoned ones—often end up throwing away MySQL's speed and other advantages due to poorly designed, inefficient databases. In many cases, they create extra work for their application (as well as themselves) due to poor choices throughout the scope of the database creation and through the way they perform operations to retrieve their data.

Given MySQL's popularity with web-based applications with PHP, we will be focusing heavily on this area. However, we will also look at other scenarios in which MySQL is employed, and most of our discussion will apply equally well to programming languages other than PHP.

What This Book Is About

This book focuses on four main themes:

- **Fundamentals**: Knowing these can save you time and trouble in creating and using MySQL databases. We'll cover MySQL query basics, data types and table types, normalization and table indexes, functions, operators, and more. Obviously a lot of this material is discussed elsewhere, but we try to present it with a special emphasis on building fast, compact databases and with a view to making it easier to use them in your applications in an efficient manner.

- **Problem areas relating to design and performance**: We'll talk about a number of these, including poor usage of data and table types. In Chapter 3, we'll get into actual database design issues as we discuss normalization and indexes—proper usage of these can speed up database performance remarkably. In Chapter 4, we'll examine MySQL's wealth of built-in functions and logical and flow-control operators, and in Chapter 5, we'll cover joins and temporary tables. All of these can help you minimize redundancy in your database and streamline queries. In Chapter 6, we'll also discuss some aspects of performance that don't relate directly to database design, including configuration and networking issues.

- **Effective use of MySQL in applications**: We'll discuss MySQL programming interfaces in Chapter 7, but we keep this issue in mind throughout this book. Part of the reason we'll spend so much time and space in earlier chapters on MySQL data types, normalization, functions, and operators is that one of the most common causes of choke points in database applications is the use of application logic to filter and process results when this can be done by the database before the data ever gets to the application.

- **New features in upcoming MySQL versions**: Over the next year or two, there will be a lot of changes in MySQL as versions 4.1 and 5.0 become ready for production. In Chapter 8, we'll examine the most important of these and show you how, once they're available, you'll be able to leverage them to write better (and often fewer) queries and do more work within the database. We'll help you get ready for these, and to use them to make your MySQL applications faster, more efficient, and more portable.

Fundamentals

While this book isn't intended for raw beginners, we do want to accommodate those whose experience with MySQL has been limited, or those who are migrating from another database. With this in mind, we'll conduct a review of SQL and MySQL basics in Chapter 1, including how to connect to MySQL and the syntax for the most common sorts of queries. We'll also discuss naming conventions, which has always seemed to us to be somewhat neglected. In Chapter 2, we'll cover all of the MySQL data types (including a couple that are unique to MySQL) and table types, and give you some tips as to when each type is most appropriate. Knowing when to use which data types can save you development time, database space, and processing time.

Problem Areas

In this book, we will help developers overcome problems in several key areas.

Poor Datatype and Database Design Decisions

We'll discuss some general good principles of database design such as efficient and appropriate use of datatypes and normalization as applied in MySQL. We'll show you ways to help you both recognize poor database design choices and do something about them.

It can be all too easy to rush into a project, and choose the improper column types, or even the wrong table types. Making poor database design choices can create a larger overhead for your application, and can hamper the performance of MySQL and your application.

We'll also point out some "gotchas" having to do with datatypes and column types. These are not necessarily bugs in MySQL; often they're features that are mentioned in the MySQL documentation but which are frequently overlooked, and then come back to haunt developers later when they result in behavior that's not expected.

Overreliance on Application Code

Overall efficiency can be greatly increased by getting the database to do your work instead of application code by writing queries that return only the data your application actually needs. It can be easy sometimes to forget that you can return the data you need directly from the database, without having to manipulate it in the application code. This can increase the speed of your application and make matters much simpler and easier on the application side.

Many application developers, including some of considerable experience, do not realize just how powerful a language SQL really is. A great deal of application logic can be subsumed into SQL logic. We'll look at how to write complex joins and to make effective use of

- MySQL string and math functions

- User variables

- CASE ... WHEN ... THEN and IN clauses

- Temporary tables

- Logical and mathematical operators

All of these features will help to cut down on the number of queries that are needed to get the data you're looking for. Knowing when and how to use these techniques in your queries can often help reduce the amount of overhead in your application by reducing multiple queries into one structured query.

Overuse, Under-Use, and Misuse of Indexes

The proper use of indexes can greatly enhance performance of MySQL and lower the processing times for queries. However, improper use of indexes can cause problems with your application. For example, many developers make the assumption that every column should be indexed and do so automatically, not realizing that they're simply using up memory for indexes that don't offer any advantage. Others simply don't understand the role that indexes play and end up writing unnecessarily complex code that, in essence, reinvents the wheel.

Beyond Design: Performance Tuning Basics

Optimization of database and table schemas, while extremely important, is by no means the only area in which improvements can be made to the performance of MySQL and applications making use of it. A great deal of useful information for pinpointing choke points and other inefficiencies can be obtained from MySQL logs and from server and status variables. Unanticipated bottlenecks and other problems can be uncovered, and knowledge of these can help solve performance issues that are not apparent on the surface of the application. In Chapter 6, we'll look at these in depth and provide some suggestions for making changes in MySQL's configuration files to improve performance in a number of different scenarios.

Looking Ahead (and Behind)

There have been quite a few changes in MySQL with the release of version 4.0; more are in store for the 4.1.x series of releases (version 4.1-alpha having been available for several months at the time of this writing), and even more new features are anticipated in MySQL 5.0 when it's released sometime in 2005 or 2006. Planning ahead and being aware of these changes can ease upgrade issues when you move your application to newer versions of MySQL.

Our "target" version of MySQL in this book is 4.0/4.1, as version 4.0 has been in production release for nearly a year as of this writing, and 4.1 is expected to reach production status before the end of 2004. However, as there are many commercial applications and web hosts still using MySQL 3.23, we'll try to indicate where a feature is new or exhibits significantly new behavior in MySQL 4.0 and 4.1.

As for what's ahead, we'll look at subqueries (also known as nested queries) in MySQL 4.1, as well as index caching and some changes in column types. The introduction of stored procedures and views in MySQL 5.0 represents a quantum leap for MySQL developers and administrators. We'll give you a solid grounding in these features, explain what they'll mean for you and your projects, and provide examples that you can try out for yourself using the pre-release versions already available. We'll also give you our best guess as to what you might expect to see in MySQL 5.1 once development on that series begins.

Who This Book Is For

You should be able to derive some benefit from reading this book if you fit into one or more of the following categories:

- Current MySQL users who can write basic SELECT, DELETE, and UPDATE queries and who want to design their own databases or make improvements in the ones they're already using

- Developers who've worked with database-enabled applications and want to improve the efficiency of their MySQL-based applications

- Developers who haven't worked with database applications before and are seeking to get started in understanding databases and how to write for them

- Users of other databases who are looking to add MySQL to their repertoire or to port existing applications to MySQL from another database

There are some things that *won't* be covered in this book:

- Beginner-level "What is a database/table/query?" sort of questions. You don't necessarily have to be experienced with MySQL in order to derive some benefit from this book; experience with another RDBMS will do. But you should be comfortable with basic database concepts and SQL syntax, or be ready to do a little supplemental reading on your own to familiarize yourself with these.

- MySQL installation—we assume that you already have access to a working MySQL installation, or are prepared to handle the setup on your own. If you're new to MySQL, this is not nearly as heartless as it might sound: as we've noted, MySQL AB provides binaries and installers for a number of platforms, and basic installation and setup is quite easy if you're using Windows, Linux, or Mac OS X.

- User and privilege administration issues. Most of the examples in this book assume that the user already has the necessary privileges to run the queries shown. Some of the issues covered with respect to logs, system and status variables, and configuration assume that you have root or superuser access. Probably the simplest way to deal with all of these issues for purposes of testing the examples provided is to install a "throwaway" copy of MySQL on your desktop and work with that.

- Transactions and replication. While both of these are important for building robust MySQL-enabled applications—and it has been argued that no "real" database doesn't make use of transactions—they really fall outside the scope that we set for ourselves when planning this book. We do discuss transactions in Chapter 5 and provide some programming examples using them in Chapter 7, but they aren't part of our main focus.

We hope that you'll find this book useful in getting the most out of MySQL.

### CHAPTER 1

Review of MySQL Basics

Before we delve into database design principles, we're going to review some MySQL basics, just to make sure that we're all roughly on the same page.

We'll start by looking at how you can connect to the MySQL database server, because that's the first thing you'll need to do if you want to be able to work with MySQL. While it's not our intention to cover administration issues in this book, we do want to make sure that you're aware of MySQL's basic requirements in this regard, because some other databases are not as rigorous as MySQL when it comes to authentication.

Once you've connected to MySQL, you'll be working with databases, tables, and columns; of course, you'll need to be able to identify these quickly and easily. Because there appears to be a lot of disparity in naming conventions for these items, we'll talk about MySQL's rules regarding identifiers, including allowed characters, case-sensitivity, and use of reserved keywords. We'll also suggest some guidelines for you to follow in naming your tables, columns, aliases, and so forth.

The rest of this chapter will consist of a review of MySQL's syntax and other rules for writing basic queries. Even if you've used MySQL before, you might want to scan this syntax review section, as there have been a few changes in MySQL 4.0 and 4.1 that you might not be aware of and can use to your advantage, such as new syntax for deleting rows from multiple tables.

We'll look at how to create and delete tables using the CREATE and DROP commands. Next, we'll go over how to retrieve data from tables using SELECT queries. In our discussion of SELECT, we'll also show you how you can order results using an ORDER BY clause and how to group related records together with GROUP BY. Then we'll cover the basics for getting data into database tables with INSERT. Sometimes, you need to change records that are already present in a table; we'll discuss how this can be done using the UPDATE command. Finally, we'll review how you can delete one or more records from a table, which can be done with DELETE. In each case, we'll provide a formal definition of the command, including its most common and useful variants where applicable, and then provide some examples so you can see just how it's used.

If any of the information in this chapter is completely new to you, you should probably consult a good introductory book or tutorial. One of the better books that we can suggest is Martin Kofler's *The Definitive Guide to MySQL, Second Edition* (Apress, 2003), which covers MySQL 4.0.

How to Connect to MySQL

Connecting to MySQL via the command line is easy. Simply type in the following command, where `username` indicates the account username:

```
> mysql -u <username> -p
```

If the MySQL server is running on a different machine than the one you're actually using, you can add the `-h` option, followed by the server name or IP address to your login:

```
> mysql -h dbserver -u dbuser -p
```

NOTE   *Throughout this book, we'll indicate the system command prompt using* shell>_. *The MySQL command prompt is always indicated using* mysql>_.

In either case, you should then be prompted with:

```
Enter password:
```

After successfully entering your password, you should see something similar to this:

```
Welcome to the MySQL monitor.  Commands end with ; or \g.
Your MySQL connection id is 42465 to server version: 4.0.15-standard
Type 'help;' or '\h' for help. Type '\c' to clear the buffer.
```

If you see something like this:

```
ERROR 1045 (28000): Access denied for user...
```

That means there's a problem with your username and/or password. Most likely you've entered one of these incorrectly.

NOTE   *Remember that on a fresh MySQL installation, the passwords for the root and anonymous user accounts are blank.*

If you have repeated login failures with a given username/password, you should check to see if the user actually exists, and if so, reset the password. (If you need help with this, ask your database administrator; if you're running your own MySQL installation, consult Kofler's *Definitive Guide to MySQL*, mentioned at the beginning of this chapter.)

NOTE *Windows users should be aware that, unlike the case with Linux, installing MySQL on Windows does not automatically add it to your system path. This means that you must either navigate to the directory where the MySQL executable is located or include the path to it when you run MySQL. If you used the default options for the installation, this directory will be* C:\mysql\bin\. *To make things easier on yourself, you can add* C:\mysql\bin\.; *to the beginning of your* PATH *environment variable (don't forget the dot and semicolon). After that, you'll be able to call* mysql *directly from anywhere on the system. (Some Windows versions may require a reboot as well.) You should also be aware that the Windows 95/98/Me series is* not *recommended for production use with MySQL; use Windows NT, 2000, XP, or 2003 instead.*

To access a particular database, you must first select it. To do this from the command line, employ the use command:

```
mysql> use dbname;
```

where dbname is the name of the database. On success, MySQL will respond with:

```
Database changed.
mysql>
```

If the database wasn't found, you'll see something like this:

```
ERROR 1049: Unknown database 'nosuchdb'
mysql>
```

To connect to a MySQL database from an application, you generally use the API functions or methods provided by the programming language or environment. The intent is the same: First connect to the MySQL server using the proper username, hostname, and password; then select the database whose tables you want to work with. For example, consider the following bit of PHP 4 code:

```php
<?php
  $host = "localhost";
  $user = "webuser";
  $pass = "53cr37p455w0rd";
  $dbname = "web01";

  $conn = mysql_connect($host, $user, $pass)
    or die("Couldn't connect to MySQL server on $host: " . mysql_error() . ".");
  $db = mysql_select_db($dbname, $conn)
    or die("Couldn't select database $dbname: " . mysql_error() . ".");

  echo "Ready for queries against database $dbname on server $host.";
?>
```

Here, we've defined some variables to hold the names of the MySQL server and database we wish to access, the username we want to log in under, and that user's password. We then call `mysql_connect()` to log in to the MySQL server. This function is equivalent to typing the following at a system prompt:

```
> mysql -u webuser -p53cr37p455w0rd
```

If the connection attempt is successful, the function returns a *connection identifier* that we can use to refer to the same connection elsewhere in this PHP script. (In the event of failure, it returns a Boolean **FALSE**.) Next, we call the `mysql_select_db()` function, which takes as arguments the name of the database we want to select and the identifier of the connection to use, and returns **TRUE** on success and **FALSE** on failure.

 NOTE *In PHP 4, the second argument for* `mysql_select_db()` *is optional. If it's omitted, PHP tries to use the connection that was most recently opened using* `mysql_connect()`. *However, it's good practice always to use both arguments. If your application is accessing multiple MySQL databases or servers, it's easy to cause errors by trying to select a database on the wrong server or by using a connection made by a user who doesn't have access to that database.*

Many of the other programming APIs for working with MySQL are similar in this regard. All of them provide some means of logging in to the MySQL server and then selecting a database against which to run queries. The equivalent to the preceding example using C is not an exact replica, but the same general concepts apply:

```
MYSQL mysql;
mysql_init(&mysql);

if(!mysql_real_connect(&mysql, "host", "user", "pass", "dbname", 0, NULL, 0))
{
    fprintf(stderr, "Database connection failed: %s\n", mysql_error(&mysql));
}
```

MySQL APIs also exist for Perl (DBD::mysql), Java (Connector/J), Python, and Tcl, among others. We'll discuss some of these in Chapter 7 of this book.

Identifiers and Naming Conventions

In order to perform useful tasks of any sort, you must be able to name the tools and materials with which you're working. This is no less true of working with relational databases than it is of building a bridge, writing a sonnet, or performing spinal surgery. In the former case, we need to be able to assign meaningful and appropriate names to databases, tables, and table columns.

As with any field of technical endeavor where computers are involved, there are certain rules for creating identifiers for these items, and these rules must be followed; otherwise, the names won't be recognized as such and errors will result. Fortunately, MySQL's rules for creating identifiers are fairly basic, and it won't take us long to go over them.

Next, we must consider the issue of naming conventions, which represent a very important step in creating efficient and normalized databases. Whereas the rules for creating identifiers are imposed by MySQL, naming conventions are rules we set for ourselves in order to make the names we create more useful. Good naming conventions help us ensure that the names we devise have these characteristics:

- Consistent

- Descriptive

- Easily understood and remembered

- Simple to use

- Minimally prone to producing errors

After looking at MySQL's rules for forming identifiers, we'll devote the rest of this section to offering you a set of guidelines for your own naming conventions.

Rather than laying out a strict set of rules as such, we'll present these guidelines as a series of do's and don'ts to consider as you choose your own rules for creating names.

MySQL Rules for Identifiers

Just for the record, Table 1-1 shows the permitted characters in the different sorts of MySQL identifiers and the maximum length of each in versions 3.23.6 and higher.

Table 1-1. Permitted Characters in MySQL Identifiers

IDENTIFIER	MAXIMUM LENGTH	PERMITTED CHARACTERS
Database	64	Any character allowed in directory names except /, \, or .
Table	64	Any character allowed in filenames, except / or .
Column	64	All characters
Alias	255	All characters

The normal character set for MySQL consists of the Latin-1 letters and numbers, plus the underscore (_) and dollar sign ($) characters. If an identifier contains any characters other than these, the identifier must be delimited using the backtick character (`). Note that it's possible to create an identifier that consists solely of digits, but in this case, it must also be set off with backticks. Because of this and the fact that it's easy to confuse such identifiers with actual numbers, we don't recommend using identifiers that consist only of digits.

Naming Conventions: Do's and Don'ts

Now we're going to look at a few things you should try to do (or try to avoid doing, as the case may be) when naming your databases, tables, and columns. These do's and don'ts are not *requirements* in the sense of "if you don't do such and so, your application will break"; rather, they're *recommendations* for what in our experience make for best practices.

The important issue is not so much that you follow all of these guidelines word for word, but that you adopt *sensible* guidelines and stick with them. In other words, choose naming conventions that will work for you, and don't try to place unreasonable restrictions on yourself in doing so. If you do, you'll find yourself needing to change them later on. On the other hand, don't be afraid to be flexible. If you find that some aspect of the naming system you've been using is causing you trouble, modify it to something that works better. Also keep in mind that different projects and applications have different requirements, so a naming convention that works well in one case may not be the best fit for another. Try to keep these things in mind as you read through our list of do's and don'ts.

Do Try to Be Consistent

It is important to keep your naming conventions consistent throughout all phases of developing your application. This will help you during the initial development and will make future maintenance of the application a lot easier as well. For example, if you decide to use lowercase table names with words separated by underscores, you should do so for all of the tables in the database. You should consider following the same convention for naming columns and any aliases you use as well.

Being inconsistent can lead to problems down the road, or even confuse someone else who may be brought in to help maintain or expand on the initial application you created. By taking a little bit of extra time in the initial development and design process, you can save yourself and any future developers or administrators who may need to work with your database a great amount of trouble.

NOTE   *In this book, we'll use uppercase for all MySQL reserved keywords and lowercase for all identifiers.*

Do Use Easily Understood, Descriptive Identifiers

Using names that are clear, distinct, and easily recognizable can help you while you are developing your application code, as well as when you are trying to pinpoint problems. Otherwise, you might spend a lot of time researching your code to identify what a particular table or column contains.

In which of the following two examples would it be easier for you to recognize the type and purpose of the data stored in the table and each of the columns referenced?

```
SELECT column1, column4, column3
FROM table4
WHERE column10 > 20
LIMIT 0, 10;
```

or

```
SELECT id, firstname, lastname
FROM customers
WHERE age > 20
LIMIT 0, 10;
```

Naturally, you would choose the second example. Just from looking at the query, you can assume with a relatively high degree of certainty that you're pulling the customer's ID number as well as the associated customer's first and last names from a table that stores customer data. The first example does not give you this sort of insight. At a later date, you probably would not remember that **column1** = customer ID, **column3** = customer's last name, **column4** = customer's first name, and so on. And even if you remembered this set of correspondences perfectly well, it would not do much good for others trying to work with your database—particularly if you were flattened by a truck on your way to the office one morning, and they didn't have you around to remind them any longer! They would need to read through a large sampling of the data in each table and column and try to infer what sort of information table4 is holding.

CAUTION   *What might seem a natural assumption to you, such as listing the column for the customer's surname before the column for the customer's given name, might not be so intuitive to someone else.*

You might say, "Well, I'd just write it all down in a table of correspondences so everyone would always know which column relates to which piece of information." (Yes, to our dismay, we've seen applications set up in such a way that the developers were *expected* to consult such tables in order to determine which columns they needed to obtain in a given query!) In which case, you would be missing the point, which is: *Never add unnecessary layers of complexity to an application.* Use clear, unambiguous identifiers. Avoid the need for correspondences tables (or other unnecessary and unreliable workarounds involving feats of memory), and realize that it's extremely likely others will consider your "natural order" to be counterintuitive.

This is not to say that you shouldn't use comments in your table definitions—that's what they're there for, after all. Nor do we mean that you shouldn't create a well-developed schema as part of your project's documentation, because you definitely should. However, you and your teammates will get heaps more work done if you don't make it necessary to consult documentation every single time a query needs to be written.

Neither is there any need to be excessively verbose. We've seen tables in which the columns were given the datatypes as part of their names, à la Hungarian notation in Visual Basic, such as **int_primary_key_customer_id**, **varchar30_customer_first_name**, and so on. This is simply wasteful, since you can find out what the datatypes are at any time by running a `SHOW CREATE TABLE customers;` from the command line or by performing the equivalent by using an API call, such as PHP 4's `mysql_field_type()`. In fact, while it's a common practice to include the table name in each column name—such as **customer_id**, **customer_firstname**, and **customer_lastname**—it can be argued that this isn't really necessary, since you can use the dot operator at any time to distinguish between like-named columns in different tables: **customers.id**, **customers.first_name**, and **customers.last_name**. There are good reasons for adopting either practice, but again, the goal is to pick one convention or the other and stick with it.

NOTE *As you'll see in Chapter 5, including the table name in the column used as a unique ID often makes it more convenient to write joins between tables.*

Don't Use Reserved Keywords

Don't use reserved keywords or commands from ANSI SQL, MySQL, or PostgreSQL when naming databases, columns, or tables. Even if such identifiers appear to work with your current MySQL installation, they may cause conflicts if you need to move to a different server, version, or configuration. In particular, using reserved words for table names is liable to cause you headaches if you try to use them on a MySQL server that's running in ANSI-compliant mode. You may consult the following references for these words:

- **ANSI SQL:** `http://developer.mimer.se/validator/sql-reserved-words.tml`

- **MySQL:** `http://www.mysql.com/doc/en/Reserved_words.html`

- **PostgreSQL:** `http://www.postgresql.org/docs/7/interactive/syntax.htm`

Of course, it's quite possible to use reserved words as identifiers; however, if you're running MySQL in ANSI mode, you'll need to set them off with backticks. Nevertheless, in the interest of minimizing the potential for errors generated if you forget to delimit them, as well as the potential for general confusion, we strongly advise that you do *not* employ reserved SQL keywords or anything else requiring the use of backticks for table or column names.

Don't Depend on Case-Sensitivity or Case-Insensitivity

An example of case-sensitivity dependency might be to name one table in a given database **productcategories** and another in the same database **ProductCategories**, and expect MySQL to regard them as distinct. The opposite situation—relying on case-*in*sensitivity—would be to name a table **ProductCategories** and then refer to it in a query as **productcategories** (or vice versa).

Relying on either of these is not really a very good idea for two reasons. One of these reasons is that case-sensitivity in MySQL is determined by two different factors:

- The case-sensitivity of the operating system on which MySQL is running

- The setting of the `lower_case_table_names` variable in the my.cnf file on Linux and other Unix-like systems.

On Windows, the latter has no effect, since names of directories and files are not case-sensitive (for example, you can't have two directories named mydir and MyDIR in the same parent directory on a Windows system, nor can there be two files named myFile.EXT and MyFile.ext in the same directory). When MySQL is running on Unix systems with `lower_case_table_names` turned on in the my.cnf file, table names are automatically converted to lowercase. Beginning with MySQL 4.0.2, this also applies to database names, and, as of MySQL 4.1.1, to table aliases as well.

The other reason you shouldn't rely on MySQL to be either case-sensitive or case-agnostic is that it encourages poor programming practice. You make it easy to make mistakes because you selected data from, say, **productcategories** rather than **ProductCategories**. Also, referring to tables with whatever case you happen to feel like at any given moment is sloppy and confuses others who need to work with your databases and/or application code. Others will waste time trying to figure out if **productcategories**, **ProductCategories**, and **PRODUCTCATEGORIES** are the same table or different tables.

If you develop on one server and then deploy your application to another (or several others), you may find that the behavior of a different configuration, MySQL version, operating system, or some combination of these breaks the application in a rather dramatic fashion. In light of all of these different possibilities, we recommend that you follow these case conventions:

- Name all databases, tables, columns, and indexes in lowercase.

- Refer to them consistently using lowercase.

This also applies to any table or column aliases you might use in your queries. If you're used to programming in a case-sensitive language such as C, PHP, Perl, Java, or JavaScript—or if you're accustomed to coding standards for other languages such as Visual Basic that allow the use of mixed-case identifiers—you may find this irritating. However, you're likely to be a lot more irritated when you find that you need to edit most or all of your queries on the eve of deploying your company's new web site or unveiling a demonstration of your new application for an important client.

Don't Use Special Characters in Identifiers

Although MySQL versions 3.23.6 and newer are extremely liberal about the characters used for identifiers, we would counsel you to err on the side of conservatism in this regard. In the first place, this makes identifiers more difficult to read. This violates our principle of keeping identifiers legible and easily understood. In addition, it introduces increased ambiguity and uncertainty. Sure, you can cleverly name a table **20$*-TWO!**, but how many people are going to recognize that as meaning "Twenty-dollar specials, this week only!" and that the table is supposed to store information about weekly specials for this client's e-commerce site? It's really much better if you dare to be mundane and name the table something like **web_weekly_specials**.

MySQL supports most accented and other special characters used in Western European languages, but it's best to avoid them in identifiers. To a German developer, it might be natural to name a table containing a list of books as **bücher**, but a programmer working for an American or Australian firm that uses the application might find it frustrating to discover that's why his query SELECT ... FROM bucher; or SELECT ... FROM bocher; doesn't work ("Fair dinkum! It sure looked like an *o*..."), and that he must use a character that's not even present on his keyboard to query the table, or to rename the table and change all of the existing queries that refer to it. He'll be even less impressed if part or all of the application is in a compiled language like C or Java and he doesn't have access to the source code.

You should also keep in mind that there's always the chance that your application might need to be compatible with a legacy database server. For all the talk we hear about progress, let's face it: The dirty secret of corporate IT is the old VAX in the payroll department—it's still running the same COBOL programs that were loaded on it when the firm's current CEO was in kindergarten. Windows developers sometimes must support DOS applications. Web developers sometimes need to support Netscape 4. You, as a MySQL developer, will almost certainly, at some point in your career, be stuck with supporting an infrastructure that is soundly grounded in MySQL 3.22 servers and clients that have been chugging along doing their job just fine for five years or longer; upgrading them will not be presented to you as an option. So, if you do choose to allow special characters in identifiers as part of your naming scheme, be prepared to run into the occasional situation where you might not have any choice in the matter.

Don't Use Spaces in Identifiers

Although MySQL will allow you to employ spaces in identifiers (so long as the identifier is set off by backticks), we strongly recommend that you do not do so. Use an underscore (_), as in **customer_first_name**, rather than **customer first name**. Otherwise, you will create numerous opportunities for yourself (and for others) to make syntactical and logical errors. Consider that this statement:

```
UPDATE `select orders` SET `order status`='S' WHERE `select order id`='20549';
```

will definitely not have the same result as this one:

```
UPDATE select orders SET order status='S' WHERE select order id='20549';
```

due to what MySQL will regard as several instances of misplaced SELECT keywords in the latter.

In addition, because MySQL saves data in directories corresponding to databases and files corresponding to tables (and named after them in both cases), you may be making trouble for yourself if you develop on an operating system that allows spaces in directory names and filenames and then try to deploy on one that doesn't allow them. The same sort of reasoning applies to special characters as well.

Do Limit Identifiers to a Sensible Length

As noted in Table 1-1, MySQL identifiers for databases, tables, and columns can be up to 64 characters in length. That doesn't mean you should go out of your way to make identifiers as long as possible, but rather that, if you actually do need to use a really long one, you're covered.

For example, in an inventory-related database, let's say you have several tables for products, categories, subcategories, availability codes, and vendor codes. Naturally, each of these tables has several columns for different sorts of data. You might be tempted to name (as some do) the columns containing unique IDs and names for product availability codes as **inventory_product_availability_code_id** and **inventory_product_availability_code_name**, but this is really not necessary. Just remember that you can select only from tables in the same database in a single query, and that dot notation and aliases are your friends. So, all you really might need to do would be to name the table **availability_codes** and the columns as **id** and **name**.

One other thing to keep in mind is that there are many occasions when you may be building queries dynamically in the application layer, so the shorter and more systematically you name tables and columns, the better.

TIP *If you don't know which database you're currently using, you can always run a* SELECT DATABASE(); *query to find out, or just send a* USE dbname; *command to force the issue.*

However, don't go to the other extreme, either. Using cryptic, one- or two-letter identifiers might be economical, but it's not very informative. The trick is to exercise some intelligent discretion and use identifiers that are long enough and distinctive enough to be descriptive, without going overboard and making extra work for yourself unnecessarily.

Do Use "id" with Primary Keys

Using an ID is a fairly well entrenched convention in database design. This is due in no small part to the fact that it simply makes sense to refer to the column that uniquely identifies each row of a table as an ID or id. Whether or not you choose to prefix all columns in a table with the name of the table (and there are good arguments for and against that practice), it's always a good idea to prefix the name of the column that serves as the table's primary key.

For example, let's say you're developing an online shopping cart system, and your database needs a **products** table to hold information about the items being offered sale. Let's suppose further that this table needs columns for a unique product ID, and the product's name, description, and unit price. Whether or not you name the remaining columns **product_name**, **product_description**, and **product_price** or simply **name**, **description**, and **price** is strictly up to you. However, you should still name the ID column **product_id**. Since this column is the one that's most likely to serve as a foreign key in another table (whether or not you actually employ foreign key constraints), if you do this, you'll be able to use abbreviated syntax for USING clauses in many of your joins (see Chapter 6 for more about joins).

Queries Review

Now let's turn our attention to the syntactical high points of MySQL's most commonly used queries and related commands. In the course of this review, we'll look at how to accomplish the following tasks:

- Create new tables with CREATE TABLE.

- Drop (delete) existing tables with the DROP TABLE statement.

- Retrieve data from tables using the SELECT command.

- Store data records in tables with INSERT queries.

- Alter existing records by means of the UPDATE command.

- Remove records from tables using DELETE queries.

For each of these commands, we'll start by showing you a formal definition of the command and then follow up with some examples illustrating its use. Where there are several common variations on the command, we'll show you each of these and explain where it's appropriate.

NOTE *Notations for definitions: Square brackets ([ ]) indicate an optional argument or clause; curly brackets ({ }) indicate a required argument; the pipe character (|) indicates a choice (read as or); quotation marks (' ') and commas (,) are required as shown. MySQL keywords, as elsewhere in this book, are capitalized; text in italics represents expressions or literal values.*

CREATE TABLE Syntax

The CREATE TABLE command is used to create new tables in a MySQL database. You can use it to create a completely new table from scratch or (beginning with MySQL 4.1) one that copies the definition of an existing table.

Definition

The CREATE TABLE statement in MySQL takes one of two forms:

```
CREATE [TEMPORARY] TABLE [IF NOT EXISTS] table_name
  [(column_definition[column_definition2,...])]
[table_option(s)] [select_statement];
```

or:

```
CREATE [TEMPORARY] TABLE [IF NOT EXISTS] table_name [() LIKE old_table_name [)];
```

Using the TEMPORARY keyword creates a table that will exist only for the lifetime of the connection during which it was made. Including IF NOT EXISTS in a table creation statement prevents the generation of an error if a table with that name already exists in the database that's currently selected.

The basic syntax for a column definition is as follows:

```
name type[(size | precision, decimals | value-list)]
       [options] [DEFAULT value] [index_type]
```

We've already discussed names of columns in the previous section. Some column types (such as CHAR, VARCHAR, and INT) require or allow a size to be specified. Floating-point number types (FLOAT, DECIMAL, DOUBLE, and so on) require or allow a degree of precision and number of decimals. The ENUM and SET types require a comma-delimited list of possible values. Options for numeric types include UNSIGNED, meaning that the values must all be nonnegative, and ZEROFILL, meaning that MySQL will fill any unused digits to the left (or right, in the case of DECIMAL) with zeros. Columns may also be specified as being NULL or NOT NULL, which determines whether or not the column may contain nulls; the default is NULL. Text columns (of type CHAR, VARCHAR, TEXT, and so on) can take the BINARY option, which forces all comparisons made with values in that column to be case-sensitive. You may also specify a default value for the column; if not specified, the default value is generally zero, an empty string, or the first value given in the value-list, depending on the column type.

CAUTION   TEXT *and* BLOB *columns cannot be given a default value.*

Indexes or keys on single columns may be specified in the same line as the column definition or on a separate line; keys on multiple columns must be defined separately. We'll discuss all of the available column types in greater detail in the next chapter, as well as a number of table creation options that we've omitted here. For now, let's just look at a few examples.

Examples

Here is the CREATE TABLE statement to create a **customers** table that we'll use in some of the examples that follow:

```
CREATE TABLE customers (
    customer_id INT(10) UNSIGNED NOT NULL AUTO_INCREMENT,
    firstname VARCHAR(35) NOT NULL,
    lastname VARCHAR(35) NOT NULL,
    sub_date DATE NOT NULL,
    PRIMARY KEY id (customer_id)
) TYPE=MyISAM COMMENT='Sample table definition';
```

This creates a table of type MyISAM. This is the normal default table type in MySQL (we'll discuss the other table types in the next chapter). The **customer_id** column is a ten-digit unsigned integer, which automatically increments for each new record that's added to this table. The **firstname** and **lastname** columns are both of type VARCHAR, and the **sub_date** column is of type DATE. Since we didn't declare default values for any of the columns, the default value for both **firstname** and **lastname** is ' ' (an empty string), and the default value for the **sub_date** column is 0000-00-00.

We could also have written the table definition like so:

```
CREATE TABLE customers (
    customer_id INT(10) UNSIGNED AUTO_INCREMENT PRIMARY KEY,
    firstname VARCHAR(35) NOT NULL,
    lastname VARCHAR(35) NOT NULL,
    sub_date DATE NOT NULL
) TYPE=MyISAM COMMENT='Sample table definition';
```

This places the primary key definition in the column on which the key is defined. We'll discuss this method of defining keys in depth in Chapter 3, which covers keys, indexes, and normalization.

Since MySQL 4.1, it's also possible to create a table that copies the structure of an existing one:

```
CREATE TABLE more_customers LIKE customers;
```

This will create a new, empty table named **more_customers** with exactly the same column definitions as **customers**, including any keys, just as if we had written this:

```
CREATE TABLE more_customers (
   customer_id INT(10) UNSIGNED NOT NULL AUTO_INCREMENT,
   firstname VARCHAR(35) NOT NULL,
   lastname VARCHAR(35) NOT NULL,
   sub_date DATE NOT NULL,
   PRIMARY KEY id (customer_id)
) TYPE=MyISAM COMMENT='Sample table definition';
```

You can also use a variation on this syntax to create a new table, some, but not all, of whose column definitions are copied from another table:

```
CREATE TABLE ex_customers (
   end_date DATE NOT NULL,
   PRIMARY KEY id (customer_id)
) TYPE=MyISAM COMMENT='Former customers'
   SELECT customer_id, firstname, lastname FROM customers;
```

This creates a new table and copies the data from the original table into it, just as if we had written this:

```
CREATE TABLE ex_customers (
   customer_id INT(10) UNSIGNED NOT NULL AUTO_INCREMENT,
   firstname VARCHAR(35) NOT NULL,
   lastname VARCHAR(35) NOT NULL,
   end_date DATE NOT NULL,
   PRIMARY KEY id (customer_id)
) TYPE=MyISAM COMMENT='Former customers';
```

followed by this:

```
INSERT INTO ex_customers (customer_id, firstname, lastname, end_date)
   SELECT customer_id, firstname, lastname, end_date FROM customers;
```

INSERT ... SELECT is used to copy records from one table into another. We describe this statement in further detail later, in the "SELECT Syntax" section.

The CREATE TABLE ... SELECT statement was implemented in MySQL 3.23.

NOTE *Unlike* CREATE TABLE ... LIKE, CREATE TABLE ... SELECT *does not copy indexes. You must define these yourself in the body of the* CREATE TABLE *statement.*

DROP Syntax

DROP statements are employed for removing databases and tables, and they are relatively simple and straightforward to understand and use. Although there are several other uses for DROP, we'll cover only two of them here.

This command deletes the database named *db_name* from the MySQL server:

```
DROP DATABASE db_name;
```

This command deletes the table named *table_name* from the current database:

```
DROP TABLE table_name;
```

You can delete multiple tables by adding their names and separating them with commas:

```
DROP TABLE table_name1, table_name2, table_name3;
```

You can ensure that you are dropping a temporary table and not one that you intended to keep by using this statement:

```
DROP TEMPORARY TABLE table_name;
```

When used with the TEMPORARY keyword, this will drop the table named in the command only if that table was created with CREATE TEMPORARY TABLE.

NOTE *Unless the temporary table is quite large or your application uses persistent connections, you won't need to drop it, as a temporary table is automatically dropped when the connection under which it was created is closed.*

You can also use the following syntax to keep from generating an error (or a note in MySQL 4.1 or above) if you attempt to delete a nonexistent table:

```
DROP TABLE IF EXISTS table_name;
```

CAUTION DROP *commands delete the database or table(s) to which they're applied along with* all *of the data contained in the database or table(s)! There is no MySQL command or function to undo a* DROP, *so don't execute one unless (a) you're absolutely positive that you'll never have any use for that data again, and (b) you keep complete and current backups.*

SELECT Syntax

SELECT statements are used to retrieve information from one or more tables in the database to which you are connected. The arguments issued with the SELECT command indicate which columns in the specified table or tables from which you wish to retrieve data, what conditions you wish to be met by the data that's returned, and what you want done with it.

It's important to remember that a SELECT statement always returns a *set* of records. Even if only one record matches the match conditions that you establish for a query, that's a set consisting of one record. If there are no matching records, the result is a set with no rows. This is the case not only for SELECT queries, but also for UPDATE and DELETE operations as well, as you'll see shortly.

Definition

The (mostly) complete definition for the SELECT statement is as follows:

```
SELECT [STRAIGHT_JOIN]
      [SQL_SMALL_RESULT] [SQL_BIG_RESULT] [SQL_BUFFER_RESULT]
      [SQL_CACHE | SQL_NO_CACHE] [SQL_CALC_FOUND_ROWS] [HIGH_PRIORITY]
      [DISTINCT | DISTINCTROW | ALL]
    column_reference(s)
    [INTO {OUTFILE | DUMPFILE} 'file_name' export_options]
    [FROM table_reference(s)
      [WHERE conditional_expression(s)]
      [GROUP BY {unsigned_integer | column_name(s) | formula} [ASC | DESC], ...
        [WITH ROLLUP]]
      [HAVING conditional_expression(s)]
      [ORDER BY {unsigned_integer | column_name(s) | formula} [ASC | DESC] ,...]
      [LIMIT [offset,] row_count | row_count OFFSET offset]
      [PROCEDURE procedure_name(argument_list)]
      [FOR UPDATE | LOCK IN SHARE MODE]]
```

We won't provide details of every single option listed in this definition here; indeed, much of what we'll be discussing later in this book will center on demonstrating many of these options and how they can be put to use in writing more complex and precise SELECT queries. There also are some additional clauses and operators not shown here that you may use with SELECT queries. We'll introduce and discuss these in more detail later in this section.

Examples

Let's look at a few basic examples of SELECT queries in use. The simplest of these is to select a single column from a given table:

```
SELECT customer_id
FROM customers
WHERE firstname = 'John';
```

This query will return a list of the customer IDs for all records from the **customers** table in which the value stored for the customer's first name is John.

To select more than one column, just add more column names, and separate them with commas:

```
SELECT customer_id, lastname, subscribed_date
FROM customers
WHERE firstname = 'John';
```

 NOTE *Spaces following commas in SQL statements are optional, and we'll use them in this book as seems appropriate.*

To retrieve *all* columns from a table in one go, just use the wildcard character:

```
SELECT *
FROM customers
WHERE firstname = 'John';
```

However, it's more efficient to retrieve only the columns that you need, and to save the wildcard for use on those occasions when you actually require all the data for the records that are returned.

Comments in MySQL

Like most other programming languages, MySQL allows you to write comments that aren't evaluated by the MySQL server, for purposes of documentation. Several commenting styles are supported. You can use # (hash mark) to start a comment that continues to the end of the line. MySQL also has a C-style comment syntax that you can employ for multiline comments or comments in the middle of a line: /* begins the comment and */ ends it.

Some other databases allow you to use — (double dash) to start a single-line comment; note that the double dash must be followed by a space character, and MySQL supports this for compatibility reasons. However, we recommend that you avoid its use, as it can easily be confused with two minus signs. (This is legal SQL syntax and may come about with dynamically generated queries.) In this book, we'll use only the # or /* . . . */ comment delimiters.

In a **customers** table containing many records, there are likely to be quite a few customers whose given name is John. You can narrow things down a bit by adding additional conditions to the WHERE clause using the logical operators AND, OR, and NOT (or !), and any of the comparison operators =, >, <, <=, >=, and <> (or !=):

```
# Get records for any customer with the first name "John" and last name "Jones"
SELECT customer_id, lastname, sub_date
FROM customers
WHERE firstname = 'John' AND lastname = 'Jones';


# Any customer with the first name "John" but whose last name is not "Smith"
SELECT customer_id, lastname, sub_date
FROM customers
WHERE firstname = 'John' AND lastname <> 'Smith';


# Any customer whose last name is "Smith" or "Jones"
SELECT customer_id, firstname, lastname, sub_date
FROM customers
WHERE lastname = 'Smith' OR lastname = 'Jones';


#Any customer with the last name "Jones" whose subscription began during 2002
SELECT customer_id, firstname, lastname, sub_date
FROM customers
WHERE lastname = 'Jones'
AND sub_date >= '2002-01-01' AND sub_date <= '2002-12-31';
```

You can employ as many conditions in a WHERE clause as are necessary to filter out unnecessary data. You can also use parentheses to group together parts of clauses to force conditions to be evaluated in the order desired. For example, to get all the data on customers who subscribed in January or March of 2003, but *not* in February of that year, you can write either of the following:

```
SELECT *
FROM customers
WHERE (sub_date >= '2003-01-01' AND sub_date < '2003-02-01')
OR (sub_date >= '2003-03-01' AND sub_date < '2003-04-01');
```

or

```
SELECT *
FROM customers
WHERE (sub_date>='2003-01-01' AND sub_date<'2003-04-01')
AND NOT(sub_date>='2003-02-01' AND sub_date<'2003-03-01');
```

> **NOTE** *The* NOT *and* ! *operators mean exactly the same thing and are completely interchangeable; the same is true with respect to the* <> *and* != *operators. We prefer* NOT *and* <>*, and these are what we'll use in this book, but feel free to use whichever ones you feel most comfortable or familiar with. However, we do suggest that you adopt one or the other of each pair of operators and use them consistently.*

In addition to tests for equality, inequality, and comparison, MySQL also allows you to do "fuzzy" matching using the LIKE operator with the _ (underscore) and % (percent sign) wildcards. LIKE tells MySQL we want to make a fuzzy or partial match against a string value. The _ stands for any single character; the % stands for any number of characters. Using these, you can build expressions for matching the beginning, end, or any other portions of a string. For instance, if we want to find all customers whose first names begin with the letter *J*, we can write:

```
SELECT *
FROM customers
WHERE firstname LIKE 'J%';
```

This will match John, James, Jeremiah, and so on. Here are a few other examples, just to give you an idea:

- The expression J%n will match John, Jen, Jon, Jan, and Joan, but not Jane.

- J_n will match Jen, Jan, and Jon, but not John or Joan.

- %n will match Jen, Ben, Jan, John, and Van, but not Jane.

LIKE is normally case-insensitive, so j_m will match Jim. To force case-sensitivity, use LIKE BINARY. Of course, you can combine LIKE conditions with other tests, including other LIKE conditions:

```
/* Obtain all data for male customers, whose initials
are "J. S.", and who subscribed prior to 01 July 1999 */
SELECT *
FROM customers
WHERE (firstname LIKE 'J%' AND lastname LIKE 'S%')
AND sub_date < '1999-07-01' AND sex = "M";
```

One other note about LIKE before we move on: if you're unsure whether or not an expression you've built will match a given string, it's easy to test this from the command line. Here are examples (also demonstrating LIKE BINARY):

```
mysql> SELECT 'John' LIKE 'j%n';
+------------------+
| 'John' LIKE 'j%n' |
+------------------+
|                1 |
+------------------+
1 row in set (0.00 sec)
mysql> SELECT 'John' LIKE BINARY 'j%n';
+-------------------------+
| 'John' LIKE BINARY 'j%n' |
+-------------------------+
|                       0 |
+-------------------------+
1 row in set (0.05 sec)
mysql>
```

NOTE *Don't forget that MySQL doesn't have a Boolean datatype as such. It returns a 1 for a logical* **TRUE** *and a 0 for* **FALSE**.

If you need to match a literal % or _ character, escape it with a backslash: \%, _. Since \ is the escape character, you'll need to escape that as well, if you want to match a literal instance of it. For example, to match the string *end\n* with any one character preceding it, you would use LIKE 'end\\n'.

Finally, it's also possible to test against a specific set of values using the IN operator. For example, to select a group of customers having any of a given set of last names, we can use this:

```
SELECT *
FROM customers
WHERE lastname IN ('Harris', 'Davies', 'Williams', 'Mills');
```

This is a convenient shorthand for queries in this form:

```
SELECT *
FROM customers
WHERE lastname = 'Harris' OR lastname = 'Davies'
OR lastname = 'Williams' OR lastname = 'Mills';
```

Either of these will return all columns for all customer records in the **customers** table where the customer's last name matches one of the names listed. The use of IN is not limited to columns containing text; it can be used to match within a set of discrete values of any type. Both LIKE and IN can be combined with number of other conditions in a WHERE clause by using logical operators:

```
SELECT *
FROM customers
WHERE lastname = 'Smith'
AND (firstname LIKE 'R%d' OR firstname LIKE 'B%d')
AND sub_date IN ('2003-10-01', '2003-10-15', '2003-11-01');
```

You should be able to figure out by now what this query will do.

As you'll see shortly, all of the WHERE clause syntax and operators that we've just looked at are equally applicable to UPDATE and DELETE queries as well as to SELECT queries.

ORDER BY and GROUP BY Clauses in SELECT Queries

Not only can you filter the results of a query using logical and comparison operators, but also you can determine the order in which records will be returned. In fact, one mistake often made by programmers who are new to working with databases is that they fail to take advantage of this capability. They're either unaware of it, or they're laboring under the mistaken impression that they'll be able to handle this issue more efficiently in their application code; thus they spend a great deal of time coding unnecessary sorting and grouping algorithms.

Suppose we want to retrieve a set of records from our **customers** table, but we would like to have them in alphabetical order. We can accomplish this easily using an ORDER BY clause:

```
SELECT customer_id, firstname, lastname, sub_date
FROM customers
ORDER BY lastname ASC;
```

All we have to do is name the column by which we wish to sort following the ORDER BY. The optional ASC keyword tells MySQL we want to sort in ascending order; to sort in reverse order, use DESC instead.

You can do a sort on practically any column type. For example, if we want to sort by the customer's subscription date, starting with the most recent and working our way back, we can use the following:

```
SELECT customer_id, firstname, lastname, sub_date
FROM customers
ORDER BY sub_date DESC;
```

You can also sort on multiple columns. For instance, if we were to run the preceding query that sorts on the last name, we might see John Smith listed before Bill Smith, because no ordering is set with regard to the given name, only to the surname. To fix this, we specify both columns:

```
SELECT customer_id, firstname, lastname, sub_date
FROM customers
ORDER BY lastname, firstname;
```

Now the results will be sorted by last name, then, within each last name, by the first name, so Bill Smith will be listed, then John Smith, then Larry Smith, and so on.

There's no practical limit on the number of columns you can specify, so it's quite possible to use something like this:

```
SELECT customer_id, firstname, lastname, sub_date
FROM customers
ORDER BY lastname ASC, firstname ASC, sub_date DESC, state_abbr ASC;
```

Notice that you can specify ASC or DESC for each column independently of the others. The order of the records returned by this query will be as follows:

- First, by last name, ascending (Jones before Smith)

- Next, by first name, ascending (Carl Jones before Don Jones)

- Next, by subscription date, descending (Carl Jones who subscribed on July 25, 2003, before a different Carl Jones, who subscribed on July 10, 2003)

- Finally, by state abbreviation, ascending (Carl Jones who subscribed on July 20, 2003, who lives in Florida [FL] before Carl Jones who also subscribed on July 20, 2003, but who lives in Georgia [GA])

You can also group records together using a GROUP BY clause and one or more of the various MySQL math and other functions. (We'll discuss functions in detail in Chapter 4.) Let's say we also have an **orders** table, which lists all orders made by customers, including the amount of each order and the customer's first and last names.

NOTE   *This particular* **orders** *table isn't a very good example from the viewpoint of achieving normalization, since we obviously have multiple records for the same customer duplicating the customer's name (and all customers having the same name will have their orders grouped together!). We'll take this up in Chapter 3. For now, just bear with us in the interest of keeping things simple for explanatory purposes.*

Now suppose we want to see how much each customer has spent with us. We can obtain this information using the SUM() function and a GROUP BY clause:

```
SELECT firstname, lastname, SUM(amount) AS total
FROM orders
GROUP BY lastname, firstname
```

The SUM() function adds together all of the amount values. Using GROUP BY allows you to specify for which groups of customers you would like to see those sums. You can specify multiple columns for the GROUP BY clause as well, as you can see from the example. This obtains the total for *each unique combination of values in those columns*, so we might get a result such as this:

```
Command Prompt - mysql -h megalon -u root -p                            _ □ X
mysql> SELECT firstname, lastname, SUM(amount) AS total
    -> FROM orders
    -> GROUP BY lastname, firstname;
+-----------+----------+---------+
| firstname | lastname | total   |
+-----------+----------+---------+
| bill      | jones    | 2920.63 |
| mary      | jones    | 1288.47 |
| John      | Lee      |  144.10 |
| Rachel    | Lewis    |  455.60 |
| bill      | smith    |  904.21 |
| john      | smith    | 3207.76 |
| mary      | smith    | 1165.73 |
| lucy      | vance    | 1128.90 |
| Jim       | Williams |  251.10 |
+-----------+----------+---------+
9 rows in set (0.00 sec)

mysql>
```

You can also use ASC and DESC in GROUP BY clauses, just as you can with ORDER BY, and you can use GROUP BY and ORDER BY in the same query as well. However, GROUP BY has the same effect on ordering as ORDER BY, so you don't need to use the latter unless you want to modify the ordering already imposed on the results using GROUP BY.

In MySQL 3.23 and newer, you can use expressions in ORDER BY or GROUP BY clauses. However, this isn't ANSI-compliant. To get around this, you can use an alias in either type of clause:

```
SELECT firstname, lastname, COUNT(*) AS ordercount, AVG(amount) AS average
FROM orders
GROUP BY lastname, firstname
ORDER BY ordercount DESC, lastname ASC, firstname ASC;
```

This query gives us the number of orders and the average amount spent per order for each customer (actually, for each unique combination of first name and last name). We specify ORDER BY ordercount DESC, using the alias we set for COUNT(*) in the SELECT clause, to give us the results sorted by greatest number of orders first. (Aliases are discussed in more detail shortly, after we look at the LIMIT clause.) Note that, because we override the GROUP BY order, we need to specify that we want the results to be sorted by last name and first name within groups of customers with the same total number of orders. The result might look something like this:

```
Command Prompt - mysql -h megalon -u root -p                          _ |□| x|
mysql> SELECT firstname, lastname,
    ->    COUNT(*) AS ordercount, AVG(amount) AS average
    -> FROM orders
    -> GROUP BY lastname, firstname
    -> ORDER BY ordercount DESC, lastname ASC, firstname ASC;
+-----------+-----------+------------+------------+
| firstname | lastname  | ordercount | average    |
+-----------+-----------+------------+------------+
| bill      | jones     |          5 | 584.126000 |
| john      | smith     |          5 | 641.552000 |
| mary      | jones     |          4 | 322.117500 |
| John      | Lee       |          2 |  72.050000 |
| Rachel    | Lewis     |          2 | 227.800000 |
| bill      | smith     |          2 | 452.105000 |
| mary      | smith     |          2 | 582.865000 |
| lucy      | vance     |          2 | 564.450000 |
| Jim       | Williams  |          2 | 125.550000 |
+-----------+-----------+------------+------------+
9 rows in set (0.01 sec)

mysql>
```

NOTE *In the example shown here, you might notice that the numbers in the **average** column have more than two digits to the right of the decimal point. This is a side effect often encountered when performing floating-point arithmetic; see the next chapter for a discussion of this.*

For a complete and up-to-date listing of MySQL functions and modifiers, see the online MySQL Manual page for these at http://www.mysql.com/doc/en/ Group_by_functions_and_modifiers.html.

We'll be discussing a good many of these functions later on in this book as well.

LIMIT Clauses in SELECT Queries

You can use a LIMIT clause to constrain the number and range of records returned by a SELECT query. The clause takes one of two forms:

LIMIT *rows_to_skip, rows_to_return*

or

LIMIT *number*

Both forms of this clause are simple to use. In the first form, *rows_to_skip* and *rows_to_return* mean pretty much what they sound like: If we imagine the rows in a resultset being indexed or numbered from 1 to the total number of rows, employing LIMIT in this fashion will return the designated subset of that resultset. For example, suppose we have a table named **friends**:

```
Command Prompt - mysql -h megalon -u root -p                    _ □ ×

mysql> SELECT * FROM friends;
+----+---------+
| id | name    |
+----+---------+
|  1 | mary    |
|  2 | jim     |
|  3 | bob     |
|  4 | rodney  |
|  5 | sally   |
|  6 | jane    |
|  7 | george  |
|  8 | joe     |
|  9 | gwen    |
| 10 | melinda |
+----+---------+
10 rows in set (0.01 sec)

mysql>
```

If we're interested in only the seven rows following the first three, we can use a LIMIT clause:

```
Command Prompt - mysql -h megalon -u root -p                    _ □ ×

mysql> SELECT * FROM friends LIMIT 3, 7;
+----+---------+
| id | name    |
+----+---------+
|  4 | rodney  |
|  5 | sally   |
|  6 | jane    |
|  7 | george  |
|  8 | joe     |
|  9 | gwen    |
| 10 | melinda |
+----+---------+
7 rows in set (0.00 sec)

mysql>
```

Notice that we don't start with the third row, but rather the fourth. Now let's suppose we want to retrieve the first five rows in the set. In this case, we need to use only a single parameter for the LIMIT clause:

```
Command Prompt - mysql -h megalon -u root -p                    _ □ ×

mysql> SELECT * FROM friends LIMIT 5;
+----+---------+
| id | name    |
+----+---------+
|  1 | mary    |
|  2 | jim     |
|  3 | bob     |
|  4 | rodney  |
|  5 | sally   |
+----+---------+
5 rows in set (0.00 sec)

mysql>
```

This has exactly the same effect as if we had used

```
SELECT * FROM friends LIMIT 0, 5;
```

Another way of thinking about this abbreviated format is to consider zero as the default value for the first argument. There is no way to specify a default value for the second argument. If we wanted to return all the records from **friends** but the first three, we would have to use something like this:

```
SELECT * FROM friends WHERE id > 3;
```

Alternatively, we could use a value guaranteed to be greater than the number of records in the table:

```
SELECT * FROM friends LIMIT 3, 1000000;
```

However, in order for this to work, we will need to have some idea how many records are actually in the table.

> **NOTE**   *A* LIMIT *clause can also be used in an* UPDATE *or* DELETE *query; see the following corresponding sections for more information.*

Aliases in SELECT Queries

An *alias* in MySQL is nothing more than a nickname or shorthand used in a SELECT query for a table, column, or SQL expression. Aliases, as shown in our earlier example with the SUM() and AVG() functions, can be employed in order to shorten repetitive references in queries, as well as to provide identifiers elsewhere in a query and in application code.

An identifier may be defined as an alias simply by using the identifier following the relevant table name, column name, or expression, optionally preceded with the AS keyword. Table aliases are most useful when selecting from multiple tables and are defined in a query's WHERE or JOIN clause. (Joins are discussed in Chapter 5.)

For example, instead of using this:

```
SELECT categories.name, products.name
FROM categories, products
WHERE products.id = 2345 AND categories.id = products.category_id;
```

We can use this:

```
SELECT c.name, p.name
FROM categories c, products p
WHERE p.id = 2345 AND c.id = p.category_id;
```

Column aliases come in particularly handy where columns in different tables may have the same name and you want to pass a unique identifier for each column in the resultset to your application code:

```php
<?php
  /*  MySQL connection & DB selection code goes here...   */

  $prodid = $_GET["prodid"];
  $query = "SELECT c.name AS cname, p.name AS pname
            FROM categories c, products p
            WHERE p.id = '$prodid' AND c.id = p.category_id";
  $result = mysql_query($query);

  $row = mysql_fetch_assoc($result);
  extract($row);

  echo "<p>PRODUCT: $pname; CATEGORY: $cname</p>\n";
?>
```

As you can see here, the column aliases are passed to PHP and can be used there as keys in an associative array or even (thanks to the PHP extract() function) as variable names. You can also see that it's perfectly legal to combine table and column aliases as well. We should point out that our own preference is to use AS when defining an alias for a column or SQL expression, and to omit it when defining a table alias, but this is just our own habit. It would have been just as correct to use this:

```
SELECT c.name cname, p.name pname
FROM categories c, products p
WHERE p.id = '$prodid' AND c.id = p.category_id;
```

or

```
SELECT c.name AS cname, p.name AS pname
FROM categories AS c, products AS p
WHERE p.id = '$prodid' AND c.id = p.category_id;
```

For this example, we used PHP to show how column aliases are made available to application code, but you'll find that this is also the case for other programming languages with MySQL-compatible APIs. We'll discuss these in Chapter 7 of this book.

Creating an alias for an SQL expression is done in the same way. You may also use previously defined aliases in ORDER BY, GROUP BY, and HAVING clauses. For example, let's consider the data shown here:

```
Command Prompt - mysql -h megalon -u root -p                    _ □ X
mysql> SELECT * FROM orders;
+----+-----------+----------+---------+----------+------------+
| id | firstname | lastname | amount  | discount | date       |
+----+-----------+----------+---------+----------+------------+
|  1 | bill      | jones    |  125.45 |     0.00 | 2003-07-15 |
|  2 | john      | smith    |  241.05 |     0.00 | 2003-06-12 |
|  3 | mary      | jones    |  335.64 |     0.00 | 2003-10-04 |
|  4 | john      | smith    | 1024.55 |     0.15 | 2003-03-24 |
|  5 | bill      | smith    |  652.02 |     0.15 | 2003-05-09 |
|  6 | mary      | jones    |   98.54 |     0.00 | 2003-06-12 |
|  7 | john      | smith    |  572.35 |     0.15 | 2003-02-11 |
|  8 | bill      | jones    |  358.17 |     0.00 | 2003-04-30 |
|  9 | mary      | jones    |  488.05 |     0.15 | 2003-02-02 |
| 10 | lucy      | vance    | 1004.65 |     0.15 | 2003-03-19 |
| 11 | john      | smith    |  704.33 |     0.15 | 2003-07-18 |
| 12 | bill      | jones    |  852.32 |     0.15 | 2003-05-14 |
| 13 | mary      | smith    |  423.51 |     0.00 | 2003-06-22 |
| 14 | mary      | jones    |  366.24 |     0.00 | 2003-08-06 |
| 15 | lucy      | vance    |  124.25 |     0.00 | 2003-09-24 |
| 16 | bill      | jones    |  279.97 |     0.00 | 2003-04-12 |
| 17 | john      | smith    |  665.48 |     0.15 | 2003-03-27 |
| 18 | bill      | smith    |  252.19 |     0.00 | 2003-06-08 |
| 19 | mary      | smith    |  742.22 |     0.15 | 2003-07-09 |
| 20 | bill      | jones    | 1304.72 |     0.15 | 2003-08-08 |
| 21 | Jim       | Williams |  125.55 |     0.00 | 2004-03-15 |
| 22 | Rachel    | Lewis    |  227.80 |     0.00 | 2004-03-18 |
| 23 | John      | Lee      |   72.05 |     0.00 | 2004-03-12 |
| 24 | Jim       | Williams |  125.55 |     0.00 | 2004-03-15 |
| 25 | Rachel    | Lewis    |  227.80 |     0.00 | 2004-03-18 |
| 26 | John      | Lee      |   72.05 |     0.00 | 2004-03-12 |
+----+-----------+----------+---------+----------+------------+
26 rows in set (0.01 sec)

mysql>
```

We can obtain a nicely formatted listing of customers' order totals using this query:

```
Command Prompt - mysql -h megalon -u root -p                    _ □ X
mysql> SELECT CONCAT(firstname, ' ', lastname) AS customer,
    ->     CONCAT('$', SUM(amount)) AS total
    -> FROM orders
    -> GROUP BY customer;
+---------------+----------+
| customer      | total    |
+---------------+----------+
| bill jones    | $2920.63 |
| bill smith    | $904.21  |
| Jim Williams  | $251.10  |
| John Lee      | $144.10  |
| john smith    | $3207.76 |
| lucy vance    | $1128.90 |
| mary jones    | $1288.47 |
| mary smith    | $1165.73 |
| Rachel Lewis  | $455.60  |
+---------------+----------+
9 rows in set (0.00 sec)

mysql>
```

The headings in the output of this query are definitely easier to read and understand than the SQL expressions they stand in for. If you were executing this query in application code, you would be able to refer to the customer and total columns in the output by those aliases there as well. As we'll be showing you throughout much of this book, operations such as concatenations are often much faster when performed in queries rather than in application code.

As shown in Table 1-1 earlier in this chapter, aliases can be up to 64 characters in length and may contain any characters. However, we recommend that you keep your aliases as short as possible and that you also observe the same naming conventions we've already suggested for MySQL identifiers with regard to aliases.

INSERT Syntax

The INSERT statement inserts new rows into an existing table in a database.

Definition

The complete definition of the INSERT statement is as follows:

```
INSERT [LOW_PRIORITY | DELAYED] [IGNORE]
  [INTO] table_name [(column_name[, ...])]
  VALUES ((expression | DEFAULT)[,...), (...), ...]
  [ON DUPLICATE KEY UPDATE column_name = expression[, ...] ]
```

or:

```
INSERT [LOW_PRIORITY | DELAYED] [IGNORE]
  [INTO] table_name [(column_name[,...])]
  SELECT select_statement
```

or:

```
INSERT [LOW_PRIORITY | DELAYED] [IGNORE]
        [INTO] table_name
        SET column_name = (expression | DEFAULT)[, ...]
```

We won't cover every aspect of this definition here, but we'll demonstrate the most common variants.

Examples

At its most basic, the INSERT query has three forms. Two of these specify which columns should receive which item of data.

Suppose we wish to insert a new record into the **orders** table (shown in the previous example) with the following data:

- First name: John

- Last name: Smith

- Order amount: $652.77

- Order date: October 12, 2003

Using the names of the columns, we can write either of the following INSERT queries:

```
INSERT INTO orders (firstname, lastname, amount, order_date)
VALUES ('John', 'Smith', '652.77', '2003-10-12');
```

or

```
INSERT INTO orders
SET firstname='John', lastname='Smith', amount='652.77', order_date='2003-10-12';
```

Since we specify the column names, we don't need to worry about the order they're specified in, or if any columns are omitted, using either of these formats. Any omitted columns will be assigned their default values (assuming that the columns actually have default values, of course).

CAUTION *MySQL can be configured so as not to provide default column values automatically unless they're specified in the definition of a table. However, if you're using the standard MySQL binaries as provided by MySQL AB, this shouldn't be a problem.*

The third form of the INSERT statement doesn't require you to name the columns:

```
INSERT INTO orders VALUES ('John', 'Smith', '652.77', '2003-10-12');
```

However, there's a trade-off involved: You must specify a value for every column in the table, and all values must be given in the order shown by a CREATE TABLE statement. Suppose we do a SHOW CREATE TABLE orders;, and MySQL displays a table creation statement:

```
Command Prompt - mysql -h megalon -u root -p                    _ □ ×

mysql> SHOW CREATE TABLE orders\G
*************************** 1. row ***************************
       Table: orders
Create Table: CREATE TABLE `orders` (
  `id` int(11) NOT NULL auto_increment,
  `firstname` varchar(25) NOT NULL default '',
  `lastname` varchar(25) NOT NULL default '',
  `amount` decimal(6,2) NOT NULL default '0.00',
  `discount` decimal(3,2) NOT NULL default '0.00',
  `date` date NOT NULL default '0000-00-00',
  PRIMARY KEY (`id`)
) ENGINE=MyISAM DEFAULT CHARSET=latin1 COMMENT='orders table'
1 row in set (0.00 sec)

mysql>
```

If this is the case, the INSERT query that we've just written will fail. It turns out that there are two other columns in the table that we didn't know about (or managed to overlook): **customer_id** and **ship_date**. All we need to do is to tell MySQL to use the default value for those columns. You can accomplish this by inserting an empty string or a NULL, although the latter will fail with an error if the column definition doesn't allow for null values:

```
INSERT INTO orders
VALUES ('', 'John', 'Smith', '','652.77', '2003-10-12', '');
```

or

```
INSERT INTO orders
VALUES (NULL, 'John', 'Smith', '','652.77', '2003-10-12', '');
```

Since **customer_id** is an auto-incrementing column, MySQL will automatically insert the next available integer for that column. Note that we *can* use NULL for this purpose with an auto-incrementing column, even though its definition contains a NOT NULL specifier. The listed default values will be inserted for the other two columns: an integer zero for the **zipcode** column, and 0000-00-00 for **ship_date**. (Presumably, we'll update these values once we have the shipping information for this order.)

Any of these three formats is equally acceptable. One might be more appropriate or easier to use than the others in different circumstances; otherwise, it's a matter of personal preference.

The other form of the INSERT query that you should be aware of is INSERT ... SELECT, which allows you to add one or more values from one table directly to another. This is particularly useful when you want to work closely with a given subset of data. For example, suppose we wish to prepare some reports on customer activity for the third quarter of 2003, based on data from the **orders** table used in previous examples. Assuming that we've already created a table named **reports** that has the appropriate column names, we can write:

```
INSERT INTO reports (c_first, c_last, amt_billed, o_date)
SELECT firstname, lastname, amount, order_date
FROM orders
WHERE order_date >= '2003-07-01' AND order_date < '2003-10-01';
```

This will insert a new record into **reports** for each record in the **orders** table that meets the criteria set in the WHERE clause. The value in a given **orders** record's **firstname** column (which we can also write as **orders.firstname**) will be inserted into the new **reports** record's **c_first** column (or more simply, **reports.c_first**); that of the **orders.lastname** column will be used for the new **reports.c_last** value; and so on. Now we can work with just the third-quarter data without needing to specify a WHERE order_date >= '2003-07-01' AND order_date < '2003-10-01' clause in every query, or to worry about making changes that will corrupt the original data.

Speaking of making changes to records, let's look at how that can be done in MySQL.

UPDATE Syntax

If you want to alter the data in an existing record (without adding a new record to the table), use the UPDATE statement.

Definition

The complete definition for UPDATE is as follows.

```
UPDATE [LOW_PRIORITY] [IGNORE] table_name[, table_name2, ...]
    SET column_name=expression [, column_name2=expression2, ...]
    [WHERE condition(s)]
    [ORDER BY column_name | alias[, column_name2 | alias2, ...]]
    [LIMIT row_count]
```

In it simplest form, as used since the release of MySQL 3.23, this statement updates the column or columns in the table *table_name* with the value or values indicated by the equal signs. You can use a WHERE clause to determine the conditions under which those columns will be updated in any given record. (You can also use LIMIT to restrict the number of rows to be updated, although this feature really didn't become useful until MySQL 4.0, as explained in the next section.)

Examples

Let's take a look at a few examples of using the UPDATE command; we'll continue to use our **orders** table. To start with, the simplest case might be something like this:

```
UPDATE orders
SET ship_date = NOW();
```

This will set the **ship_date** column in every record of the table to today's date.

To set the **ship_date** for only those records in which this column hasn't yet been set, we would use this form:

```
UPDATE records
SET ship_date = NOW()
WHERE ship_date = '0000-00-00';
```

An expression used in the SET clause to change the value of a particular column may be self-referential. For example, let's assume that all of the dollar amounts stored in the table include 10% goods and services tax (GST) and, due to a change in the firm's bookkeeping practices, we now want to start storing those exclusive of any tax:

```
UPDATE orders
SET amount = amount / 1.1;
```

As a slightly different scenario, let's say that another department had already adopted this practice, but nobody bothered to send us a copy of the memo until ten weeks after the fact. Therefore, we want to update only the amounts in the records for orders made prior to September 14, 2003:

```
UPDATE orders
SET amount = amount / 1.1
WHERE order_date < '2003-09-14';
```

Of course, we can also update multiple columns in a single query. Suppose we discover that the name of one of our customers has been misspelled by someone during data entry, and we've been asked to change all order records showing the name Donald Johnson to show the orders as having been made by Ronald Johnston. This isn't terribly difficult to accomplish:

```
UPDATE orders
SET firstname = 'Ronald', lastname = 'Johnston'
WHERE firstname = 'Donald' AND lastname = 'Johnson';
```

Newer versions have introduced new features for updates to make them much more powerful. Beginning with MySQL 4.0, it's possible to update multiple tables with a single statement:

```
UPDATE customers c, orders o
SET o.ship_date = NOW(), c.last_order_date = o.ship_date
WHERE o.ship_date = '' AND c.lastname = o.lastname;
```

As of MySQL 4.0.4, it's also possible to use an ORDER BY clause with UPDATE queries, so LIMIT becomes rather more useful with updates than in previous versions. Suppose our **customers** table contains a **discount** field that's used to determine when selected customers are eligible for a special discount. We can offer a 15% discount to the ten customers with the highest cost per order with this statement:

```
UPDATE customers
SET discount = 0.15
ORDER BY amount DESC
LIMIT 10 ;  /* or: LIMIT 0, 10  */
```

And we can give a 5% discount to the next ten highest spenders like this:

```
UPDATE customers
SET discount = 0.05
WHERE discount <> 0.15
/* So we don't decrease the discount for any customers
   who also happen to be in the next 10! */
ORDER BY amount DESC
LIMIT 11, 20;
```

Of course, there's much more you can do with SELECT queries. We'll discuss more powerful options and commands in later chapters.

DELETE Syntax

The other major type of query used in MySQL (and in SQL in general) is the DELETE query, which you can use to remove records from a table.

Definition

In MySQL, there are three main variations on the syntax that can be employed for writing a DELETE query:

```
DELETE [LOW_PRIORITY] [QUICK]
  FROM table_name
  [WHERE condition(s)]
  [ORDER BY order_clause]
  [LIMIT row_count]
```

or:

```
DELETE [LOW_PRIORITY] [QUICK] table_name[.*] [, table_name2[.*] ...]
  FROM table_reference(s)
  [WHERE condition(s)]
```

or:

```
DELETE [LOW_PRIORITY] [QUICK]
  FROM table_name[.*] [, table_name2[.*] ...]
  USING table_reference(s)
  [WHERE condition(s)]
```

CAUTION   *Issuing a* DELETE *command with no* WHERE *clause will result in all rows being deleted from the table specified in the query. You can prevent this from happening by using the* --safe-updates *or* --i-am-a-dummy *configuration option in a my.cnf or my.ini file.*

Examples

The first of the variants represents the quickest and simplest form of this command:

```
DELETE FROM customers
WHERE customer_id = '101';
```

Assuming that the **customer_id** column value is unique for each record in the **customers** table, this will delete a single record from that table: the record for which **id** has the value shown. All rows meeting the condition will be deleted from the table, and it's up to you to make sure that only one record matches that condition if you wish to delete a single row.

NOTE *Using **id** as the name or part of the name of a column in and of itself does not give the column any special properties; this is a somewhat common misapprehension. Uniqueness must be guaranteed by making the column a unique or primary key and (optionally) using the* AUTO_INCREMENT *attribute for the column definition. (See Chapter 3 for more information about keys and column attributes.)*

Suppose we back up the **customers** table at the beginning of each quarter, and for efficiency, we keep in the active database only those records from the last two quarters. In such a case, we could, after making our backup at the beginning of the third quarter of 2003, delete all records to be "aged out" from the **orders** table by using a single query:

```
DELETE FROM orders
WHERE order_date < '2003-01-01';
```

This would expunge the records for all orders made prior to January 1, 2003 from the "live" database.

Of course, you're not limited to specifying a single condition in the WHERE clause. For example, in the **reports** table we created using a SELECT ... INSERT query (in the examples of the INSERT syntax earlier in this chapter), we could delete all records for sales more than 90 days in the past that were also for amounts under $100 by using this statement:

```
DELETE FROM reports
WHERE amt_billed < 100
AND o_date < (NOW() - INTERVAL 90 DAY);
```

(For more information about MySQL's time and date functions, see the appropriate section of Chapter 4.)

NOTE *If you delete a large portion of a table that is of type MyISAM, it may be necessary to run the MySQL table optimization command afterwards to prevent performance drops due to fragmented datafiles and to free disk space. To issue this command, simply use the syntax* OPTIMIZE TABLE *table_name;*.

While we're reviewing DELETE syntax, it's probably appropriate to discuss another option that is often more effective than DELETE FROM table_name; when you wish to remove all the data from a specified table: the TRUNCATE command. This handy Oracle SQL extension was added in MySQL 3.23.28.

Its syntax is quite simple:

```
TRUNCATE [TABLE] table_name;
```

TIP *In MySQL versions 3.23.28 through 3.23.32, the optional* TABLE *keyword must be omitted from* TRUNCATE *commands.*

However, there are a few differences in behavior that distinguish TRUNCATE from DELETE:

- TRUNCATE removes all data by performing a DROP TABLE command and then re-creating the table. This means that the numbering of any auto-incrementing column that might be in the table will be reinitialized, which is not the case with DELETE.

- TRUNCATE is *not* transaction safe. If there is an active transaction or table-lock, this command will return an error.

- The number of deleted rows is not returned, so if you need to know this, use DELETE FROM table_name; or run a SELECT COUNT(*) FROM table_name; query immediately prior to issuing the TRUNCATE command.

NOTE DELETE *queries without a* WHERE *clause return zero affected rows in MySQL 3.23. Another* DELETE *option will delete all rows from a table* and *cause the correct number of deleted rows to be returned in MySQL 3.23, but it's not usually recommended because it's almost always slower. This is* DELETE FROM table_name WHERE 1 > 0;. *MySQL 4.0 and above do not have this issue and will always report the number of deleted rows correctly, whether or not a* WHERE *clause was used.*

In MySQL 4.0, support for ORDER BY clauses was added to DELETE. For example, in MySQL 4.0, you can delete the records for the 50 smallest orders (by amount spent) from the **orders** table like this:

```
DELETE FROM orders
ORDER BY amount ASC
LIMIT 50;
```

You can also use `LIMIT` with `DELETE` queries to segment deletions of very large numbers of records from a table in a very busy database, when used in conjunction with a programming language's `wait` or similar command. For example, in PHP you could write something like this:

```
$affected = 100;
$query = "DELETE FROM orders
          WHERE (order_date + INTERVAL 30 DAY) < NOW() AND confirmed = 'N'
          ORDER BY order_date
          LIMIT 100";
while($affected >= 100)
{
  $result = mysql_query($query);
  $affected = mysql_affected_rows($result);
  sleep(60);
}
echo "Deletion of unconfirmed orders over 30 days old has been completed.";
```

In MySQL 4, two new forms of this command providing the capability to delete from multiple tables in a single query have been added. Beginning with MySQL 4.0, you can perform deletions such as this:

```
DELETE orders, customers
FROM orders, customers, regions
WHERE orders.customer_id = customers.customer_id
AND regions.region_id = customers.region_id
AND regions.region_id = 4;
```

This will delete all records in the **orders** and **customers** tables linked to customers in region 4. Notice that records are deleted only from the tables listed *before* the `FROM` clause.

MySQL 4.0.2 introduced a variation on this syntax that you might find a bit easier to read and use:

```
DELETE FROM orders, customers
USING orders, customers, regions
WHERE orders.customer_id = customers.customer_id
AND regions.region_id = customers.region_id
AND regions.region_id = 4;
```

You may also sometimes see an optional dot-syntax, as in the following:

```
# Either...
DELETE FROM orders.*, customers.*
USING orders, customers, regions
WHERE orders.customer_id = customers.customer_id
AND regions.region_id = customers.region_id
AND regions.region_id = 4;
# or...
DELETE orders.*, customers.*
FROM orders, customers, regions
WHERE orders.customer_id = customers.customer_id
AND regions.region_id = customers.region_id
AND regions.region_id = 4;
```

In both cases, adding the .* has no effect; this feature is present only to make it easier to port code from other databases (most notably Microsoft Access), and you may safely omit it unless this will be a concern in your application.

Summary

We've reviewed some MySQL basics in this chapter for those of you who have not used MySQL before or haven't used it in a while. First, we covered how to establish a connection with MySQL by logging in with a username and password, which is absolutely essential if you're going to accomplish anything useful with it, whether you're using the MySQL Monitor or accessing a MySQL database from application code.

Next, we discussed naming conventions. Because MySQL, depending on the platform on which it's being used and how it's configured, may or may not be case-sensitive with regard to table and column names, we recommended the use of lowercase identifiers. In addition, although it's possible to use other characters in MySQL identifiers, we also recommended that you stick with letters with or without numbers, and (possibly) the underscore character, and that you avoid the use of reserved keywords.

Finally, we provided a review of the basic syntax and usage for some of the most important types of queries used in MySQL: CREATE TABLE, DROP, SELECT, INSERT, UPDATE, DELETE, and TRUNCATE. In the course of our discussion, we covered the most relevant and useful changes and additions to these commands in MySQL 4.0 and 4.1, including multitable deletes and the use of ORDER BY clauses in UPDATE and DELETE queries.

We also discussed the use of table, column, and expression aliases. These can save a great deal of repetition (and typing) in long queries and can be quite helpful in database application programming.

What's Next

Before you can begin building databases, you need to consider the categories or formats in which data can be stored. While some developers may have a "one size fits all" philosophy regarding datatypes, this is simply not the case. Effective use of datatypes *does* matter and *can* make a tremendous amount of difference in your MySQL-backed applications, and we'll discuss some of the many reasons this is so in Chapter 2.

MySQL supports most of SQL-standard datatypes and has a couple of unique ones of its own. We'll examine all of these, looking at the capabilities and limitations of each one, and try to provide you with some useful and practical advice that will help you determine when a given MySQL datatype is most appropriate. In keeping with the idea that one of the characteristics of a well-tuned database is that it exhibits an economical use of disk space, we'll also go into some detail about the space requirements of each datatype.

MySQL is somewhat unusual among relational databases in that it supports a number of database engines and corresponding table types, including ISAM, MyISAM, InnoDB, and Berkeley DB, among others. No useful book on building and using MySQL databases would be complete without a discussion of MySQL table types and their characteristics.

In Chapter 2, we'll examine each of these table types in terms of their capabilities, availability, requirements and relative strengths and weaknesses. We'll also pay special attention to changes in table types and how they're supported in different MySQL versions, including version 5.0.

CHAPTER 2

MySQL Column and Table Types

To begin with the obvious, the purpose of a database is to provide a place where you can store data now and retrieve it reliably at some time in the future. In this chapter, we'll look at and try to answer two key questions that follow from this premise:

- What types of data can you store?

- What kinds of structures can you use to store this data?

Like any other modern relational database, MySQL offers a rich selection of datatypes for storing different kinds of data of various shapes and sizes. The greater part of this chapter will be spent reviewing MySQL's datatypes and their storage requirements. In fact, we'll go into excruciating detail at some points. While this may not sound particularly exciting (unless you like the idea of "excruciating"), it's very important that you be familiar with these types, because you simply can't design effective tables and databases unless you know what column types go best with what sort of data.

We'll begin with what can be thought of as MySQL's two "simple" classes of datatypes: numbers and character data. Then, at roughly the midpoint of our discussion of datatypes, we'll take a time-out to talk about a special value with which you may already be familiar from elsewhere in your computing experience: a *null value*, which is quite often a source of confusion. Although its definition is a fairly simple one, it is still often misunderstood and misused, even by experienced database developers and programmers. We'll provide this simple definition, and then discuss just what NULL is, what it isn't, and when you should and should not use it. After that, we'll tackle the two more complex sorts of data that MySQL can work with: date and time types, and grouping types. Under the "Groupings" heading, we'll also look at some ways in which you might solve a fairly common problem, which is that MySQL has no true Boolean datatype.

The coverage of the second main topic of this chapter is quite a bit shorter than the one covering datatypes and associated issues, but it's no less important. Once you've determined the best datatypes for storing your data, you need to think about the sort of table of which those columns of data will be a part. MySQL supports several different table types, each with its own characteristics, and we'll offer an overview of MySQL's table types, their capabilities, and how and when they can and ought to be used.

But before we begin going into all of those "excruciating" details, let's talk about why you should even care about datatypes.

Why Datatypes Matter

Because each column in a table must be declared as being of a particular type and thereafter will hold data only of that particular type, it's necessary to make the right choice of column type right from the start. Of course, it's possible and even sometimes necessary to change the datatype for a column (using one or more ALTER commands) after the table containing that column has been created, but you'll make it much easier on yourself and any developers working with your databases if you can keep this to an absolute minimum.

NOTE *We use the terms* datatype *and* column type *more or less interchangeably throughout this chapter. Strictly speaking, a column type refers to the datatype that the column is intended to contain; in other words, a column is declared to be of a particular datatype.*

As you'll see shortly, data comes in four basic varieties insofar as MySQL is concerned: numbers, strings (character data), dates and times, and groupings (sets). Each of MySQL's datatypes belongs to one of these. Each datatype has a particular purpose or provides a best fit when modeling one or more objects or situations in the real world. For example, exact numeric types (also known as integer types) are best suited for indexing or counting discrete objects, approximate types (such as floating-point numbers) should be used for storing values containing fractions, and so on. As we go over each datatype, we'll try to provide some examples illustrating where it's best used. Each datatype also has specific storage requirements, and we'll provide details on these as well.

Using the wrong datatype, such as storing numbers in a column designated as containing character data, is usually not a good idea. Following our discussion of the datatypes themselves, we'll also look at some common mistakes made in choosing datatypes, and what you can do to correct them or, better yet, to avoid making them in the first place. Getting rid of bloat isn't the only rationale for making effective use of MySQL datatypes; there are at least two other reasons for doing so:

- Trying to perform certain operations on some types of data, like attempting to multiply a number by a string value, can lead to unexpected and usually erroneous results.

- Some MySQL datatypes have special properties or special functions associated with them. If you declare a column as some other type, and then try to make use of these, you will quickly find that they don't work.

A Few Words from Chad Russell

One of the main things that sticks in my mind, when I think back to when I first started designing databases, was how much other developers would stress out over using the appropriate column type. At first, I wasn't quite sure why they made a big deal over the way a certain column type handles the appropriate stored data. Over the years, I have encountered so many poor choices that other developers have made when choosing their column types and developing their databases, that I now understand what all the fuss was about.

Knowing the column types that are available to you on the database platform that you're running, and knowing the right situations to use them in, can greatly improve the performance of your database. Although some these differences may not appear to be great, they can and will compound as database size and traffic increase.

Another thing to keep in mind is to use the appropriate column size for the respective data you are storing. Although this may take some extra time in planning, it will help you avoid many performance issues in the end. I once had to redesign a database that had been created by another developer. When I first examined the database structure, I found that the every column field was either CHAR(100) or INT; the database took up approximately 750MB. After being restructured to conform to appropriate datatypes and sizes, the size of the database was reduced by nearly 90%, to only about 9MB.

And from Jon Stephens

I could recount a datatype horror story or two of my own. However, I think that Chad's already made the point: While there are many other factors to weigh when designing a database, it is very important to keep in mind that "one size fits all" does *not* apply when it comes to choosing datatypes. Trying to implement this notion as a design decision will almost invariably lead to bloat, and bloat leads to poor performance.

The fact that so many database administrators and developers seem to believe that it's okay to use any old datatype for any old type of data is one of our pet peeves when dealing with other people's databases, and it's one of the things that inspired us to write this book. You're going to hear us say many, many times throughout the first part of this chapter, "Datatypes *do* matter; your choices in this regard *will* make a difference." It's a message that we firmly believe can't be repeated often enough, and it's one that we ourselves try to keep in mind whenever we're designing a new database or trying to give a facelift to an existing one.

We're not promising that you'll see such dramatic results as Chad describes in every single case. Nevertheless, we *can* tell you that by spending even a little time getting better acquainted with what MySQL has to offer in terms of datatypes, and applying this knowledge, you'll be able to see improvements with regard to both space requirements and performance under load, and that as your data and traffic requirements scale upwards, so will those improvements.

It's true that sometimes compromises need to be made, and that a few bytes here and there aren't likely to make that large a difference in the overall scheme of things. However, as in the scenario that Chad described, it's also true that using a CHAR(100) column to store a six-digit number (and wasting 85 to 90 bytes of space per table row!) is just not sensible. Multiply this mistake by a dozen columns in a dozen tables, and then by many thousands of records, and you have a lot of wasted space.

MySQL Column Types

Each piece of data stored in a MySQL database must be of a particular type. If you've programmed in a strongly typed language such as C++ or Java, you should already be comfortable with this concept. Even if your programming experience is limited to weakly typed scripting languages such as JavaScript or PHP, you've almost certainly run into datatype-related "gotchas."

For a very simple example, consider the following JavaScript function:

```
function myFunction() { return val + val; }
```

Now let's call the function twice, with values that look similar, but are of different types:

```
var resultOne = myFunction(11);
var resultTwo = myFunction("11");
```

The value that's computed for **resultOne** (the integer 22) is definitely not the same value that's computed for **resultTwo** (the string "1111")! Much the same holds true in MySQL (and most, if not all, other relational databases). Many scripting languages (such as JavaScript or PHP) will attempt to convert values of types that don't actually fit the operation you're trying to perform on them. For instance, if you try to add a number to a string in JavaScript, the interpreter will convert the number into a string, and then concatenate the two values. MySQL will also attempt to convert datatypes and column types, but this often isn't terribly efficient, as you'll see shortly.

MySQL column types can be divided into four broad categories:

- **Numeric types:** Integer, floating-point, and decimal numbers

- **Character/text types:** Character, text, and binary data

- **Date/time types:** For working with calendar dates, clock times, and time-stamps

- **Logical/grouping types:** Sets, enumerated values, and ways to represent Boolean values

Storing Numbers: Numeric Column Types

When working with numbers (or any datatype, for that matter), it is very important to choose the appropriate column type. You should always store numeric data in a numeric column type, unless there is a chance that your data may include nonnumeric characters, as in the case of ISBN or UPC numbers.

MySQL's numeric column types can be divided into two categories:

- Exact types (sometimes also referred to as integer types), which may contain only whole numbers

- Approximate types (also known as decimal or floating-point types), which can be used to store fractional values

We'll look at each of these in turn—first the exact, and then the approximate numeric types.

Exact Numeric (Integer) Column Types

The first of MySQL's two categories of numeric column types stores integer values, which are most often employed for indexing records and for holding counts of discrete objects. In other words, the exact numeric column types are used to store data that helps answer questions like "How many copies of *Pride and Prejudice* did this customer order?" An integer is, of course, simply a whole number; you can't store a fractional value in an integer column.

MySQL has a number of column types for storing integers according to their size. While extremely large integers can be stored (much greater than a trillion, which is a pretty big number already), there are also many occasions when you wish to store values of a much more modest size. For example, there's really no need to allow for the event that you'll need to store a number like 5,875,890,421 in an **items_in_stock** column when it's impossible for there to be so many items in your entire inventory. MySQL has column types to accommodate these as well. It's to your advantage to use these whenever possible, because you can save overhead by not allocating memory for values that aren't ever going to be used. In addition, you can cut down on the amount of erroneous data being stored by *disallowing* the storage of values that are extreme or even nonsensical in a given situation.

You'll also see how it's possible to specify the *signedness* of integers; that is, you can state in a column definition whether you're going to permit negative values to be stored in that column. Not allowing this to happen when it's not necessary can sometimes save space in a database. It can also prevent the storing of impossible values. For instance, you're certainly never going to have a situation where a customer might order negative 17 copies of *Pride and Prejudice* from your bookstore, so you shouldn't allow such an impossible scenario to be modeled in the bookstore's database.

Next, we'll look at display issues with regard to integers in MySQL. Sometimes, for various reasons, you need to guarantee that an integer is displayed with a certain minimum number of digits, which you can accomplish by specifying a display width in conjunction with the ZEROFILL modifier. We'll also consider what happens when you try to store a value that is too large (or small) for a given column, both in terms of its magnitude and the number of digits it contains.

As you read over the next dozen or so pages, it may seem like a lot of space to devote to something as simple as integers. Just keep in mind that all of this material does have its uses, and familiarizing yourself with it now will very likely—sometime, somewhere—help to save you time and trouble in designing an efficient MySQL database.

Size and Sign

MySQL supports several integer column types, which are distinguished by the sizes of the ranges of values that can be stored in each. As we've stated already, using the proper integer type for the task at hand will not only save you space, but also help to prevent insertion into a table of "junk" data, with unlikely or even useless values. There are actually five of these integer types, whose characteristics are summarized in Table 2-1.

Table 2-1. MySQL Integer Types

COLUMN TYPE	STORAGE REQUIRED	MINIMUM VALUE	MAXIMUM VALUE	RANGE
TINYINT	1 byte	−128	127	2^8
SMALLINT	2 bytes	−32,768	32,767	2^{16}
MEDIUMINT	3 bytes	−8,388,608	8,388,607	2^{24}
INT	4 bytes	−2,147,483,648	2,147,483,647	2^{32}
BIGINT	8 bytes	−9,223,372,036,854,775,808	9,223,372,036,854,775,807	2^{64}

Integer values are *signed* by default; that is, they can contain positive and negative values. MySQL supports an UNSIGNED extension, which you can use to specify that a column contain only positive values. This can be useful in cases where you know in advance that a particular item of data is not going to be negative.

For example, suppose you're doing a population study and need to store birth data for different demographic areas. You're never going to encounter a situation where a negative number of children were born. This also increases the maximum value that you can insert into an integer column. However, the *range* of values remains the same, as shown in Table 2-1. For example, if you declare a column like this:

```
births SMALLINT UNSIGNED
```

Then **births** can contain values between 0 and 65,535 inclusive, but the range of values is still two to the sixteenth power (2 bytes).

On the other hand, to store the net change in population for a given area, you wouldn't want to do this, since it's quite possible that there might be more deaths than births, or that a large number of people might move out of the area, so using UNSIGNED for a **net_population_change** column wouldn't make much sense.

> **NOTE** INTEGER *is just a synonym for* INT. *To MySQL, they mean exactly the same thing.*

Choose the size that's most suitable for the type of data you'll be storing in the column. For instance, if you're designing a database for an online retail bookstore web site, chances are that no single customer is going to order more than 255 copies of the same book, so you're probably safe using something like this in an **orders** table:

```
number_of_copies TINYINT UNSIGNED
```

To provide a somewhat extreme example, let's suppose you define this column using BIGINT instead of TINYINT. Once you've recorded 100,000 orders, you will have wasted 700KB on a single column reserving space for data you'll never use. This isn't a huge amount in and of itself, but when multiplied by several columns in several tables, it will start to add up quickly.

On the other hand, suppose you decide later that the site is going to start catering to the bookseller trade (in the vernacular, you are migrating the original B2C business model to a B2B model). Now you need to be able to accommodate orders for several hundred or even thousands of copies of a single book. At that point, you could alter the **orders** table structure and change the TINYINT column type to SMALLINT, without losing the data that's already in the table.

> **CAUTION** *You can always change a smaller integer column type to a larger one without penalty. However, the reverse is not true: if you change a larger integer type to a smaller one, you'll truncate any existing values that are larger than the maximum allowed by the new column type.*

A common practice is to define a table's primary key as INT, but very often, SMALLINT or MEDIUMINT will do. Your objective should be to model the requirements for your application in a realistic fashion, keeping in mind that MySQL will allow you to extend a good table design and doesn't require you to rebuild the whole thing from scratch just because you need larger numbers in one or two places.

Stored vs. Displayed Values

Now let's discuss two issues we often come across when dealing with numeric values in computing: padding and truncation. The first of these concerns what you do when a value takes up fewer digits than needed for some purpose, and the second describes what happens when a value is larger than the maximum allowed for a particular column type.

Padding is what you do when you display a number that takes up fewer places than a given minimum in order to make it "fit" that minimum number, which you accomplish by filling the empty positions with zeros. When working with integers, you're concerned with only left padding (adding zeros to the left of the significant digits), as adding them to the right side would change the value of the number.

In order to pad integers in MySQL, you use a MySQL extension for integer types: the optional *display width* argument. Before we continue, however, we need to clear up a common misconception about it. A great many MySQL users, even experienced ones, have the mistaken idea that this value represents the maximum value or number of digits allowed in the column. Nothing could be further from the truth, as we can prove very quickly and easily. Let's create a simple **ints** table:

```
CREATE TABLE ints (
  val INT(3)
);
```

What we've done here is to create a table with a single column that can contain an integer value between –999 and 999 inclusive, right? Wrong, as we can see by inserting some sample data and then selecting it again.

```
Command Prompt - mysql -h megalon -u root -p
mysql> INSERT INTO ints (val) VALUES (9), (99), (999), (9999);
Query OK, 4 rows affected (0.06 sec)
Records: 4  Duplicates: 0  Warnings: 0

mysql> SELECT val FROM ints;
+------+
| val  |
+------+
|    9 |
|   99 |
|  999 |
| 9999 |
+------+
4 rows in set (0.00 sec)

mysql>
```

The display width makes no difference in the fact that the value1 column is of type INT and can, therefore, contain a value much larger than 999. Another way of thinking about the display width is that it represents a *minimum* number of digits; if the actual value takes fewer than that number of digits, MySQL will make up the difference using zeros.

This argument is really useful only in conjunction with another MySQL extension: ZEROFILL. Let's modify the definition of the **ints** table to include a ZEROFILL, and then see what happens when we rerun the same query.

```
Command Prompt - mysql -h megalon -u root -p
mysql> ALTER TABLE ints MODIFY COLUMN val INT(3) ZEROFILL;
Query OK, 4 rows affected (0.10 sec)
Records: 4  Duplicates: 0  Warnings: 0

mysql> SELECT val FROM ints;
+------+
| val  |
+------+
|  009 |
|  099 |
|  999 |
| 9999 |
+------+
4 rows in set (0.03 sec)

mysql>
```

NOTE *MySQL will supply a default value for each integer column subtype, whether or not you've specified ZEROFILL in an integer column definition.*

Using a display width can be handy for data such as zip codes or post codes that must contain a certain number of digits:

```
zipcode SMALLINT(5)
```

Of course, you'll need to enforce any maximum length restrictions in your application code if you decide to go this route.

Another common use for display widths occurs when doing LOAD DATA on fixed-width files. MySQL can import data from these files, as long as the display width of each numeric column in the table into which you're importing the data matches that of the corresponding column in the source file.

Otherwise, you don't need to include a display width.

Let's create a table with five columns, one of each integer type, and then see what MySQL has to tell us about those columns when we ask it for the table definition using the DESCRIBE command.

```
Command Prompt - mysql -h megalon -u root -p                    _ □ x
mysql> CREATE TABLE ints2 (
    -> value1 TINYINT,
    -> value2 SMALLINT,
    -> value3 MEDIUMINT,
    -> value4 INT,
    -> value5 INT
    -> );
Query OK, 0 rows affected (0.01 sec)

mysql> DESCRIBE ints2;
+--------+-------------+------+-----+---------+-------+
| Field  | Type        | Null | Key | Default | Extra |
+--------+-------------+------+-----+---------+-------+
| value1 | tinyint(4)  | YES  |     | NULL    |       |
| value2 | smallint(6) | YES  |     | NULL    |       |
| value3 | mediumint(9)| YES  |     | NULL    |       |
| value4 | int(11)     | YES  |     | NULL    |       |
| value5 | int(11)     | YES  |     | NULL    |       |
+--------+-------------+------+-----+---------+-------+
5 rows in set (0.05 sec)

mysql>
```

NOTE   *In each case, the default display width is* decreased *by one if you declare an integer column to be* UNSIGNED.

In fact, there's no rule that says you can't use a display width that's greater than the number of places the maximum value for an integer column would take up. You can see in the next example what happens if you try this. First, we create a table with a single column of type TINYINT (maximum value 255); then we insert a value and perform a SELECT query. The result is as shown.

```
Command Prompt - mysql -h megalon -u root -p                    _ □ x
mysql> CREATE TABLE ints3 (
    -> value1 TINYINT(8) ZEROFILL
    -> );
Query OK, 0 rows affected (0.02 sec)

mysql> INSERT INTO ints3 (value1) VALUES (23);
Query OK, 1 row affected (0.00 sec)

mysql> SELECT value1 FROM ints3;
+----------+
| value1   |
+----------+
| 00000023 |
+----------+
1 row in set (0.00 sec)

mysql>
```

It's also important to know that if you attempt to store a value greater than the maximum allowed value for that type (or less than the minimum allowed value), the value is *truncated* to the maximum (or minimum). For example, let's create a table **ints4** that contains two columns. Both columns are of type TINYINT, but one of these is signed and the other is unsigned. Next, we'll insert some values that we know will exceed the upper and lower bounds for both columns.

```
Command Prompt - mysql -h megalon -u root -p                        _ □ ×
mysql> CREATE TABLE ints4 (
    -> value1 TINYINT,
    -> value2 TINYINT UNSIGNED
    -> );
Query OK, 0 rows affected (0.02 sec)

mysql> INSERT INTO ints4 (value1, value2)
    -> VALUES (-1000, -1000), (1000, 1000);
Query OK, 2 rows affected, 4 warnings (0.05 sec)
Records: 2  Duplicates: 0  Warnings: 4

mysql>
```

Notice that MySQL generates four warnings for the INSERT query: one warning for each value that exceeded the limit imposed by the column type. If you're running MySQL 4.1 or later, you can retrieve the warnings generated by the previous command or query from within MySQL by using the SHOW WARNINGS command.

```
Command Prompt - mysql -h megalon -u root -p                        _ □ ×
mysql> SHOW WARNINGS\G
*************************** 1. row ***************************
  Level: Warning
   Code: 1263
Message: Data truncated, out of range for column 'value1' at row 1
*************************** 2. row ***************************
  Level: Warning
   Code: 1263
Message: Data truncated, out of range for column 'value2' at row 1
*************************** 3. row ***************************
  Level: Warning
   Code: 1263
Message: Data truncated, out of range for column 'value1' at row 2
*************************** 4. row ***************************
  Level: Warning
   Code: 1263
Message: Data truncated, out of range for column 'value2' at row 2
4 rows in set (0.01 sec)

mysql>
```

Regardless of the MySQL version, if we select both columns from the records that were just inserted, this is what's retrieved:

```
Command Prompt - mysql -h megalon -u root -p                        _ □ ×
mysql> SELECT value1, value2 FROM ints4;
+--------+--------+
| value1 | value2 |
+--------+--------+
|   -128 |      0 |
|    127 |    255 |
+--------+--------+
2 rows in set (0.00 sec)

mysql>
```

You can see an example of a common "gotcha" here: A column is declared as UNSIGNED, and then later someone attempts to store a negative number in it. The result is that a zero is stored instead. A related problem often occurs when application code tests whether a given value retrieved from this column is less than zero, and never executes because no nonnegative values can be stored there.

One other common error is the belief that you can somehow "expand" a column definition by using a sufficiently large value for its display width. Let's reuse the **ints3** table from the previous example. First, we'll clear all records (one record in this case) from this table, verify with a SELECT query that the table is empty, and then attempt to insert a value greater than 255 (the maximum for TINYINT).

```
Command Prompt - mysql -h megalon -u root -p                    _ □ ×
mysql> DELETE FROM ints3;
Query OK, 1 row affected (0.00 sec)

mysql> SELECT value1 FROM ints3;
Empty set (0.01 sec)

mysql> INSERT INTO ints3 (value1) VALUES (500);
Query OK, 1 row affected, 1 warning (0.00 sec)

mysql>
```

You can see that MySQL 4.1 (and later) reports an "out of range" warning, and that the value is in fact truncated to 255, even though the display is still padded out to eight digits.

```
Command Prompt - mysql -h megalon -u root -p                    _ □ ×
mysql> SHOW WARNINGS\G
*************************** 1. row ***************************
  Level: Warning
   Code: 1263
Message: Data truncated, out of range for column 'value1' at row 1
1 row in set (0.00 sec)

mysql> SELECT value1 FROM ints3;
+----------+
| value1   |
+----------+
| 00000255 |
+----------+
1 row in set (0.00 sec)

mysql>
```

A final observation before we move on: Don't use display width and ZEROFILL unless you actually need them for a reason. If the leading zeros aren't required and you're forced to remove them, you'll merely create an extra, unnecessary step in your application code. Whether you use string methods or a regular expression to strip them off, the result is still wasted code, wasted resources, and decreased efficiency.

 CAUTION *Using* ZEROFILL *in a column definition automatically implies that the column values are unsigned and any negative values you attempt to insert into that column will be truncated to zero, whether or not you've actually used the* UNSIGNED *keyword.*

Approximate (Floating-Point) Numeric Column Types

Now that we've examined the datatypes MySQL has for working with whole numbers, it's time to move on to those used to store numbers that contain a fractional part. We refer to these as "approximate" column types. There are three sorts of approximate numeric column types used in MySQL for varying purposes:

- FLOAT: These are most often used for storing single-precision floating-point numbers. There are some alternative forms for the FLOAT column type, which we'll also present in our discussion in this section, since you may encounter them in working with existing databases, and one of these actually causes MySQL to store numbers declared to be FLOAT as double-precision. However, we feel that it's much simpler to use FLOAT for single-precision numbers only.

- DOUBLE: These are always double-precision values. Their display width and number of digits following the decimal point can be specified if so desired. In MySQL, the names REAL, DOUBLE, and DOUBLE PRECISION all mean exactly the same thing. We prefer to use DOUBLE, and suggest that you do likewise, since this is how the equivalent datatype is referred to in C, Java, and many other programming languages.

- DECIMAL: These are actually stored as strings and can be specified in terms of a mantissa and an exponent. They're most useful in situations where a fixed number of decimals is required, such as when performing monetary calculations. Arithmetic with DECIMAL types is done as double-precision math. The terms DECIMAL, DEC, NUMERIC, and FIXED are synonymous in MySQL.

We'll look at each of these in greater detail shortly, but before we do that, we should talk about just what we mean by the terms *single-precision* and *double-precision*. It's important to remember that single-precision and double-precision numbers are defined in terms of binary numbers and are represented as decimals only for the convenience of humans (by MySQL and countless other databases and programming languages). A single-precision number is represented internally as a 4-byte (32-bit) binary number, and is broken down as follows:

- The first bit is called the *sign bit*; if it's a zero, the number is positive; if it's a one, the number is negative.

- The next 8 bits (1 byte) represent an exponent in the range of zero to binary 1111 1111 (decimal 255), from which we subtract 0111 1111 (decimal 127) to give us an effective range of –126 to 128 (–0111 1111 to 1000 0000 binary).

- The remaining 23 bits represent a binary fraction.

Figure 2-1 shows a diagram that might help to make things a bit clearer.

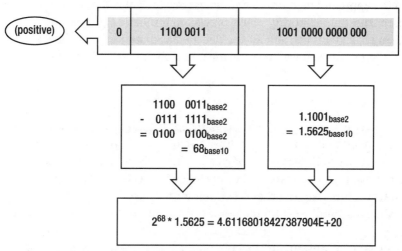

Figure 2-1. A computer's internal representation of a single-precision floating-point number

A double-precision number is similarly constructed, except that it's 8 bytes long (64 bits): the exponential portion is 11 bits, and the fractional part is 52 bits long.

Without regard to sign, the smallest possible nonzero single-precision number is 2^{-126}, or approximately 1.17549435E–38 decimal, and the largest possible single-precision value is $(2 - 2^{-23}) * 2^{127}$, or roughly 3.40282347E+38 decimal. For double-precision numbers, the minimum nonzero value is 2^{-1022}, or approximately 2.22507386E–308, and the maximum is $(2 - 2^{-52}) * 2^{1023}$, which is roughly equal to 1.79769313E+308.

Now we're ready to discuss the three kinds of approximate number types supported in MySQL: FLOAT, DOUBLE, and DECIMAL.

NOTE *Beginning with MySQL 4.0.2, all floating-point column types can be declared as* UNSIGNED. *As with unsigned integer columns, negative values cannot be stored in unsigned floating-point columns. However, unlike the case with integer types, the upper ranges of these types are* not *extended when declared as unsigned. Floating-point columns may also be declared as* ZEROFILL.

Single-Precision Numbers: The FLOAT Type

The first of the approximate number datatypes we'll look at is the FLOAT type, which is used (mostly) for storing single-precision numbers. This type can be a bit confusing because it can actually be declared and used in three different ways, but the simplest (and we think the most useful) of these is like so:

```
avalue FLOAT
```

This declares **avalue** as a single-precision (4-byte) floating-point value.

We recommend that you stick with this form of FLOAT. If you need double-precision numbers, use DOUBLE; if you need greater precision than that, use DECIMAL (these two types are discussed in the following sections). We're going to concentrate on this simple sort of FLOAT, but for the sake of completeness, we'll show you later in this section the other two ways this type can be declared and used.

Floats are generally useful for storing noninteger values where you're not overly concerned with exact precision. Let's look at an example or two. First, let's create a table floats1 containing a single FLOAT column, insert a few values into it, and then display them again using a SELECT query.

```
Command Prompt - mysql -h megalon -u root -p

mysql> CREATE TABLE floats1 (
    -> value1 FLOAT
    -> );
Query OK, 0 rows affected (0.03 sec)

mysql> INSERT INTO floats1 (value1)
    -> VALUES (123456789), (123.456789), (.123456789);
Query OK, 3 rows affected (0.01 sec)
Records: 3  Duplicates: 0  Warnings: 0

mysql> SELECT value1 FROM floats1;
+-------------+
| value1      |
+-------------+
| 1.23457e+008 |
|     123.457 |
|    0.123457 |
+-------------+
3 rows in set (0.00 sec)

mysql>
```

As you can see, MySQL does a lot of rounding here. In fact, as you work with these values, you'll find even more rounding is liable to take place. For an example, let's see what happens when we select the column values divided by other numbers (first a thousand, and then a million).

```
Command Prompt - mysql -h megalon -u root -p                    _ □ x
mysql> SELECT value1 / 1000 FROM floats1;
+--------------------+
| value1 / 1000      |
+--------------------+
|         123456.792 |
|     0.12345678710937 |
|   0.00012345679104328 |
+--------------------+
3 rows in set (0.04 sec)

mysql> SELECT value1 / 1000000 FROM floats1;
+--------------------+
| value1 / 1000000   |
+--------------------+
|         123.456792 |
|    0.0001234567871093 |
|    1.2345679104328e-007 |
+--------------------+
3 rows in set (0.01 sec)

mysql>
```

From this, you might deduce a general rule of thumb: You can't depend on a FLOAT value to be accurate after the first eight digits or so. However, rounding errors can creep in even faster than you might expect, as we can observe from creating a new table containing a FLOAT column, inserting some values into it, and then performing a few simple mathematical operations on them. (There's no reason why we can't create this table in a single line of SQL, and since it's a fairly short one, we do just that.)

```
Command Prompt - mysql -h megalon -u root -p                    _ □ x
mysql> CREATE TABLE floats2 (value1 FLOAT);
Query OK, 0 rows affected (0.03 sec)

mysql> INSERT INTO floats2 (value1)
    -> VALUES (100.00), (200.00), (10000.00), (10.5), (-505.05);
Query OK, 5 rows affected (0.00 sec)
Records: 5  Duplicates: 0  Warnings: 0

mysql>
```

You can probably sum these up in your head to obtain the value 9805.45. If you want to double-check using a pen and paper, go ahead. You can even use the MySQL command line as a calculator to verify the result.

```
Command Prompt - mysql -h megalon -u root -p                    _ □ x
mysql> SELECT 100.00 + 200.00 + 10000.00 + 10.5 - 505.05;
+---------------------------------------------+
| 100.00 + 200.00 + 10000.00 + 10.5 - 505.05 |
+---------------------------------------------+
|                                     9805.45 |
+---------------------------------------------+
1 row in set (0.01 sec)

mysql>
```

However, when we use the SUM() function to total up the same numbers after they've been stored as type FLOAT, the results might not be quite what you were expecting.

```
Command Prompt - mysql -h megalon -u root -p               _ □ ×
mysql> SELECT SUM(value1) FROM floats2;
+------------------+
| SUM(value1)      |
+------------------+
| 9805.450012207   |
+------------------+
1 row in set (0.06 sec)

mysql>
```

When we take the average of these five numbers, we should obtain 1961.09. If we sum the values directly, and then divide the result by 5, that's exactly what we get. But once again, if we use the stored FLOAT representations of these numbers, a margin of error quickly makes itself apparent, as you can see in the two queries and their results shown here.

```
Command Prompt - mysql -h megalon -u root -p               _ □ ×
mysql> SELECT (100.00 + 200.00 + 10000.00 + 10.5 - 505.05) / 5;
+-----------------------------------------------------+
| (100.00 + 200.00 + 10000.00 + 10.5 - 505.05) / 5    |
+-----------------------------------------------------+
|                                          1961.0900  |
+-----------------------------------------------------+
1 row in set (0.03 sec)

mysql> SELECT AVG(value1) FROM floats2;
+------------------+
| AVG(value1)      |
+------------------+
| 1961.0900024414  |
+------------------+
1 row in set (0.00 sec)

mysql>
```

This apparent discrepancy is due to the fact that MySQL treats all values as double-precision values when performing floating-point arithmetic.

As we've already said, we think it's best to use the simple form of the FLOAT type (and reserve this type for storing single-precision numbers), but since MySQL provides two other forms of it that you may see in use from time to time, let's discuss those briefly before moving on. The first of these takes this form:

FLOAT(p)

where p is the number of precision bits used. However, you can't alter the range of the exponent. If p is less than 24, the value for the exponent is 8 bits (range is 2^{-126} to 2^{127}); if it's between 24 and 52, the exponent is 11 bits (2^{-1022} to 2^{1023}). In addition, if p is less than 24, the column value is single-precision and requires 4 bytes of storage; if it's between 24 and 52, the column value is a double-precision number and takes up 8 bytes in memory. If you use FLOAT(p) where p is greater than 24, then the value will be treated as a double-precision number, and the results of calculations will be much more reliable. It's simpler just to use DOUBLE.

The other alternative method of declaring a FLOAT creates a column that stores single-precision numbers, and involves two arguments, like so:

FLOAT(w, d)

where *w* represents the display width, and *d* is the number of decimals used for the values stored. These are similar to the arguments used with the DECIMAL type (discussed next). If you specify a width smaller than the number of decimals, MySQL automatically sets $w = d + 1$.

If you declare a column as FLOAT, FLOAT(w, d), or FLOAT(p) where *p* is less than 25, and then later change the column type to FLOAT(p) where *p* is 25 or greater, the values already stored in that column will *not* be updated and will still be subject to rounding errors. Here is an example of this:

```
Command Prompt - mysql -h megalon -u root -p
mysql> CREATE TABLE floats3 (value1 FLOAT);
Query OK, 0 rows affected (0.01 sec)

mysql> INSERT INTO floats3 (value1)
    -> VALUES (100.00), (200.00), (10000.00), (10.5), (-505.05);
Query OK, 5 rows affected (0.00 sec)
Records: 5  Duplicates: 0  Warnings: 0

mysql> ALTER TABLE floats3 MODIFY COLUMN value1 FLOAT(32);
Query OK, 5 rows affected (0.04 sec)
Records: 5  Duplicates: 0  Warnings: 0

mysql> SELECT SUM(value1), AVG(value1) FROM floats3;
+----------------+----------------+
| SUM(value1)    | AVG(value1)    |
+----------------+----------------+
| 9805.450012207 | 1961.0900024414 |
+----------------+----------------+
1 row in set (0.00 sec)

mysql>
```

This is an easy mistake to make. Remember that if you're using a single-precision column and later discover that you need the accuracy of double-precision values, you'll need to update the values stored in the column after changing the column type.

TIP *Numbers in columns declared using either* FLOAT *or* FLOAT(w, d) *syntax are always stored as single-precision values. Numbers stored in columns declared as* FLOAT(p) *where* p ≥ 25 *are always double-precision. In general, we recommend using* FLOAT *(with no parameters) for single-precision numbers and* DOUBLE *for double-precision numbers.*

Double-Precision Numbers: The DOUBLE Type

Sometimes, you need more accuracy with floating-point numbers than the (roughly) eight significant digits supported by single-precision types. In such a case, you might wish to consider using a double-precision (8-byte) column type, which is roughly 10^{10} times more accurate than single-precision. MySQL has three different synonyms for double-precision floating-point numbers: DOUBLE, DOUBLE PRECISION, and REAL. We prefer to use DOUBLE, but you are free to use whichever name you prefer, just as long as you recognize that all three of them mean the same thing.

 TIP   *If you need to export MySQL double-precision values to a different database engine, you may want to declare them as* DOUBLE PRECISION *for maximum portability.*

These three types don't take any kind of a precision argument; they're always double-precision numbers and always require 8 bytes of storage. (See the discussion of double-precision numbers under the heading "Approximate (Floating-Point) Numeric Column Types" earlier in this chapter for more details.) If we repeat our experiment with obtaining sums and averages of decimal numbers from the previous section, we find that using a double-precision column for the floating-point values gives us much better results than we got using a FLOAT (single-precision) column.

```
Command Prompt - mysql -h megalon -u root -p                    _ □ ×
mysql> CREATE TABLE doubles1 (value1 DOUBLE);
Query OK, 0 rows affected (0.01 sec)

mysql> INSERT INTO doubles1 (value1)
    -> VALUES (100.00), (200.00), (10000.00), (10.5), (-505.05);
Query OK, 5 rows affected (0.01 sec)
Records: 5  Duplicates: 0  Warnings: 0

mysql> SELECT SUM(value1), AVG(value1) FROM doubles1;
+-------------+-------------+
| SUM(value1) | AVG(value1) |
+-------------+-------------+
|     9805.45 |     1961.09 |
+-------------+-------------+
1 row in set (0.01 sec)

mysql>
```

In fact, these are exactly the values you would expect.

DOUBLE columns (including DOUBLE PRECISION and REAL) may optionally be declared with two additional arguments in the format DOUBLE(w, d) where w is the display width and d is the number of digits to the right of the decimal point. This does *not* affect the amount of space required to store values in these columns. The width argument has no effect unless you also declare the column as ZEROFILL, in which case any empty positions to the left of the decimal (up to that number) will be filled with zeros.

CAUTION *Attempting to use a single argument with any of the* DOUBLE *column types will result in a syntax error. If you want to specify the width or the number of digits, you must specify both.*

Whether or not the column is declared as ZEROFILL, if the DOUBLE(w, d) form is used, any empty places up to the *d* position to the right of the decimal will be filled with zeros, and any extra digits in excess of that number will be truncated. Like the other numeric column types, DOUBLE columns can be declared as UNSIGNED. Here is a brief example:

```
Command Prompt - mysql -h megalon -u root -p

mysql> CREATE TABLE doubles2 (
    -> value1 DOUBLE(4, 4),
    -> value2 DOUBLE(4, 4) ZEROFILL,
    -> value3 DOUBLE(4, 4) UNSIGNED ZEROFILL
    -> );
Query OK, 0 rows affected (0.02 sec)

mysql> INSERT INTO doubles2 (value1, value2, value3)
    -> VALUES (12345.12345, 3.05, -2.045);
Query OK, 1 row affected, 1 warning (0.00 sec)

mysql> SHOW WARNINGS\G
*************************** 1. row ***************************
  Level: Warning
   Code: 1263
Message: Data truncated, out of range for column 'value3' at row 1
1 row in set (0.00 sec)

mysql> SELECT * FROM doubles2;
+------------+--------+--------+
| value1     | value2 | value3 |
+------------+--------+--------+
| 12345.1234 | 3.0500 | 0.0000 |
+------------+--------+--------+
1 row in set (0.00 sec)

mysql>
```

As you can see here, the fifth digit for the first value is dropped, the second value is padded with zeros to four decimal places, and the third value is truncated to zero.

NOTE *Beginning with MySQL 4.0.2, floating-point column types can be declared as* UNSIGNED *or* ZEROFILL*. Previous to this, only integer column types could be so modified.*

The DECIMAL Type

The third and last of the approximate numeric datatypes we'll discuss is the DECIMAL column type. This type is also known as DEC, NUMERIC, or FIXED. We use (and recommend that you use) DECIMAL, but you can choose whichever of these names that you like, as long as you're consistent and you remember what it means. FIXED was added in MySQL 4.1, so if you're using an earlier version, that option isn't available to you.

DECIMAL column types have the same range of values by default as double-precision types. Unlike the case for values stored as DOUBLE, however, DECIMAL types can be (and usually are) specified with regard to both their overall length and the number of digits to the right of the decimal point (if any). This makes them useful for monetary and other calculations requiring a fixed fractional part. For example, consider this the column definition:

```
price DECIMAL(5,2)
```

All values stored in the **price** column will be exactly five digits long, with exactly two of those digits following the decimal point. (Any missing digits to the right of the decimal will automatically be filled with zeros.)

The storage required for a DECIMAL column value is calculated using a formula, which we can express using the following pseudocode:

```
if(W >= D)
{
  if(D > 0)
    S = W + 2
  else
    S = W + 1
}
else
  S = D + 2
```

where S is the space required in bytes, W is the width of the column, and D is the number of decimal digits. Using this formula, you can determine that each record in the **price** column we just defined will require seven bytes of storage.

NOTE *If you don't specify a number of decimals for a DECIMAL column, the default is value is zero (0). If you don't specify a width, the default is 10.*

When using DECIMAL column types, excess digits to the right of the decimal point are dropped, and when the width of the value exceeds what was declared for the column, MySQL truncates it to the largest number that will fit. Let's see how this works by creating a table with a DECIMAL column and inserting some numbers into it.

```
Command Prompt - mysql -h megalon -u root -p                          _ □ X
mysql> CREATE TABLE decimals1 (value1 DECIMAL(5, 2));
Query OK, 0 rows affected (0.03 sec)

mysql> INSERT INTO decimals1 (value1)
    -> VALUES
    -> (3.25), (23.255), (123.5), (-123.5), (1234.5), (-1234.5);
Query OK, 6 rows affected, 1 warning (0.01 sec)
Records: 6  Duplicates: 0  Warnings: 1

mysql> SHOW WARNINGS\G
*************************** 1. row ***************************
  Level: Warning
   Code: 1263
Message: Data truncated, out of range for column 'value1' at row 6
1 row in set (0.00 sec)

mysql>
```

MySQL generated a data truncation warning for the last of the values we inserted. Here are the values as stored in the table:

```
Command Prompt - mysql -h megalon -u root -p                          _ □ X
mysql> SELECT value1 FROM decimals1;
+---------+
| value1  |
+---------+
|    3.25 |
|   23.25 |
|  123.50 |
| -123.50 |
| 1234.50 |
| -999.99 |
+---------+
6 rows in set (0.00 sec)

mysql>
```

MySQL doesn't include the minus sign, so the greatest negative value that can be inserted into a DECIMAL column with whose width is five digits and with two decimals places is –999.99.

In the following command-line example, we perform a couple of basic operations on some DECIMAL values. First, we drop the current values stored in the **decimals1** table and insert some new ones, performing a SELECT query to verify that we've replaced the old values with the new ones.

```
Command Prompt - mysql -h megalon -u root -p                          _ □ X
mysql> TRUNCATE decimals1;
Query OK, 0 rows affected (0.00 sec)

mysql> INSERT INTO decimals1 (value1)
    -> VALUES (12.25), (12.27), (12.27), (12.25);
Query OK, 4 rows affected (0.00 sec)
Records: 4  Duplicates: 0  Warnings: 0

mysql> SELECT value1 FROM decimals1;
+--------+
| value1 |
+--------+
|  12.25 |
|  12.27 |
|  12.27 |
|  12.25 |
+--------+
4 rows in set (0.00 sec)

mysql>
```

When we sum or average the new values, we get pretty much what we would expect.

```
Command Prompt - mysql -h megalon -u root -p                    _ □ x
mysql> SELECT SUM(value1) FROM decimals1;
+-------------+
| SUM(value1) |
+-------------+
|       49.04 |
+-------------+
1 row in set (0.00 sec)

mysql> SELECT AVG(value1) FROM decimals1;
+-------------+
| AVG(value1) |
+-------------+
|   12.260000 |
+-------------+
1 row in set (0.00 sec)

mysql>
```

Now let's find out what happens when we update a couple of the stored values in such a way that the average will require more decimal places to represent it accurately than were set in the column definition.

```
Command Prompt - mysql -h megalon -u root -p                    _ □ x
mysql> UPDATE decimals1
    -> SET value1 = 12.26
    -> WHERE value1 = 12.25;
Query OK, 2 rows affected (0.04 sec)
Rows matched: 2  Changed: 2  Warnings: 0

mysql> SELECT SUM(value1) FROM decimals1;
+-------------+
| SUM(value1) |
+-------------+
|       49.06 |
+-------------+
1 row in set (0.01 sec)

mysql> SELECT AVG(value1) FROM decimals1;
+-------------+
| AVG(value1) |
+-------------+
|   12.265000 |
+-------------+
1 row in set (0.00 sec)

mysql>
```

This leads us to suspect that MySQL is actually performing double-precision arithmetic behind the scenes. To confirm this, let's multiply the average by an arbitrarily large value (say 1,000,000), and see what MySQL shows as the result.

```
Command Prompt - mysql -h megalon -u root -p                    _ □ x
mysql> SELECT AVG(value1) * 1000000 FROM decimals1;
+-----------------------+
| AVG(value1) * 1000000 |
+-----------------------+
|        12265000.000000 |
+-----------------------+
1 row in set (0.01 sec)

mysql>
```

There are three points to consider here:

- You will often obtain much greater precision when using stored values in calculations than that used to store those values. This means that you don't need to worry about rounding errors in many cases (but see our earlier discussion of the FLOAT type).

- You can sometimes save storage space due to this fact. For example, if we used DOUBLE instead of DECIMAL(5,2) for the single column in the **decimals1** table, we would use 8 bytes per value instead of 7. This may not seem like much, but when used in a table with 100,000 records where there's also an index on this column, this will save approximately 1.1MB of space.

- However, this also means you must take responsibility for any truncation and rounding requirements. You can handle this in your application code, but you might find it more efficient to take care of this in the query itself by using something like SELECT ROUND(AVG(value1)) FROM decimals1; or SELECT TRUNCATE(AVG(value1), 2) FROM decimals1;. We'll discuss the issues accompanying the use of such functions in Chapter 4.

There's a lot to know about MySQL's numeric datatypes, and we've thrown a lot of background information at you during our discussion of these. We don't expect you remember every last detail from what you've just read, especially after just one sitting. We *would* like for you to remember that MySQL has a number of options for you to consider whenever you need to store numbers, and that finding the right one is often a matter of balancing both memory and the need for accuracy.

Storing Character Data: CHAR, VARCHAR, TEXT, and BLOB

Just as with numerical data, you should store character data in columns defined for that specific purpose. You should also exercise caution and plan how many characters your column is going to hold. MySQL features four different column types for strings, and your choice for the most appropriate one to use will depend on the size and variability of the character data that you intend to store. The character datatypes are as follows:

- CHAR: All strings to be stored are of the same fixed length of 0 to 255 characters.

- VARCHAR: The strings to be stored may vary in length, but none of them is longer than the stated maximum for the column, which can be up to 255 characters.

- TEXT: The character data to be stored includes strings that are greater than 255 characters in length; case-sensitivity with regard to sorting the data is not an issue.

- BLOB: The same as TEXT, except that the data stored in a BLOB column can be sorted in a case-sensitive fashion.

TEXT and BLOB columns each come in several different varieties, which differ in the maximum length of the strings that they can accept. We'll provide details in the upcoming discussions of these column types.

The process by which you can decide which character column type is best to use for a given column is illustrated as in Figure 2-2.

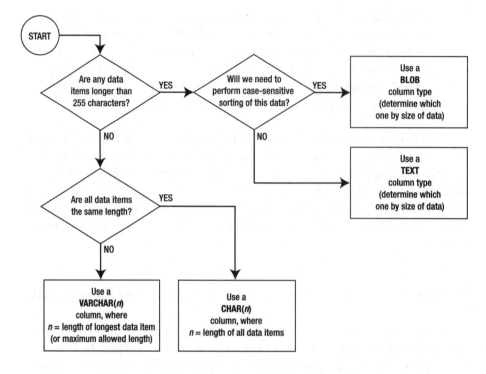

Figure 2-2. Determining the best character datatype for a column

Now we're going to look at the characteristics of each of these four column types in more depth, starting with the CHAR type. Since the TEXT and BLOB column types are virtually identical (except for their sorting characteristics), we'll examine those two together.

Short, Fixed-Length Strings: The CHAR Type

CHAR can be used to store values from 0 to 255 characters, and it should be employed when storing short strings of a fixed length. For example, suppose you're constructing a table for storing data about books that includes an **isbn** column for holding the ISBN (International Standard Book Number) of each book. An ISBN is an alphanumeric value that is always 10 characters in length, so a column definition such as the following is an appropriate choice:

```
isbn CHAR(10) NOT NULL
```

NOTE *The range of possible widths for a* CHAR *is shown as 0 to 255, and not 1 to 255. The zero is not a misprint, and later on in this chapter, we'll show you an instance where you might actually wish to use a* CHAR(0) *column. (See the discussion of Booleans in the "True and False—Accommodating Boolean Values" section later in this chapter.)*

The storage space required for a CHAR column is always the number of bytes equal to the declared width of the column. So our **isbn** column as defined in this example will use 10 bytes per record stored.

When a string that is shorter than the assigned maximum value of the column is inserted into a CHAR column, MySQL will right-pad it with spaces to the specified length, and then remove those spaces once the value is retrieved from the database. For this reason, you usually shouldn't use CHAR for variable-length strings; you'll just be wasting space. In other words, if you define a column like this:

```
firstname CHAR(35)
```

And then store the string "William" in it, you'll still be using 35 bytes for storage, even though "William" is only seven characters (7 bytes) in length.

MySQL can scan tables in which all columns are of fixed widths faster than it can one in which some or all the columns are variable-length types. However, with proper indexing, table scans can be greatly reduced or even eliminated. We'll touch on these issues again in Chapters 3 and 6.

TIP *Beginning with MySQL 4.1.0, it's possible to specify the character set for an individual* CHAR *or* VARCHAR *column using the* ASCII *or* UNICODE *modifier.* ASCII *will assign the Latin-1 character set, and* UNICODE *will assign the Unicode (UCS-2) character set.*

Short, Variable-Length Strings: The VARCHAR Type

VARCHAR is shorthand for *VAR*iable-length *CHAR*acter. Similar to the CHAR column type, VARCHAR can be used to store strings that are from 1 to 255 characters in length. This type is useful when storing strings that you know will vary in length. Note that MySQL does *not* pad VARCHAR entries, and trailing spaces are removed when the value is stored.

The advantage to using VARCHAR over CHAR is that VARCHAR uses just enough space to store the value actually inserted into the column. For example, we could define a **firstname** column like this:

```
firstname VARCHAR(35)
```

Then the column's capacity would still be set to 35 characters (just as using CHAR(35) would do). However, storing the string "William" would then require just 8 bytes: 1 byte per character, plus an additional byte to record the length of the string. In this case, we save 27 bytes over what we would use to store the same string in a CHAR column of the same size.

Neither CHAR nor VARCHAR is case-sensitive by default with respect to comparing or sorting values. To force case-sensitivity, declare the column as CHAR BINARY or VARCHAR BINARY.

TIP *Beginning with MySQL 4.1.0, you may also use* CHAR BYTE *in place of* CHAR BINARY, *and* VARCHAR BYTE *for* VARCHAR BINARY.

Just to make sure this distinction with regard to sorting behavior is clear, let's look at an example. First, we'll create two tables named strings1 and strings2, each of which contains two VARCHAR columns. These tables are identical, except that the columns in **strings2** will be declared as BINARY. We'll insert identical data into each table as well.

```
Command Prompt - mysql -h megalon -u root -p

mysql> CREATE TABLE strings1 (
    -> value1 VARCHAR(10),
    -> value2 VARCHAR(10)
    -> );
Query OK, 0 rows affected (0.01 sec)

mysql> CREATE TABLE strings2 (
    -> value1 VARCHAR(10) BINARY,
    -> value2 VARCHAR(10) BINARY
    -> );
Query OK, 0 rows affected (0.02 sec)

mysql> INSERT INTO strings1 (value1, value2)
    -> VALUES ('apple', 'Orange');
Query OK, 1 row affected (0.01 sec)

mysql> INSERT INTO strings2 (value1, value2)
    -> VALUES ('apple', 'Orange');
Query OK, 1 row affected (0.00 sec)

mysql>
```

Recall that the expression value1 < value2 will evaluate to 1 (Boolean **TRUE**) if the first of the two strings value1 and value2 is sorted first, and 0 (Boolean **FALSE**) if the opposite is true. In other words (as we can see by the first SELECT query in the next example), the expression 'a' < 'b' will evaluate as 1. Let's see what happens when we compare the strings stored in each of the two tables.

```
Command Prompt - mysql -h megalon -u root -p                        _ □ ×
mysql> SELECT value1 < value2 FROM strings1;
+-----------------+
| value1 < value2 |
+-----------------+
|               1 |
+-----------------+
1 row in set (0.00 sec)

mysql> SELECT value1 < value2 FROM strings2;
+-----------------+
| value1 < value2 |
+-----------------+
|               0 |
+-----------------+
1 row in set (0.00 sec)

mysql>
```

Note that this does *not* mean that case isn't preserved in strings stored in VARCHAR columns, whether or not they're declared as BINARY. We can easily prove this by performing a simple SELECT from both tables.

```
Command Prompt - mysql -h megalon -u root -p                        _ □ ×
mysql> SELECT s1.value1, s1.value2, s2.value1, s2.value2
    -> FROM strings1 s1, strings2 s2;
+--------+--------+--------+--------+
| value1 | value2 | value1 | value2 |
+--------+--------+--------+--------+
| apple  | Orange | apple  | Orange |
+--------+--------+--------+--------+
1 row in set (0.01 sec)

mysql>
```

NOTE *A column declared as simply* CHAR *(with no width specified) is the same as declaring it as* CHAR(1). *A* VARCHAR *column must have its width specified (failure to do so will result in a syntax error). Both column types will trim characters in excess of the stated width (or 1 in the case of* CHAR *with no width specified).*

Long Strings: The TEXT and BLOB Types

When you want to store large strings of text (longer than the 255-character maximum for CHAR and VARCHAR), you'll need to use a TEXT or BLOB column type. TEXT and BLOB column types are basically the same; however, the TEXT types are not case-sensitive with regard to sorting behavior, whereas the BLOB types are. (BLOB is an acronym for *Binary Large Object*.) There are actually four column types to choose from for each of the TEXT and BLOB types; these vary in the number of characters that they can hold, as shown in Table 2-2.

Table 2-2. TEXT and BLOB Column Types

TEXT Column Type	BLOB Column Type	Number of Characters (Bytes)	Storage Required (L = Length of Stored Value)
TINYTEXT	TINYBLOB	255 ($2^8 - 1$)	L + 1 bytes
TEXT	BLOB	65,535 ($2^{16} - 1 = 64KB - 1$)	L + 2 bytes
MEDIUMTEXT	MEDIUMBLOB	16,777,215 ($2^{24} - 1 = 16MB - 1$)	L + 3 bytes
LONGTEXT	LONGBLOB	4,294,967,295 ($2^{32} - 1 = 4GB - 1$)	L + 4 bytes

These types are very similar to CHAR and VARCHAR, except that the TEXT and BLOB types have much greater capacities. However, you cannot assign a display width to a TEXT or BLOB column, and MySQL will not remove trailing spaces from strings stored in columns of either type, as it does with VARCHAR.

NOTE *Beginning with MySQL 4.1, you can also use* LONG *or* LONG VARCHAR *to declare a column of type* MEDIUMTEXT. *This was introduced to enhance compatibility with other databases. Note that you may not declare a column as* LONG VARCHAR BINARY!

The value stored in a column of either of these types is basically a binary object. Not only can you store large amounts of text, but you can also store binary data, such as that for an image or PDF file. It is sometimes customary, especially among web developers, to declare columns used to store data for assets like image or sound files as one of the BLOB types; however, this isn't really necessary, and you can use the same-sized TEXT column type to achieve the same result.

CAUTION *Although* MEDIUMTEXT, MEDIUMBLOB, LONGTEXT, *and* LONGBLOB *columns can hold fantastically large amounts of data, the number of bytes that can actually be stored by a client application in a single* INSERT *query is limited by the* max_allowed_packet *configuration variable. You can check this value by using* SHOW VARIABLES LIKE 'max_allowed_packet'; *in the MySQL Monitor. You can change it either by editing the my.cnf file (or possibly my.ini on Windows), or by starting MySQL with* mysqld −max_allowed_packet=number. *The default value is approximately 10MB (10,484,736 bytes).*

Silent Changes of Column Types

There are several cases where MySQL converts columns declared as one datatype into a different (but related) type. Normally, this is not a great cause for concern, but you should be aware that it does happen, so you aren't confused by it.

A VARCHAR column whose length is less than 4 is converted to CHAR. Conversely, if a table contains any variable-length columns (TEXT or BLOB types), then any CHAR column with a length of greater than 3 in that table is automatically converted to VARCHAR. This will not affect your applications in any noticeable way regarding how you must program them, but it does save space.

Beginning with MySQL 4.1, it is possible to declare CHAR and VARCHAR columns with lengths greater than 255. However, these are automatically converted to TEXT columns.

MySQL allows you to use a number of column types from other databases when defining columns, but converts these to MySQL column types when the tables using them are created, as shown in the following list:

Other Vendor's Column Type	MySQL Column Type
BINARY(N)	CHAR(N) BINARY
CHAR VARYING(N)	VARCHAR(N)
FLOAT4	FLOAT
FLOAT8	DOUBLE
INT1	TINYINT
INT2	SMALLINT
INT3	MEDIUMINT
INT4	INT
INT8	BIGINT
LONG VARBINARY	MEDIUMBLOB
LONG VARCHAR	MEDIUMTEXT
MIDDLEINT	MEDIUMINT
VARBINARY(N)	VARCHAR(N) BINARY

You can easily determine whether or not MySQL has performed a silent column change by performing a SHOW CREATE TABLE or DESCRIBE query. When MySQL performs a column change in this manner, it will issue a warning, as you can see in the following example. (This example uses \G instead of a semicolon to terminate a query, which causes the output to be formatted vertically instead of in a horizontal tabular layout, and thus makes it easier to read in some cases.)

```
Command Prompt - mysql -h megalon -u root -p                    _ □ ×
mysql> CREATE TABLE text1 (value1 VARCHAR(300));
Query OK, 0 rows affected, 1 warning (0.03 sec)

mysql> SHOW WARNINGS;
+---------+------+----------------------------------------------+
| Level   | Code | Message                                      |
+---------+------+----------------------------------------------+
| Warning | 1245 | Converting column 'value1' from CHAR to TEXT |
+---------+------+----------------------------------------------+
1 row in set (0.00 sec)

mysql> SHOW CREATE TABLE text1\G
*************************** 1. row ***************************
       Table: text1
Create Table: CREATE TABLE `text1` (
  `value1` text
) ENGINE=MyISAM DEFAULT CHARSET=latin1
1 row in set (0.01 sec)

mysql>
```

However, when MySQL changes only the name of another vendor's column type to its MySQL-native equivalent, no actual change is made in the type of data that the column may store, and so no warning is issued, as you can see in this example:

```
Command Prompt - mysql -h megalon -u root -p                    _ □ ×
mysql> CREATE TABLE text2 (value1 LONG VARCHAR);
Query OK, 0 rows affected (0.02 sec)

mysql> SHOW CREATE TABLE text2\G
*************************** 1. row ***************************
       Table: text2
Create Table: CREATE TABLE `text2` (
  `value1` mediumtext
) ENGINE=MyISAM DEFAULT CHARSET=latin1
1 row in set (0.00 sec)

mysql>
```

There is no way to override MySQL's behavior in this regard, short of modifying the source code and recompiling it yourself.

Much Ado About Nothing: What Is NULL?

We're now roughly midway through our discussion of MySQL's datatypes, and it occurred to us you might like to take a break before we move on to tackle the more complex date-related and grouping types. While you might be thinking in terms of not having to read about anything, we've decided (with the sense of the perverse that doesn't seem uncommon among those who spend too much time getting their tans from the glare of a computer monitor) to have you take a working holiday and spend a little time reading and thinking about Nothing. While this may seem only an attempt at bad humor, we actually have a serious purpose in mind. The matter of Nothing is quite a serious one in MySQL, as it is in computing in general. In this "time-out" section, we're going to discuss a special value that can literally be taken to mean nothing, the reasons why we need such a value, and how it works in MySQL.

Sometimes, you need a way to describe a value that isn't actually a value, that denotes the absence of a value, or that indicates that the value is unknown. For example, suppose we're recording contact data about a firm's customers in a **customers** table for use in a number of applications. As part of this scenario, the firm mails each customer a printed monthly newsletter. Management would like to cut costs by encouraging customers to receive an e-mail version of the newsletter instead. The first step in the conversion process is to add a new column to the **customers** table:

```
ALTER TABLE customers ADD COLUMN email varchar(75) NULL;
```

> **NOTE** *If you don't specify either* NULL *or* NOT NULL *in a column definition, by default, the column can accept* NULL *values. However, there's nothing wrong with making the choice an explicit one.*

When we execute this ALTER TABLE command, all existing records in the table will start out having NULL for the value of the **email** column. This is exactly what we want; at that point, every record in the **customers** table says, "We don't know anything yet about the e-mail address for this customer."

People often have a misconception as to what exactly a NULL value is. Many newcomers to SQL often think that NULL is the same thing as ' ' (an empty string) or zero, and even experienced MySQL users sometimes forget that there's a difference. However, this is not the case.

These two INSERT queries are completely different with regard to the value that each inserts for the e-mail address:

```
INSERT INTO customers (fname, lname, email) VALUES ('John', 'Smith', NULL);
INSERT INTO customers (fname, lname, email) VALUES ('John', 'Smith', '');
```

The first one uses a NULL value, which can be regarded as, "We don't know Smith's e-mail address (or even whether or not he has one)." The second represents the statement, "We know that John Smith has no e-mail address."

NULL is a value that is not equal to any value, *including itself.* Another way of stating this is that NULL compared to any other value, even itself, is NULL.

```
Command Prompt - mysql -h megalon -u root -p                       _ □ ×
mysql> SELECT 0 = NULL, 2 = NULL, 'jon' = NULL, NULL = NULL;
+----------+----------+--------------+-------------+
| 0 = NULL | 2 = NULL | 'jon' = NULL | NULL = NULL |
+----------+----------+--------------+-------------+
|     NULL |     NULL |         NULL |        NULL |
+----------+----------+--------------+-------------+
1 row in set (0.00 sec)

mysql>
```

To determine in MySQL whether or not a value is NULL, you can use one of the two operators: IS NULL or IS NOT NULL. For example, to get a list of customers whose e-mail addresses we don't know, we can use this:

```
SELECT fname, lname, addr1, addr2, city, state, zip
FROM customers
WHERE email IS NULL;
```

Then we can send a postcard to all of the customers in this set, asking them if they have e-mail addresses. To get a list of customers whom we know not to have e-mail addresses, so that we can mail the printed version of the newsletter to them, we would use this:

```
SELECT fname, lname FROM customers WHERE email <> '';
```

A common error is to insert or test for the string 'NULL', thinking that it's the same thing as working with the NULL keyword. As you can see by means of the simple query shown here, these are not the same thing at all:

```
Command Prompt - mysql -h megalon -u root -p                       _ □ ×
mysql> SELECT NULL IS NULL, 'NULL' IS NULL;
+--------------+----------------+
| NULL IS NULL | 'NULL' IS NULL |
+--------------+----------------+
|            1 |              0 |
+--------------+----------------+
1 row in set (0.02 sec)

mysql>
```

PHP programmers seem especially prone to trying to use something like this:

```
$query = "SELECT name, email FROM customers WHERE email = 'NULL'";
$result = mysql_query($query);
if(mysql_num_rows($result) == 0)
{
    echo "<p>All customer emails have been checked.</p>\n";
}
```

And then discovering later that 1,500 customers are still receiving the printed newsletter. You may be tempted to declare a column NOT NULL and then use the string 'NULL' to indicate a NULL value. This is another common error, because then you won't be able to use IS NULL, IS NOT NULL, or IFNULL(); you're required to test the column against a particular string value instead. What's even worse is that another developer, not knowing that you've designed your database and application in such a fashion, may try to use these standard methods of testing for NULL values and immediately run into trouble.

MySQL also supports a "NULL-safe" comparison operator, <=>, as shown in the next example. However, It's preferable to use IS [NOT] NULL, particularly if you need to be compatible with other databases, as this is standard SQL (<=> is specific to MySQL).

You can also use the IFNULL() function to return one of two expressions depending on whether or not the first expression is a NULL. For example, to return either the e-mail address if it's known or the string 'UNKNOWN' if it isn't, use this:

```
SELECT fname, lname, IFNULL(email,'UNKNOWN') FROM customers;
```

Don't confuse this with the NULLIF() function, which returns the NULL value if its two arguments are equal.

Speaking of functions, we should mention that NULL values are ignored by such aggregate functions as SUM(), MIN(), MAX(), and AVG() (used in GROUP BY queries). We'll discuss all of these functions in detail in Chapter 4.

TIP   *The COUNT() function is affected by NULL values. For example, consider the query SELECT COUNT(*), COUNT(email) FROM customers;. The first column of the resultset will be the number of all customer records in the table, and the second will be the number of customers whose e-mail address is a non-NULL value. In other words, the expression COUNT(email) gives exactly the same result that you would obtain using SELECT COUNT(*) FROM customers WHERE email IS NOT NULL;.*

Before we resume our discussion of datatypes, we should note that the NULL value has two additional special uses in MySQL:

- When inserted into an AUTO_INCREMENT column, NULL causes the next available value to be stored in the column, whether or not the column has been declared NOT NULL.

- You can also insert a NULL into a TIMESTAMP column in order to force its value to be updated to one that corresponds to the current date and time.

 TIP   *If you don't need* NULL *values in a column, declaring it as* NOT NULL *will save you 1 byte of storage space per row.*

Storing Dates and Times

A recurring issue in software development has to do with the treatment of dates and times. We need to know when orders are placed and shipped, when people will be available for meetings, how long it has been since subscribers last paid their membership fees, and so on. MySQL helps us deal with these sorts of problems by supporting several column types related to dates and times. (As you'll see in Chapter 4, there are also a number of special functions in MySQL to work with values of these types.) The following are the column types for date and time storage:

- DATE: Stores a calendar date (year, month, and day of month) in *YYYY-MM-DD* format.

- TIME: Stores a clock time (hours, minutes, and seconds) in 24-hour format: *HHH:MM:SS*. For hour values less than 100, the leading zero is suppressed.

- YEAR: Stores a four-digit year.

- DATETIME: Stores a complete date and time in the format *YYYY-MM-DD HH:MM:SS*. Basically, this column type combines the DATE and TIME types.

- TIMESTAMP: Similar in some ways to DATETIME, but with some additional special properties. The format and behavior of this column type have changed considerably beginning with MySQL 4.1, and its use is not recommended for new databases.

Although we referred to these types earlier as examples of "complex" datatypes in MySQL, they are actually fairly simple to understand and use, as you'll see in our discussion of each of them over the next few sections.

CAUTION *The MySQL documentation suggests that any delimiters can be used to separate the individual parts making up* DATE, TIME, *and* DATETIME *values. In other words, it should be legal to store a value such as '2003*06+25' in a* DATE *column and have it understood by MySQL that you mean "25th June 2003" (2003-06-25). However, in practice, we've found that this behavior is not reliable or consistent across different MySQL versions and operating platforms. We therefore strongly suggest that you use only dashes (-) to separate the month, day, and year portions of dates, and only colons (:) to separate hours, minutes, and seconds in time values.*

DATE

The DATE type is used when storing dates without a time value. MySQL stores DATE values as strings in the format: 'YYYY-MM-DD'. The value range that this column type can handle is from '1000-01-01' to '9999-12-31'. DATE values use 3 bytes of storage.

It is best to use this format when dealing with dates, rather than having your application code convert the date, and then storing it in a CHAR or VARCHAR column. This will help reduce extra coding in your application, as well as provide a standard for your application, if you ever need to share the data with another application. This is a fairly common error in database and application design, and we'll provide a more detailed explanation and example later in this chapter.

MySQL requires that you store DATE values as strings:

```
INSERT INTO somedates (adate) VALUES ('2004-01-01');
```

If you don't use the quotes, MySQL will regard this as an error. The same is true with TIME and DATETIME values as well. It is *sometimes*, but not *always* true for TIMESTAMP values (see the later discussion of TIMESTAMP for details).

The following is an example of how to store the current date in a DATE column using the NOW() function and how it's displayed when we retrieve it.

```
Command Prompt - mysql -h megalon -u root -p                    _ □ ×
mysql> CREATE TABLE dates1 (value1 DATE);
Query OK, 0 rows affected (0.02 sec)

mysql> INSERT INTO dates1 (value1) VALUES (NOW());
Query OK, 1 row affected (0.04 sec)

mysql> SELECT value1 FROM dates1;
+------------+
| value1     |
+------------+
| 2004-08-01 |
+------------+
1 row in set (0.00 sec)

mysql>
```

TIME

The TIME datatype is, in a manner of speaking, the opposite of DATE. It's used when you need to store only a time value, without a corresponding date. MySQL stores this value in the format 'HHH:MM:SS', and it may range anywhere from '-838:59:59' to '838:59:59'. Like DATE, a TIME column requires 3 bytes of memory to store each value.

As with the DATE type, you should use this column type when you are storing specific time values in your application, and not try to devise your own structures for this purpose. The following is an example of how to define a TIME column, store the current time in it, and retrieve it.

```
Command Prompt - mysql -h megalon -u root -p                    _ □ ×
mysql> CREATE TABLE times1 (value1 TIME);
Query OK, 0 rows affected (0.02 sec)

mysql> INSERT INTO times1 (value1) VALUES (NOW());
Query OK, 1 row affected (0.03 sec)

mysql> SELECT value1 FROM times1;
+----------+
| value1   |
+----------+
| 22:28:23 |
+----------+
1 row in set (0.00 sec)

mysql>
```

YEAR

If you need to store data that represents only the year portion of a date, you can use the YEAR column type. This type occupies only 1 byte, and will store years in the range of 1901 to 2155, inclusive. You can insert a value into a YEAR column as either an integer or a string. If you attempt to insert a floating-point number (or the string representation of one) into a YEAR column, MySQL will silently ignore the decimal point and any digits to the right of it. You can use the NOW() function to insert the current year into a YEAR column, although this will prompt a warning.

In addition, it's also possible to insert a number in the range 1 to 99 or a two-digit string into a YEAR column. In this case, MySQL will attempt to convert the value to a four-digit year. MySQL regards numbers in the range of 70 to 99 as the years 1970 through 1999, and numbers in the range 1 through 69 as the years 2000 through 2069.

 CAUTION *Inserting the strings '0' or '00' into a* YEAR *column will be interpreted as the year 2000; inserting an integer zero (0) will be interpreted as the value 0000. MySQL 4.1 and later will not issue a warning when this occurs.*

Any illegal values will be truncated to 0000; MySQL 4.1 and above will issue a warning when this happens, as you can see in the following example.

```
Command Prompt - mysql -h megalon -u root -p

mysql> CREATE TABLE years1 (value1 YEAR);
Query OK, 0 rows affected (0.03 sec)

mysql> INSERT INTO years1 (value1)
    -> VALUES (NOW()), ('1997'), ('19978');
Query OK, 3 rows affected, 2 warnings (0.00 sec)
Records: 3  Duplicates: 0  Warnings: 2

mysql> SHOW WARNINGS\G
*************************** 1. row ***************************
  Level: Warning
   Code: 1264
Message: Data truncated for column 'value1' at row 1
*************************** 2. row ***************************
  Level: Warning
   Code: 1263
Message: Data truncated, out of range for column 'value1' at row 3
2 rows in set (0.00 sec)

mysql> SELECT value1 FROM years1;
+--------+
| value1 |
+--------+
|   2004 |
|   1997 |
|   0000 |
+--------+
3 rows in set (0.00 sec)

mysql>
```

 NOTE *MySQL will attempt to store, compare, and sort two-digit years in* YEAR *columns according to the rules given in this section; however, it's best to use four-digit years and avoid the possibility of unpleasant surprises.*

DATETIME

You should use the DATETIME column type when you need to store both time and date values in single column. The standard format MySQL uses for this type is 'YYYY-MM-DD HH:MM:SS'. The supported range of values is '1000-01-01 00:00:00' to '9999-12-31 23:59:59'. DATETIME records require 8 bytes of storage for each value, so don't use it if your application requires only dates. Otherwise, you're just wasting 5 bytes for every record in the table.

Values must be inserted into DATETIME columns as strings. They must consist of a complete date or a complete date and time. Attempting to insert a time value alone will cause the value to be coerced to '0000-00-00 00:00:00'; beginning with MySQL 4.1, the server will issue a warning if this happens. (Note that SHOW WARNINGS doesn't report anything when this occurs.) You can use NOW() to insert the current date and time.

Here is a simple example of creating a table with a DATETIME column, inserting some values into it, and retrieving them:

```
Command Prompt - mysql -h megalon -u root -p

mysql> CREATE TABLE datetimes1 (value1 DATETIME);
Query OK, 0 rows affected (0.02 sec)

mysql> INSERT INTO datetimes1 (value1) VALUES
    -> (NOW()), ('2005-01-15 11:25:15'), ('2005-01-15'), ('11:25:15');
Query OK, 4 rows affected (0.01 sec)
Records: 4  Duplicates: 0  Warnings: 1

mysql> SHOW WARNINGS\G
Empty set (0.00 sec)

mysql> SELECT value1 FROM datetimes1;
+---------------------+
| value1              |
+---------------------+
| 2004-08-01 22:33:43 |
| 2005-01-15 11:25:15 |
| 2005-01-15 00:00:00 |
| 0000-00-00 00:00:00 |
+---------------------+
4 rows in set (0.01 sec)

mysql>
```

 CAUTION   *MySQL does not compensate for Julian dates in use prior to the adoption of the Gregorian calendar. This occurred in Catholic Europe ca. 1582, but Protestant England (and its American colonies) held out for 170 years before making the change. Russia did not change over until 1918; in fact, (according to the calendar used in the West) the "October Revolution" actually took place in November.*

TIMESTAMP

We are not going to spend a great deal of time with the TIMESTAMP datatype, other than to advise you to discontinue its use in existing databases where possible, and not to use it in new ones. One of the reasons for this is that its behavior changes radically in MySQL 4.1. Beginning with MySQL 4.1.0, it is stored and displayed more or less identically to DATETIME. Another is that its behavior in MySQL 4.1 and later depends on whether you're running MySQL in MAXDB mode.

A TIMESTAMP column is chiefly useful in that you can insert a NULL into it, and the current date and time will be recorded, which is handy for logging changes. However, when running MySQL in MAXDB mode, TIMESTAMP does not do this. We suggest instead that you use either DATETIME or INT columns for such purposes and use the NOW() function:

```
UPDATE orders
SET status = 'SENT', last_update = NOW()
WHERE orderid = 23335;
```

A TMESTAMP column requires 4 bytes of storage.

Some databases allow you to define a DATE, TIME, or DATETIME column using NOW() or an equivalent function or expression. MySQL does not permit this. We've observed people (including authors of some books about MySQL!) defining a **timestamp** column using something like the following:

```
CREATE TABLE timestamps (
  id INT,
  ts TIMESTAMP NOT NULL DEFAULT 'NOW()'
);
```

This is in the mistaken belief that it will force the column to store the current time, and only the current time, at the time the record is inserted into the table. In earlier MySQL versions (up to 4.1), you could do this, but whenever you updated an existing record, the timestamp would be updated as well. What's really happening here is that the default value specified is incompatible with the column type and is, thus, ignored. In MySQL 5.0, this is illegal, and the following example shows what happens if you try it.

```
Command Prompt - mysql -h megalon -u root -p
mysql> CREATE TABLE timestamps (
    -> id INT,
    -> ts TIMESTAMP NOT NULL DEFAULT 'NOW()'
    -> );
ERROR 1067 (42000): Invalid default value for 'ts'
mysql>
```

If you need to store timestamps, a much better solution used by many developers working with MySQL is to use an INT column and store the value generated by the UNIX_TIMESTAMP() function. The following is a simple example of this. Note that the warning here is generated by inserting an empty string into the **id** column, and has nothing to do with the **ts** column used for storing the timestamp.

```
Command Prompt - mysql -h megalon -u root -p                                    _ □ x
mysql> CREATE TABLE timestamps2 (
    -> id INT AUTO_INCREMENT PRIMARY KEY,
    -> ts INT
    -> );
Query OK, 0 rows affected (0.01 sec)

mysql> INSERT INTO timestamps2 (id, ts) VALUES ('', UNIX_TIMESTAMP());

Query OK, 1 row affected, 1 warning (0.06 sec)

mysql> SHOW WARNINGS\G
*************************** 1. row ***************************
  Level: Warning
   Code: 1264
Message: Data truncated for column 'id' at row 1
1 row in set (0.00 sec)

mysql> INSERT INTO timestamps2 (id, ts) VALUES ('', UNIX_TIMESTAMP());

Query OK, 1 row affected, 1 warning (0.00 sec)

mysql> INSERT INTO timestamps2 (id, ts) VALUES ('', UNIX_TIMESTAMP());

Query OK, 1 row affected, 1 warning (0.00 sec)

mysql> SELECT id, ts FROM timestamps2;
+----+------------+
| id | ts         |
+----+------------+
|  1 | 1091363920 |
|  2 | 1091363940 |
|  3 | 1091363944 |
+----+------------+
3 rows in set (0.00 sec)

mysql>
```

NOTE   *If you find yourself working with a legacy database that uses the* TIMESTAMP *column type, you can obtain more information about it from the MySQL documentation.*

Working with Sets of Values: ENUM, SET, and Boolean Values

Sometimes, it can be convenient to have a column that is restricted to an arbitrary range of values. MySQL has two special column types for working with sets of values:

- ENUM: This column type allows you to store any one value from a list that you've defined for that column.

- SET: This type is similar to ENUM in that you're permitted to define a list of custom values, but differs in that you can store one *or more* values from the list.

Neither of these column types is usually available in other databases. We'll examine both of them in this section.

The ENUM Type

One scenario involving a set of predefined and mutually exclusive values might involve the status of tests done on products under development, where you know that the set of possible values is not likely (or extremely unlikely) to change over the lifetime of the application. In this case, the status of each test (to be stored in the **qa_status** column in our example) will be one of the following four values: PENDING, IN PROGRESS, PASS, or FAIL.

This represents a fairly simple and straightforward scheme: Once a product is ready for testing, it's PENDING; when testing begins, it's IN PROGRESS until completed; and once the test is concluded, the product's status is either PASS or FAIL. What sort of datatype would make for the best "fit" here? Let's look at the two most likely alternatives.

INT (or more likely TINYINT) has one main advantage: It doesn't require much space (1 byte per record). The problem is that we would either need to hard-code the human-readable status names into the application or use a status codes lookup table. The first is inefficient, and the second seems like overkill for a range of four possible values. Another possible solution might be to use queries containing fairly lengthy CASE ... WHEN constructs (see Chapter 4), but this also seems like a lot of work in order to distinguish just a few values.

CHAR or VARCHAR requires more memory than TINYINT, but by using words from everyday language, we make it quite easy to write queries to obtain answers to basic questions such as, "Which products have passed QA testing over the last week?"

```
SELECT product_name
FROM qa_tests
WHERE qa_status='PASS' AND TO_DAYS(test_date) > TO_DAYS(NOW()) - 7;
```

The other potential source of trouble presented by both choices is that they make it easy to insert meaningless values into the **qa_status** column. We could use an integer-type column that links to a status codes table (and possibly a foreign key constraint based on this as well), but this seems like a lot of work for four static values. Using a character-type column would force us to check values in the application logic before inserting them. (Otherwise, we could run into problems when somebody decided to start inserting, say, PASSED instead of PASS.) This, however, is not as efficient as it could be, and developers could circumvent this easily.

However, there is another possibility: the enumerated (ENUM) type allows you to specify a set of possible values for a column:

```
CREATE TABLE qa_tests (
  #  other column definitions...
  test_status ENUM('PENDING','IN PROGRESS','PASS','FAIL')
);
```

NOTE *You may use spaces and other nonalphanumeric characters in enumerated values; however, we advise that you do not use any characters other than alphanumeric characters, underscores, and spaces.*

Let's incorporate this column definition into a working table that's part of a database for a firm that markets some of the very interesting products one sees sold on broadcast television during the early morning hours. While we're at it, let's insert some suitable data for illustrative purposes. (The warnings are generated by inserting empty strings into the auto-incrementing **qa_test_id** column.)

```
Command Prompt - mysql -h megalon -u root -p
+---------------------------+
| version()                 |
+---------------------------+
| 5.0.0-alpha-max-nt-log    |
+---------------------------+
1 row in set (0.00 sec)

mysql> CREATE TABLE qa_tests (
    ->    id INT NOT NULL AUTO_INCREMENT PRIMARY KEY,
    ->    product_name VARCHAR(30) NOT NULL,
    ->    last_update DATE NOT NULL,
    ->    qa_status
    ->      ENUM('PENDING', 'IN PROGRESS', 'PASS', 'FAIL') NOT NULL
    -> );
Query OK, 0 rows affected (0.02 sec)

mysql> INSERT INTO qa_tests VALUES
    -> ('', 'Souper Soup Dehydrator', '2004-05-10', 'IN PROGRESS'),
    -> ('', 'Ants Ants Revolution', '2004-05-12', 'PASS'),
    -> ('', 'Churn-O-Bill Butter Churn', '2004-05-18', 'FAIL'),
    -> ('', 'Congeal-O-Meal', '2004-05-16', 'PENDING'),
    -> ('', 'Thrash-O-Matic', '2004-06-02', 'FAIL'),
    -> ('', 'Gas-Powered Turnip Slicer', '2004-05-20', 'IN PROGRESS'),
    -> ('', 'Personal Breathalyser', '2004-06-05', DEFAULT),
    -> ('', 'INTERCAL Home Study Course', '2004-06-04', 'PASS');
Query OK, 8 rows affected, 8 warnings (0.01 sec)
Records: 8  Duplicates: 0  Warnings: 8

mysql>
```

If it is not declared NOT NULL, an ENUM column can contain NULL values. Unless a different value is declared as the default, the default value is the first value listed in the column definition. Notice that the next-to-last record in the INSERT query shown in the example uses the DEFAULT keyword (introduced in MySQL 4.0.3) for the value of the **qa_status** column. We can easily verify that the correct value was inserted.

```
Command Prompt - mysql -h megalon -u root -p
mysql> SELECT * FROM qa_tests;
+----+----------------------------+-------------+-------------+
| id | product_name               | last_update | qa_status   |
+----+----------------------------+-------------+-------------+
|  1 | Souper Soup Dehydrator     | 2004-05-10  | IN PROGRESS |
|  2 | Ants Ants Revolution       | 2004-05-12  | PASS        |
|  3 | Churn-O-Bill Butter Churn  | 2004-05-18  | FAIL        |
|  4 | Congeal-O-Meal             | 2004-05-16  | PENDING     |
|  5 | Thrash-O-Matic             | 2004-06-02  | FAIL        |
|  6 | Gas-Powered Turnip Slicer  | 2004-05-20  | IN PROGRESS |
|  7 | Personal Breathalyser      | 2004-06-05  | PENDING     |
|  8 | INTERCAL Home Study Course | 2004-06-04  | PASS        |
+----+----------------------------+-------------+-------------+
8 rows in set (0.00 sec)

mysql>
```

Predefined values for enumerated columns must always be passed to MySQL as strings.

```
Command Prompt - mysql -h megalon -u root -p                          _ □ ×
mysql> UPDATE qa_tests SET qa_status = FAIL WHERE id = 6;
ERROR 1054 (42S22): Unknown column 'FAIL' in 'field list'
mysql> UPDATE qa_tests SET qa_status = 'FAIL' WHERE id = 6;
Query OK, 1 row affected (0.01 sec)
Rows matched: 1  Changed: 1  Warnings: 0

mysql> SELECT * FROM qa_tests;
+----+--------------------------+-------------+-------------+
| id | product_name             | last_update | qa_status   |
+----+--------------------------+-------------+-------------+
|  1 | Souper Soup Dehydrator   | 2004-05-10  | IN PROGRESS |
|  2 | Ants Ants Revolution     | 2004-05-12  | PASS        |
|  3 | Churn-O-Bill Butter Churn| 2004-05-18  | FAIL        |
|  4 | Congeal-O-Meal           | 2004-05-16  | PENDING     |
|  5 | Thrash-O-Matic           | 2004-06-02  | FAIL        |
|  6 | Gas-Powered Turnip Slicer| 2004-05-20  | FAIL        |
|  7 | Personal Breathalyser    | 2004-06-05  | PENDING     |
|  8 | INTERCAL Home Study Course| 2004-06-04 | PASS        |
+----+--------------------------+-------------+-------------+
8 rows in set (0.00 sec)

mysql>
```

Because the values are indexed, it is also possible to insert numbers into ENUM columns as part of INSERT or UPDATE queries, with the indexing beginning at 1 for the first value in the column definition. The following shows a couple of sample queries and the updated table data.

```
Command Prompt - mysql -h megalon -u root -p                          _ □ ×
mysql> INSERT INTO qa_tests VALUES
    -> ('', 'Bass Blaster Fishing Mortar', NOW(), 1);
Query OK, 1 row affected, 1 warning (0.00 sec)

mysql> SHOW WARNINGS\G
*************************** 1. row ***************************
  Level: Warning
   Code: 1264
Message: Data truncated for column 'id' at row 1
1 row in set (0.00 sec)

mysql> UPDATE qa_tests SET qa_status = 3 WHERE id = 7;
Query OK, 1 row affected (0.00 sec)
Rows matched: 1  Changed: 1  Warnings: 0

mysql> SELECT * FROM qa_tests;
+----+--------------------------+-------------+-------------+
| id | product_name             | last_update | qa_status   |
+----+--------------------------+-------------+-------------+
|  1 | Souper Soup Dehydrator   | 2004-05-10  | IN PROGRESS |
|  2 | Ants Ants Revolution     | 2004-05-12  | PASS        |
|  3 | Churn-O-Bill Butter Churn| 2004-05-18  | FAIL        |
|  4 | Congeal-O-Meal           | 2004-05-16  | PENDING     |
|  5 | Thrash-O-Matic           | 2004-06-02  | FAIL        |
|  6 | Gas-Powered Turnip Slicer| 2004-05-20  | FAIL        |
|  7 | Personal Breathalyser    | 2004-06-05  | PASS        |
|  8 | INTERCAL Home Study Course| 2004-06-04 | PASS        |
|  9 | Bass Blaster Fishing Mortar| 2004-08-01| PENDING     |
+----+--------------------------+-------------+-------------+
9 rows in set (0.00 sec)

mysql>
```

However, this isn't normally recommended practice, since it could easily lead to confusion. The index of NULL (if the column definition allows NULL values) is NULL. In the event that a value is inserted that's not present in the value list, MySQL inserts an empty string (and beginning with version 4.1.0, issues a warning as well). The empty string value always has an index of zero.

ENUM columns can also be sorted according to the order of the values in the definition. This means we can use the column in an ORDER BY query.

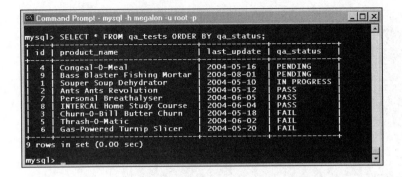

However, making direct comparisons gets a little trickier. For example, given the definition for the **qa_status** column in our example, this clause:

```
SELECT * FROM qa_tests WHERE qa_status > 'PASS';
```

returns data for all tests whose status is 'PENDING', because this string sorts alphabetically after 'PASS'. Recalling that 'PASS' is the third value in the list we defined for the **qa_status** column, we could use the index for this value:

```
SELECT * FROM qa_tests WHERE qa_status > 3;
```

In this instance, we'll obtain the records whose status is 'FAIL', because 'FAIL' is the fourth item in the enumeration list. Since this might be a little confusing, let's see exactly what output we obtain from these two queries.

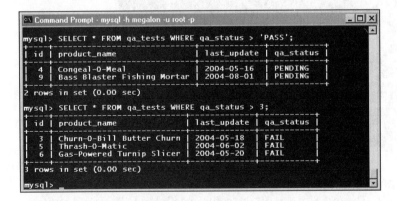

According to the MySQL documentation, ENUM columns will *not* be sorted in alphabetical order unless they are listed in alphabetical order in the column declaration. However, our experience shows that in MySQL 4.0 and later, ENUM columns *are* in fact sorted in alphabetical order. To avoid confusion, you may want to define ENUM lists with the values in alphabetical order.

CAUTION   *Even if you're using numbers as values in an* ENUM *column, they must be specified as strings. For example, trying to declare a column as* mycol ENUM(3,6,9) *instead of* mycol ENUM('3', '6', '9') *will cause an error. We recommend that you avoid this potential pitfall by not using numbers for* ENUM *column values. In addition, when declaring a default value for an* ENUM *column, don't forget that it must also be specified as a string; otherwise, it will be (silently!) ignored.*

ENUM columns can actually have quite a large number of enumerated values—up to 65,535 of them. They are also economical in terms of storage space. An ENUM column defined with $n<=255$ possible values requires just 1 byte of storage; one with $255<n<65,535$ values uses 2 bytes. This means it's easy for you to add new values (say, 'CANCELED') to the list, without needing to make changes anywhere else in the database, such as in a linked table.

Enumerated values are case-insensitive, but they are returned in the same case used in the column definition. We generally employ, and recommend that you use, all uppercase for ENUM values, as this is accepted usage for distinguishing constants in many programming languages such as C, Java, Perl, PHP, and Visual Basic.

The SET Type

The last of MySQL's column types that we'll look at is also probably the least well known, the least often used, and the least understood. The SET type is a complex type. Although its values are set as strings, they're actually stored behind the scenes as numbers, and we'll show exactly how this is done and how to turn this knowledge to your advantage if you find yourself using a table containing a SET column.

The SET datatype is similar in some ways to ENUM; however, where ENUM allows just one choice from a predetermined list to be used as a column value, SET allows for *multiple* values from the list to be used in the same record. In other words, the column values are not mutually exclusive. For example, let's suppose we're designing a web application whose users may speak one or more of three languages: English, German, and Spanish. To accommodate this, we might an **app_users** table with a **language** column, defined as follows:

```
language SET('ENGLISH', 'GERMAN', 'SPANISH') NOT NULL;
```

(We name the table **app_users** rather than **users** in order to avoid any confusion with MySQL's own **mysql.user** table.) The following shows the creation and population of this table.

```
Command Prompt - mysql -h megalon -u root -p                        _ □ ×

mysql> CREATE TABLE app_users (
    ->     app_user_id INT AUTO_INCREMENT NOT NULL PRIMARY KEY,
    ->     username VARCHAR(16) NOT NULL,
    ->     language SET('ENGLISH', 'GERMAN', 'SPANISH')
    -> );
Query OK, 0 rows affected (0.03 sec)

mysql> INSERT INTO app_users (app_user_id, username, language) VALUES
    ->     ('', 'georgeb72', 'ENGLISH'),
    ->     ('', 'pablo337', 'ENGLISH,SPANISH'),
    ->     ('', 'marie421', 'ENGLISH,GERMAN'),
    ->     ('', 'heinrich052', 'GERMAN'),
    ->     ('', 'roberto611', 'SPANISH,GERMAN'),
    ->     ('', 'luciana62', 'SPANISH,ENGLISH');
Query OK, 6 rows affected, 6 warnings (0.01 sec)
Records: 6  Duplicates: 0  Warnings: 6

mysql>
```

If you look carefully, you'll see that we inserted user pablo337's language preference as 'ENGLISH,SPANISH' but used the value 'SPANISH,ENGLISH' for user luciana64. This isn't a problem, as you can see when we select all the table data.

```
Command Prompt - mysql -h megalon -u root -p                        _ □ ×

mysql> SELECT * FROM app_users;
+-------------+-------------+-----------------+
| app_user_id | username    | language        |
+-------------+-------------+-----------------+
|           1 | georgeb72   | ENGLISH         |
|           2 | pablo337    | ENGLISH,SPANISH |
|           3 | marie421    | ENGLISH,GERMAN  |
|           4 | heinrich052 | GERMAN          |
|           5 | roberto611  | GERMAN,SPANISH  |
|           6 | luciana62   | ENGLISH,SPANISH |
+-------------+-------------+-----------------+
6 rows in set (0.00 sec)

mysql>
```

MySQL puts the language choices back into the correct order. The same thing is true for UPDATE queries.

```
Command Prompt - mysql -h megalon -u root -p                        _ □ ×

mysql> UPDATE app_users
    -> SET language = 'ENGLISH,GERMAN'
    -> WHERE username = 'georgeb72';
Query OK, 1 row affected (0.00 sec)
Rows matched: 1  Changed: 1  Warnings: 0

mysql> UPDATE app_users
    -> SET language = 'GERMAN,ENGLISH'
    -> WHERE username = 'heinrich052';
Query OK, 1 row affected (0.00 sec)
Rows matched: 1  Changed: 1  Warnings: 0

mysql> SELECT * FROM app_users;
+-------------+-------------+-----------------+
| app_user_id | username    | language        |
+-------------+-------------+-----------------+
|           1 | georgeb72   | ENGLISH,GERMAN  |
|           2 | pablo337    | ENGLISH,SPANISH |
|           3 | marie421    | ENGLISH,GERMAN  |
|           4 | heinrich052 | ENGLISH,GERMAN  |
|           5 | roberto611  | GERMAN,SPANISH  |
|           6 | luciana62   | ENGLISH,SPANISH |
+-------------+-------------+-----------------+
6 rows in set (0.00 sec)

mysql>
```

Notice that the inserted or updated values are contained together within a *single* set of quotes, separated by a comma. (For this reason, no element in the value list for a SET column may contain a comma.)

In order to select rows by the values in a SET column, you can use a LIKE clause, as shown here:

You can also use the FIND_IN_SET() function for this purpose. This function takes a string as its first argument and a list as its second argument. It returns the index at which the string is found in the list or a zero if it's not found.

As you can see, the results of both SELECT queries are exactly the same.

Because the set's values are always stored in order in which they were defined, you can obtain matches on multiple values, as demonstrated in the following example.

```
Command Prompt - mysql -h megalon -u root -p
mysql> SELECT * FROM app_users
    -> WHERE language LIKE '%ENGLISH%SPANISH%';
+-------------+-----------+-----------------+
| app_user_id | username  | language        |
+-------------+-----------+-----------------+
|           2 | pablo337  | ENGLISH,SPANISH |
|           6 | luciana62 | ENGLISH,SPANISH |
+-------------+-----------+-----------------+
2 rows in set (0.00 sec)

mysql>
```

This query will return the set of users who speak both English and Spanish. In order to consider how you might easily determine which users speak English *or* Spanish, we need to digress for just a moment.

Like the values in enumerated column definitions, SET values are indexed. However, the indexing scheme is based on binary numbers. The first value corresponds to the first bit of the binary value number, the second value to the second bit, and so on. The indexing for the values defined for the language column in our example is as follows:

VALUE	BINARY INDEX	DECIMAL EQUIVALENT
ENGLISH	001	1
GERMAN	010	2
SPANISH	100	4

The index value stored for multiple values is just their sum, and you can use this value in INSERT and UPDATE queries, just as you can use the string values. For example, the following:

```
UPDATE users SET user_language = 6 WHERE username = 'erick428';
```

is equivalent to this:

```
UPDATE users SET user_language = ('GERMAN,SPANISH') WHERE username = 'erick428';
```

because GERMAN sets the twos bit, SPANISH sets the fours bit, and the sum of 2 and 4 is 6.

Before continuing, let's update the language preferences using this query:

Now let's check the result.

This gives us a slightly better spread of values than we had previously for purposes of the next couple of examples. This also gives us the chance to show you how to select the index value stored for a SET column (this trick of adding zero to the column in the SELECT works for ENUM column values as well).

You can perform more sophisticated selection of data from SET columns using binary operators such as & and | (see Chapter 4 for more information about these operators). For example, if we want to see which users have English or Spanish (or both languages) among their chosen languages, we can use the & operator with the sum of their index values (1 and 4):

```
SELECT * FROM app_users WHERE lanuage & 5;
```

Let's see what happens when we actually try this.

```
mysql> SELECT * FROM app_users WHERE language & 5;
+-------------+------------+-------------------------+
| app_user_id | username   | language                |
+-------------+------------+-------------------------+
|           2 | pablo337   | ENGLISH,GERMAN          |
|           3 | marie421   | SPANISH                 |
|           4 | heinrich052| ENGLISH,SPANISH         |
|           5 | roberto611 | GERMAN,SPANISH          |
|           6 | luciana62  | ENGLISH,GERMAN,SPANISH  |
+-------------+------------+-------------------------+
5 rows in set (0.02 sec)

mysql>
```

To obtain a list of users whose language choices include English or Spanish, but not both, we would need to include an AND in the WHERE clause:

```
SELECT * FROM app_users WHERE language & 5 AND language <> 5;
```

There are some other tricks you can perform in queries against SET columns using binary operators; see Chapter 4 for more ideas about what's possible.

SET is fairly economical in terms of memory requirements. The amount of storage used by a SET column varies with the length of the value list, as shown in Table 2-3.

Table 2-3. SET Column Type Storage Requirements

NUMBER OF ELEMENTS IN SET	NUMBER OF BYTES PER ROW
1 – 8	1
9 – 16	2
17 – 24	3
25 – 32	4
33 – 64	8

There are a few drawbacks to using SET:

- It means that your data isn't normalized. As you'll see in the next chapter, what you should use in a scenario like this one (in what's known as a *many-to-many relationship* between users and languages) is three separate tables: one for the users, one for the language options, and one linking the two together.

- You often can't index SET columns effectively. This means that SELECT queries against them are not going to be as fast as they could be. (You can create an index against a SET column, but it refers to the column as a whole, rather than to its individual elements.) It's also fairly meaningless to try to sort against a SET column.

- The maximum number of values that can be listed in a SET declaration is 64, so if you want more than that, you'll need to use multiple SET columns or to implement a normalized schema for your database.

However, there are some advantages to using SET:

- As we noted when discussing the ENUM column type, it seems a bit silly to maintain extra tables in order to accommodate a property that can take on only a very few values.

- SET is extensible; that is, you can redefine a SET column to include new values without disrupting the data already stored in it, as long as you add them to the end of the listing, and you can make this change to only a single table.

- You can do comparisons on multiple values using a few arithmetic and binary operators, without performing complicated multiple-table joins.

NOTE *Like* ENUM, *the* SET *datatype is unique to MySQL and has no equivalent in other common databases such as Oracle, Microsoft SQL Server, or PostgreSQL.*

True and False: Accommodating Boolean Values

The last datatype we'll look at isn't a true column type at all, at least not in MySQL. However, it's so common in computing, that we would be doing you a grave disservice if we didn't discuss it at all. This datatype is the Boolean datatype, which is

pretty much the simplest type you can have. It has just two values, **TRUE** and
FALSE (three values if you include the **NULL** value).

As of this writing (MySQL 5.0.0-alpha having just been released), MySQL still
doesn't have a true Boolean datatype, although MySQL AB says that one will be
added in the future. MySQL does have a BOOL or BIT column type. As of MySQL
4.1, you may also refer to this type using the BOOLEAN keyword. This type is actually
equivalent to TINYINT(1), the idea being that you use a 1 for a Boolean TRUE, and a
0 for Boolean FALSE. We can verify this as shown in the next example.

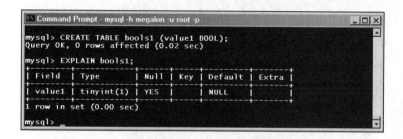

```
mysql> CREATE TABLE bools1 (value1 BOOL);
Query OK, 0 rows affected (0.02 sec)

mysql> EXPLAIN bools1;
+--------+------------+------+-----+---------+-------+
| Field  | Type       | Null | Key | Default | Extra |
+--------+------------+------+-----+---------+-------+
| value1 | tinyint(1) | YES  |     | NULL    |       |
+--------+------------+------+-----+---------+-------+
1 row in set (0.00 sec)

mysql>
```

We don't find this a very satisfying solution, and look forward to seeing a
true Boolean implemented in MySQL. The reason for this is that it's possible to
insert values other than 0 or 1 (or possibly the NULL value).

For example, suppose that someone runs an EXPLAIN, DESCRIBE, or SHOW CREATE
TABLE query on **bools1** (the table in the previous example). This person sees that
value1 is a TINYINT(1) and thinks that it's okay to write a routine that inserts integers other than 0 or 1. Then, later on, someone else comes along and says, "Oh,
that's supposed to be Boolean column and somebody messed it up by inserting
values greater than 1. I'll just fix that with an UPDATE SET value1=1 WHERE value1>1;
query." Then the first someone's code gets broken.

A better solution is to prevent those sorts of problems by using a datatype that
doesn't allow out-of-range values to be inserted in the first place. Unfortunately,
even if you're using MySQL 4.1 (or later), the BOOL type does allow just that.

NOTE *The SQL standard (SQL99) defines a BOOLEAN datatype that
can take one of the values **TRUE, FALSE**, or **UNKNOWN (NULL)**.
However, at present, only PostgreSQL actually supports such a
datatype. Like MySQL, SQL Server and Oracle do not support a
true Boolean datatype.*

In the meantime, while we're waiting for a true Boolean type to be implemented, what other alternatives are there? One method that's sometimes
employed is to define a true/false column as something like this:

```
gets_newsletter ENUM('F','T') NOT NULL
```

This isn't so bad, is it? Let's give it a try.

```
Command Prompt - mysql -h megalon -u root -p                        _ □ ×
mysql> CREATE TABLE bools2 (value1 ENUM('F', 'T') NOT NULL);
Query OK, 0 rows affected (0.01 sec)

mysql> INSERT INTO bools2 (value1) VALUES
    -> ('F'), ('T'), (NULL), (''), ('G');
Query OK, 5 rows affected, 3 warnings (0.00 sec)
Records: 5  Duplicates: 0  Warnings: 3

mysql> SHOW WARNINGS\G
*************************** 1. row ***************************
  Level: Warning
   Code: 1262
Message: Data truncated, NULL supplied to NOT NULL column 'value1' at
row 3
*************************** 2. row ***************************
  Level: Warning
   Code: 1264
Message: Data truncated for column 'value1' at row 4
*************************** 3. row ***************************
  Level: Warning
   Code: 1264
Message: Data truncated for column 'value1' at row 5
3 rows in set (0.00 sec)

mysql> SELECT value1 FROM bools2;
+--------+
| value1 |
+--------+
| F      |
| T      |
|        |
|        |
|        |
+--------+
5 rows in set (0.01 sec)

mysql>
```

Can you see what the problem is here? If we insert a value other than 'F' or 'T', the column winds up containing an empty string. Of course, you can design your application in such a way that it's impossible for an end user to insert any value other than the two in the enumeration list, but that won't stop other programmers from writing applications that don't prevent this. Another possibility is that you set up an automated task (a cron job on Unix or a scheduled task on Windows platforms) to run an update on the table periodically and set all empty columns to the default enumerated value. On the other hand, defining a "Boolean" column in this way allows for the empty string to be treated as the unknown value required in SQL99, and we're then guaranteed that any value not explicitly true or false will be regarded as unknown.

Another method of simulating a Boolean type would be to define the column as CHAR(0). Such a column has two, and only two, permitted values: an empty string or NULL. Given that an empty string is stored for any non-NULL value, it makes sense (to us, at least) to regard NULL as "true" and ' ' as "false." In this way, a value corresponding to "true" will be stored in the column if, and only if, a NULL is inserted. Of course, if the demands of your application are otherwise, you're free to interpret these in the opposite fashion. A CHAR(0) column is also extremely economical, as it requires only 1 bit of storage; both BOOL and ENUM('F', 'T') require 1 byte per record. The drawback with this approach is that there's no provision for the **UNKNOWN** value that's stipulated by SQL99.

Why Datatypes Do Matter, Revisited

You've now seen that it's easy for your data to become "polluted" without you realizing it. MySQL will often attempt to convert between types for you, which can lead to maddening silent errors. For example, let's see what happens when we try to use VARCHAR for fields intended to store numbers. First, we'll create a table, and then insert two rows into it. The second row contains an erroneous piece of data: a letter instead of a number.

```
Command Prompt - mysql -h megalon -u root -p                          _ □ ×

mysql> CREATE TABLE numbers (value1 VARCHAR(5), value2 VARCHAR(5));
Query OK, 0 rows affected (0.02 sec)

mysql> INSERT INTO numbers (value1, value2)
    -> VALUES ('2', '5'), ('a', '10');
Query OK, 2 rows affected (0.00 sec)
Records: 2  Duplicates: 0  Warnings: 0

mysql> SELECT value1, value2 FROM numbers;
+--------+--------+
| value1 | value2 |
+--------+--------+
| 2      | 5      |
| a      | 10     |
+--------+--------+
2 rows in set (0.00 sec)

mysql>
```

Because the letter 'a' in the second row is character data, there's no error or warning for MySQL to report.

Now let's perform a query involving a simple calculation.

```
Command Prompt - mysql -h megalon -u root -p                          _ □ ×

mysql> SELECT value1, value2, value1 * value2 AS product
    -> FROM numbers;
+--------+--------+---------+
| value1 | value2 | product |
+--------+--------+---------+
| 2      | 5      |      10 |
| a      | 10     |       0 |
+--------+--------+---------+
2 rows in set (0.01 sec)

mysql>
```

Because MySQL automatically casts the nondigit character to a zero, we might not even be aware that there's an erroneous value in the first column, if we were to simply obtain the product of the two columns. At least, not until we discovered later that, in spite of the test we're performing to make sure that only nonzero values are being inserted into both columns, the product of **value1** and **value2** is still zero.

In large tables, using VARCHAR or TEXT—rather than INT, FLOAT, or DECIMAL—can be extremely wasteful of space. For example, an eight-digit integer requires only 4 bytes to store, but the same number in a TEXT column requires 10 bytes. This may seem very small considering that you are using only 6 bytes extra; however, if you multiply that by the five columns in which you are storing integers as text, and then multiply it by the 50,000 records in the table, you'll see that you've wasted 1.5MB of space!

Not only does the use of unsuitable column types waste space and leave you open to type-conversion errors, but it can also create much more work for you. Suppose your application calls for dates to be displayed in *dd-mm-yyyy* format (for example, 01-02-2004 for February 1, 2004). You might be tempted to create a date column using this format:

```
start_date CHAR(10)
```

This requires 10 bytes of storage per record, as opposed to 3 bytes per record for this version of the column:

```
start_date DATE
```

and 2 bytes of the difference are spent just storing the two dash characters—hardly economical, especially when you start multiplying by many thousands of records (or more). But that's not the only problem. Because the values are not true date values, you encounter issues with comparison and sorting as well.

Let's create two tables, each containing two columns, which we'll use for storing date information.

```
Command Prompt - mysql -h megalon -u root -p

mysql> CREATE TABLE real_dates (
    -> start_date DATE,
    -> end_date DATE
    -> );
Query OK, 0 rows affected (0.03 sec)

mysql> CREATE TABLE fake_dates (
    -> start_date CHAR(10),
    -> end_date CHAR(10)
    -> );
Query OK, 0 rows affected (0.02 sec)

mysql>
```

In **real_dates**, we define the dates as the DATE type. In **fake_dates**, we define them as strings (CHAR(10)). Now let's store the date values corresponding to January 2, 2003, and February 1, 2004, in both tables, and then compare them using the < operator (recall that MySQL returns a 1 for Boolean **TRUE** and a 0 for **FALSE**). The INSERT and SELECT queries are shown in the following example.

```
Command Prompt - mysql -h megalon -u root -p                    _ □ ×

mysql> INSERT INTO real_dates (start_date, end_date)
    -> VALUES ('2003-01-02', '2004-02-01');
Query OK, 1 row affected (0.01 sec)

mysql> INSERT INTO fake_dates (start_date, end_date)
    -> VALUES ('02-01-2003', '01-02-2004');
Query OK, 1 row affected (0.00 sec)

mysql> SELECT start_date < end_date FROM real_dates;
+-----------------------+
| start_date < end_date |
+-----------------------+
|                     1 |
+-----------------------+
1 row in set (0.01 sec)

mysql> SELECT start_date < end_date FROM fake_dates;
+-----------------------+
| start_date < end_date |
+-----------------------+
|                     0 |
+-----------------------+
1 row in set (0.01 sec)

mysql>
```

Because we declared the columns in **fake_dates** as the CHAR type, they're sorted and compared in character order, not in date order. In order to perform a true date-based comparison, we would need to write a fairly complex query or use extra middleware code. In addition, using the CHAR columns in this case makes it very easy to insert "junk" data into **fake_dates**. In fact, we can insert *any* string whose length is less than or equal to 10, even something utterly ridiculous like *94WerV=&*. There's no simple way to test for integrity. On the other hand, if we attempt to insert inappropriate values into **real_dates**, MySQL will instead truncate these to '0000-00-00', which we can easily test for, and in MySQL 4.1 and later, we'll receive a warning if this happens. Let's delete the existing data from both tables, and then try to insert some junk into **real_dates**.

```
Command Prompt - mysql -h megalon -u root -p                    _ □ ×

mysql> DELETE FROM real_dates;
Query OK, 1 row affected (0.01 sec)

mysql> DELETE FROM fake_dates;
Query OK, 1 row affected (0.00 sec)

mysql> INSERT INTO real_dates VALUES ('blah', 'blah');
Query OK, 1 row affected, 2 warnings (0.00 sec)

mysql> SHOW WARNINGS\G
*************************** 1. row ***************************
  Level: Warning
   Code: 1264
Message: Data truncated for column 'start_date' at row 1
*************************** 2. row ***************************
  Level: Warning
   Code: 1264
Message: Data truncated for column 'end_date' at row 1
2 rows in set (0.00 sec)

mysql>
```

However, we'll receive no such warning if we insert the same values into the **fake_dates** table. As you can see in the next example, MySQL says, in effect, "You're inserting text into CHAR columns, and that's just as it should be."

```
Command Prompt - mysql -h megalon -u root -p                    _ □ ×
mysql> INSERT INTO fake_dates VALUES ('blah', 'blah');
Query OK, 1 row affected (0.00 sec)

mysql>
```

Here are the values that are actually stored in the two tables:

```
Command Prompt - mysql -h megalon -u root -p                    _ □ ×
mysql> SELECT d1.start_date, d1.end_date, d2.start_date, d2.end_date
    -> FROM real_dates d1, fake_dates d2;
+------------+------------+------------+----------+
| start_date | end_date   | start_date | end_date |
+------------+------------+------------+----------+
| 0000-00-00 | 0000-00-00 | blah       | blah     |
+------------+------------+------------+----------+
1 row in set (0.00 sec)

mysql>
```

This means that, while you don't need to do anything other than check the values in **real_dates** to ensure that they're not equal to '0000-00-00', you can't trust the values stored in **fake_dates** at all. You would need to use regular expressions or some other form of pattern-matching to ensure that the values fit the format.

Finally, if we don't store dates as DATE values, we can't use MySQL's time and date functions with them.

```
Command Prompt - mysql -h megalon -u root -p                    _ □ ×
mysql> SELECT YEAR(d1.start_date) AS y1, YEAR(d2.start_date) AS y2
    -> FROM real_dates d1, fake_dates d2;
+------+------+
| y1   | y2   |
+------+------+
|    0 | NULL |
+------+------+
1 row in set (0.01 sec)

mysql>
```

We'll discuss in greater detail the functions and operators that can be used in MySQL queries in Chapter 4. For now, the point that we're trying to get across is this: Just because you refer to something as a "date" (or any other type of data) doesn't mean that MySQL automatically treats it as one. A much better alternative to creating your own conventions is to learn MySQL's datatypes and understand how to work with them effectively.

MySQL Table Types

Now that we've discussed the MySQL column types in some detail, we're ready to consider what sorts of tables those columns will make up. Most databases use a single data storage engines and, thus, all tables have the same basic characteristics and support the same features. MySQL is quite different (and possibly unique) in this regard. It can work with several different storage engines, and thus, several different table types. When designing your MySQL database and application structure, you have a number of choices. In this section, we'll compare the capabilities, strengths, and limitations of each type, and discuss how to decide which table type is most appropriate to use in a given situation.

Basically, MySQL can be considered to have two varieties of tables: transactional tables (InnoDB and BDB) and nontransactional tables (ISAM, MyISAM, HEAP, and MERGE).

Advantages of using transactional tables include the following:

- They're "safer" than nontransactional tables; by this, we mean that, if your system crashes, you can recover your data either by automatic recovery or by using a backup plus the transaction log.

- If an UPDATE fails, you can easily restore to the previous state; with nontransactional tables, all changes that have taken place are permanent.

- Transactional tables provide more accurate data reads (if tables are consistently updated).

- You can combine many statements using COMMIT.

- You can roll back your changes using ROLLBACK (MySQL must not be running in auto-commit mode in order for this to work).

The advantages of using nontransactional tables are as follows:

- They're much faster than transactional tables.

- They require less disk space than transactional tables.

- They use fewer system resources than transactional tables.

ISAM and MyISAM Tables

Since the ISAM table type is considered deprecated as of MySQL version 4.1, it is not compiled into the default MySQL database engine. As of MySQL 5.0, ISAM is no longer supported or included at all. MyISAM tables are the replacement for this table type and are based on the ISAM code.

MyISAM is the default table type for MySQL as of version 3.23. So, if you create your tables with no table type defined (and you have not specified a different default table type in your my.cnf or my.ini file), MySQL will create it as the MyISAM type.

TIP *You can easily convert any ISAM tables that you might still be using to MyISAM format by running one of the* mysql_convert_table_format *scripts, which can be found in the scripts directory of your MySQL installation. The version of the script with the .sh extension is a Unix bash script; the other is written in Perl and should run on any system where Perl is installed.*

MySQL uses three files for each MyISAM table. The first file, *tablename*.MYI, contains the table indexes. The second file, *tablename*.MYD, contains the table data. The third, *tablename*.frm, contains the table definition. MySQL includes tools for checking, optimizing, and recovering MyISAM tables (myisamchk) and for compressing MyISAM table data to use less space (myisampack). (Chapter 3 includes a description of how to compress tables with MyISAM tables with myisampack.)

Although we won't go into this in complete detail, we wouldn't be doing our job as authors of a book about MySQL if we didn't mention the most noteworthy features of MyISAM tables:

- **Crash recovery:** There is a flag in the MyISAM file that indicates if the table was closed correctly. If you pass the –myisam-recover option to mysqld on startup, the server daemon will automatically check to see if the table was closed correctly and repair if it necessary.

- **Concurrent** INSERT **statements:** You can insert a row into a table even if data is being read from that table by another user.

- **Support for large files:** MyISAM tables provide 64-bit file support on filesystems and operating systems (OSs) that support big files.

- **Portability:** All data in a MyISAM table is stored with the low byte first. This makes the data machine- and OS-independent. The only requirement for binary portability is that the machine uses two's-complement signed integers (as nearly every computer manufactured the last 20 years has) and IEEE floating-point format (also dominant among mainstream machines). (In other words, you can copy the files used by MySQL to store tables directly between many different types of machines running different OSs.) There are no major performance issues that surround using this type of data storage.

- **Good index compression:** All number keys are stored high byte first, which gives fast compression on indexes.

- **AUTO_INCREMENT capability:** MyISAM provides internal handling of one auto-incrementing column. MySQL will automatically update this when rows are inserted or updated; it can be reset using the myisamchk tool included with MySQL. This makes the AUTO_INCREMENT columns quite fast.

- **Optimized inserts:** When data is inserted in sorted order (as when using an AUTO_INCREMENT column), the key tree will be split, so that the high node will contain only one index. This will provides better space utilization in the key tree.

- TEXT **column indexes:** Both BLOB and TEXT columns may be indexed.

The index files for MyISAM tables are also smaller than for ISAM tables. Although extra processing time is needed for INSERT or UPDATE operations, MyISAM tables provide faster return of data because they use less disk space, thus reducing the amount of disk time MySQL needs to access the data from the index.

InnoDB Tables

The InnoDB table type provides MySQL with a transaction-safe (ACID-compliant) table to use for your applications that require transaction support. This will give your COMMIT, ROLLBACK, and crash-recovery support, as well as row-level locking and nonlocking reads using SELECT, such as Oracle uses. These features help improve multiuser concurrency, performance, and accuracy with critical data.

 NOTE *ACID stands for* Atomic – Consistent – Isolated – Durable, *and is used to describe the necessary conditions of database transactions. We'll discuss these conditions when we talk about programming with MySQL transactions in Chapter 7.*

What Kinds of Tables Are Available on My Server?

To see what types of tables are enabled on your MySQL installation, run the following command from within the MySQL Monitor:

```
SHOW VARIABLES LIKE '%have%';
```

You should receive output similar to what's shown here (although the individual YES and NO values may differ somewhat according to your MySQL version and the options enabled in your configuration):

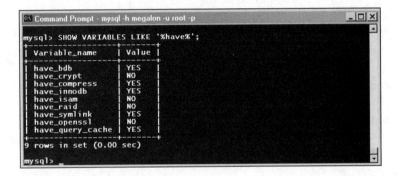

Note that MyISAM support isn't listed because it's always available.

It is important to verify that MySQL support for a desired table type is turned on before trying to create a table of that type, because MySQL will not display any sort of error or warning messages if that type isn't available. Instead, MySQL will silently apply the default table type (normally MyISAM).

You can change the default table type by setting `default-table-type=tabletype` in your my.cnf or my.ini file. However, we recommend that you don't change it on multiuser systems without a very good reason, as most users will be accustomed to MyISAM as the default.

InnoDB tables are good at handling large amounts of data, as well as data that is constantly being read from or updated by multiple users. For example, if you're building an ordering system for your web site, InnoDB would be ideal for storing order information relating to areas such as billing and shipping. However, if you're storing data that's updated only relatively infrequently, such as product data, you might want to choose a nontransactional table type, such as MyISAM, in order to save storage space.

TIP   *You're not restricted to a single table type within any given database—far from it. In fact, this versatility is one of MySQL's unique advantages. Tables for which transaction support is critical can be of type InnoDB or BDB; tables that don't need transactions or that you wish to use for storing data for full-text searches can be made MyISAM; temporary tables can be HEAP tables. You can use whatever combination of table types best suits your needs and those of your application.*

InnoDB tables have the following limitations:

- InnoDB tables do not support full-text indexes. If your application requires full-text indexes, you will need to use MyISAM tables to store the data that you wish to search.

- InnoDB tables tend to be fairly slow compared with MyISAM or HEAP tables. Don't use InnoDB unless your application requires transaction support or you intend to enforce foreign keys.

- The Windows version of MySQL stores InnoDB tables with lowercase table names. If you are trying to move databases in binary format from Unix (Linux) to Windows, you need to make sure they are changed to lowercase before doing so. (This is another good reason to use lowercase names, as we discussed in Chapter 1.)

- Using InnoDB tables can require some extra setup in the my.cnf (or my.ini) file. In MySQL 4.0 and earlier, you must tell MySQL the location of the InnoDB datafile on the system. You should also include directives specifying the size of data and log files, and allocating memory for InnoDB to use. In MySQL 4.1 and later, this is done for you, but you may need to modify the default values.

- The SHOW TABLE STATUS command is not accurate for InnoDB tables, other than with regard to the physical size that is reserved by that table. For row counts, it provides only estimates.

CAUTION   *Be sure to read the MySQL documentation for information about how to specify the size of data and log files in InnoDB tables. Don't depend on MySQL's defaults to provide what you'll need to run InnoDB on a production server, as failure to allocate sufficient memory will result in drastically decreased performance.*

It is worth noting that when performing any CREATE INDEX, DROP INDEX, and ALTER TABLE commands on an InnoDB table, the entire table will be re-created. If the table is very large, this can take a considerable amount of time.

To obtain InnoDB runtime information, use the following command from the MySQL Monitor command line:

```
SHOW INNODB STATUS;
```

(You may want to use the \G line terminator for this command to make the output more easy to read.)

In MySQL 5.0, this command has changed:

```
SHOW ENGINE INNODB STATUS;
```

BDB Tables

Berkeley DB tables (more commonly referred to as BDB) provide another transaction-safe table type for MySQL. BDB is included in MySQL versions 3.23.34 and later. Like InnoDB tables, which have largely superseded them, they provide COMMIT and ROLLBACK methods. Unlike InnoDB tables, BDB tables don't support foreign key constraints.

To determine whether your MySQL installation supports BDB tables, use the SHOW VARIABLES LIKE '%have%' command. If have_bdb is set to NO, then BDB is not available on your MySQL server. To enable BDB, you will need to run the mysqld-max binary instead of the binary you're currently using, or you'll need to recompile MySQL from source, using the --with-bdb flag.

BDB provides a page-level lock when performing operations on tables. (A *page* in this context means a group of rows that varies depending on the number of rows in the table, the OS being used, and several other factors.) When a transaction is being processed, MySQL will lock the particular page of data in relation to the query, and all other data in the table will be ready for additional queries. Although this method is not better for performance than the row-level locking provided by InnoDB tables, it is much superior to the table-level locking used by MyISAM tables. This also improves concurrency for your database in a multiuser environment.

Here are a few other points to keep in mind about BDB tables:

- BDB tables have a very high probability of surviving crashes.

- If you don't want or need BDB tables for your applications, you can start MySQL with the --skip-bdb option to disable them and save considerable amounts of memory.

- As with InnoDB tables, each BDB table is required to have a primary key, and MySQL will define one for you, if you fail to do so. This hidden primary key for BDB tables comes at a cost of 5 bytes' storage per row (for InnoDB tables, the storage requirement for this will vary).

- Aggregate functions depending on the number of rows in the table such as COUNT() and AVG() tend to be rather slow, especially as BDB tables increase in size, and may not be completely accurate after a large number of INSERT and DELETE operations have been run. You can force the count to be updated by issuing an ANALYZE TABLE or OPTIMIZE TABLE command.

- A BDB table tends to take up more space than the equivalent MyISAM table.

You should also note that BDB tables are not currently supported for Linux on non-Intel platforms, or on Mac OS X, so be sure to keep this in mind for situations where your application may be deployed on platforms other than the one you're using for development.

 TIP *For efficiency when using InnoDB or BDB tables, you should always try to minimize the number of separate transactions required by your application, and to maximize the number of operations performed per transaction. We'll discuss this more in Chapter 7.*

HEAP Tables

The HEAP table type employs hashed indexes and stores them in memory. This allows HEAP tables to be extremely fast. However, in the event of a crash (of either MySQL itself or the machine that it's running on), you'll lose all of your data.

You should also remember for safety's sake always to set a value for MAX_ROWS when creating a HEAP table in order not to use too much memory. Note that you can't create a HEAP table larger than the size that's set in the max_heap_table_size configuration variable in any case. You should normally leave this set at its default (approximately 10% of system RAM), and not increase it unless you really need to.

You should also use DROP TABLE, TRUNCATE, or DELETE FROM on a HEAP table just as soon as you no longer need its data. Of course, if you've used CREATE TEMPORARY TABLE to create the table, it will automatically be dropped when the current connection to MySQL is closed.

Here are some additional facts about HEAP tables that may prove useful:

- The memory required by each row in a HEAP table can be found by summing the lengths of all keys plus 8 bytes per key, and then adding the length of the row multiplied by 4 bytes to this sum. (On 64-bit systems, these two numbers will be 16 bytes and 8 bytes, respectively.)

- HEAP tables use fixed record lengths and are dynamic; in other words, they don't easily become fragmented.

- HEAP tables provide no support for TEXT and BLOB column types.

- HEAP tables provide no support for AUTO_INCREMENT.

- HEAP tables provide no support for indexes on NULL columns before MySQL 4.0.2.

- Indexes are used only for WHERE clauses involving the = and <=> operators.

HEAP tables are most useful when employed to store intermediate results in temporary tables. Don't forget to plan ahead and make sure that you won't have so many HEAP tables open simultaneously that all of the system's memory will be used up, and be sure that your system has enough RAM to meet your projected HEAP table memory requirements.

Summary

Databases are for storing data in discrete and well-defined "packages" (columns) in an ordered fashion. In the context of working with databases, these are referred to as *datatypes* or *column types*, and you can't begin to organize data into an efficient database unless you have a solid understanding of what sorts of "packages" or "boxes" are available to fit things into. We devoted the first (and larger) portion of this chapter to examining MySQL's many datatypes, both simple (numbers and character data) and complex (dates and groupings of predefined values), in terms of the sorts of data they're best suited to represent and the amount of space that's required to store them. We tried to emphasize throughout this discussion that data of a given type is best stored in a column corresponding to that type, and showed some examples illustrating why it's usually a poor decision to do otherwise. For example, if you choose to store and retrieve dates as strings, you'll usually wind up using more space than you would have if you had used the appropriate date type (such as TIME or DATE), and you won't be able to take advantage of MySQL's functionality that's particular to dates.

Any serious application is going to involve working with numbers, and MySQL features a wide range of numeric types. We covered these in depth, along with such related topics as the definitions of single-precision and double-precision numbers, the precision to which MySQL performs calculations with various number types, and ways to economize on space while ensuring sufficient accuracy in computations. Strings are also (obviously!) quite important, and MySQL offers a number of different choices with regard to size and static versus dynamic storage options for these.

MySQL is not alone in its use of the null value (NULL), which is found in nearly all other databases, as well as in most programming languages. MySQL developers are not alone in that many of them often misunderstand what it is and how it's useful. NULL is not zero, and it's not the string composed of the letters *N-U-L-L*; it's literally *nothing*. We also mentioned how it affects indexing and storage requirements.

We also examined two unique datatypes that MySQL offers for handling columns whose possible values are limited to a specific range or list. In the case of ENUM, the column may contain one value. SET columns may contain a subset of the allowed values. For those of you already familiar with First Normal Form, it may seem like the SET type violates this by definition, but if you examine how SET works beneath the surface, you can see that you really aren't storing multiple values in a single column; it just looks that way. (We'll come back to this in the next chapter, when we cover database normalization.) We also pointed out that MySQL doesn't have (as of this writing) a true Boolean datatype, and we examined some alternatives for simulating a Boolean column.

Along the way, we pointed out some common "gotchas" (due to MySQL's unusual handling of certain situations), as well as some common conceptual errors made by developers using MySQL. For example, many MySQL users misunderstand the purpose and effects of width arguments for numeric types, and we tried to lay as many of these misunderstandings to rest as possible.

Once you've decided which datatypes will be used for columns, you're ready to store records. However, you need to consider what sort of tables those records will be a part of. MySQL is unique in that it offers a number of different table types and that it's possible to use more than one type of table in a single database. We looked at each of MySQL's table types and talked about the different characteristics of each. The usefulness of some of these capabilities will become more apparent later on, after we've talked about issues like indexing and foreign keys in the next chapter, and temporary tables in Chapter 6.

What's Next

We've laid some groundwork for building a good MySQL database by discussing how to store data in table columns appropriately and effectively, and what sorts of tables are available to use. In Chapter 3, we'll discuss actual database design, which involves identifying the entities or objects to be represented and their relationships, determining the most suitable datatypes (a fair amount of which we've just covered in the current chapter), imposing data integrity, establishing keys, and deriving a coherent model of the database. Database design is more often than not an iterative process. Using normalization techniques, we'll show you how you can improve an initial model in a series of steps to arrive at an efficient and extensible database. We'll also discuss some common errors in database design, and what you can do to correct them, and possibly to avoid making them in the first place.

CHAPTER 3

Keys, Indexes, and Normalization

A DATABASE HAS two primary functions: to store data and to return data. In this chapter, we're going to look at three related topics in database design: *keys* (or *constraints*), *indexes*, and *normalization*. All three of these things help us to accomplish two goals:

- To minimize the amount of space required to store data

- To minimize the amount of time and effort required to execute queries and return useful results from them

Many of the concepts that we'll discuss are common to all relational databases but, naturally, we'll focus on their application in MySQL.

We'll start things out by discussing a pattern we've noticed time and time again in dealing with "fixing" databases created by others that we've inherited in our work, and particularly in adapting datastores supplied by vendors. The mind-set evidenced by some of the databases with which we've been confronted we have come to call the Spreadsheet Syndrome. While it may work well in some situations, it does not embody a good methodology for database design. We feel that this "spreadsheet state of mind" is responsible for a great many of the problems encountered in badly designed databases.

We'll also review the rules defining a relational database, because understanding just what a relational database management system (RDBMS) is supposed to be and how it's supposed to function can't help but improve your ability to make effective use of one.

Next, we'll delve into what is probably *the* core concept of relational database design. Normalization is the process of applying a series of rules, known as *normal forms*, to the design of a database in order to eliminate redundant data. Each of these normal forms is the formalization of a rule for modeling data. The concept of *foreign keys* is essential to building a normalized database, as these allow you to impose constraints on values in one table in terms of the values found in columns of one or more different tables. Not all of the table types found in MySQL support explicit foreign key constraints, but no matter which type of table you're using, you still can (and should!) apply normalization principles in designing databases.

Indexes and key constraints can speed up queries and help you to organize data more efficiently, as well as to guarantee data integrity. We'll also examine a greatly underutilized feature, which is the ability to create indexes on multiple columns in the same table. These can often be used to dramatically speed up repeated queries against multiple columns.

Next, we'll cover a command that should be part of your regular MySQL toolkit. EXPLAIN SELECT provides a wealth of useful information about queries, which you should take advantage of if you're serious about getting the best performance from MySQL. This includes whether or not MySQL is using your indexes to optimize queries, and if so, which ones, as well as the types of joins it will try to use. Join types are not created equal when it comes to speed of execution, and being able to recognize them will help you pinpoint bottlenecks where unnecessary table rows are being read, discover where indexes should be created, and see where indexes that you have created aren't being used.

Finally, we'll look at some common errors we've observed in the creation of indexes and in normalizing databases. We'll also revisit the Spreadsheet Syndrome at that point.

Beyond the Spreadsheet Syndrome

Spreadsheets can be a wonderful and useful thing, and the rise of electronic spreadsheet programs such as VisiCalc and Lotus 1-2-3 (along with word processors) helped fuel the desktop computer revolution of the 1980s. Spreadsheets are very handy for producing two-dimensional views or groupings of related data and obtaining calculations based on numbers stored in the same columns or rows. Their capabilities have been greatly extended over the last couple of decades; you can perform sorts, produce graphs and charts, change formatting on the fly, and so on.

However, at their core, spreadsheets are still basically an electronic model of the old-time paper ledger. In those ledgers, human beings needed to keep running totals and to repeat important data items on every page. This was because each page had to present a large enough subset of all the data so that human beings wouldn't lose track of what it represented. In other words, a spreadsheet exhibits a very high degree of *redundancy*.

Figures 3-1 and 3-2 show portions of a typical spreadsheet depicting payroll for a firm with 11 employees.

3324-payroll.xls

	A	B	C	D	E	F	G	H	I	J
1	Empl. Name	Job Title	Pay Pd. Beg.	Pay Pd. End	Hrly.Rt.	Tot. Hrs.	Reg. Hrs.	O/T Hrs.	Reg. Pay	O/T Pay
2	Smith, John	Sales Asst.	June 1, 2002	Jun 15, 2002	$12.65	88.15	80.00	8.15	$1,012.00	$154.65
3	García, Jane	Exec. Secy.	June 1, 2002	Jun 15, 2002	$13.45	82.90	80.00	2.90	$1,076.00	$58.51
4	Davis, David	Sales Asst.	June 1, 2002	Jun 15, 2002	$12.85	78.65	78.65	0.00	$1,010.65	$0.00
5	Doe, John	Whse./Del.	June 1, 2002	Jun 15, 2002	$9.75	84.50	80.00	4.50	$780.00	$65.81
6	Williams, Lois	Sales Asst.	June 1, 2002	Jun 15, 2002	$11.35	82.25	80.00	2.25	$908.00	$38.31
7	Sung, William	Shift Mgr.	June 1, 2002	Jun 15, 2002	$15.45	81.60	80.00	1.60	$1,236.00	$37.08
8	Voegel, Jay	Store Mgr.	June 1, 2002	Jun 15, 2002	$16.25	92.40	80.00	12.40	$1,300.00	$302.25
9	Giuliani, Regina	Shift Mgr.	June 1, 2002	Jun 15, 2002	$15.75	76.50	76.50	0.00	$1,204.88	$0.00
10	Elshemy, Kamel	Sales Asst.	June 1, 2002	Jun 15, 2002	$12.25	82.35	80.00	2.35	$980.00	$43.18
11	Morgan, Debora	Sales Asst.	June 1, 2002	Jun 15, 2002	$11.25	78.50	78.50	0.00	$883.13	$0.00
12	Jones, Richard	Sales Asst.	June 1, 2002	Jun 15, 2002	$11.55	84.20	80.00	4.20	$924.00	$72.77
13										
14	TOTALS:					912.00	873.65	38.35	$11,314.65	$772.55
15										
16	AVERAGE:				$12.96	82.91	79.42	3.49	$1,028.60	$70.23

Figure 3-1. A portion of a typical spreadsheet showing gross wages calculation

3324-payroll.xls

	A	C	D	K	L	M	N	O	P
1	Empl. Name	Pay Pd. Beg.	Pay Pd. End	Gross Pay	# Dep.	Tax Pct.	Tax Ded.	Tax Amt.	This Chk.
2	Smith, John	June 1, 2002	Jun 15, 2002	$1,166.65	1	25%	5%	$233.33	$933.32
3	García, Jane	June 1, 2002	Jun 15, 2002	$1,134.51	0	25%	0%	$283.63	$850.88
4	Davis, David	June 1, 2002	Jun 15, 2002	$1,010.65	3	25%	15%	$101.07	$909.59
5	Doe, John	June 1, 2002	Jun 15, 2002	$845.81	2	15%	10%	$42.29	$803.52
6	Williams, Lois	June 1, 2002	Jun 15, 2002	$946.31	2	15%	10%	$47.32	$898.99
7	Sung, William	June 1, 2002	Jun 15, 2002	$1,273.08	3	25%	15%	$127.31	$1,145.77
8	Voegel, Jay	June 1, 2002	Jun 15, 2002	$1,602.25	0	25%	0%	$400.56	$1,201.69
9	Giuliani, Regina	June 1, 2002	Jun 15, 2002	$1,204.88	3	25%	15%	$120.49	$1,084.39
10	Elshemy, Kamel	June 1, 2002	Jun 15, 2002	$1,023.18	1	25%	5%	$204.64	$818.55
11	Morgan, Debora	June 1, 2002	Jun 15, 2002	$883.13	1	15%	5%	$88.31	$794.81
12	Jones, Richard	June 1, 2002	Jun 15, 2002	$996.77	0	15%	0%	$149.51	$847.25
13									
14	TOTALS:			$12,087.20				$1,798.45	$10,288.75
15									
16	AVERAGE:			$1,098.84	1.45	21.36%	7.27%	$163.50	$935.34

Sheet1 \ Sheet 1 [2] \ Sheet 2 \ Sheet 3 /

Figure 3-2. A portion of a typical spreadsheet showing payroll taxes calculation

For a small number of employees, this is fairly workable. It's the sort of information that needs to be printed on payroll checks and pay stubs. It's easy to read and print out, it doesn't take up a great deal of disk space (less than 35KB for a single pay period), and it's easy to make changes if and when they're required. However, when the developers try to scale up this application, either in terms of the number of employees represented or when they broaden the scope of the application itself, they start to run into problems.

In a nutshell, relational databases and spreadsheets both support a row-and-column view of data, but the resemblance ends there. Let's look at some key points differentiating spreadsheets from databases:

> **Separation of data from code and presentation:** What makes a spreadsheet so easy to use—the fact that all formatting, data, and programming logic are provided in the same context—is also what makes it difficult to maintain. A well-designed database, on the other hand, stores data in the most generic possible form, without any formatting or programming code included. Thus, developers are free to create applications using whatever logic or formatting is desired by the programmer, without needing to remove preexisting formatting or code first. Experienced programmers are aware that separation of data, code, and presentation makes for more efficient and maintainable applications than trying to mix them all up together. As you'll see shortly, this is a key point in good database design as well.

> **Redundancy:** A spreadsheet has a great deal of data that's either repetitive or that can be derived easily from other data in the same spreadsheet. Looking at the example in Figure 3-1, for instance, you can see that the starting and ending dates for all 12 rows are the same, and that some employees have the same job title. In addition, the values in the total hours, regular hours, and overtime hours columns are interdependent, and all of the values in the three pay columns can be derived from one or more of the hours columns and the pay rate column. In Figure 3-2, which represents a second sheet from the same spreadsheet, you can see that four of the columns from the first sheet are repeated. A well-designed database doesn't have this problem; each item of data is distinct and unique. Data that's the same for multiple records can be placed elsewhere and related to the appropriate records in the current table. In other words, you can put repeating data in a separate table and link to it from the current one using a *foreign key constraint*. Columns that depend on one another are either reduced to their distinguishing values or are removed. In a normalized database, we would most likely remove the regular hours and overtime hours columns, for example. We could derive those values from the total hours columns as needed, using a formula based on the fact that any number of hours less than or equal to 80 is considered regular time, and hours in excess of 80 are considered overtime.

Shared access: Spreadsheets are subject to a second form of redundancy. If your "Human Resources department" consists of a single secretary or accountant whose main function in this regard is preparing the payroll, then sharing a spreadsheet isn't a problem. However, when your firm employs thousands, there will be many different individuals needing to work with the data at the same time. With a spreadsheet, you're limited to a single file that can be in use by only one person at a time. The only way to support simultaneous users is to have multiple copies of the spreadsheet file. A database supports concurrent users who can operate on any records in the database at will; the only restrictions they're subject to are those imposed by the database authorization or privilege system. The database engine—not a separate application or OS extension working at the filesystem level—handles any conflicts arising from simultaneous attempts to access or change the same data.

Security issues: Spreadsheets feature only rudimentary security protections, and generally speaking, your choices are often limited to allowing read/write, read-only, or no access at all to the entire body of data in a single file. Some spreadsheet programs (including the popular Microsoft Excel) have somewhat more sophisticated permissions schemes than this (individual sheets within a spreadsheet can be protected, and individual columns can be write-protected), but this is still in sharp contrast to the permissions model of a typical database. By design, a good database engine supports concurrent users with different permission levels and modes of access. The database ensures that only users with the necessary permissions can perform requested operations. The MySQL database engine provides a very fine-grained permissions matrix, with databases, tables, and columns making up one axis and the full range of SQL operations making up the other. While we won't go into the details concerning MySQL's privileges system in this book, it is something you should keep in mind as you plan and deploy MySQL-backed applications.

Rules for Relational Databases

The conceptual foundations for the modern relation database can be found in the work of Dr. E. F. Codd, an IBM researcher who wrote a number of seminal works in the 1960s and 1970s outlining database principles, as well as defining normalization and normal forms (which we'll look at later in this chapter). In 1985, he published a set of rules, or guidelines, defining the ideal relational database, which we list in this section. Some of these rules we've already touched on to one degree or another; others we'll cover in this chapter or later in the book. The names (in bold) are Dr. Codd's; the formulations of these rules (italics) and accompanying explanations (plain type) represent our own interpretations of these guidelines. Usually referred to as Codd's Twelve Rules, there are actually 13 of them:

0. **Rule 0:** For a system to qualify as an RDBMS, that system must use its relational facilities to manage the database. In other words, database management should take place from within the database itself, employing the same relational language (SQL) that's used to manipulate data. In theory, the system should use only its relational facilities to manage the database, but in practice, nearly all modern databases provide some external tools as well. This is also true of MySQL, due to the presence of utilities such as `mysqladmin`, `mysqlshow`, and `myisamchk`. Older versions of MySQL were somewhat lacking in their adherence to this guideline, but beginning with the 3.23.*XX* series, it's possible to handle nearly all database management from within the MySQL Monitor.

1. **The Information Rule:** *Data must be logically represented and systematically accessible.* A table consists of rows and columns. A row corresponds to an individual record; the data items belonging to each record are organized into fields (or columns). A column defines the type and characteristics of data that may be stored in it. All records in a table share a common set of columns, and each column definition is the same for all records.

2. **The Guaranteed Access Rule:** *Data will be accessible in a logical fashion by table, primary key, and column.* Another way of saying this is that any item of data in the database should be logically identifiable according to the name of the column it occurs in, the value of the primary key for the record of which it's a part, and the name of the table where this row and column are found. This has been extended in most database implementations (including MySQL) to provide for access to databases as supersets of tables. A corollary of this rule is that each database on the same database server must be uniquely named, as must each table within the same database. Each column of a given table must also be uniquely identified. As long as at least one column in a table is either a primary or unique key, we can access any desired row in that table in MySQL.

3. **Systematic Treatment of Null Values:** *The empty or null value must be treated uniformly as an unknown or missing value; we must not make a substitution such as an empty string, blanks, or zero for this unique value.* An accepted corollary of this rule is that null values may not serve as primary keys. (See the relevant section in the previous chapter for more detailed information about how MySQL treats this value.) In addition, most databases (including MySQL) also allow a column to be constrained from holding any null values. In MySQL, the NOT NULL constraint is used for this purpose.

4. **Dynamic On-Line Catalogue Based on the Relational Model:** *Metadata* (that is, data about the database) *is to be stored in the database.* Another way of stating this rule is that the database must permit us to access its structure using the same tools that we use to access its data. In MySQL, this is accomplished by means of the grant tables and other system tables.

5. **The Comprehensive Data Sublanguage Rule:** *We must be able to define data, constraints, access permissions, views, transactions, and data manipulation in a single language.* The most common language for doing this is SQL (Structured Query Language), originally developed by IBM in the late 1970s, and today, most databases support one dialect of it or another. Using MySQL's variant of SQL, it's possible to perform any of these tasks outlined in this rule. In MySQL 5.0, it's also possible to create stored procedures and user-defined functions using SQL syntax (we'll look at these in Chapter 8).

6. **The View Updating Rule:** *Views must reflect changes in their base tables, and vice versa.* A *view* acts like a table but is defined by a SELECT query. Beginning with MySQL 3.23, temporary tables were available to take on some of the functions of views. Support for derived tables (sometimes known as unnamed views) was introduced in MySQL 4.1. Unlike views, neither derived tables nor temporary tables are persistent, and they do not transmit updates back to their parent tables. Support for views is expected to be added to MySQL in version 5.1. We discuss temporary tables in Chapter 6. In Chapter 8, we'll discuss derived tables as implemented in MySQL 4.1 onwards. Also in Chapter 8, we'll take a look at how actual views (that is, persistent virtual tables) might be handled in future releases.

7. **High-Level Insert, Update, and Delete:** *We must be able to insert, retrieve, update, or delete data with a single operation.* This means is that we should be able to operate on sets of data derived from multiple rows (and possible multiple tables as well) and that we shouldn't be limited to working with one row at a time. We're already seen that this is the case for operating on multiple rows in a single table in MySQL, and we'll extend this to rows from more than one table when we discuss joins in Chapter 6.

8. **The Physical Data Independence Rule:** *Operations on the database by users or applications must be independent of the physical aspects of data storage and access.* Database users must able to work with data without needing to worry about hardware or how the database interacts with it. For example, let's suppose we find that we're running out of space on the disk where the mysql/data directory is located. We can shut down

MySQL, move this directory to a different disk (or even a different machine, through the use of symbolic links), update the MySQL configuration file, and then restart the server. In such a case (provided we follow these steps correctly), users will see no difference in the structures of the databases and tables they were working with prior to the change.

9. **The Logical Data Independence Rule:** *Operations on the database must be able to effect changes in the database schema without having to recreate it or the applications built upon it.* The view that users have of the data in a database should not change due to a change in the logical structure of the database. In other words, if table structures are altered, users should not notice the difference. Note that this guideline is very difficult to implement, and few (if any) databases currently in use do so.

10. **The Integrity Independence Rule:** *It must be possible to guarantee data integrity within the context of the database and its metadata; it should not be a requirement of applications to impose such constraints.* In most relational databases (including MySQL), this boils down to two principal constraints that can be imposed using SQL: No primary key can depend upon a null value, and if a foreign key is defined in one table, any value it takes on must be that of a primary key in another table. We'll see how MySQL fulfills these requirements later in this chapter. (As for datatype constraints, MySQL is changing in versions 4.1 and 5.0 to provide better handling of these than the silent failures and/or conversions that were the norm in MySQL 3.23 and 4.0.)

11. **The Distribution Independence Rule:** *The language used to manipulate data should not be impacted by the manner in which data is physically stored.* Users of the database should not have to be concerned whether or not data storage is in a single physical location or is distributed across multiple locations. This is handled for the most part in MySQL by configuration settings that are insulated from database users and vice versa.

12. **The Non-Subversion Rule:** *Any row processing* (that is, procedural programming) *done in the system must follow the rules that set-processing operations obey with regard to data integrity.* In other words, there should be no way to violate constraints on table columns or to alter them, other than through the use of SQL or another similar set-processing language to alter the table structure. In theory, it might be possible to write a program to manipulate MySQL's table datafiles in such a way as to break this rule, but that would require working with the files on the binary level, and chances are that doing so would simply make the table unusable in MySQL.

No existing database implements all of Codd's Rules to the letter, of which fact partisans of other RDBMS who belittle MySQL in newsgroups, mailing lists, and web discussion sites sometimes need to be reminded. For example, no current database provides full update and delete capabilities with respect to logical views.

Another criticism often directed against MySQL is its lack of transactions, views, stored procedures, cursors, or triggers. In the first case, such criticisms are at least three years out of date, transactions having been available in production releases since the beginning of 2001. Temporary tables were also implemented some time ago, and derived tables became supported in MySQL 4.1. With regard to the remaining three items, none of these is mandated by Codd's Rules, although they are all present in the SQL 92 and subsequent ANSI SQL standards. Stored procedures and basic cursors are implemented in MySQL 5.0; triggers and possibly views are expected in MySQL 5.1.

The chief shortcoming of MySQL, in our view, is with regard to the Integrity Independence Rule: The current production version (4.0) sometimes performs datatype substitutions without warning the user of these. However, as we've noted previously, newer releases handle such situations more rigorously, with more (and increasingly precise) warnings being issued and better API access to these warnings.

Our point here is that MySQL complies with these rules about as well as any other RDBMS that's currently in widespread use. Despite what some might say, MySQL is a "real" relational database. If you're going to use it in your applications, you should treat it like one.

Normalization and Data Modeling

A database is defined as a set of related tables. It's entirely possible to use more than one database in a single application. Whether or not it's desirable to do so is another matter entirely, and like many other aspects of database design, the answer is somewhat subjective and depends on the types of data being used, their relationships to one another, and the needs of the developer, application, and client.

If your payroll application requires that you build tables of employees, job positions, wage rates, and days/hours worked, you might be better off using a single payroll database for all of them, even if it's used for several different clients, as long as you're performing essentially the same task for each client. If your accounting firm is keeping patient records for a veterinarian, tracking inventory for a bakery, and doing taxes for private individuals—that is, performing a collection of fairly disparate tasks—perhaps it would be more appropriate to keep records relating to each client in a separate database.

Another point to consider is that MySQL stores datafiles for different databases in separate directories. If you're using symbolic links to one or more of these, or if the partition in which your data directory is stored spans multiple physical drives, then accessing several databases concurrently may impede performance.

Database design is something of an art as well as a science. However, there are certain well-defined principles that are essential to building an efficient database. *Normalization* can be summed up as the process by which redundancy is removed from a database, so that each piece of data is necessary, separate, and unique. This process tends to have the effect of minimizing space and other resource requirements and maximizing efficiency. It also helps you to focus on the precise relationships between different items of data, and decide whether or not the database provides an accurate and complete representation of the system that you're trying to model.

NOTE   *The design of a database or table is often referred to as a database or table* schema.

The goals of normalization can be enumerated as follows:

- Ensure that all data required for the application model is stored in the database.

- Minimize the presence of redundant data and relationships.

- Allow for the data in the database to be updated as efficiently as possible.

- Prevent the loss of essential data while guarding against the retention of data that's no longer needed.

Proper normalization not only economizes on the amount of space used for storing data, but it also helps prevent anomalies from occurring when we perform updates; that is, it helps ensure that when we add, update, or delete a record in the database, all necessary data relating to that record is also added, deleted, or updated. This helps to prevent corruption of the database. It is also much easier to modify the structure of a normalized database than it is to change an unnormalized one. Because normalized tables represent discrete entities, we can often add or delete entities from the data model by creating or dropping tables, rather than by making changes in the structure of existing tables.

In a normalized database, information belonging to a given item is stored in a single record. Since we don't need to change data in multiple locations (tables) in order to achieve a complete update, this reduces the possibility of leaving unneeded information "stranded" in the database. An example of this sort of anomaly would be where we delete a customer's name but fail to delete her address. As a result, we now have an address record that's no longer associated with a customer in any meaningful way. In other words, since each customer has an address and that address is usually unique to the customer, we should store addresses with customer records and not separately. It is this type of situation that normalization strives to avoid. It also achieves this goal in part by breaking down an overly complex table into a number of simpler ones, with each table containing data items that have a set of closely related attributes. In other words, each table should represent a single concept, entity, or relationship.

NOTE *The conversion of a single table with many columns into a number of tables (each with fewer columns) is also known as* decomposition.

Normal Forms

Normalization is a *process*. In order to eliminate duplicated data, we must go through a series of steps or levels, with each step depending on the previous one. These steps are known as *normal forms*. There are at least six of them, listed here with their common abbreviations:

- First Normal Form (1NF)

- Second Normal Form (2NF)

- Third Normal Form (3NF)

- Boyce-Codd Normal Form (BCNF)

- Fourth Normal Form (4NF)

- Fifth Normal Form (5NF)

Normal forms can be thought of as a series of prescriptions for the way in which data should be stored in a database. Their origins can be traced to a set of papers written by E. F. Codd between 1969 and 1972, which introduced the relational data model (including the "Twelve Rules" we looked at earlier in this chapter) and the concept of normalization, and provided the first formal definitions for what are now known as First, Second, and Third Normal Forms.

Since that time, additional normal forms have been devised. In fact, there are even more than those we've listed here, such as Sixth Normal Form (6NF) and Domain-Key Normal Form (DKNF), but these tend to be fairly esoteric and are often not applicable to situations commonly encountered in everyday database design and development. In practice, the vast majority of database developers normalize only through Third (or possibly Bryce-Codd) Normal Form.

We'll cover the first three normal forms in this chapter. (If you're interested in learning about the remaining normal forms, see Appendix A.) Over the next few sections, we'll apply each normal form in turn to the same set of data. For this example, we'll use a collection of data about some university students, originally ordered as shown here:

Students
Name
Year
Major
Minor
Classes & Hours
Course Load
GPA

A few typical entries in this dataset might look like Table 3-1.

While the language used to describe the normal forms is often rather esoteric (unless you happen to be highly conversant with logical and set notation), their aims and the basic processes for achieving these forms are not that difficult to understand. What follows is a brief attempt to convey the principles of and concepts behind normalization in something approaching ordinary language.

Table 3-1. Sample Student Data

Name	Year	Major	Minor	Classes and Hours	Course Load	GPA
Mary-Ann Sukoto	Senior	Art	Spanish	Modern American Poets/3, Classic Castilian Literature/3, Studio Painting/5, 20th Century Europe/3	14	3.86
Joseph Miller	Sophomore	Computer Science	Mathematics	Programming Data Structures/3, Java Swing GUIs/4, Linear Algebra/4, 20th Century Europe/3	14	3.78
Julia Shapiro	Senior	Sociology	Geology	Senior Sociology Research Project/5, Introduction to Probability and Statistics/4, Mineralogy of Western North America/3	12	3.92
Hakim Ferris	Freshman	Undecided	Undecided	English Composition/3, 20th Century Europe/3, Intro to Ecology/4, Music Appreciation/3	13	0.00

First Normal Form

First Normal Form says that each attribute in a table can't be further subdivided. More formally, we can say that a table is in First Normal Form if meets the following three conditions:

- There are no duplicated rows in the table. In other words, the table must have a primary key (which can consist of one or more columns, as we've seen). Note that this does not mean that two or more rows cannot have the same value in the same column, only that each row taken as a whole must be distinguishable in some way from all other rows.

- All entries in the same column are of the same logical type. Declaring a column as CHAR(50) and then storing disparate values such as "123 Main St.", "3388 5555", and "Frank" in it does *not* mean that the table is in First Normal Form just because the column has a single datatype.

- Each cell of the table is single-valued (no repeating groups or arrays). This requirement is also often stated as "All attributes must be atomic."

How do we apply these rules to our student data? We could satisfy the first rule in one of two ways: We can either place a uniqueness constraint on the table, or we can add a unique key. None of the existing columns can be guaranteed to be unique in and of itself, and there really are no guarantees that any combination of columns will be unique, either: there could easily be two sophomores named Joseph Miller, majoring in Computer Science and minoring in Mathematics. In fact, it's not outside the realm of possibility that both these students are taking the same courses this semester and that both have the same grade-point average. So the best solution here is to add a Student ID column (an auto-incrementing integer type) to the table to serve as the table's primary key.

Fortunately, the second rule is already satisfied; we don't have any values in any of the columns that don't logically fit in with the others. All of the Name entries look and act reasonably like the names of persons, all of the Year entries contain a designation for a student's year in university, and so on.

When we come to the third rule, we run into some problems. The Classes and Hours column as used can contain multiple values. We could conceivably deal with this issue by adding several additional columns and naming them something like Classes and Hours 1, Classes and Hours 2, Classes and Hours 3, and so on. However, we would need to make sure that we allowed enough columns. And if we have just one student taking more classes than we've allowed columns for, we would be forced to alter the design of the table, which is a very inefficient way of doing things. In addition, we would invariably wind up with a large number of null values, because not every student would sign up for the maximum possible number of classes. While nulls are not evil in and of themselves (after all, all relational databases are supposed to accommodate their existence), they do take up space, so it seems prudent not to design a large number of them into the database if we can avoid doing so.

This type of situation—where one student can sign up for several classes and many students can sign up for the same class—is quite common in database design, and it is known as a *many-to-many relationship*. A better solution is to create a separate Classes table, put the class data into it, and then create a lookup table to create a separate link between each student and each class, independent of any other student's classes or any other class's students. In other words, we reduce the many-to-many relationship to a set of one-to-one relationships.

Now, when a student signs up for or drops a class, we need only drop the corresponding record in the lookup table. Because a student cannot be signed up for the same class more than once, each combination of student and class is unique. We'll make the Classes table's primary key on both sets of columns.

When we move the Classes and Hours entries to the Classes table, we notice that we have a case where two different kinds of data are merged into a single column. Each class has a name and is known to be worth a certain number of credit hours. Looking back at our original dataset, we can see that we'll be expected to work with those numbers of hours apart from the names of the classes and as hours (that is, as numbers), and so separating them into two columns only makes sense.

Sometimes, however, the question of divisibility depends largely on how we intend to use the data. For example, suppose we have an address field into which we intend to place string values such as "52 Kookaburra Lane, Waterford West 4133 QLD". If all we're ever going to do with this bit of information is print address labels in some order that doesn't depend on information contained within the address itself, then this is probably adequate. However, if we'll later need to create a list based on city, state, or post code, we would need to split up the address field value programmatically to get at these pieces of data. So, in this case, we've violated First Normal Form. This is *very* inefficient, since we could end up needing to perform string operations on the results of a large number of queries. In addition, validation of this sort of "vague" data is more difficult, whereas verifying (for example) the entry in the post code field as a four-digit number is relatively quick and painless. The way to solve this problem would be to use separate fields for the street address, city name, post code, and state.

Looking back at the Students table, we can envision situations where we'll be expected to separate the first and last names. So we will use separate fields for these.

The resulting set of tables and their relationships are shown in the diagram in Figure 3-3.

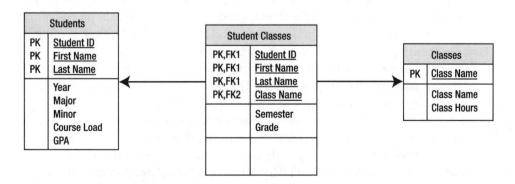

Figure 3-3. The student data in First Normal Form

NOTE *You may notice that the primary key for the Students table consists of three columns: Student ID, First Name, and Last Name. There is no rule that says you can't create a key on more than one column, and you'll see later that there are times when this is actually desirable. This is not one of those times, and we'll explain why and take steps to correct the problem in our discussion of Second Normal Form.*

In many cases, a date and time are stored together in a single column. This might seem to be a violation of First Normal Form, but it's really our perception that they're somehow different that's in error here. The SQL datetime datatype's representation of a date and time using "0000-00-00 00:00:00" notation is just a convenience provided for humans who are used to making things overly complicated. From the database's point of view, it's just another number of seconds or milliseconds.

To summarize, it's almost always less time-consuming to store and retrieve data in the form that's most "friendly" to your application than it is to use your middleware to bludgeon poorly defined data into shape. Conversely, it's nearly always a mistake to combine different sorts of data into a single column in order to save space.

TIP *The rule to follow in achieving First Normal Form can be stated in a general fashion as: **Separate use—separate column**.*

Second Normal Form

In order to be in *Second Normal Form*, a table must be in First Normal Form, and then all non-key attributes in the table must depend on the entire key. In other words, information in a row should not depend on only part of that row's primary key. For example, storing the date of an order as part of that order's primary key is generally not a good idea, since another order made the same day will contain the same date as part of its primary key. This is wasteful, because the date in this case isn't serving to identify the order uniquely, and if we're storing the date *only* as part of this key and must extract it from that column's value to determine the date the order was made, then we've violated First Normal Form.

If in looking at Figure 3-3, you thought it appeared a bit cluttered, then your intuition is serving you well. The Students table violates Second Normal Form because only part of the primary key is guaranteed unique. Neither the

First Name nor the Last Name column contributes to the uniqueness of the key. Because we're linking the Student Classes table to the Students table, and its primary key depends in part on the primary key of Students, it also breaks Second Normal Form. The solution to this problem is to remove the First Name and Last Name columns from the primary key. The Student ID is already unique and therefore sufficient as the primary key of the Students table. When we do this, we no longer need to link to the extraneous columns from the Student Classes table, and removing them satisfies Second Normal Form for that table also.

Our updated database schema is shown in Figure 3-4.

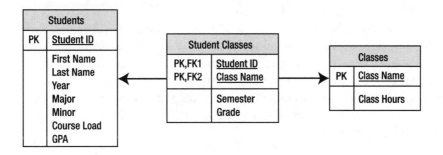

Figure 3-4. The student data in Second Normal Form

TIP   *The rule for Second Normal Form might be stated as:* **Make sure that the primary key is truly unique for each row in the table**.

Third Normal Form

Third Normal Form is, in some respects, a more general way of restating the rule for Second Normal Form. It says that information in any key other than the primary key should contribute to describing that key (or rather, the entity that the primary key represents), and if it doesn't, it should be moved to another table. We have just seen this type of situation with regard to the Student Classes table: The Course Name column doesn't describe the relationship between a student and a course; it actually describes a class. We should therefore add a separate primary key to the Classes table and link to this key from the Student Classes table. Doing this also eliminates redundant data—there's no need to duplicate the names of classes. In addition, the Students table now satisfies Second Normal Form, but we have two columns in it that break Third Normal Form.

In both the Major and Minor columns, we have data that doesn't describe a student; rather, it describes courses of study.

If we could be positive that each and every student had one and only one major and one and only one minor throughout his or her university career, we could possibly consider the course of study as an attribute of students. However, real life shows that this is seldom the case. We should also consider the fact that, should there happen to be no Archaeology majors or minors taking any classes this semester, there would be no representation for that course of study anywhere in our schema! The best way to resolve these issues is to create a Courses table containing the names of all the degree concentrations offered by the university, and link to it from the Students table.

The Course Load and GPA columns should also be eliminated from the Students table, since they describe information about the classes being taken (or that have been taken) by the student, and this is true for most, if not all, calculated values. We can provide a mechanism for obtaining these values by augmenting the Student Classes table with Semester and Grade columns. Using MySQL-compatible column names, the query for obtaining a given student's course load might be written like this:

```
SELECT SUM(c.class_hours) AS course_load
FROM classes c
JOIN students s
USING (student_id)
WHERE s.first_name = 'Rhoda' AND s.last_name='Mirebelli';
```

And the query for the same student's GPA might look like this:

```
SELECT ROUND(( SUM(c.class_hours * c.grade) / SUM(c.class_hours) ), 2 ) AS gpa
From classes c
JOIN students s
USING (student_id)
WHERE s.first_name = 'Rhoda' AND s.last_name='Mirebelli';
```

In MySQL 5.0, it is quite easy to convert these into a single stored procedure (for more information about stored procedures, see Chapter 8).

The new table arrangement complying with Third Normal Form is shown in Figure 3-5.

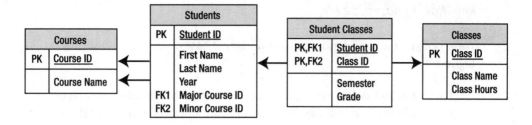

Figure 3-5. The students data in Third Normal Form

 TIP *Another way to sum up Third Normal Form rule is:* ***All columns that are not part of the primary key must relate directly to the primary key and must not depend on any other columns.***

Denormalization

If you've spent any time at all working with databases, you may have encountered the term *denormalization*, which is usually defined as, "Moving from a higher to a lower normal form in order to speed up database access." What do we need denormalization for, anyway? Is there such a thing as too much normalization? If so, how do we know when we've normalized enough, but not too much?

First of all, we need to be very careful to distinguish between the terms *denormalized* and *unnormalized*. When we speak of a denormalized database, this means that that we've normalized a database to at least Third Normal Form, and then removed specific normalizations for the purpose of increasing performance. An unnormalized database is one for which the normalization process outlined in the previous sections has not been performed at all. You can't denormalize an unnormalized database.

The theory behind denormalization goes something like this: Normalization ensures that any given fact gets stored in one place and one place only, which is great for inserting or updating data. But it also means that retrieving the data that we want can often require complicated queries and joins, and these naturally run more slowly than a simple SELECT.

Why Not Denormalize?

We're not great fans of denormalization in most cases. Here's the reasoning behind that:

Lack of principles: We've seen numerous articles and books purporting to explain the Principles of Denormalization; however, not one of these describes the same set of principles. Most of them aren't even close to one another. We believe that the reason for this is that there really *aren't* any principles of denormalization—any more than there is a set of principles to go by when tearing down a house, other than those of the "Don't let loose beams fall on you" variety. While it's true that a lot of texts on normalization don't agree exactly on which normal forms are which, the *principles* of normalization are well known and agreed on by database professionals.

Uneven results: Communication with a database goes in both directions: in and out. Applications do not only store data or only retrieve data; they do both. This means that denormalization is by necessity a robbing-Peter-to-pay-Paul proposition. If you denormalize in order to speed up some SELECT queries, you will slow down some INSERT and UPDATE queries in turn. Perhaps the particular script or program you're working on today only extracts data, but next week you'll find that updating those same records takes longer. Or someone else who is responsible for writing program code to update the database will find performance has fallen off in that regard.

Other optimization tools: There are already methods for optimizing database input and output, both of which are discussed in this chapter. These are, respectively, normalization and indexing. Our experience has shown that using these together in an intelligent manner will take care of the vast majority of database performance issues that you're likely to encounter. Instead of looking for a "magic bullet" to cure performance problems, we suggest that you employ these tools for the purposes for which they're intended.

MySQL's design: MySQL was originally designed to be and continues to be optimized for speed. When set up and used properly, MySQL is already one of the fastest databases available today, consistently outperforming many others (including Oracle).

In short, your best bet for performance is usually going to be a database in which there's no redundant data; that is, one that's normalized through Third Normal Form (or possibly higher in some cases).

When Might You Want to Denormalize?

Having said all of these things, we can't ignore the fact that there *are* times when certain denormalization techniques can give you a speed boost. Here are some of them:

> **Split tables:** This can sometimes be useful when a table contains variable-width (VARCHAR, TEXT, or BLOB) columns. MySQL works most efficiently with tables that are made up completely of fixed-width columns. However, this isn't always possible, particularly if you need to store large amounts of text or binary data and access it frequently. In such cases, it may be possible to split a table into two, one of which contains only fixed-width columns, and both having an indexed, fixed-width column in common (a column declared as INT AUTO_INCREMENT PRIMARY KEY being an obvious choice). You can then use the indexes on the fixed-width table and get the data from the records with matching indexes in the table with the variable-width column or columns. (For more about joins between multiple tables, see Chapter 6.) Another instance where it might be beneficial to split a table is when you frequently get data from only some of the columns.

NOTE *There is almost never any need to split a table simply because it has a large number of columns or rows.*

> **Calculated values:** If you frequently need to refer to results of calculations involving a great many rows, such as counts and sums, it may be faster to keep these values in a separate table and update them as needed, instead of recalculating them every time they're used.

> **Hash columns:** When you have a situation where you frequently need to use a single index on several columns, you may find that SELECT queries are faster if you create a separate index column and store a hashed value based on those column values. Since most programming languages have hashing functions, it then becomes fairly easy to pass queries such as (using PHP syntax)

```
$query = "SELECT * FROM mytable WHERE hashcol = '" . md5($val1.$val2) . "'".
```

> **Statistical reporting:** It's often faster to update summary tables for use in report generation than it is to create report data. Unless "live" statistical data is essential to your application, consider using summaries instead and updating them periodically.

Storing as BLOB: Occasionally, you may run into a situation where data to be stored simply doesn't fit easily into a well-defined table structure. In these cases, it could be more efficient to store it in a BLOB column. If you want to do this, be aware that you'll need to write code that packs and unpacks the data stored in this fashion.

In all of these cases, remember: *You must begin any denormalization from a normalized database whose tables have proper indexes.* Normalize, then add indexes, then test those indexes using EXPLAIN. (In the next section, we'll discuss these topics.) Otherwise, you're simply wasting your time by making a bad situation worse.

Compressed Tables

If your application is such that all or most of the data is inserted periodically in a batch (say, once a week or less often), and then read out frequently in between these times, consider using compressed tables for an additional speed boost. These can be generated from MyISAM tables using the myisampack utility, which can normally be found in the mysql/bin directory. From a system shell or DOS prompt, navigate to the appropriate database directory, and then use the following command:

```
shell> myisampack table_name
shell> myisamchk -rq -analyze -sort-index table_name.MYI
```

(You may need to include the path to your mysql/bin directory in calling these utilities if it's not part of your system path.) Of course, there's no reason why you can't automate this procedure using a Unix cron job or the Task Scheduler on Windows systems.

Using myisamchk after myisampack re-creates the indexes on the table *table_name*. The myisampack utility will reduce the size of the datafile by 40 to 70 percent, and will speed up SELECT queries by 15% to 25%, even on tables without any indexes. When used on well-indexed tables and with queries making proper use of those indexes, the results may be little short of dramatic.

Keys, Indexes, and Constraints

In the previous chapter, we discussed datatype constraints, where the allowed range of values for a given column is restricted by type, length, and whether or not the column may take a null value. Now we'll talk about constraints based on other values in the same or different columns, and even in different tables.

Keys and Indexes Defined

The terms *key* and *index* are to some extent interchangeable in ordinary language, and even in informal database parlance, but they don't mean exactly the same thing, nor are the MySQL KEY and INDEX keywords used in precisely the same way. Let's discuss each of these.

An *index* as used in a database is analogous to the index of a book. A book's index speeds up the search for pages containing a specific word or phrase. For example, if you're writing a program in Python, and you can't remember the exact number and order of arguments for the eval() function, you pull out your trusty copy of *Practical Python*, turn to the "E" section of the index, and find the listing "eval function, evaluating a Python expression with. . .," which points to page 126 where the description of the function is located. This is much faster than starting at the beginning of the book and scanning through 120 pages to find what you're looking for. In much the same way, when you issue a query to MySQL requiring a match on a specific value in a given column, MySQL must start first with the first row and check each row in the table sequentially until it finds the one where the column matches the desired value. When you create an index on the column, you tell MySQL to write an ordered list of all values for the specified column, which it can then search very quickly to find matching rows, regardless of their positions in the table. We'll go a bit more into the specifics of how MySQL does this shortly.

A *key*, on the other hand, is an index that also serves as a constraint on a column's value. MySQL has three types of keys:

- **Unique:** This specifies that each row in the table must contain a unique value for the column on which the unique key is created.

- **Primary:** This creates a unique, non-null key constraint on the desired column.

- **Foreign:** This specifies that any value found in this column must match a value in a unique column in the table to which the foreign key refers.

In the case of a unique key or primary key, attempting to insert a new record with a value duplicating that found in the same column of a different record in the same table results in an error, and the INSERT query terminates immediately. The same is true with regard to row updates. You can suppress the error message using INSERT IGNORE or UPDATE IGNORE, in which case operations on any rows containing duplicate values fail silently, and the query will continue. In the case of an UPDATE query, this means that MySQL will perform the update on any rows not containing values that conflict.

INDEX Syntax

You can create indexes on columns at the time the table is created or add indexes later (as part of an ALTER TABLE statement), and you may index any column type. At a minimum, all MySQL table types (MyISAM, InnoDB, BDB, and so on) can support 16 indexes per table and a total index length of at least 256 bytes.

You can create or add an index using one of three methods:

- Define it at the time the table is created, as part of the CREATE TABLE statement.

- Add the index using an ALTER TABLE statement.

- Add the index using a CREATE INDEX statement.

To define an index as part of a table creation statement, add a line in this form:

```
INDEX [index_name] (column_name[(prefix_length)])
```

For example, the following CREATE TABLE statement creates the **pets** table with an index on the **name** column:

```
CREATE TABLE pets (
   name VARCHAR(30),
   species VARCHAR(15),
   age TINYINT(2),
   INDEX (name(5))
);
```

This index uses only the first five characters in the **name** column value. You may also use KEY in lieu of INDEX in this setting, and if you run a SHOW CREATE TABLE query on a table containing indexes, this is just what MySQL displays: the column definitions followed by the definitions for any indexes that may exist for this table.

```
Command Prompt - mysql -h megalon -u root -p                    _ □ ×
mysql> SHOW CREATE TABLE pets\G
*********************** 1. row ***************************
       Table: pets
Create Table: CREATE TABLE `pets` (
  `name` varchar(30) default NULL,
  `species` varchar(15) default NULL,
  `age` tinyint(2) default NULL,
  KEY `name` (`name`(5))
) ENGINE=MyISAM DEFAULT CHARSET=latin1
1 row in set (0.01 sec)

mysql>
```

We could also create the **pets** table without the index, and then add the index at a later time, using either of the following two statements:

```
ALTER TABLE pets ADD INDEX petname (name(5));
```

or

```
CREATE INDEX petname ON pets (name(5));
```

In either case, the output of the SHOW CREATE TABLE command will be the same as shown in the previous example.

 CAUTION *Specifying an index name is optional when creating an index using a* create table *or* ALTER TABLE *statement. However, the name must be specified when using* CREATE INDEX. *As you'll see shortly, there are some very good reasons for naming your indexes.*

F̶ . . . VARCHAR, you may optionally specify a prefix le̶n̶g̶ . . . g so reduces the amount of space required for the . . . creation when a new index is added on a table with . . . may slow down SELECT queries somewhat, it is also . . . PDATE queries. This is because not as much data nee . . . ex file when rows are added or modified.

Inde̶ . . . or BLOB column could potentially take up very large amounts of . . . e. Because of this, you're required to specify an index length when creating an index on a column of either of these two types. The maximum index length allowed is 255 characters. However, in the vast majority of cases, 5 to 15 characters should be sufficient.

NOTE *Don't try to specify the index length when creating or adding a full-text index. This is because full-text indexes are automatically defined for the entire column.*

You can specify that an index is to be sorted in ascending or descending order using the ASC or DESC keyword when you're creating or adding an index. The default is ASC. Employing DESC might speed up queries a bit when you know that your application will be selecting values entirely or primarily from the upper end of the column's range of values.

```
ALTER TABLE pets ADD INDEX petname (name(5) DESC);
```

It's also possible to drop indexes from tables when they're no longer needed using an ALTER TABLE command. To drop the **petname** index from the **pets** table, use this:

```
ALTER TABLE pets DROP INDEX petname;
```

Note that in order to drop an index, you must either have named the index when you added it or be prepared to re-create the table from scratch. You may also use DROP KEY instead of DROP INDEX, but we prefer and advise you to use the latter. The other way to drop an index is to use this form:

```
DROP INDEX petname ON pets;
```

You must use DROP INDEX and not DROP KEY in this case.

CAUTION *A common error is to assume that dropping an index removes the column on which the index was built. This is not the case; if you wish to remove a column, you must use* ALTER TABLE... DROP COLUMN....

How Do Indexes Work?

Many developers working with MySQL (and other databases) don't bother with column indexes because they're either unaware of them or fail to see any advantage to be gained from using them. Others may use primary keys, but neglect indexes and unique keys for the same reasons. If you fall into either category, don't skip this section. What we're about to discuss in the following paragraphs will hopefully encourage you to think a bit differently about indexes.

Indexes can help speed up several different sorts of queries in several different ways when applied to the relevant columns:

Finding matching rows for WHERE **clauses:** This includes clauses using comparison operators (=, <>, >, >=, <, <=, IS NULL, IS NOT NULL, <=>, BETWEEN, IN). It also includes LIKE clauses that match against a string pattern. In other words, a query using LIKE 'MYSQL%' or LIKE 'M%SQL%' will be optimized, but one using a column name will not be optimized. Beginning with MySQL 4.0, a pattern beginning with a wildcard will also be optimized, but still won't make use of indexes.

Finding MAX() **and** MIN() **values:** If your query involves calling one or both of these functions on only indexed columns, and the WHERE clause compares only indexed columns with constant values, then MySQL can look up a single key and return a result directly from the index file.

Sorting and grouping using ORDER BY **and** GROUP BY**:** If the column used for sorting or grouping is indexed, then MySQL does not need to perform a sort before returning the rows, as they're already ordered. When ordering or grouping by multiple columns, some benefit is derived if all the columns have indexes; MySQL will still need to perform a sort of the combined values, but this will still be faster than if one or more of the columns aren't indexed at all. The query will be even faster if all of the columns form a left prefix for a single index (as described in the "Indexes on Multiple Columns" section later in this chapter); in this case, all the keys are already ordered.

Fetching rows from other tables when performing joins: If your database is normalized, joins will tend to use only indexed columns in "foreign" tables. This means that MySQL won't need to sort the rows in those tables before returning them. (If you need to join or order against a column in a foreign table where that column is not already a primary key of the foreign table or already indexed, you probably should add an index on that column.) We'll talk more about this in the next chapter.

Suppose we have a table that stores data about fish, defined as:

```
CREATE TABLE fish (
  species VARCHAR(30) NOT NULL,
  size ENUM('TINY', 'SMALL', 'MEDIUM', 'LARGE') NOT NULL,
  friendly ENUM('YES', 'NO') NOT NULL
);
```

Let's assume further that we've inserted the data shown in Table 3-2, in the order shown in the table.

Table 3-2. Data for the Fish Table

(Record #)	Species	Size	Friendly
(1)	haddock	MEDIUM	YES
(2)	tuna	LARGE	YES
(3)	guppy	TINY	YES
(4)	barracuda	MEDIUM	NO
(5)	grouper	LARGE	YES
(6)	mackerel	SMALL	YES
(7)	swordfish	LARGE	NO
(8)	flounder	SMALL	YES
(9)	stonefish	SMALL	NO
(10)	cod	MEDIUM	YES
(11)	pike	MEDIUM	NO
(12)	sardine	TINY	YES
(13)	catfish	SMALL	NO
(14)	bass	SMALL	YES
(15)	perch	SMALL	YES

Note that MySQL does *not* actually number the rows in this table as we've defined it (we would need to use an AUTO_INCREMENT column for that to happen); we've just indicated the order of insertion in Table 3-2 for easy reference.

Leaving aside for a moment the issue of what happens when records are deleted and new ones added, we can state MySQL stores records in the order in which they were inserted into the table. What transpires when we want to retrieve a row corresponding to a particular species, such as in the query shown here?

```
SELECT * FROM fish WHERE species='CATFISH';
```

The answer is that MySQL will scan every record in the table in the order stored until it finds the match. In this particular case, it scans 13 records including the one that satisfies the query's WHERE clause. Now let's add a unique index on the **species** column:

```
ALTER TABLE fish ADD UNIQUE( species(10) );
```

Here, we don't worry about naming the index, and we specify it on the first ten characters in the column value. (This just happens to be the length of the longest species name used; in practice, we would probably use about half that many characters for the length of the prefix, as that would normally be enough to distinguish the elements in this particular list of words.) When we create the index, MySQL sorts all of the column values in order and stores the ordered list. Along with each item in the list, it also stores a pointer to the corresponding record. This list is stored in the form of a *balanced tree* (or B-tree), which lends itself to finding matching records extremely quickly. Figure 3-6 shows what the B-tree looks like for this example.

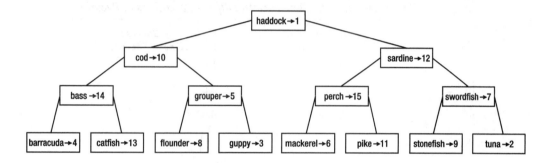

Figure 3-6. The B-tree for the species column

This tree is organized in such a fashion that lower values are always on the left and higher values will be found on the right. The root node of this tree, which holds the middle value of the list, is our starting point. In this case, its value is "haddock". The value we're seeking ("catfish") comes before the midpoint value, so we move to the left. The next node contains the value "cod". Again, our target value comes before this one, so we take the next left branch, which leads to a node containing the value "bass". Bass comes before the target value, so we follow the branch leading right. This path connects to a node containing the desired value and pointer to the corresponding record in the **fish** table (the thirteenth row in that table). Using the B-tree index has cut the number of steps required to find the record we wanted from 13 to 4, or by a factor of 3.25.

What's interesting about the balanced search is that its relative efficiency actually *increases* with the number of records to be searched. We can demonstrate this by means of the following algorithm:

1. Set M = number of rows to be searched; set $N = 0$.

2. Increment N by 1; set $M = M / 2$.

3. If $M > 1$, go to step 2. Otherwise, return N. N will be the maximum number of steps required either to find a matching row or to exhaust the tree (and show that there are no matching rows).

Plugging an arbitrary set of values into this formula will yield results such as those shown in Table 3-3.

Table 3-3. Efficiency Ratios for B-trees with Different Numbers of Records

Number of Records	Maximum Number of Search Steps	Efficiency Increase (Approximate Factor)
5	3	1.67
10	4	2.5
50	6	8.33
100	7	14
500	9	55
1,000	10	100
5,000	13	385
10,000	14	714
50,000	16	3,125
100,000	17	5,882
500,000	19	26,316
1,000,000	20	50,000
5,000,000	23	217,391
10,000,000	24	416,667
100,000,000	27	3,703,704
1,000,000,000	30	33,333,333

While you might not ever work with tables containing 100 million rows or more, you can see that a considerable savings can be realized through the use of indexes in tables having just a few thousand records. Of course, when dealing with extremely large tables, other factors such as limitations imposed by the server hardware and OS (as well as the size of the indexes themselves) will intervene to reduce the speed gains suggested in Table 3-3. Nonetheless, on average, a query that uses an index on the appropriate column can be expected to run about 10 to 100 times faster than the same query without the index.

TIP *If you need to create indexes on tables containing a great many records, it's usually much faster to create the table first without any indexes, insert all of the records, and then as the final step add the index. This is due to the fact that when inserting rows into a table with an existing index, MySQL must update that index for each row inserted before adding the next record.*

UNIQUE KEY Syntax

Specifying a unique key on a column guarantees that there will be no duplicate values for that column anywhere in the table. You can specify that a column is to contain only unique values in several ways. You've already seen one way to do this at the time a table is created:

```
CREATE TABLE fish (
   species VARCHAR(30) NOT NULL UNIQUE KEY,
   size ENUM('TINY', 'SMALL', 'MEDIUM', 'LARGE') NOT NULL,
   friendly ENUM('YES', 'NO') NOT NULL
);
```

You can also declare the unique key in a separate clause of the CREATE TABLE statement:

```
CREATE TABLE fish (
   species VARCHAR(30) NOT NULL,
   size ENUM('TINY', 'SMALL', 'MEDIUM', 'LARGE') NOT NULL,
   friendly ENUM('YES', 'NO') NOT NULL,
   UNIQUE KEY fishspecies (species)
);
```

Here, the KEY keyword is optional, as is the name of the index. The complete syntax for this type of clause is as follows:

```
[CONSTRAINT [symbol]] UNIQUE [KEY] [index_name] (col_name[, col_name2, ...])
```

The CONSTRAINT keyword is supplied for compatibility with other databases that require it. You may also use UNIQUE INDEX rather than UNIQUE KEY.

To add a unique index to an existing table, you can use ALTER TABLE or CREATE INDEX. Assuming that the **fish** table had been created without the unique key on the **species** column, we could add it using this statement:

```
ALTER TABLE ADD UNIQUE (species);
```

The complete syntax for adding a unique key in this way is as follows:

```
ALTER TABLE ADD [CONSTRAINT [symbol]]
    UNIQUE [index_name] (col_name[, col_name2, ...]);
```

(As is usual in the syntax definitions in this book, the keywords and identifiers in square brackets are optional.)

Here is the syntax for using a CREATE INDEX command to add a unique key to an existing table:

```
CREATE UNIQUE INDEX index_name ON table_name (col_name[, colname2, ...]);
```

Note that the INDEX keyword is required here; you cannot use KEY in its place.

If you try to insert a value into a column that is a unique key and that value already exists in that column, the query will fail with an error. Any attempt to add a unique key on a column containing duplicate values will also fail. Such errors can be read from your applications by calling an API function such as mysql_error(). (See Chapter 7 for more information about obtaining MySQL error and warning messages in your programs.)

NOTE *It is possible to specify an index length for a unique key. However, doing so has no effect.*

If you need to drop a unique key, just use DROP INDEX. Assuming that we named the unique key we created on the **species** column, for example, we could remove it again by means of this ALTER TABLE statement:

```
ALTER TABLE fish DROP INDEX fishspecies;
```

PRIMARY KEY Syntax

A primary key is basically a unique key with the further requirement that the primary key column may not contain any null values. For this reason putting a NOT NULL constraint on a primary key column is redundant, and declaring such a column as NULL is not allowed. A table may not contain more than one primary key. (However, it is possible to create a single primary key on multiple columns, as you'll see in the "Multiple-Column Primary Keys" section a bit later in this chapter.) The restrictions on unique key columns regarding duplicate values (see the preceding section) also apply to primary keys.

The simplest way to create a primary key at the time a table is created is shown here:

```
CREATE TABLE fish (
    species VARCHAR(30) PRIMARY KEY,
    size ENUM('TINY', 'SMALL', 'MEDIUM', 'LARGE') NOT NULL,
    friendly ENUM('YES', 'NO') NOT NULL
);
```

This causes the **species** column to be the primary key of the **fish** table. We can also create the primary key in a separate clause:

```
CREATE TABLE fish (
    species VARCHAR(30),
    size ENUM('TINY', 'SMALL', 'MEDIUM', 'LARGE') NOT NULL,
    friendly ENUM('YES', 'NO') NOT NULL,
    PRIMARY KEY (species)
);
```

We can optionally precede PRIMARY KEY in this instance with the CONSTRAINT keyword and an optional symbol name; this syntax is provided for compatibility reasons. Primary keys are not named in MySQL.

To add a primary key, use an ALTER TABLE statement:

```
ALTER TABLE fish ADD PRIMARY KEY (species);
```

You can also use the CONSTRAINT keyword (with an optional symbol or constraint name) before the PRIMARY KEY keyword when altering a table in this way; again this syntax is not required, but supported to make it easier to import table structures from other databases. There is no equivalent to the CREATE INDEX statement for adding a primary key to a table.

To drop the primary key on the **fish** table, simply use this statement:

```
ALTER TABLE fish DROP PRIMARY KEY;
```

 CAUTION *If you don't create a primary key for a table, MySQL will automatically regard the first unique key defined in the table (if there is one) as its primary key. If you use DROP PRIMARY KEY on such a table, MySQL will drop the unique key that it regards as the primary key instead.*

Unique Keys, Primary Keys, and NULL

It is entirely possible to add a unique index on a NULL column. If you do so, you need to keep in mind that null values in MyISAM and InnoDB tables are ignored by the uniqueness constraint. This means that:

- More than one row may have NULL as its value for the unique column.

- These rows have no effect on and are ignored by aggregate functions such as COUNT() and AVG().

This can have entirely unintended consequences. For example, let's create a table containing one column that is declared as NULL, on which we create a unique key and then insert a few rows containing the null value.

```
Command Prompt - mysql -h megalon -u root -p

mysql> CREATE TABLE uniquenulltest (id INT NULL UNIQUE KEY);
Query OK, 0 rows affected (0.01 sec)

mysql> INSERT INTO uniquenulltest (id)
    -> VALUES (NULL), (NULL), (NULL);
Query OK, 3 rows affected (0.01 sec)
Records: 3  Duplicates: 0  Warnings: 0

mysql>
```

As you can see, MySQL has no problem letting us have as many rows as we want that contain NULL for that column. Just to make sure, let's retrieve all the rows from the table.

```
Command Prompt - mysql -h megalon -u root -p
mysql> SELECT * FROM uniquenulltest;
+------+
| id   |
+------+
| NULL |
| NULL |
| NULL |
+------+
3 rows in set (0.00 sec)

mysql>
```

We inserted three rows, and we retrieved three rows. Now let's get a count of those rows using the COUNT() function. The result should be 3, right?

```
Command Prompt - mysql -h megalon -u root -p
mysql> SELECT COUNT(id) FROM uniquenulltest;
+-----------+
| COUNT(id) |
+-----------+
|         0 |
+-----------+
1 row in set (0.00 sec)

mysql>
```

Guess again! Because we used the name of the nullable column as the argument to COUNT(), the nulls didn't get counted. However, if we use the * wildcard instead, we obtain the expected result.

```
Command Prompt - mysql -h megalon -u root -p
mysql> SELECT COUNT(*) FROM uniquenulltest;
+----------+
| COUNT(*) |
+----------+
|        3 |
+----------+
1 row in set (0.00 sec)

mysql>
```

This can be very handy in some circumstances, but don't allow yourself to be tricked by the difference.

CAUTION *There's an exception to these rules regarding the counting of null values: Berkeley DB tables allow only one null value in a* NULL *column that has a unique key. However, just as is the case with other table types, the row containing the* NULL *is not counted in aggregate functions.*

A primary key cannot be created on a NULL column. This is true of any relational database, not just of MySQL. As a primary key is intended to uniquely identify *every* row in a table, this is a completely logical and reasonable requirement.

FULLTEXT Indexes

A full-text index can be used with MyISAM tables (and *only* MyISAM tables!) in order to facilitate natural-language full-text searching, which we'll discuss in detail in the next chapter. A FULLTEXT index may be created on CHAR, VARCHAR, and the other text-type columns, but not on any other column type.

Let's suppose we've added a **description** column to the fish table defined as type VARCHAR(255). To create a full-text index on this column when we create the table, our table creation statement might look something like this:

```
CREATE TABLE fish (
    species VARCHAR(30) PRIMARY KEY,
    size ENUM('TINY', 'SMALL', 'MEDIUM', 'LARGE') NOT NULL,
    friendly ENUM('YES', 'NO') NOT NULL,
    description VARCHAR(255),
    FULLTEXT INDEX (description)
);
```

We could also add the full-text index after creating and populating the table, and as we've mentioned, this might be preferable if the table contains many records. We can do this in two ways:

```
ALTER TABLE fish ADD FULLTEXT (description);
```

or

```
CREATE FULLTEXT INDEX descr_index ON fish (description);
```

As when adding other types of indexes, you can use an optional index name in the ALTER TABLE statement, and an index name is required when using CREATE INDEX. In addition, with any of these three methods, you can optionally specify a sort order (ASC or DESC) for the index.

FOREIGN KEY Syntax

As you saw when we discussed normalization earlier in the chapter, you'll often need to associate a column in one table with a column in another (*foreign*) table. Another way of saying this is that the column on which you create the foreign key *references* the column in the foreign table. We speak of these two tables as having a *parent-child relationship*: We refer to the table in which the foreign key is created as the *child* of the referenced table, and to the referenced (foreign) table as the *parent* table. We may also say that the column having the foreign key in the child table *depends* on the referenced column in the parent.

When applied to a table column, a foreign key constraint adds the requirement that any value found in the column must match a value from the referenced column in the foreign table, and that the referenced column must be guaranteed unique; in other words, there must be a unique key or primary key constraint on the column in the foreign table. In addition, both columns must be of compatible types:

- With respect to integer types, both columns must be the same size and both must be either signed or unsigned.

- Corresponding string columns are not required to be of the same length.

NOTE *As of this writing, only InnoDB tables supported foreign key constraints in MySQL. Creating a foreign key in a MyISAM column, while not producing any errors, has no effect. Foreign key support for MyISAM tables may be added at some stage during the development of the MySQL 5.X series.*

While the minimum required syntax for creating a foreign key is fairly simple, there are a number of variations. Let's look first at a basic example. Suppose we're working on a management application for a firm with a number of departments, names, and other data relating to each department stored in a **departments** table, which has this partial definition:

```
CREATE TABLE departments (
  dept_name VARCHAR(30) NOT NULL UNIQUE KEY
) TYPE=INNODB;
```

The CREATE TABLE statement necessary to create our **employees** table might look something like this:

```
CREATE TABLE employees (
  first_name VARCHAR(30) NOT NULL,
  last_name VARCHAR(30) NOT NULL,
  department VARCHAR(30)
) TYPE=INNODB;
```

The objective here is to guarantee that department names that don't exist in the **departments** table are not entered into the **employees** table. We do this by creating a foreign key on the **employees.department** column and referencing the **departments.dept_name** column. We can accomplish this in one of two ways. The first is to add a clause to the second CREATE TABLE statement before executing it:

```
CREATE TABLE employees (
  first_name VARCHAR(30) NOT NULL,
  last_name VARCHAR(30) NOT NULL,
  department VARCHAR(30),
  FOREIGN KEY (department) REFERENCES departments (dept_name)
) TYPE=INNODB;
```

We could also create both of the tables, using the first two CREATE TABLE statements shown in the preceding example, and then add the foreign key constraint to **employees** with an ALTER TABLE command:

```
ALTER TABLE employees
  ADD FOREIGN KEY (department)
  REFERENCES departments (dept_name);
```

When using the second method, we must ensure that there are no values in **employees.department** that don't match up to values found in **departments.dept_name**. Otherwise, the ALTER TABLE statement will fail with an error. However, you may declare the child table column as NULL or allow it to be NULL by default, as we've done.

 TIP *Beginning with MySQL 4.0.13, you can use* SHOW INNODB STATUS; *to display the most recent error or errors encountered when working with InnoDB tables.*

The complete syntax for a foreign key constraint is as follows:

```
[CONSTRAINT [name]] FOREIGN KEY (column_list)
  REFERENCES table_name (column_list)
  [ON DELETE {CASCADE | SET NULL | NO ACTION | RESTRICT}]
  [ON UPDATE {CASCADE | SET NULL | NO ACTION | RESTRICT}]
```

Any of the possible legal variations on this syntax may be used as part of either a CREATE TABLE or an ALTER TABLE ... ADD ... statement.

The CONSTRAINT keyword is optional. However, using this keyword permits you to specify a name for the foreign key constraint.

The remaining two optional constraints allow you to determine what happens in the child table's foreign key column if a value in the referenced parent table column is deleted or changed. Each of these requires the additional use of one of the four constraint specifiers shown. Table 3-4 shows the values for ON DELETE and ON UPDATE constraints, along with the version of MySQL in which they were introduced. The default value is RESTRICT.

NOTE   *Don't forget that in MySQL versions prior to 4.0, you must run the -max binary in order to have support for InnoDB tables.*

Table 3-4. Values for ON DELETE and ON UPDATE Constraints

Constraint	Effect	MySQL Version
ON DELETE CASCADE	When a row in the parent table is deleted, any rows in the child table that have matching values on the foreign key column are deleted.	3.23.50-max
ON DELETE SET NULL	When a row in the parent table is deleted, the dependent column value is set to NULL in any rows in the child table having values matching that of the referenced column in the parent.	3.23.50-max
ON DELETE NO ACTION	When a row in the parent table is deleted, no changes occur in the child table.	3.23.43b-max
ON DELETE RESTRICT	Rows in the parent table with values matched by rows in the child table cannot be deleted.	3.23.43b-max
ON UPDATE CASCADE	When a value in the referenced column is updated, values in the dependent column matched by the original value in the parent table column are updated to match the new value in the parent.	4.0.8

(Continued)

Table 3-4. Values for ON DELETE and ON UPDATE Constraints (Continued)

Constraint	Effect	MySQL Version
ON UPDATE SET NULL	When a value in the referenced column is updated, all values in the dependent column matched by the original value of the parent column are set to NULL.	4.0.8
ON UPDATE NO ACTION	When a value in the parent column is updated, no changes take place in the child table.	4.0.8
ON UPDATE RESTRICT	Values in the parent column having matching values in the child column cannot be updated.	4.0.8

Indexes on Multiple Columns

It is entirely possible, and sometimes very appropriate, to create indexes or keys on multiple columns. Any type of index or key may be created on multiple columns. Perhaps the best way to explain why and how this might be done would be to provide a couple of examples, so let's do that right now.

Example 1: Basic Multiple-Column Index

Just as you can speed up queries against one column by creating an index on that column, you can speed up queries on multiple columns by creating an index spanning all those columns. For this example, we'll define a simple **students** table as follows:

```
CREATE TABLE students (
    firstname varchar(30) NOT NULL,
    lastname varchar(30) NOT NULL,
    year ENUM('FRESHMAN','SOPHOMORE','JUNIOR','SENIOR') NOT NULL,
    gpa decimal(3,2) UNSIGNED NOT NULL
);
```

An application using this table might reasonably be expected to make a lot of queries against both the **firstname** and **lastname** fields, like this:

```
SELECT * FROM students WHERE firstname='William' AND lastname='Johnson';
```

We created this table, and then populated it with 100,000 randomly generated records using this off-the-cuff PHP4 script:

```php
<?php
  mysql_connect("localhost", "zontar", "******");
  mysql_select_db("mdbd");

  function random_name()
  {
    $output = "";
    $num = rand(1, 20);

    for($i = 0; $i < $num; $i++)
      $output .= chr( rand(65, 90) );

    return $output;
  }


  for($i = 0; $i < 100000; $i ++)
  {
    $firstname = random_name();
    $lastname = random_name();
    $year = rand(1, 4);
    $gpa = rand(200, 400) / 100;

    $query = "INSERT INTO students (firstname,lastname,year,gpa)
                  VALUES ('$firstname','$lastname','$year','$gpa')";

    echo "<p>$query</p>";

    mysql_query($query)
      or die( mysql_error() );
  }
?>
```

The populated MyISAM table takes up about 3.5MB on disk. We picked an arbitrary **firstname-lastname** pair from close to the end of the table and ran a SELECT query matching those two values; it took MySQL 0.79 second to return 39 matching rows. (The fact that, out of 100,000 pairs of strings of randomly determined length made up of randomly determined characters, we had that many matches should tell you that the PHP rand() function is not really all that random! Use mt_rand() instead if you need real randomness.) This might not seem very slow, but when you consider that such a table in a real-world setting would likely have 20 or 30 columns, hold tens of thousands of rows, and might have several dozen (or even a hundred or more) concurrent users, it's evident that it would be nice if we could speed things up a bit.

We have three alternatives here for adding indexes:

- Add an index on either the **firstname** or **lastname** column.

- Add indexes on both columns.

- Add a single index on both columns.

Let's see what happens with each of these.
First, let's add an index on the **firstname** column:

```
CREATE INDEX fname ON students (firstname(10));
```

On one of our test systems (an old Compaq ProLiant server with dual 200MHz Pentiums and 160MB RAM, running Windows 2000 Server, IIS 5.0, PHP 4.3.3, MySQL 5.0.0-alpha, and very little else), this index takes about 3 seconds to create and requires approximately 540KB of disk space. When we reran the query, we got back the results in 0.28 second; we increased the speed of the query by a factor of about 2.8. On your own server, the space requirements should be about the same, although the times required will vary with your hardware and other factors.

Next, we create a second index, whose prefix length is the same size as the first, on the **lastname** column:

```
CREATE INDEX lname ON student (lastname(10));
```

The **lname** index takes about the same amount time to create as **fname**, and requires about the same amount of space. When we reran the same SELECT query after adding this index, it took just 0.07 second, which is about four times faster than with the previous index, and which represents a nearly twelve-fold speed increase over the same query with no indexes whatsoever. We should note, however, that MySQL actually uses only *one* index for this query, and you'll soon see how you can verify this for yourself using the EXPLAIN command.

Finally, we'll drop the two indexes we previously created (note that a separate ALTER TABLE statement is required for each index that we wish to drop):

```
ALTER TABLE students DROP INDEX fname;
ALTER TABLE students DROP INDEX lname;
```

Then we add a single index covering both columns:

```
CREATE INDEX fullname ON students (firstname(10), lastname(10));
```

This two-column index requires about 10.5 seconds to create and took up 1.5MB on disk. When we ran the SELECT query this time, however, the results were better than with two separate indexes on each column by a factor of 3.5. The query took just 0.02 second to complete in this case—nearly 40 times faster than with no indexes at all. This is not the ideal factor of nearly 6,000 to 1 that we saw for 100,000 records in Table 3-3, but it does represent a substantial speed increase in line with the factor of 10 to 100 that we said was usual for well-implemented indexes. Part of the reason for this is that it does take MySQL time to read the index file.

The order in which the columns are listed can be very important in determining how useful a given index is. MySQL creates multicolumn indexes in such a way that the leftmost prefixes will be used where appropriate. To illustrate what we mean by this, let's start again with the basic **students** table (without any indexes). This time, we'll create an index on three columns:

```
CREATE INDEX ind_student ON students (lastname(10), firstname(10), year);
```

Note carefully the order in which the columns are listed in the definition. We've now created an index on **students** that can be used to optimize the following three queries:

- Against the leftmost column in the index:

    ```
    SELECT * FROM students
    WHERE lastname='Jones';
    ```

- Against the leftmost *two* columns from the index:

    ```
    SELECT * FROM students
    WHERE firstname='Marvin' AND lastname='Jones';
    ```

- Against all three columns:

    ```
    SELECT * FROM students
    WHERE lastname='Jones' AND firstname='Marvin' AND year='SOPHOMORE';
    ```

In the second example here, we've reversed the order of the **firstname** and **lastname** columns in the WHERE clause. All other things being equal, this won't affect the speed of the query. What matters is that that the two columns we're matching against form a *leftmost prefix* of the index.

However, this query won't be optimized by the index we've created:

```
SELECT * FROM students WHERE firstname='Marvin';
```

This is due to the fact that the column being selected against is not the leftmost column in the index.

However, these two queries *can* take advantage of the index:

```
SELECT * FROM students WHERE lastname='Jones' AND year='SOPHOMORE';
SELECT * FROM students WHERE lastname='Jones' AND gpa>3.35;
```

In both of these cases, the first column being selected against is the leftmost column, so MySQL will use that portion of the index, and then scan the table for the matching year or GPA.

Example 2: Multiple-Column Unique Key

This example will be relatively brief. Let's suppose we have a table containing customer data for a mail-order sales firm, something like this:

```
CREATE TABLE customers (
    firstname VARCHAR(30) NOT NULL,
    lastname VARCHAR(30) NOT NULL,
    suffix ENUM('SR', 'JR', 'III', 'IV') NOT NULL,
    street VARCHAR(50) NOT NULL,
    city VARCHAR(30) NOT NULL,
    state CHAR(2) NOT NULL,
    zipcode INT(4) ZEROFILL
);
```

In this example, our objective is to ensure that there is one and only one **customers** record per customer. To accomplish this, we need some sort of unique key for this table. However, different customers might share the same first name, last name, or even both. So if you're thinking that a unique key on both name fields would be a good idea, that's a start in the right direction, but we also need to consider the fact that there could well be a John Smith in New York City and another in Boston. So perhaps we need to create the key on the **firstname**, **lastname**, and **city** columns? That seems workable, until we realize that we have a Mary Richards in Houston, Texas, and another Mary Richards in Houston, Ohio (yes, there really such is a town; in fact, Jon grew up near there). So perhaps we should use a unique index on the four columns **firstname**, **lastname**, **city**, and **state**? Actually, the good people at the U.S. Post Office have taken care of the city/state issue by issuing zip codes that are unique to each city or town in the entire country.

NOTE *In the U.S., each zip code is guaranteed unique to each town or city. However, the same isn't always the case for postal or mail codes in other countries. For example, a search at* http://www.auspost.com.au/ *reveals that Australian postcode 4133 is common to 4 neighboring municipalities on the south side of Brisbane (Chambers Flat, Logan Reserve, Waterford, and Waterford West). So what might be wasteful in one locale could be necessary in another.*

Problem solved—we can just use the first and last names and the post code, right? Not so fast. . . A look in the telephone directory for any medium to large city will eventually yield at least one or two instances where two people with the same first and last names live in the same postal district. However, it is unlikely that they will live at the same address, so there's another column we can use. Finally, there's the problem caused by people naming their children after themselves: we'll take care of what happens when George Johnson, Senior and George Johnson, Junior live in the same house by including the **suffix** column as well. We can create the unique key as follows:

```
CREATE UNIQUE INDEX u_cust ON customers
  (firstname, lastname, suffix, address, postcode);
```

Now we can rest assured that each customer account record will correspond to one and *only* one actual customer; that is, that there's a one-to-one relationship between real customers and records in the **customers** table.

As you can see here, in cases where the distinctiveness of each record in a table needs to be ensured, and no single column exists whose value is guaranteed unique, creating a unique index on several columns can sometimes be a viable alternative to creating a separate unique or primary key.

Multiple-Column Primary Keys

Contrary to what many database developers and programmers seem to think, creating a primary key on more than one column is not only possible, it's actually preferable to creating a separate primary key column. If all of the following conditions are true, you should seriously consider making the index a primary key:

- All of the columns to be indexed are `NOT NULL`.

- You need any possible combination of values for those columns to be unique.

- There is no existing primary key in that table.

Some of you who have been using MySQL or another database for a while might take exception to this, and say that a primary key should always be declared as a single column integer with an `AUTO_INCREMENT` constraint. This is a very common methodology that has the following advantages:

- Joins on integer columns tend to be faster than joins on other column types.

- `WHERE` clauses are shorter (for example, `WHERE customer_id=334` versus `WHERE firstname='Marvin' AND lastname='Jones' AND address='1234 East River Drive' AND zipcode=45365`).

- Users can alter the data, but they can't alter the key. However, you should be aware that some APIs (such as Microsoft's ADO with ODBC) do require a single-column primary key.

While all of these things are true, they don't tell the whole story. Here's why:

Comparisons: In most cases, in order to be useful, a `WHERE` clause must contain a comparison with the value(s) of one or more table columns, such as `WHERE lastname LIKE 'J%'`. In order to optimize a query that searches on data given column, you need to have an index on that column. This means you've lost any advantage you thought you had gained by creating the single-column integer index.

Comprehensibility: `WHERE` clauses that use only single integer keys are shorter, but they are also more difficult for humans to understand. This is because their values are based on the order in which the rows are inserted, not on the data; they cloud the meaning of our queries with an extra and unnecessary level of abstraction. In other words, when you're debugging an application, something like

```
SELECT * FROM companies WHERE company_name='OurCo';
```

is easier to read than

```
SELECT * FROM companies WHERE company_id='45874';.
```

Duplication: Using auto-incrementing primary keys without placing a unique key on the columns on which the distinctiveness of the rows depends means that duplicate records can be inserted into the table, unless you enforce the uniqueness constraint in the application rather than in the database. This is very, very bad. The alternative is to have what are essentially two unique keys in order to enforce a single uniqueness constraint, which isn't much better.

Key protection: If you're using InnoDB tables and all of their foreign keys are defined with the proper ON DELETE and ON UPDATE constraints, you don't need to worry about users updating the keys, because the integrity of the data and of relationships between tables is already protected.

Consider that MySQL's own system tables (including the grant tables) make no use of auto-incrementing columns whatsoever, but instead have multicolumn primary keys.

Giving every table an auto-incrementing primary key made more sense in earlier versions of MySQL when the standard distribution didn't implement foreign keys (and even where present, they had only limited support for cascades). However, these are no longer issues. As MySQL has matured, so perhaps should our habits. This isn't to say that we want you to believe that using INT AUTO_INCREMENT PRIMARY KEY is somehow evil in and of itself, but we do want you to be aware that there are alternatives worth considering when designing your database.

EXPLAIN SELECT

You can find out which indexes if any (and lot of other useful information) will be used to perform a given query using EXPLAIN SELECT. Let's bring back the **students** table we used earlier, including the unique key named **u_student** defined on the **lastname**, **firstname**, and **year** columns:

```
CREATE TABLE students (
    firstname varchar(30) NOT NULL,
    lastname varchar(30) NOT NULL,
    year ENUM('FRESHMAN','SOPHOMORE','JUNIOR','SENIOR') NOT NULL,
    gpa decimal(3,2) UNSIGNED NOT NULL,
    UNIQUE `u_student` (`lastname`(10),`firstname`(10),`year`)
);
```

Using EXPLAIN SELECT is simple. All you need to do is prefix the SELECT query you wish to analyze with the EXPLAIN keyword. Here are the results when we EXPLAIN two different queries against the **students** table.

```
Command Prompt - mysql -h megalon -u root -p
mysql> explain select * from students where lastname='jones'\G
*************************** 1. row ***************************
           id: 1
  select_type: SIMPLE
        table: students
         type: ref
possible_keys: u_student
          key: u_student
      key_len: 10
          ref: const
         rows: 1
        Extra: Using where
1 row in set (0.06 sec)

mysql> explain select * from students where firstname='marvin'\G
*************************** 1. row ***************************
           id: 1
  select_type: SIMPLE
        table: students
         type: ALL
possible_keys: NULL
          key: NULL
      key_len: NULL
          ref: NULL
         rows: 49997
        Extra: Using where
1 row in set (0.01 sec)

mysql>
```

In the first case, MySQL is able to use **u_student** as an index for a query against the **lastname** column. In the second case, it doesn't find any indexes to use at all (hence the NULL entry for the value of *key*). You can also see that it searched nearly every row in the table before finding a matching value.

The output from this command also shows the type of query being analyzed, the length of the key being used, and the number of rows that will need to be checked. Table 3-5 describes the output of EXPLAIN SELECT. (Some of this information applies to joins on multiple tables, which we'll discuss in Chapter 6; you might want to bookmark this page so you can refer back to it from there.)

NOTE   *The **id** and **select_type** fields were added to* EXPLAIN SELECT *output in MySQL 4.1.*

Table 3-5. Fields and Values Returned by EXPLAIN SELECT

FIELD	MEANING	VALUES
id	Identifier (number of the SELECT within the query)	An integer (always 1 in a single-table select).
select_type	Type of SELECT statement	SIMPLE: No use of UNION or subqueries.

Table 3-5. Fields and Values Returned by EXPLAIN SELECT (Continued)

FIELD	MEANING	VALUES
		PRIMARY: Outermost table in a union or join.
		UNION: Inner table(s) in a UNION query.
		DEPENDENT UNION: Inner table(s) in a UNION query dependent on an outer subquery.
		SUBQUERY: First SELECT in a subquery.
		DEPENDENT SUBQUERY: First SELECT dependent on an outer subquery.
		DERIVED: Derived table SELECT (subquery in a FROM clause).
Table	The table to which the output row refers	Name of table.
type	Join type	system: The table has only a single row (special case of const).
		const: The table has at most one matching row. Used when comparing all prefixes of a unique or primary key with constants. This is the best possible value to see reported for type.
		eq_ref: Only one row will be read from this table for each combination of rows from previous tables. This is also good to see.
		ref: All rows with matching index values for each combination of rows from previous tables will be read from the current table. If only a few rows are matched, this means the query will be reasonably speedy, although not quite as fast as eq_ref.

(Continued)

Table 3-5. Fields and Values Returned by EXPLAIN SELECT (Continued)

FIELD	MEANING	VALUES
		ref_or_null: Like ref, except an extra search will be done for rows containing null values, and so the query will be a bit slower than one that uses a ref join.
		range: Only rows with values within a given range will be used. range can be employed when the indexed column is compared to a constant.
		index: The entire index file will be scanned for matches. Not as fast as the other join types, but usually still faster than ALL, since the index file is typically smaller than the datafile.
		ALL: The entire datafile will be scanned for matches. This is as slow as it gets; if you see this for a query you intend to use frequently, it's time to create one or more indexes.
possible_keys	What keys can be used by MySQL to optimize the query.	If no keys can be used, this value will be NULL (and the join type will be ALL).
key	The key used by MySQL to optimize the query.	This will be NULL if no key was used. (To force MySQL to use a particular key, you can add USE KEY or IGNORE KEY to your query.
key_len	Length of the key used.	NULL if no key was used. (Tip: You can deduce from this value how many parts of a multipart key were used.)
ref	Shows which columns or constraints were used with key to select rows.	Name of column or constraint, or NULL if no key was used.
rows	Number of rows to be scanned by MySQL in executing the query.	Same as the number of rows in the table if no index was used; generally speaking, the lower this number is in relation to the number of rows in the table, the better.

Table 3-5. Fields and Values Returned by EXPLAIN SELECT (Continued)

FIELD	MEANING	VALUES
Extra	Provides additional information about how MySQL has tried to optimize the query.	`Distinct`: MySQL will stop searching once it has found a matching row.
		`Not exists`: MySQL was able to convert this query into a `LEFT JOIN` and so won't need to check any more rows in this table after the first match is found.
		`Range checked for each record...`: An optimal or close to optimal index couldn't be found to use for all rows. Instead, MySQL will check all relevant combinations of rows from the previous tables and determine the best index to use with each. Not ideal in terms of speed, but still faster than not using any index at all.
		`Using filesort`: An extra sort will be required before the rows can be returned in the order requested. If you see this and/or `Using temporary`, you may not be using a good index; it's also possible that your query is returning many rows that you don't really need.
		`Using temporary`: MySQL will create a temporary table to hold intermediate results. You'll often see `Using temporary` and `Using filesort` on `GROUP BY` queries where there's an `ORDER BY` clause using a different column, and sometimes when grouping on multiple columns as well.
		`Using where`: A `WHERE` clause is being used to restrict the rows returned. If the value of `type` is `ALL` or `index`, you may want to create a more suitable index for this table, as this means you're returning all of its rows (unless this is what you intended to do).

Whenever you're working with any but the most trivially obvious queries and indexes, you should always examine your queries with EXPLAIN SELECT. When you see a join type of anything other than system, const, or eq_ref, it's quite likely that your query can be optimized, by adding or modifying indexes, or by rewriting the query itself. Ideally, given enough testing, you should be able to have all of your queries using one of these three join types.

TIP *Try to keep* EXPLAIN SELECT *fresh in your mind, or at least bookmark that section of this chapter. You may want to refer to it again in Chapter 6 when we discuss multiple-table joins.*

We could provide several pages of additional examples illustrating the use of EXPLAIN SELECT, but the best way to become familiar with it is simply to use it. Every time you write a query, ask MySQL to EXPLAIN it to you. Before long, you'll start to see where you're most likely to be coming up short on your use of indexes. Don't forget, however, that indexes will only be effective when employed with normalized tables. Normalize your database to Third Normal Form or better, write your SELECT queries, and then index the columns those queries use. If you follow this methodology, you should find that most of your queries are already optimized.

Common Problems and Errors

There's a world of mistakes that can be made in setting up databases. Generally these fall into two categories: duplicate indexes and unnecessary indexes. We'll discuss these and few other common errors in the following sections.

Duplicate Indexes

Quite often, we've seen MySQL tables created with SQL statements that look something like this:

```
CREATE TABLE books (
    book_id INT AUTO_INCREMENT NOT NULL,
    title VARCHAR(50) NOT NULL,
    author VARCHAR(75) NOT NULL,
    PRIMARY KEY (book_id),
    INDEX (book_id)
);
```

or this:

```
CREATE TABLE books (
  book_id INT AUTO_INCREMENT NOT NULL,
  title VARCHAR(50) NOT NULL,
  author VARCHAR(75) NOT NULL,
  PRIMARY KEY (book_id),
  UNIQUE KEY (title, author),
  INDEX (title,author)
);
```

There are similar issues in both cases: we've created a second index on the same column in both tables. A primary key is an index and so is a unique key; there's no need to create a separate index on the same column.

Unnecessary Indexes

We've also seen some books and tutorials that recommend creating an index on every column. For example, we've seen something like this proposed as the structure for a **books** table to be used in the database backing an online bookstore:

```
CREATE TABLE books (
  book_id INT AUTO_INCREMENT NOT NULL,
  isbn VARCHAR(13) NOT NULL,
  title VARCHAR(50) NOT NULL,
  author VARCHAR(75) NOT NULL,
  area ENUM('FICTION', 'NONFICTION'),
  subject ENUM('GENERAL', 'HISTORY', 'SCIENCE', 'POLITICS' /* etc. */) NOT NULL,
  format ENUM('HARDBACK', 'PAPERBACK') NOT NULL,
  list_price DECIMAL(5,2),
  wholesale_price DECIMAL(5,2),
  PRIMARY KEY (book_id),
  UNIQUE KEY (isbn),
  UNIQUE KEY (author, title),
  INDEX (book_id),
  INDEX (isbn),
  INDEX (title),
  INDEX (author),
  INDEX (area),
  INDEX (subject),
  INDEX (format),
  INDEX (list_price),
  INDEX (wholesale_price)
);
```

Not only does this employ unnecessary indexes as in the previous example, it also compounds the issues raised by doing so—how often are we likely to select from the entire **books** table by format or wholesale price? In addition, we have three unique columns, which is also wasteful. An arrangement like this one is likely to be just as useful, will require less space, and will update more quickly:

```
CREATE TABLE books (
    isbn VARCHAR(13) NOT NULL,
    title VARCHAR(50) NOT NULL,
    author VARCHAR(75) NOT NULL,
    format ENUM('HARDBACK', 'PAPERBACK', 'TRADE EDITION') NOT NULL,
    list_price DECIMAL(5,2),
    wholesale_price DECIMAL(5,2),
    PRIMARY KEY (isbn),
    INDEX (author, title),
    INDEX (subject, author)
);
```

Now we have a single unique column (the primary key), and we've reduced the number of indexes considerably. Due to the ordering of the index columns, we've already optimized any filtering to be done by author, author and title, subject, or subject and author. (Of course, in the real world, we might want to perform some additional normalization with regard to subjects, binding formats, and perhaps authors, but this should serve to get the point across.) It's likely that a prospective customer will want to search by some combination of subject, author, and title first, and then be concerned with pricing and possible formats afterward. In this sort of situation, what might work best to load a result set from a "first pass" into a temporary table, and then allow the user to choose based on price, binding format, and other characteristics that might be considered of secondary interest.

Clever Hacks That Aren't So Clever

One "clever" hack is to create your own datatype when MySQL provides a perfectly useful one. This occurs most often with regard to dates. One common mistake is to use a CHAR or VARCHAR column for storing dates. As we mentioned in our discussion of MySQL datatypes in Chapter 2, this can lead to a lot of unnecessary work, either in queries or in application code, and can lead to hard-to-spot errors as well (see the example of using dates in the "Why Datatypes Do Matter, Revisited" section in Chapter 2).

The other common error of this type is to do something like this:

```
CREATE TABLE orders (
  order_id INT AUTO_INCREMENT NOT NULL PRIMARY KEY,
  customer_id INT NOT NULL,
  order_day TINYINT(2) NOT NULL DEFAULT 1,
  order_month TINYINT(2) NOT NULL DEFAULT 1,
  order_year SMALLINT(4) NOT NULL DEFAULT 2000
);
```

instead of

```
CREATE TABLE orders (
  order_id INT AUTO_INCREMENT NOT NULL PRIMARY KEY,
  customer_id INT NOT NULL,
  order_date DATE NOT NULL DEFAULT '2000-01-01'
);
```

There are at least four problems with the first of these two tables that aren't encountered with the second one:

- Constraints that can't be enforced within the database; instead, you must depend on application code to impose necessary restrictions on any values that you wish to store.

- Extraneous application code (or a stored procedure in MySQL 5) is required to perform updates and retrievals.

- Three columns are required instead of one. Depending on your application's requirements, you may also need more than a single index (which is all that's required if you need to sort on the **order_date** column in the second version of the table).

- You cannot take advantage of any of MySQL's built-in date-calculation or date-formatting functions; if you need the equivalent of one, you'll need to code it yourself.

Too Many Tables

One other common error we've seen appears to arise out of a misunderstanding of how normalization works. There appears to be widespread but mistaken belief that it's better to create several tables with fewer columns, period. Or perhaps this is another symptom of "spreadsheet-itis." For example, suppose we're given a collection of comma-separated-value files, which, based on the column names given as the first row of each file, we can represent as shown in Figure 3-7.

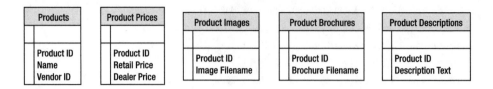

Figure 3-7. Data for a products database

At first glance, it might seem that these are intended to be imported into a group of linked tables, and we might be tempted to do just that, as shown in Figure 3-8.

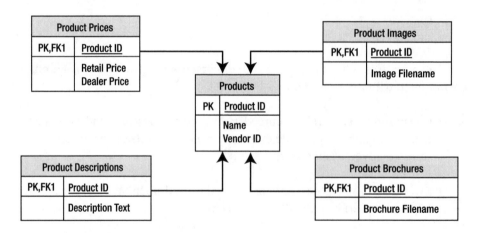

Figure 3-8. Dividing the data into separate tables

But let's think for a moment about what this data actually represents. Each product is not very likely to have more than one set of prices (unless there's some other factor at work here). Nor is it likely to have more than one description—and if it does, it makes more sense to combine the descriptions for each product into one, unless there are clearly different *sorts* of descriptions, such as a long description and a short description, or translation of product descriptions in different languages. In addition, a price should be considered to be an attribute of a product, rather than as an entity on its own. So it's much more reasonable to consider prices and descriptions of products as product attributes, and to place them into a single **products** table.

What about the product images and product brochures data? Should these be kept in separate tables, or added to the **products** table? The only way to

answer this question is to create **product_images** and **product_brochures**
tables, import the data into these, and then to subject them to a bit of analysis.
The question we need to answer here is this: Is the relationship between products and product images one-to-one, one-to-many, or many-to-many? We can
run the following query to help us do so:

```
SELECT product_id, COUNT(product_id)
FROM product_images GROUP BY product_id;
```

If we see any values greater than 1 in the second column of the output, we know
there's a one-to-many relationship between products and product images.

In addition, we can run this query:

```
SELECT image_filename, COUNT(image_filename)
FROM product_images GROUP BY image_filename;
```

If there are any values greater than 1 in the second column of the output, we
know there's a one-to-many relationship between product images and products.

If *either* (exclusive OR) of these conditions is true, we should retain a separate
product_images table. If *both* conditions are true, we know that a many-to-
many relationship exists, and we not only need the **product_images** table, but
we also need a lookup table between **product_images** and **products** as well.

If *neither* condition is true, we should move the data for product image filenames directly into the **products** table.

Summary

In this chapter, we've discussed how to optimize the two most important tasks
performed by MySQL (or any relational database): getting data into the database
and storing it efficiently, and getting it back out again as quickly and efficiently
as possible. The procedure for optimizing a database's "input-friendliness" is
known as *normalization*. As for improving the speed of retrieving data, you can
accomplish this by adding indexes to the appropriate columns and groups of
columns. We also discussed Codd's Rules for Relational Databases to provide
some background, as well as insights into what it is that a database is supposed
to do and how it is supposed to do it.

A lot of people—even those who've worked with MySQL or another RDBMS
for some time—confuse a database with a spreadsheet. This tendency we sometimes like to call the Spreadsheet Syndrome, which is typified by a tendency to
repeat data in at least two different ways: by storing the same data in different
locations and by storing data items that can be derived (directly or indirectly)
from other data. Normalization is the process by which you eliminate redundant
data, and the steps in this process are known as *normal forms*.

We covered the three normal forms that permit database designers to eliminate redundant data and reduce all data relationships to one-to-one correspondences. An added benefit to database normalization is that it helps to preclude update anomalies. That is, it provides a way to deal with issues of the sort we encounter when a student is listed as studying French 101 in a Students table, and the corresponding entry for the French 101 class is deleted from a Classes table.

Sometimes, in order to speed up queries, you can employ a technique known as *denormalization*, which is defined as removing normalizations from a database.

Indexes can dramatically speed up data retrieval, and we provided some behind-the-scenes information about how indexes actually work. The creation of indexes, contrary to how it may be practiced by some, is not something that should be done by rote. Rather, you should use indexes judiciously, in conjunction with those queries that are necessary to an application or are likely to be made when it is used, and thus which columns and groups of columns are most likely to be searched, sorted, or grouped against. Fortunately, MySQL provides an excellent tool for such analysis in the form of the EXPLAIN SELECT query, which tells us how MySQL is attempting to optimize the query, providing information about the type of join employed, possible indexes, indexes used (and, by extension, indexes that *aren't* being used), and how effective those used actually are. This is a grossly underused feature of MySQL and one that you should definitely add to your own toolkit if it's not there already.

Finally, we looked at some errors commonly encountered in creating indexes. We provided an example of the "spreadsheet state of mind" in use and offered some suggestions as to what to do about it when you run across it, as well as some simple analysis techniques that you can employ in deciding how to set up your database tables.

What's Next

In developing and maintaining database-backed applications, we often find ourselves expending time and effort in manipulating data after it has been retrieved but before we can make active use of it. A lot of this "massaging" of data is really unnecessary when we consider the wealth of logical, mathematical, string, and other operators and functions that are available in MySQL. It can also be exasperating (not to mention wasteful) when we seem to be obliged to return data that we're not actually going to use, doing so only in order to sift through it to see which data we actually need for a given purpose. Most, if not all, of this post-retrieval "sifting" can be eliminated by employing MySQL's wealth of flow-control structures that (sadly) often go unused. In Chapter 4, we'll look at how these functions and operators can help us achieve our goal of returning data that's ready for immediate use in applications.

CHAPTER 4

Optimizing Queries with Operators, Branching, and Functions

IN THIS CHAPTER, we're going to explore the central premise of this book: It is almost *always* the best course of action to make the database perform as much work as possible, thus minimizing the amount of filtering and manipulating data that you do in your programming code. Another way of saying this is that by replacing program logic with SQL logic, it is possible to gain significant optimization benefits. A strong working knowledge of operators, branching, and functions in MySQL, with this optimization goal in mind, is a key part of your database skills.

While the SQL dialect supported in MySQL isn't a complete programming language in and of itself, it does provide many capabilities for manipulating and filtering data. These include logical and arithmetic operators, functions for working with strings and numbers, and branching operators that allow you to make and act on decisions within queries. As you'll see in this chapter, using these, you can create powerful queries and open new optimization opportunities.

We'll start out the chapter by demonstrating that it's possible to replace a lot of your program logic with SQL logic and achieve optimization benefits. Then we'll cover the following MySQL features:

- Logical, arithmetic, and comparison operators

- Math functions

- Functions for manipulating strings

- Date and time functions

- User-defined variables

- Decision-making and flow-control constructs

With the possible exception of the basic operators, these are among MySQL's most underused and underappreciated features.

By the time you've finished this chapter, you'll be familiar with most of these features, and you'll be able to understand their role in optimizing your own projects to improve their performance.

Replacing Program Logic with SQL Logic: A Demonstration

Many application developers don't seem to realize that SQL, while not a complete programming language in its own right, still has a wealth of constructs that can be used to fine-tune queries so that only necessary data is returned by them. Quite often, we've seen cases where programmers will return overly large result-sets, and then filter or modify them in program code.

For example, consider a scenario in which we wish to output to a web page a list of the members of some organization. Let's suppose the member data is stored in a **members** table that was created using this statement:

```
CREATE TABLE members (
    firstname VARCHAR(30) NOT NULL,
    lastname VARCHAR(30) NOT NULL,
    #  possibly more column definitions that don't relate to this example...
    dob DATE NOT NULL
);
```

We want to format the listing nicely as an HTML table with the full name of each member in one of two columns and an age range in the other. Here's one way we could do that using PHP 4:

```
<!DOCTYPE HTML PUBLIC "-//W3C//DTD HTML 4.01 Transitional//EN"
    "http://www.w3.org/TR/html4/loose.dtd">
<html>
<head>
<meta http-equiv="Content-Type" content="text/html; charset=iso-8859-1">
<title>List All Members With Age Ranges [PHP4 / Logic In PHP Code]</title>
</head>
<body>
<?php
    //  establish a connection to MySQL, and select the proper database...
    $connection = mysql_connect("localhost", "jon", "mypass");
    mysql_select_db("mydb", $connection);
    //  get the current year for the age calculation below...
    $year = (int) date("Y");
```

```php
  //  submit a query...
  $query = "SELECT firstname, lastname, dob FROM members ORDER BY lastname";
  $result = mysql_query($query);
?>


<!-- begin table display -->
<table cellpadding="5" cellspacing="0" border="1">
  <tr><th colspan="2">MEMBERS BY AGE GROUP</th></tr>
  <tr><th>Name</th><th>Age Group</th></tr>
<?php
  //  for each row returned from the database...
  while($row = mysql_fetch_assoc($result))
  {
    extract($row);
    //  get the year of birth from the birthdate column
    //  get the age by subtracting it from the current year
    $age = $year - (int) substr($dob, 0, 4);
    //  determine the age range based on the year
    if($age >= 65)
      $age_range = "Over 65";
    elseif($age >= 45)
      $age_range = "45-64";
    elseif($age >= 30)
      $age_range = "30-44";
    elseif($age >= 18)
      $age_range = "18-29";
    else
      $age_range = "Under 18";
    //  output the resulting age range along with the member's name
    echo "<tr><td>$firstname $lastname</td><td>$age_range</td></tr>\n";
  }
?>
</table>
<!-- end table display -->

</body>
</html>
```

NOTE *Anyone who is familiar with PHP might wonder why we didn't
use a* switch ... case *block instead of the* if ... elseif ... else.
*The reason is that Python doesn't have an analogue to the former.
And the reason why we care about this will become apparent shortly.
So please bear with us.*

There's nothing really wrong with this approach (it does work, after all), but notice that we need to process each row of the result set *as part of the output loop*. Wouldn't it be nice if we could obtain *exactly* the data we needed from the database, formatted *exactly* as we would like to use it in the output?

It turns out that we can do exactly that, by moving the formatting and decision-making functionality into the query that we send to MySQL:

```
<!DOCTYPE HTML PUBLIC "-//W3C//DTD HTML 4.01 Transitional//EN"
    "http://www.w3.org/TR/html4/loose.dtd">
<html>
<head>
<meta http-equiv="Content-Type" content="text/html; charset=iso-8859-1">
<title>List All Members With Age Ranges [PHP4 / Logic in SQL]</title>
</head>
<body>
<?php
  // connect and select...
  $connection = mysql_connect("localhost", "jon", "mypass");
  mysql_select_db("mydb", $connection);

  // new and improved query, which handles the logic and formatting
  $query = "SELECT
                CONCAT(firstname, ' ', lastname) AS name,
                CASE
                  WHEN (@age := YEAR(CURRENT_DATE) - YEAR(dob)) > 65 THEN 'Over 65'
                  WHEN @age >= 45 THEN '45-64'
                  WHEN @age >= 30 THEN '30-44'
                  WHEN @age >= 18 THEN '18-19'
                  ELSE 'Under 18'
                END AS age_range
                FROM members ORDER BY lastname";
  $result = mysql_query($query);
?>

<!-- begin table display -->
<table cellpadding="5" cellspacing="0" border="1">
  <tr><th colspan="2">MEMBERS BY AGE GROUP</th></tr>
  <tr><th>Name</th><th>Age Group</th></tr>
<?php
  // for each record returned by the query...
  while($row = mysql_fetch_assoc($result))
  {
    // extract and output the data
    extract($row);
```

```
      echo "<tr><td>$name</td><td>$age_range</td></tr>\n";
   }
?>
</table>
<!-- end table display -->

</body>
</html>
```

By the time you reach the end of this chapter, you'll be able to come back to this example and see exactly what the complex query does, as well as write your own. For now, just assume that we know what we're doing, and that the end result is the same as in the first example.

This second method has three main optimization advantages. We'll cover each advantage one by one now in some detail, as they support the central premise that we are conveying to you in this chapter. We'll also revisit this example at the end of the chapter.

Optimization 1: Separation of Logic and Formatting

First, we can separate the logic required for formatting the data that's retrieved from the display loop. This is much cleaner code and makes it easier to modify either the data being passed to the display loop (by modifying the query) or the display loop itself.

For example, if we decide to output the names as *lastname, firstname*, rather than *firstname lastname*, we simply change the relevant part of the query to `CONCAT(lastname, ', ', firstname) AS name`, without needing to touch the PHP code. If we do need to alter the presentation, we can tweak the display code without fear of messing up the derivation of the data or formatting of the data itself.

As an added bonus, you'll often find that your code is a bit shorter as well, because you can write fewer and/or shorter loops.

Optimization 2: Speed

This method is also faster. If you're retrieving only a few records, the difference in speed between these two PHP scripts might not be very noticeable, but increase that number to, say, 50,000 records, and you'll see that the second version executes about 10% to 15% more quickly than the first. Naturally, any improvements you might see in your own applications from adopting this methodology are going to be affected by a wide range of variables, but in an enterprise setting with vast amounts of data and many users, or on a busy web site with hundreds or even thousands of simultaneous visitors, any performance gain you can muster becomes important.

 TIP *You can often pick up an additional speed boost by making use of the query-caching capabilities available in MySQL 4.0 and later. See Chapter 6 for a discussion of query caching.*

Optimization 3: Portability

Finally, this method is also more portable. Suppose we're told that (a) we need to port this script to (just for the sake of example) Python and (b) this really needed to be done yesterday. Which version of the PHP script would you prefer to work from—particularly if you're not a Python expert?

Working from the second version of the PHP script plus a rudimentary knowledge of Python, a copy of the Python documentation, and the MySQLdb module (http://sourceforge.net/projects/mysql-python), Jon was able to produce a working script in about 30 minutes (including the time required to download, install, and configure ActivePython and MySQLdb):

```python
#!/usr/bin/python
import cgi
import MySQLdb

# connect to MySQL and create a cursor
db = MySQLdb.connect(host="localhost", user="zontar", passwd="mypass", db="mdbd")
cursor = db.cursor(cursorclass=MySQLdb.cursors.DictCursor)

# the same query used in the "improved" PHP 4 example
query = "SELECT \
            CONCAT(firstname, ' ', lastname) AS name, \
            CASE \
              WHEN (@age:=YEAR(CURRENT_DATE) - YEAR(dob)) > 65 THEN 'Over 65' \
              WHEN @age >= 45 THEN '45-64' \
              WHEN @age >= 30 THEN '30-44' \
              WHEN @age >= 18 THEN '18-29' \
              ELSE 'Under 18' \
            END AS age_range \
            FROM members \
            ORDER BY lastname, firstname"
```

```
#   submit the query and store the result set
cursor.execute(query)
result = cursor.fetchall()

#   begin HTML output
print "Content-Type: text/html"
print
print "<!DOCTYPE HTML PUBLIC \"-//W3C//DTD HTML 4.01 Transitional//EN\" \
          \"http://www.w3.org/TR/html4/loose.dtd\">\n\
<html>\n<head>\n\
<meta http-equiv=\"Content-Type\" content=\"text/html; charset=iso-8859-1\">\n\
<title>List All Members With Age Ranges [Python-CGI / Logic in SQL]</title>\n\
</head>\n<body>"

#   begin HTML table display
print "<table cellpadding=\"5\" cellspacing=\"0\" border=\"1\">\n\
      <tr><th colspan=\"2\">MEMBERS BY AGE GROUP</th></tr>\n\
      <tr><th>Name</th><th>Age Group</th></tr>"

#   display result rows in HTML table rows
for row in result:
  print "<tr><td>%s</td><td>%s</td></tr>" % (row[0], row[2])

# end table display
print "</table>"

#   end HTML page
print "</body>n\</html>"
#   end of script
```

The query does all the hard work of calculation, decision-making, string manipulation, and so forth. This means that the tasks remaining for the script in Python (or whatever language the boss told us to use) are easy to implement, almost trivially so:

1. Send the query.

2. Receive the result.

3. Generate the dynamic output by looping through the result set.

Notice that no heavy-duty parsing, calculation, or string-manipulation code is required; we've already done all that using nothing but SQL. In other words, *we've abstracted all of those tasks out of our display code and into the query.*

Figure 4-1 shows the output of the Python script in a web browser.

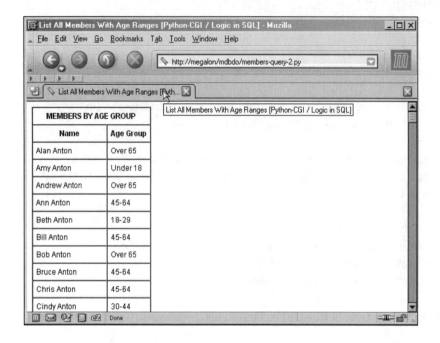

Figure 4-1. Output of the demonstration example

NOTE *If you haven't encountered Python before and are interested in checking it out, you can obtain the latest version (Python 2.3.4 as of this writing) for a variety of platforms from either* http://www.python.org/ *(Unix source code; Windows and Mac OS X binaries) or* http://activestate.com/Products/ActivePython/ *(installers for Windows, Linux, and Solaris). You might also want to pick up a copy of Magnus Lie Hetland's* Practical Python *(Apress, 2002), which we've read and can highly recommend.*

MySQL Operators

As we stated at the beginning of this chapter, our central premise is that it is almost *always* the best course of action to make the database perform as much work as possible, thus minimizing the amount of filtering and manipulating data that you do in your programming code. Simply put, a strong working knowledge of operators increases your options when it comes to replacing your programming logic with SQL logic.

NOTE   *Most of the functions and operators that we'll look at in this chapter can be used in* SELECT, INSERT, *and* UPDATE *queries, either as column values or in* WHERE *clauses. We'll provide you with examples of all of these.*

Most of MySQL's arithmetic and logical operators are likely to be familiar to you, as they're more or less the same as you'll find in most common programming languages. So we won't spend a great deal of time with them, but we will go over them and point out their MySQL-specific eccentricities where necessary.

NOTE   *Like most programming languages, MySQL uses parentheses for grouping to force the order in which operations are performed. You can use these whenever you want to override the normal precedence of MySQL operators, which we'll discuss later in this chapter.*

Logical Operators

MySQL has the basic logical operators you would expect to find in any scripting or programming language. The list was completed in MySQL 4.0.2, when support for XOR was added.

Logical operators always evaluate to **TRUE**, **FALSE**, or **NULL**. As we've mentioned before, MySQL doesn't have a Boolean datatype as such; instead, it uses 1 for Boolean **TRUE** and 0 for Boolean **FALSE**.

NOT (!): Negates the condition it precedes. Generally speaking, MySQL doesn't care whether you use ! or NOT, so you can write whichever suits you.

AND (&&): In order for an AND comparison to be true, both conditions to be tested must be true. You may use AND and && interchangeably. Note that 1 AND NULL returns NULL, and 0 AND NULL returns 0 (**FALSE**).

OR (||): Is true if at least one of the operands is true. 1 OR NULL returns 1 (**TRUE**), and 0 OR NULL returns NULL. OR and || are synonyms, so you can use either of them as you prefer.

XOR (^): Yields a true result if *one and only one* of the operands is true. Any value XOR'ed with NULL yields NULL. XOR and ^ are synonyms.

We recommend that you use AND and OR rather than && and || in order to pre-clude the possibility of accidentally leaving out one of the doubled symbols and so writing a bitwise operator instead of a logical operator.

 NOTE *Bitwise operators aren't used that often, and we don't cover them here. If you need to find out about them, consult the MySQL Manual or other reference.*

In addition, the double-pipe version of OR also serves as a concatenation operator when running MySQL in ANSI mode, and it can be used in this manner in Oracle and PostgreSQL as well.

The rules for resolving expressions containing logical operators are shown as in Table 4-1.

Table 4-1. Truth Tables for MySQL Logical Operators

OPERATOR	TRUE	FALSE	NULL
AND			
TRUE	TRUE	FALSE	NULL
FALSE	FALSE	FALSE	FALSE
NULL	NULL	FALSE	NULL
OR			
TRUE	TRUE	TRUE	TRUE
FALSE	TRUE	FALSE	NULL
NULL	NULL	NULL	NULL
XOR			
TRUE	FALSE	TRUE	NULL
FALSE	TRUE	FALSE	NULL
NULL	NULL	NULL	NULL
NOT	FALSE	TRUE	NULL

While you may have seen these before, you may not be familiar with how they act on NULL values in MySQL. Basically, the negation of NULL is NULL, and NULL used with any logical operator and any other value also results in NULL, with one exception: A value of **FALSE**, when AND'ed with NULL, results in a Boolean **FALSE**.

Arithmetic Operators

As in the case of logical operators, MySQL's arithmetic operators are fairly standard. Here they are, along with a few "gotchas" to watch for:

+ **(addition / unary positive):** Add two numbers together. A *unary plus sign* can be used to denote a positive number (basically, it is ignored). Note that, unlike the case with some scripting languages and Microsoft SQL Server, you cannot use the plus sign to concatenate strings! (See the notes about type conversion in the next section.)

- **(subtraction / unary negative or additive inverse):** Subtracts one number from another. Used with a single number, it causes that number to be negative.

* **(multiplication):** Gets the product of two numbers. The order of the arguments does not affect the value returned.

/ **(division):** Indicates a floating-point division: for example, 3 / 5 returns the value 0.6.

DIV **(integer division):** Indicates an integer division; all fractions are rounded down. For example, 5 DIV 3 returns 1, and 3 DIV 5 returns 0. This operator was added in MySQL 4.1.

% **(modulus):** Performs a division and returns the remainder. For example, 5 % 3 yields 2. If the *first* argument is negative, a negative value is returned, so that -10 % -3 and -10 % -3 both return –1, but 10 % -3 returns 1. Note that where ABS(a) < ABS(b), a % b simply returns *a*; for example, 3 % 10 evaluates to 3, and -3 % 10 evaluates to –3. You may also use the MOD() function for this; for example, MOD(5, 3) returns 2. Beginning with MySQL 4.1, you may also write 5 MOD 3 instead of MOD(5, 3).

ABS(N) returns the absolute value of a number: if *N* is positive, the returned value is simply *N*; if *N* is negative, the function returns –*N*. In case you're unfamiliar with absolute values, we show a quick example here.

```
Command Prompt - mysql -h megalon -u root -p                    _ |□| X|
mysql> SELECT 5, ABS(5), -5, ABS(-5);
+---+--------+----+---------+
| 5 | ABS(5) | -5 | ABS(-5) |
+---+--------+----+---------+
| 5 |      5 | -5 |       5 |
+---+--------+----+---------+
1 row in set (0.24 sec)

mysql> _
```

Type Conversions with Logical and Arithmetic Operators

Here are a few rules to keep in mind when working with logical and arithmetic operators in MySQL:

- Any nonzero integer used with a logical operator evaluates as **TRUE**, even if it has a negative value.

- When used with logical operators, fractional values are rounded to the nearest integer. This means that any *N* where $0.5 > \text{ABS}(N) \geq 0$ evaluates as **FALSE**. (In other words, any number whose absolute value is less than 0.5 is rounded to 0 when used with a logical operator.)

- When adding, subtracting, multiplying, or dividing a mix of integers and decimals, the result will always be a decimal; `3 * 2.33` returns 6.99, and the expression `2.1 + 1.145 - 3.245` yields 0.000.

- Any string value used in a logical or arithmetic context always evaluates to 0 (**FALSE**). For example, `'a' AND 1` returns 0 (**FALSE**) and `'b' + 4` returns 4.

- Any arithmetic expression containing `NULL` returns `NULL`. This includes the expressions `+NULL` and `-NULL`.

- Division by zero produces a `NULL` result.

- Operators (like all MySQL keywords) are case-insensitive. So it makes no practical difference whether you write `A AND B`, `A and B`, or `A && B`. However, as stated elsewhere, we generally use uppercase for MySQL keywords throughout this book for the sake of easy recognition and consistency.

While this may all look quite familiar, be aware that what is true in your programming or scripting language of choice may not be so in MySQL. So, if you encounter what seems to be a bug in using arithmetic operators in a query, it may just be that MySQL behaves a bit differently than what you're used to.

Comparison Operators

Like all programming languages, MySQL's dialect of SQL has a more or less usual set of comparison operators, as well as a few unusual ones. The equals sign (=) serves as both the equality operator and the assignment operator, and an expression containing it evaluates to **TRUE** (1) if the operands are the same, and **FALSE** (0) if they're not. If at least one of the operands is NULL, then the result is always NULL.

As mentioned in our discussion of datatypes in Chapter 2, a special "null-safe" comparison operator, <=>, returns 1 (**TRUE**) if the arguments are equal values or if both values are NULL, and 0 (**FALSE**) otherwise. In other words, 1 <=> 1 returns **TRUE** (1), 1 <=> NULL returns **FALSE** (0), and NULL <=> NULL returns **TRUE** (1). (Remember that the NULL value is not equal to any other value, not even itself.)

TIP *You may also wish to use* IS [NOT] NULL *for testing whether or not a value is* NULL, *as discussed in Chapter 3.* IS NULL *can also be written as* ISNULL(); *for example,* SELECT ISNULL(1); *returns 0. You are likely to find that* ISNULL() *is more portable to and from other databases than* IS NULL *or the* <=> *operator. In addition, MySQL supports the* IFNULL() *and* NULLIF() *flow-control operators that can be used in connection with null values, as discussed in the "Branching: Making Choices in Queries" section later in this chapter.*

There are two ways of writing the inequality comparator. You may use either != or <>; they're exactly the same so far as MySQL is concerned. The <> notation seems to be more common, and it's what we prefer to use ourselves, but the choice is entirely up to you. (As always, we recommend you choose one or the other, and stick with it.) Note that NULL compared with any value—even itself—using <> or != yields the null value. However, when performing branching operations, you're generally checking to see whether a condition is true or not, and since NULL isn't true, a null result still causes you to follow the "false" branch.

```
Command Prompt - mysql -h megalon -u root -p
mysql> SELECT IF(1 = NULL, '"True" branch', '"False" branch');
+-------------------------------------------------+
| IF(1 = NULL, '"True" branch', '"False" branch') |
+-------------------------------------------------+
| "False" branch                                  |
+-------------------------------------------------+
1 row in set (0.06 sec)
mysql>
```

We'll discuss IF() and the other branching operators later in this chapter.

NOTE *Both forms of the inequality operator (<> and !=) are standard SQL and supported by most other relational databases.*

MySQL also has greater-than, less-than, greater-than-or-equal, and less-than-or-equal operators, which are written (in order) >, <, >=, and <=. These behave more or less just as you would expect. As with the equality and inequality operators, any comparison involving NULL and using one of these operators will always yield a NULL result.

CAUTION *Some relational databases provide additional comparison operators meaning "not greater than" (!> or />) and "not less than" (!< or /<). These are not part of the SQL standard and are not currently supported in MySQL.*

There's also a shortcut for determining whether a given value lies within a certain range. The BETWEEN operator is used as shown here.

```
Command Prompt - mysql -h megalon -u root -p
mysql> SELECT 5 BETWEEN 2 AND 7;
+-------------------+
| 5 BETWEEN 2 AND 7 |
+-------------------+
|                 1 |
+-------------------+
1 row in set (0.01 sec)
mysql> SELECT 5 BETWEEN 2 AND 4;
+-------------------+
| 5 BETWEEN 2 AND 4 |
+-------------------+
|                 0 |
+-------------------+
1 row in set (0.01 sec)
mysql>
```

BETWEEN can also be used with nonnumeric datatypes such as strings. Note that (as usual) string comparisons are case-insensitive unless you employ the BINARY modifier.

```
Command Prompt - mysql -h megalon -u root -p
mysql> SELECT 'MAN' BETWEEN 'maid' AND 'mate';
+-------------------------------+
| 'MAN' BETWEEN 'maid' AND 'mate' |
+-------------------------------+
|                             1 |
+-------------------------------+
1 row in set (0.00 sec)
mysql> SELECT BINARY 'MAN' BETWEEN 'maid' AND 'mate';
+----------------------------------------+
| BINARY 'MAN' BETWEEN 'maid' AND 'mate' |
+----------------------------------------+
|                                      0 |
+----------------------------------------+
1 row in set (0.00 sec)
mysql>
```

Dates as well as strings can be compared.

```
Command Prompt - mysql -h megalon -u root -p                          _ □ ×
mysql> SELECT '2004-06-10' BETWEEN '2004-05-15' AND '2004-07-01';
+-----------------------------------------------------------+
| '2004-06-10' BETWEEN '2004-05-15' AND '2004-07-01' |
+-----------------------------------------------------------+
|                                                         1 |
+-----------------------------------------------------------+
1 row in set (0.00 sec)

mysql>
```

If the value immediately before the AND is not less than the value following it, then 0 will be always be returned.

NOTE *There's an additional operator for use in comparing strings. The LIKE operator allows you to do "fuzzy" matching with wildcards to find strings that are similar to one another. We'll discuss LIKE in more detail in the "String Functions and Regular Expressions" section later in this chapter.*

Operators for Working with Sets

MySQL also has several operators and functions for use with sets of values. The IN operator answers the question, "Does value *N* match at least one of the values in the set *A, B, C, D*...?" Here are some examples:

```
Command Prompt - mysql -h megalon -u root -p                          _ □ ×
mysql> SELECT 'jon' IN ('Mary', 'bob', 'Jon', 'Sue');
+--------------------------------------+
| 'jon' IN ('Mary', 'bob', 'Jon', 'Sue') |
+--------------------------------------+
|                                    1 |
+--------------------------------------+
1 row in set (0.00 sec)
mysql> SELECT BINARY 'jon' IN ('Mary', 'bob', 'Jon', 'Sue');
+---------------------------------------------+
| BINARY 'jon' IN ('Mary', 'bob', 'Jon', 'Sue') |
+---------------------------------------------+
|                                           0 |
+---------------------------------------------+
1 row in set (0.01 sec)
mysql> SELECT 5 IN (34, 5, 'Jon', 'Sue');
+----------------------------+
| 5 IN (34, 5, 'Jon', 'Sue') |
+----------------------------+
|                          1 |
+----------------------------+
1 row in set (0.00 sec)
mysql> SELECT 5 IN (34, '5', 'Jon', 'Sue');
+------------------------------+
| 5 IN (34, '5', 'Jon', 'Sue') |
+------------------------------+
|                            1 |
+------------------------------+
1 row in set (0.00 sec)
mysql> SELECT 5 IN (34, 6, 'Jon', 'Sue');
+----------------------------+
| 5 IN (34, 6, 'Jon', 'Sue') |
+----------------------------+
|                          0 |
+----------------------------+
1 row in set (0.00 sec)
mysql>
```

You should note the following points when using the IN operator:

- The IN operator returns 1 if a match is found (as in the first and third examples) and 0 if no match is found (as in the second and fourth examples).

- You can use any datatypes for the value to be found and for the values in the list to be searched, and you can mix datatypes in the list.

- When trying to match a string, comparisons are case-insensitive, unless you use the BINARY qualifier. (Compare the first two examples.)

- MySQL will attempt to perform a type conversion between strings and numerals, and vice versa. Hence, the number 5 is matched by the string '5' in the fourth example (but see the rules in the following "Type Conversions in Comparisons" section).

IN can be used in place of (and is basically shorthand for) multiple OR operators in a WHERE clause. For example, this query:

```
SELECT lastname, dob
FROM members
WHERE firstname IN ('Bill', 'Mary', 'George');
```

produces the same result as this one:

```
SELECT lastname, dob
FROM members
WHERE firstname='Bill' OR firstname='Mary' OR firstname='George';
```

The IN operator can also be extremely useful when used with subqueries in MySQL 4.1 and above. Let's return for a moment to our **members** table from the "Replacing Program Logic with SQL Logic: A Demonstration" section earlier in this chapter. Suppose that now we would like to know if any members were born in the year 1961. If you're a programmer, you might have visions of writing some sort of for or while loop that iterates over the dates extracted from a query. Or you might be thinking that you could use something like this to accomplish this task:

```
SELECT COUNT(*) FROM members WHERE YEAR(dob)='1961';
```

You could do that, but you would be getting your original question answered only in an indirect fashion; you would still need to test the result to see whether the result was greater than zero. By using IN and a subquery, however, you can obtain a *Yes* or *No* (actually 1 or 0) answer:

```
SELECT '1961' IN (SELECT YEAR(dob) FROM members);
```

The inner SELECT returns a list of years, and the outer SELECT looks for a match in that list. By the way, the inner SELECT must return a single column; otherwise, MySQL will signal an error.

> **NOTE**   *Subqueries were introduced in MySQL 4.1. We'll discuss them in more detail in Chapter 8.*

In place of IN, you can also use a comparison operator followed by either of the keywords ANY or SOME.

```
Command Prompt - mysql -h megalon -u root -p

mysql> SELECT 'Bill' = SOME(SELECT firstname FROM members);
+-----------------------------------------------+
| 'Bill' = SOME(SELECT firstname FROM members)  |
+-----------------------------------------------+
|                                            1  |
+-----------------------------------------------+
1 row in set (0.20 sec)

mysql> SELECT COUNT(firstname) > 0 FROM members
    -> WHERE firstname = 'Bill';
+----------------------+
| COUNT(firstname) > 0 |
+----------------------+
|                    1 |
+----------------------+
1 row in set (0.05 sec)

mysql>
```

We show an equivalent using the COUNT() function and a comparison operator in the same example. This example can be thought of as saying, "Is there some member whose first name is Bill? Yes, there is someone in the members list whose first name is Bill."

The following query and result can be thought of as saying, "There is not any member whose first name is Andy, correct? Yes, that's correct."

```
Command Prompt - mysql -h megalon -u root -p

mysql> SELECT 'Andy' <> ANY(SELECT firstname FROM members);
+-----------------------------------------------+
| 'Andy' <> ANY(SELECT firstname FROM members)  |
+-----------------------------------------------+
|                                            1  |
+-----------------------------------------------+
1 row in set (0.06 sec)

mysql>
```

> **CAUTION**   *Through MySQL 5.0.0, it is not possible to use a* LIMIT *clause in a subquery following an* IN, ANY, *or* SOME *clause.*

You can use any of the comparison operators =, !=, <>, <, <=, >, and >= with ANY or SOME. (You cannot use <=>.) Here's an example:

```
Command Prompt - mysql -h megalon -u root -p                       _ □ ×
mysql> SELECT '1922' >= ANY(SELECT YEAR(dob) FROM members);
+--------------------------------------------------+
| '1922' >= ANY(SELECT YEAR(dob) FROM members) |
+--------------------------------------------------+
|                                             0 |
+--------------------------------------------------+
1 row in set (0.20 sec)

mysql>
```

This is equivalent to asking the question, "Do we have any members who were born in the year 1922 or earlier?" and getting the answer, "No."

Finally, you can find the greatest and least values in a set by using GREATEST() and LEAST(). They're used in a similar fashion: each accepts a comma-delimited set of values and returns the largest or smallest value from the set. The following is an example of using both of these functions.

```
Command Prompt - mysql -h megalon -u root -p                       _ □ ×
mysql> SELECT GREATEST(3.1, 388, 7.995, -23, 12),
    -> LEAST(3.1, 388, 7.995, -23, 12)\G
*************************** 1. row ***************************
GREATEST(3.1, 388, 7.995, -23, 12): 388.000
   LEAST(3.1, 388, 7.995, -23, 12): -23.000
1 row in set (0.00 sec)

mysql>
```

Note that since we've mixed integer and decimal values, the result is expressed as a decimal with a precision equal to that of the argument with the greatest number of decimals.

NOTE *The order in which arguments are passed to* GREATEST() *and* LEAST() *has no effect on the result.*

You can also use the GREATEST() and LEAST() functions with strings:

```
Command Prompt - mysql -h megalon -u root -p                       _ □ ×
mysql> SELECT GREATEST('ban', 'Bat', 'band', 'Ball'),
    -> LEAST('ban', 'Bat', 'band', 'Ball')\G
*************************** 1. row ***************************
GREATEST('ban', 'Bat', 'band', 'Ball'): Bat
   LEAST('ban', 'Bat', 'band', 'Ball'): Ball
1 row in set (0.00 sec)

mysql>
```

Both functions are case-insensitive. Although you can use the BINARY modifier with either one of them without generating any errors, doing so has no effect on the result.

```
Command Prompt - mysql -h megalon -u root -p                          _ □ ×
mysql> SELECT BINARY GREATEST('ban', 'Bat', 'band', 'Ball'),
    -> BINARY LEAST('ban', 'Bat', 'band', 'Ball')\G
*************************** 1. row ***************************
BINARY GREATEST('ban', 'Bat', 'band', 'Ball'): Bat
   BINARY LEAST('ban', 'Bat', 'band', 'Ball'): Ball
1 row in set (0.00 sec)

mysql>
```

It's possible to use both numeric and string arguments in one call to GREATEST()
or LEAST(), but all of the strings are converted to 0.

```
Command Prompt - mysql -h megalon -u root -p                          _ □ ×
mysql> SELECT GREATEST(5, 'band', 88, 'bat'),
    -> LEAST(5, 'band', 88, 'bat');
+--------------------------------+-----------------------------+
| GREATEST(5, 'band', 88, 'bat') | LEAST(5, 'band', 88, 'bat') |
+--------------------------------+-----------------------------+
|                             88 |                           0 |
+--------------------------------+-----------------------------+
1 row in set (0.00 sec)

mysql>
```

 CAUTION   *In older versions of MySQL (prior to 3.23), it was possible
to use* MAX() *and* MIN() *as synonyms for* GREATEST() *and* LEAST(),
*and you may see this usage in older references. This is no longer the
case, and attempting to use one of these functions on a set will cause
an error.*

Finally, there are two functions for working with sets of values: ELT() and
FIELD(), which complement one another. ELT() is used to retrieve the value of
the element at the specified index within a set. FIELD() finds the position or
index of a given value within a set. Each takes as parameters a set of values, all
of which except the first make up a list to be tested.

For ELT(), the first element in the set is the index of the value to be retrieved.

```
Command Prompt - mysql -h megalon -u root -p                          _ □ ×
mysql> SELECT ELT(3, 'cat', 'dog', 'bird', 'fish', 'wombat');
+------------------------------------------------+
| ELT(3, 'cat', 'dog', 'bird', 'fish', 'wombat') |
+------------------------------------------------+
| bird                                           |
+------------------------------------------------+
1 row in set (0.00 sec)

mysql>
```

The first argument used with ELT() must be an integer; if it is less than 1 or
greater than the number of elements in the list, the function returns NULL. Note
that using 1 for the first argument will return the first element in the list that follows it. You can think of this function as working like an array index does in most
programming languages.

The FIELD() function attempts to match the first argument in the list that follows it. Here, too, the numbering of the list starts with 1.

```
Command Prompt - mysql -h megalon -u root -p                          _ □ x
mysql> SELECT FIELD('fish', 'cat', 'dog', 'bird', 'fish', 'wombat');
+-------------------------------------------------------------+
| FIELD('fish', 'cat', 'dog', 'bird', 'fish', 'wombat') |
+-------------------------------------------------------------+
|                                                           4 |
+-------------------------------------------------------------+
1 row in set (0.00 sec)

mysql>
```

Note that these two functions are usually employed with lists of strings, but it's also possible to use them with numbers, as shown in the next example.

```
Command Prompt - mysql -h megalon -u root -p                          _ □ x
mysql> SELECT ELT('2', 'joe', 45, 'bob', 6, 'fred');
+-------------------------------------------+
| ELT('2', 'joe', 45, 'bob', 6, 'fred') |
+-------------------------------------------+
| 45                                        |
+-------------------------------------------+
1 row in set (0.00 sec)
mysql> SELECT FIELD(6, 'joe', 45, 'bob', 6, 'fred');
+-------------------------------------------+
| FIELD(6, 'joe', 45, 'bob', 6, 'fred') |
+-------------------------------------------+
|                                         4 |
+-------------------------------------------+
1 row in set (0.00 sec)

mysql>
```

As you can likely deduce from these examples, the value used for the first argument to ELT() can be a string, as long as that string contains only digits, and the first argument to FIELD() can be a number.

Type Conversions in Comparisons

Here are few points to keep in mind when comparing values of different types using any of the comparison operators =, <>, !=, >, >=, <, and <=:

- Comparing any value with the null value returns NULL.

- String comparisons are case-insensitive unless you use the BINARY qualifier in the query or in the definition of the column whose value is being compared: 'a' = 'A' returns 1 (Boolean **TRUE**), and BINARY 'a' = 'A' returns 0 (Boolean **FALSE**).

- When comparing a string with a number, any leading spaces in the string are discarded, then any leading digits in the string that remains are converted to a number and any remaining (trailing) characters are dropped, so both 5 < '8a' and ' 15x' = 15 return 1. If the string does not begin with a digit, the string is evaluated as 0, so both the expressions 5 < 'a8' and ' x15' = 15 return 0. And 3.0 >= '2f5' evaluates as **TRUE** (returns 1) and 14 < '311mft7' is **FALSE**.

- When comparing strings and numbers, if the string (after any leading spaces are dropped) begins with one or more digits followed by a decimal point and then by one or more digits, any additional characters following the second set of digits are dropped; for example, all three of the expressions '3.28' = 3.28, '3.28.6' = 3.28, and 3.28 = '3.28x' will evaluate to **TRUE** (1).

Operator Precedence

When multiple operators are involved in a single expression, things can get a bit complicated. For example, how should MySQL resolve an expression like 2 + 3 AND 1? Should this evaluate to 3 (3 AND 1 evaluates to 1; 2 + 1 is equal to 3) or to 1 (2 + 3 is equal to 5; 5 AND 1 evaluates as 1)? Of course, you can test this directly, as shown here:

However, it isn't really practical to take the time to do this every time you encounter such an expression, not to mention the fact that, in real life, such expressions are likely to be working with values that aren't known ahead of time. Fortunately, there's a set order of precedence that determines which operations are to be done first.

The order of precedence for operators in MySQL is almost identical to that found in ANSI SQL. Table 4-2 shows the order of precedence from highest to lowest.

Table 4-2. MySQL Operator Precedence

OPERATOR	DESCRIPTION
( )	Parentheses (force grouping)
+, -; ~	Unary plus and minus; bitwise inverse
*, /, % / MOD( ) / MOD, DIV	Multiplication and division
+, -	Addition and subtraction
<=>	Null-safe comparison
=, <>, !=, >=, <=	Comparison
&, |, ^	Bitwise AND, OR, and exclusive OR (XOR)
NOT / !	Logical negation
AND / &&	Logical AND
OR / ||; IN, SOME, ANY; LIKE	Logical OR; set membership; "fuzzy" (wildcard) comparison
<<, >>	Bitwise shift
=	Variable assignment

If you want operations to be performed in some other order, you can always force the issue by using parentheses.

When evaluating complex expressions involving parentheses, MySQL follows what's sometimes known as the "inside-outside" rule: operations inside the innermost set(s) of parentheses are performed first, followed by the next set outward, and then by the next set outward from that, and so on. If you've written code in practically any other modern programming or scripting language, you should be used to this already.

MySQL Functions

We are now going to look at a number of MySQL functions. Again, the focus here is on the central premise of this chapter: replacing programming logic with SQL logic is a key optimization skill, and it is almost *always* the best course of action to make the database perform as much work as possible. You want to minimize the amount of filtering and manipulating data that you do in your programming code.

Of course, MySQL has quite a large number of built-in functions, and some of them have a great many possible arguments as well. We won't attempt to catalog all of them here—that's what the MySQL Manual is for, after all—but we will discuss and demonstrate those functions that, in our experience, have proved to be the most important and useful in terms of replacing programming logic with SQL logic.

Math Functions

MySQL has most of the standard mathematical functions you would expect to find in any programming language. These include rounding functions, exponential and logarithmic functions, and even trigonometric functions.

Rounding Functions

All of the following functions round a floating-point number to one with fewer digits to the right of the decimal point or to an integer in one way or another:

CEILING(): Returns the smallest integer that is not less than the argument. CEILING(2.45) returns 3; CEILING(-2.45) returns –2. It can also be written as CEIL() in MySQL 4.0.6 and later.

FLOOR(): Returns the largest integer that's smaller than the argument. FLOOR(2.65) yields 2; FLOOR(-2.65) returns –3.

TRUNCATE (N, D): Returns *N* truncated to *D* decimal places. TRUNCATE (2.45, 1) returns 2.4; TRUNCATE(-2.45, 1) yields –2.4. It is possible for *D* to be larger than the number of decimals in *N*; for example, TRUNCATE(2.45, 3) returns 2.450. Note that both arguments are required; TRUNCATE(2.45, 0) evaluates to 2. By using a negative value for *D*, you can round to the left of the decimal point as well; TRUNCATE(542.5, -1) yields 540 and TRUNCATE(542.5, -2) returns 500.

ROUND(*N*[, *D*]): Rounds *N* to *D* decimal places; if *D* isn't specified, then 0 is implied. Note that the manner in which rounding is performed is system-dependent. If portability is an issue for your application, or if you need to be able to depend on the exact behavior, consider using TRUNCATE(), FLOOR(), or a user-defined function (UDF) instead. Beginning in MySQL 5.0, you can also define a stored procedure or function that implements the exact rounding algorithm desired. (See Chapter 8 for information about user-defined functions and stored procedures.)

TIP *MySQL also has a convenient function for formatting numbers for display:* FORMAT(N, D) *returns a number* N *formatted in comma-separated format truncated to D decimal places. For example,* FORMAT(23456.789, 2) *returns the string* '23,456.78'.

Powers, Exponents, and Logarithms

To obtain powers of numbers in MySQL, you can use the POW() or POWER() function (the two function names are synonymous). For example, 10 to the power of 2 (that is, 10 * 10 or 10²) can be found using POW() as shown here:

```
Command Prompt - mysql -h megalon -u root -p

mysql> SELECT POW(10, 2);
+------------+
| POW(10, 2) |
+------------+
| 100.000000 |
+------------+
1 row in set (0.00 sec)

mysql>
```

The logarithm of *X* to the base *Y* is defined as the power to which *Y* must be raised is order to produce *X*. For example, the logarithm of 100 to the base 10 is 2, because 10 to the power of 2 is 100. Using mathematical notation, we would write this relationship as this:

$$\log_{10}100 = 2 \Leftrightarrow 10^2 = 100$$

The most frequently used base for logarithms in mathematics, physics, and engineering is the special value *e*, where *e* is calculated by this series:

$$\sum_{k=0}^{\infty}\frac{1}{k!} = \frac{1}{0!} + \frac{1}{1!} + \frac{1}{2!} + \frac{1}{3!} + \frac{1}{4!} + \ldots = \frac{1}{1} + \frac{1}{1} + \frac{1}{2} + \frac{1}{6} + \frac{1}{24} + \ldots \approx 2.71828$$

Logarithms to the base *e* are known as *natural logarithms* (log$_e$, often written as ln) and can be obtained in MySQL using the LOG() function. Enterprise applications don't have that many uses for natural logarithms. However, it can sometimes be quite handy to be able to calculate base-2, base-8, base-10, or base-16 logarithms, which you can do by making use of the fact that $\log xy = \ln y / \ln x$. Here is an example, in which the second result tells us that we need six digits to express the base 10 number 100 in binary notation.

```
Command Prompt - mysql -h megalon -u root -p                          _ |□| x|
mysql> SELECT LOG(100) / LOG(10);
+--------------------+
| LOG(100) / LOG(10) |
+--------------------+
|         2.00000000 |
+--------------------+
1 row in set (0.00 sec)
mysql> SELECT LOG(100) / LOG(2);
+-------------------+
| LOG(100) / LOG(2) |
+-------------------+
|        6.64385619 |
+-------------------+
1 row in set (0.00 sec)
mysql>
```

NOTE *The logarithm of 1 to any base is always 0; the logarithm of any number less than or equal to 0 (to any base) is always undefined and in MySQL will return* NULL. *Attempting to obtain a logarithm to the base 1 or 0 will also yield a* NULL *result.*

In MySQL 4.0.3, logarithmic functions were improved in a number of ways. The function LN() was added as another means for calculating natural logarithms, and the LOG() function was enhanced so that it became possible to find logarithms bases other than 2 without needing to perform division using the notation LOG(base, value). Here are a couple examples:

```
Command Prompt - mysql -h megalon -u root -p                          _ |□| x|
mysql> SELECT LOG(10, 100);
+--------------+
| LOG(10, 100) |
+--------------+
|     2.000000 |
+--------------+
1 row in set (0.01 sec)
mysql> SELECT LOG(8, 512);
+-------------+
| LOG(8, 512) |
+-------------+
|    3.000000 |
+-------------+
1 row in set (0.00 sec)
mysql> SELECT LOG(100), LN(100);
+----------+----------+
| LOG(100) | LN(100)  |
+----------+----------+
| 4.605170 | 4.605170 |
+----------+----------+
1 row in set (0.00 sec)
mysql>
```

When used with a single argument, LOG() still returns the natural logarithm. The LN() function may take only a single argument and always return the natural logarithm.

TIP   *To learn more about natural logarithms and e, a good place to start is on the MathWorld web site at* http://mathworld.wolfram.com/e.html.

The functions LOG2() (logarithm to the base 2) and LOG10() (logarithm to the base 10) were also added in MySQL 4.0.3.

To get the value of a number raised to the power of *e*, use the EXP() function, as shown in the next example.

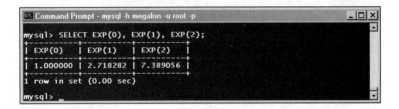

```
Command Prompt - mysql -h megalon -u root -p
mysql> SELECT EXP(0), EXP(1), EXP(2);
+----------+----------+----------+
| EXP(0)   | EXP(1)   | EXP(2)   |
+----------+----------+----------+
| 1.000000 | 2.718282 | 7.389056 |
+----------+----------+----------+
1 row in set (0.00 sec)

mysql>
```

NOTE   POW(), EXP(), *and* LOG() *always return decimal values, even if all arguments are integers.*

Trigonometric Functions

The trigonometric functions are useful for calculating lengths, arcs, and angles, as well as plotting curves and performing complex calculations involving waves.

NOTE   *We won't attempt to provide definitions or to explain trigonometry here. If you don't already know what they are or how to use them, check out the MathWorld web site, starting from* http://mathworld.wolfram.com/Trigonometry.html.

MySQL provides the following trigonometric functions, where *X* is an angle expressed in radians:

SIN(*X*): Sine of *X*

COS(*X*): Cosine of *X*

TAN(*X*): Tangent of *X*

COT(*X*): Cotangent of *X*

NOTE *The secant and cosecant trigonometric functions (often written as* sec *and* csc *in mathematical notation) can be obtained in MySQL by using the expressions* 1 / COS(*X*) *and* 1 / SIN(*X*), *respectively.*

The radian is a unit of angular measure defined such that 180 degrees is equal to π (pi) radians. (The number π is represented in MySQL as PI().) To convert radians to degrees, you can use the DEGREES() function, and to convert from degrees to radians, use the RADIANS() function.

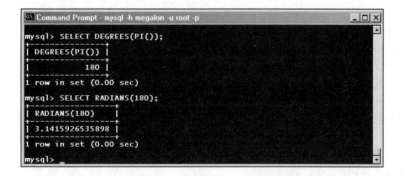

The inverse trigonometric functions all return angle values expressed in radians:

ASIN(*X*): Arcsine of *X*

ACOS(*X*): Arccosine of *X*

ATAN(X): Arctangent of X

ATAN(X, Y) or ATAN2(X, Y): Arctangent of *Y* / *X*

NOTE *MySQL stores π and e as double-precision floating-point values. This should be of sufficient accuracy for 99% of all applications requiring the use of these values.*

Other Math Functions

As noted earlier, ABS() returns the absolute value of its argument. The SIGN() function (known in mathematics as the *signum* function and often written sgn(x)) tests the sign of its argument, and returns 1 if the argument is positive, –1 if it's negative, and 0 if the argument is 0.

To obtain the square root of a number, use the SQRT() function, as shown here:

```
Command Prompt - mysql -h megalon -u root -p                              _□×
mysql> SELECT SQRT(2), SQRT(4), SQRT(16);
+----------+----------+----------+
| SQRT(2)  | SQRT(4)  | SQRT(16) |
+----------+----------+----------+
| 1.414214 | 2.000000 | 4.000000 |
+----------+----------+----------+
1 row in set (0.00 sec)

mysql>
```

It's often useful or necessary in programming to generate random numbers. MySQL provides this capability using the RAND() function, which returns a pseudo-random floating-point value from 0 to 1. An integer may be passed to this function as an optional argument; this serves to "seed" the function and allows you to produce a fairly random but repeatable sequence of values. You can also use RAND() to obtain a set of values in random order from a query by including it in an ORDER BY clause.

```
Command Prompt - mysql -h megalon -u root -p                              _□×
mysql> SELECT firstname, lastname
    -> FROM members
    -> WHERE dob > '1980-01-01'
    -> ORDER BY RAND() LIMIT 10;
+-----------+----------+
| firstname | lastname |
+-----------+----------+
| Mary      | Webster  |
| Rhonda    | Lane     |
| Martin    | Anton    |
| Stuart    | James    |
| Harold    | Robbins  |
| Ann       | Buckman  |
| Mary      | Davis    |
| Jill      | Jackson  |
| Nancy     | Nelson   |
| Chris     | Thomas   |
+-----------+----------+
10 rows in set (0.07 sec)

mysql>
```

Conversion Functions

In nearly any programming application, you encounter situations in which it's necessary to convert data from one type to another. For example, you may have a variable whose value is the string "535", and you may need to be able to treat this like the number 535 in order to multiply it by another value. Much the same is true in MySQL. In many cases, MySQL handles the conversion for you. For example, if you try to multiply the number 5 by the string "5", the latter is automatically converted to a number, so that the result is the number 25. However, there are times when MySQL's built-in type conversions don't do what you want them to, and you need to force the issue.

MySQL has two types of conversion functions for this purpose: the first is for casting datatypes to other datatypes (and in MySQL 4.01 and newer, for converting strings in one character set to another), and the second is for converting numbers in one base to another.

Type Conversions

While MySQL generally does a pretty good job of converting between datatypes, there may be times when it's necessary to perform such conversions explicitly. Beginning in MySQL 4.0.2, two functions are provided for this purpose. Both CAST() and CONVERT() take an argument of one type and attempt to return the same value converted to a different datatype. As of MySQL 4.1, CONVERT() can also be used to convert strings from one character set to another.

The CAST() function has the following syntax:

```
CAST(expression AS type)
```

where *expression* is a value or an expression that evaluates to a value, and *type* is one of the following datatypes:

- BINARY (Note that BINARY *colname* is an alias for CAST(*colname* AS BINARY))

- CHAR (available in MySQL 4.0.6 and later)

- DATE

- DATETIME

- SIGNED or SIGNED INTEGER

- TIME

- UNSIGNED or UNSIGNED INTEGER

When used to convert between datatypes, the CONVERT() function has this syntax:

```
CONVERT(expression, type)
```

This function can use any of the same values for *type* as CAST() does.

These functions are most useful when creating a new table using CREATE ... SELECT ... or copying data between tables using an INSERT ... SELECT ... query. For instance, suppose that you have a TEXT column in a table that you would like to have sorted using case-sensitivity. Instead of using BINARY *textcol* in each of your queries, you can copy the table definition and use this statement:

```
CREATE newtable SELECT CAST(textcol AS BINARY) FROM oldtable;
```

or this one:

```
INSERT INTO newtable SELECT CAST(textcol AS BINARY) FROM oldtable;
```

In the latter case, you'll need to make sure that the column into which you're selecting was declared as BINARY. (If you copied the definition of the old table, you'll need to change the column type using ALTER TABLE.)

The second form of CONVERT() has the following syntax:

```
CONVERT(expression USING encoding)
```

where *encoding* is the name of a character set, such as in this example:

```
SELECT CONVERT('I like MySQL' USING utf8);
```

You can see which character sets are available on your installation by using SHOW CHARACTER SET;.

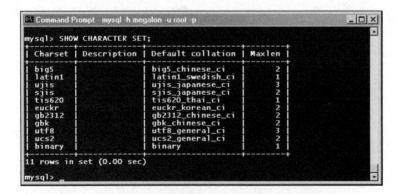

```
Command Prompt - mysql -h megalon -u root -p

mysql> SHOW CHARACTER SET;
+----------+-------------+--------------------+--------+
| Charset  | Description | Default collation  | Maxlen |
+----------+-------------+--------------------+--------+
| big5     |             | big5_chinese_ci    |   2    |
| latin1   |             | latin1_swedish_ci  |   1    |
| ujis     |             | ujis_japanese_ci   |   3    |
| sjis     |             | sjis_japanese_ci   |   2    |
| tis620   |             | tis620_thai_ci     |   1    |
| euckr    |             | euckr_korean_ci    |   2    |
| gb2312   |             | gb2312_chinese_ci  |   2    |
| gbk      |             | gbk_chinese_ci     |   2    |
| utf8     |             | utf8_general_ci    |   3    |
| ucs2     |             | ucs2_general_ci    |   2    |
| binary   |             | binary             |   1    |
+----------+-------------+--------------------+--------+
11 rows in set (0.00 sec)

mysql>
```

NOTE *In this book, we assume the use of the default Latin 1 (latin1) character set and* latin1_swedish_ci *collation. For information about configuring other character sets and collations, consult the MySQL Manual.*

Conversion of Numbers Between Bases

Four functions convert numbers from one base to another:

BIN(*X*): Converts a base-10 number *X* to binary form (base 2).

CONV(*X*, *N*, *M*): Converts the number *X* from base *N* to base *M*. The minimum allowed value for *N* or *M* is 2; the maximum value for either one is 36 (10 digits + 26 letters of the Latin alphabet for "digits" greater than 9).

HEX(*X*): Converts a base-10 number *X* to its hexadecimal equivalent (base 16).

OCT(*X*): Converts a base-10 number *X* to octal (base 8).

All four of these functions return their result as a *string*. More often than not, when you use these functions within more complex expressions, MySQL will automatically convert the result to a number, as shown in the following example.

```
Command Prompt - mysql -h megalon -u root -p                    _ □ ×
mysql> SELECT HEX(16) + HEX(32) AS b16,
    -> CONV(HEX(16) + HEX(32), 16, 10) AS b10;
+------+------+
| b16  | b10  |
+------+------+
|   30 |   48 |
+------+------+
1 row in set (0.00 sec)

mysql>
```

Keep in mind that numbers containing characters other than the digits 0 through 9 need to be quoted.

```
Command Prompt - mysql -h megalon -u root -p                    _ □ ×
mysql> SELECT CONV(1A, 16, 10);
ERROR 1054 (42522): Unknown column '1A' in 'field list'
mysql> SELECT CONV('1A', 16, 10);
+--------------------+
| CONV('1A', 16, 10) |
+--------------------+
| 26                 |
+--------------------+
1 row in set (0.00 sec)

mysql>
```

CAUTION *Do not confuse* CONV() *with the* CONVERT() *function! The latter is used to convert between datatypes, or to convert strings from one character set to another (see the previous section).*

Encryption and Encoding Functions

Several MySQL functions encrypt or encode data. You can use these functions for purposes such as keeping passwords secure and ensuring that critical data hasn't been corrupted.

MD5() and SHA1() are one-way hashing algorithms that are useful for safeguarding application passwords and other sensitive data, as is ENCRYPT() on Unix systems. ENCODE()/DECODE(), AES_ENCRYPT()/AES_DECRYPT(), and DES_ENCRYPT()/DES_DECRYPT() provide keyword-based encryption and decryption. PASSWORD() and OLD_PASSWORD() duplicate the algorithms used to encrypt MySQL's own passwords. COMPRESS() can be used to compress lengthy strings prior to storage and so save on space.

Here's some additional information about MySQL's encryption and encoding functions:

MD5(): Calculates a 128-bit checksum for a string and returns it as a 32-digit hexadecimal number using the RSA-MD5 Message Digest Algorithm. This function is supported in or has been ported to a number of programming languages, including C, Java, PHP, Perl, Visual Basic, and even JavaScript. For more information about MD5 and links to ports of it in various languages, visit http://userpages.umbc.edu/~mabzug1/cs/md5/md5.html.

SHA1(): Calculates a 160-bit hash for a string and returns it as a 40-bit hexadecimal number. Like the MD5 algorithm, the Secure Hashing Algorithm 1 (SHA1) has been implemented in a number of different programming languages. For more information about the SHA1 algorithm, see http://www.faqs.org/rfcs/rfc3174.html.

ENCODE() **and** DECODE(): ENCODE() takes as arguments a data string to be encoded and a password string, and returns a binary-encoded version of the data string that's the same length as the original. (If you wish to store the encoded string, be sure to use a BLOB column rather than a CHAR or VARCHAR column.) DECODE() also takes two arguments—the encoded string and the same password that was used to encode it—and returns the original string.

ENCRYPT(): Uses the Unix crypt() system call to encrypt a string. This function can take an optional second parameter in addition to the string to be encrypted, a "seed" string of two or more characters. This function does not work on Windows and other operating systems that don't support the crypt() system call; on these systems, it always returns NULL.

AES_ENCRYPT() **and** AES_DECRYPT(): Implement the U.S. Government's Approved Encryption Standard, also known as FIPS-197, and are the most cryptographically secure encoding functions available in MySQL as of this writing. Like ENCODE() and DECODE(), these functions require two arguments; the second argument is a password. For more information, see the AES home page at http://csrc.nist.gov/CryptoToolkit/aes/. This pair of functions was added in MySQL 4.0.2.

DES_ENCRYPT() **and** DES_DECRYPT(): Implement the U.S. National Institute of Standards and Technology's Triple-DES algorithm and are available only if MySQL has been compiled with Secure Sockets Layer (SSL) support. For more information, check the MySQL Manual or http://csrc.nist.gov/CryptoToolkit/Encryption.html#a3DES.

PASSWORD(): Same as that used by MySQL to encrypt passwords set using GRANT commands. It is strongly recommended that you do *not* use it in your application code, since it is liable to change between major releases. Prior to MySQL 5.0, this function returns a 16-digit hexadecimal number; starting in MySQL 5.0, the algorithm for PASSWORD() has changed, and the function returns a 41-character string that begins with the '*' (asterisk) character followed by a 40-digit hexadecimal number.

OLD_PASSWORD(): In MySQL 5.0, emulates the behavior of PASSWORD() in previous versions of MySQL.

COMPRESS() and UNCOMPRESS(): In MySQL 4.1.1 and later, COMPRESS() compresses a string using the zlib or equivalent library. The compressed string must be stored in a BLOB column. This can be useful for storing large amounts of textual data. The inverse of the COMPRESS() function is UNCOMPRESS(), which was also added in MySQL 4.1.1. You can find out how long a compressed string will be when uncompressed by using UNCOMPRESSED_LENGTH() on it before uncompressing it. If zlib functionality is not available, these functions will return NULL.

TIP *It's usually better to compress data before trying to encrypt it.*

CRC32(): Calculates a 32-bit cyclic redundancy check (CRC) for a string. This can be used as a hedge against data corruption. However, be aware that multiple errors can cancel each other out, so it is not 100% foolproof. (On the other hand, it's fairly reliable, and the larger the block of data, the less likely this is to happen.) If you're interested in knowing more, the MathWorld web site has some good technical information on CRCs and how they work at http://mathworld.wolfram.com/CyclicRedundancyCheck.html.

String Functions and Regular Expressions

Another way that you can save on programming logic in MySQL-based applications, and gain optimization benefits, is by performing string manipulations as part of your queries. MySQL provides a large number of string operations and supports regular expressions as well. First, let's look at some of the string functions.

String Operations

MySQL has functions for joining strings, finding and extracting substrings, and performing other useful string operations. To obtain the length of a string (that is, the number of characters it contains), you can use the LENGTH() function for single-byte character sets. For multibyte characters, you must use CHAR_LENGTH(). If internationalization is likely to be a concern in your application, you should definitely use CHAR_LENGTH().

For joining strings together, you might be tempted to use the + operator. Several programming languages allow you to do this, but when we try it in MySQL, here's what happens:

In MySQL, the + operator can be used *only* for adding numbers, and (as we discussed earlier) any strings occurring in an expression involving addition are automatically converted to zero. Instead, use either CONCAT() or CONCAT_WS().

Both of these functions concatenate strings, but in slightly different ways. CONCAT() takes two or more quoted strings separated by commas and returns a single string containing all of them joined together.

```
Command Prompt - mysql -h megalon -u root -p
mysql> SELECT CONCAT('I', 'like', 'MySQL');
+------------------------------+
| CONCAT('I', 'like', 'MySQL') |
+------------------------------+
| IlikeMySQL                   |
+------------------------------+
1 row in set (0.00 sec)

mysql>
```

This is a bit better, but is probably not exactly what we had in mind in this case. One possible solution is to insert a new string containing a space in between the strings we're already using, as shown in this example:

```
Command Prompt - mysql -h megalon -u root -p
mysql> SELECT CONCAT('I', ' ', 'like', ' ', 'MySQL');
+----------------------------------------+
| CONCAT('I', ' ', 'like', ' ', 'MySQL') |
+----------------------------------------+
| I like MySQL                           |
+----------------------------------------+
1 row in set (0.00 sec)

mysql>
```

This is a little more like it. But there's a better way: using the CONCAT_WS() function. The "WS" stands for "with separator" and indicates that the first argument is to be inserted as a separator or delimiter between each of the strings to be joined.

```
Command Prompt - mysql -h megalon -u root -p
mysql> SELECT CONCAT_WS(' ', 'I', 'like', 'MySQL');
+--------------------------------------+
| CONCAT_WS(' ', 'I', 'like', 'MySQL') |
+--------------------------------------+
| I like MySQL                         |
+--------------------------------------+
1 row in set (0.00 sec)

mysql>
```

You can see another example of using CONCAT() in the "improved" PHP 4 and Python coding examples in the "Replacing Program Logic with SQL Logic: A Demonstration" section at the beginning of this chapter.

NOTE   *Unlike many programming languages, MySQL does not have a concatenation operator like the & operator in Visual Basic or the . operator in PHP or Perl; you must use CONCAT() or CONCAT_WS() to join strings.*

To extract substrings from strings, use SUBSTRING(), whose syntax can take either of the forms shown here:

```
SUBSTRING(string, position[, length])
SUBSTRING(string FROM position[ FOR length])
```

This function returns the next *length* characters of *string* beginning with the character at *position*, with the first character in *string* at position 1. If *length* is unspecified, then all remaining characters of *string* are included in the returned substring. Here are some examples:

```
Command Prompt - mysql -h megalon -u root -p                    _ □ ×

mysql> SELECT SUBSTRING('crowd', 2);
+-----------------------+
| SUBSTRING('crowd', 2) |
+-----------------------+
| rowd                  |
+-----------------------+
1 row in set (0.00 sec)

mysql> SELECT SUBSTRING('crowd' FROM 2);
+---------------------------+
| SUBSTRING('crowd' FROM 2) |
+---------------------------+
| rowd                      |
+---------------------------+
1 row in set (0.00 sec)

mysql> SELECT SUBSTRING('crowd', 2, 3);
+--------------------------+
| SUBSTRING('crowd', 2, 3) |
+--------------------------+
| row                      |
+--------------------------+
1 row in set (0.00 sec)

mysql> SELECT SUBSTRING('crowd' FROM 2 FOR 3);
+---------------------------------+
| SUBSTRING('crowd' FROM 2 FOR 3) |
+---------------------------------+
| row                             |
+---------------------------------+
1 row in set (0.00 sec)

mysql>
```

There are no differences in behavior between the forms using commas and those using FROM and (optionally) FOR. However, the latter syntax is SQL-92 standard and thus more portable between different databases. In the SQL-92 form, the FROM clause is required.

NOTE MID() *is a synonym for* SUBSTRING(), *takes the same arguments, and works in the same way. However, it's not part of the SQL standard, and so is not likely to be supported in databases other than MySQL.*

You can use a variation on this function, SUBSTRING_INDEX(), to indicate a starting point for a substring in terms of where a given delimiter occurs within the string. Although it's not standard and not found in any other widely used database, it can be extremely handy on occasion. The syntax for calling this function is as follows:

```
SUBSTRING_INDEX(string, delimiter, index)
```

Here, *string* represents the string from which you wish to extract a substring, *delimiter* the delimiter string, and *index* how many occurrences of the *delimiter* to count. If index is positive, the delimiter count is from the left, and everything to the left of the final delimiter is returned; if it is negative, the delimiter count is from the right, and the substring returned is taken from the right of this delimiter, as you can see in the following examples.

```
Command Prompt - mysql -h megalon -u root -p                          _ □ ×
mysql> SELECT
    -> SUBSTRING_INDEX('www.mysite.com/dir/page.html', '/', 1);
+-------------------------------------------------------------+
| SUBSTRING_INDEX('www.mysite.com/dir/page.html', '/', 1) |
+-------------------------------------------------------------+
| www.mysite.com                                              |
+-------------------------------------------------------------+
1 row in set (0.00 sec)
mysql> SELECT
    -> SUBSTRING_INDEX('www.mysite.com/dir/page.html', '/', -1);
+-------------------------------------------------------------+
| SUBSTRING_INDEX('www.mysite.com/dir/page.html', '/', -1) |
+-------------------------------------------------------------+
| page.html                                                   |
+-------------------------------------------------------------+
1 row in set (0.00 sec)
mysql>
```

Another way to extract a substring is by using the RIGHT() function. It takes two arguments—a *string* and an integer *length*—and returns the rightmost *length* characters from *string*.

```
Command Prompt - mysql -h megalon -u root -p                          _ □ ×
mysql> SELECT RIGHT('drawbridge', 6);
+----------------------+
| RIGHT('drawbridge', 6) |
+----------------------+
| bridge               |
+----------------------+
1 row in set (0.00 sec)
mysql>
```

For locating a substring within a given string, you can use LOCATE(), INSTR(), and POSITION(). LOCATE() has this form:

```
LOCATE(substring, string[, position])
```

The function returns the position at which the first occurrence of *substring* is found in *string*. If *position* is specified, the function returns the position at which the first occurrence of *substring* is found in *string* following *position*.

```
Command Prompt - mysql -h megalon -u root -p                          _ |□| x|
mysql> SELECT LOCATE('al', 'alfalfa');
+--------------------------+
| LOCATE('al', 'alfalfa') |
+--------------------------+
|                        1 |
+--------------------------+
1 row in set (0.01 sec)
mysql> SELECT LOCATE('al', 'alfalfa', 2);
+-----------------------------+
| LOCATE('al', 'alfalfa', 2) |
+-----------------------------+
|                           4 |
+-----------------------------+
1 row in set (0.00 sec)
mysql>
```

INSTR() works like LOCATE() with two arguments, except that the order of the arguments is reversed.

```
Command Prompt - mysql -h megalon -u root -p                          _ |□| x|
mysql> SELECT INSTR('alfalfa', 'al');
+-----------------------+
| INSTR('alfalfa', 'al') |
+-----------------------+
|                      1 |
+-----------------------+
1 row in set (0.00 sec)
mysql>
```

The POSITION() function works similarly, except that it has the following syntax:

POSITION(*substring* IN *string*)

```
Command Prompt - mysql -h megalon -u root -p                          _ |□| x|
mysql> SELECT POSITION('al' IN 'alfalfa');
+----------------------------+
| POSITION('al' IN 'alfalfa') |
+----------------------------+
|                           1 |
+----------------------------+
1 row in set (0.00 sec)
mysql>
```

Prior to MySQL 4.0, the functions LOCATE(), INSTR(), and POSITION() were case-sensitive. Since then, they are case-sensitive only if at least one of the *string* or *substring* arguments is a binary string.

NOTE POSITION() *is standard SQL.* LOCATE() *is specific to MySQL.* INSTR() *is supported for compatibility with Oracle.*

Now let's look at some ways to modify strings. These are similar to some of the string-handling functions found in programming languages like Perl, PHP, Visual Basic, and others.

To change the case of a string to uppercase, use UCASE() or UPPER(). To convert it to lowercase, use LCASE() or LOWER().

NOTE UPPER() *and* LOWER() *are standard SQL.* UCASE() *and* LCASE() *are for compatibility with Oracle.*

A common task you'll encounter when working with strings is trimming excess spaces from the beginning or end of a string (or both). LTRIM() returns a string with all leading spaces removed; RTRIM() returns a string with all trailing spaces removed. TRIM() is a bit more sophisticated; it can be used to trim all leading or trailing occurrences of any substring from a string. Here's the complete syntax:

```
TRIM([[LEADING | TRAILING | BOTH] [substring] FROM] string)
```

The best way to explain how this function works is simply to provide a few examples. If *substring* is not specified, a space character is assumed:

```
Command Prompt - mysql -h megalon -u root -p                        _ |□| x|
mysql> SELECT TRIM(LEADING FROM '       b      ') AS s;
+--------+
| s      |
+--------+
| b      |
+--------+
1 row in set (0.01 sec)
mysql> SELECT TRIM(TRAILING FROM '       b      ') AS s;
+--------+
| s      |
+--------+
|       b |
+--------+
1 row in set (0.00 sec)
mysql> SELECT TRIM(BOTH FROM '       b      ') AS s;
+---+
| s |
+---+
| b |
+---+
1 row in set (0.00 sec)
mysql>
```

If LEADING, TRAILING, or BOTH is not specified, BOTH is assumed:

```
Command Prompt - mysql -h megalon -u root -p                        _ |□| x|
mysql> SELECT TRIM('       b      ') AS s;
+---+
| s |
+---+
| b |
+---+
1 row in set (0.00 sec)
mysql>
```

The *substring* may be any group of one or more characters:

```
mysql> SELECT TRIM(LEADING 'x' FROM 'xyzxbxxyzxyz') AS s;
+-------------+
| s           |
+-------------+
| yzxbxxyzxyz |
+-------------+
1 row in set (0.00 sec)

mysql> SELECT TRIM(LEADING 'xyz' FROM 'xyzxbxxyzxyz') AS s;
+-----------+
| s         |
+-----------+
| xbxxyzxyz |
+-----------+
1 row in set (0.00 sec)

mysql> SELECT TRIM(TRAILING 'xyz' FROM 'xyzxbxxyzxyz') AS s;
+--------+
| s      |
+--------+
| xyzxbx |
+--------+
1 row in set (0.00 sec)

mysql> SELECT TRIM('xyz' FROM 'xyzxbxxyzxyz') AS s;
+-----+
| s   |
+-----+
| xbx |
+-----+
1 row in set (0.00 sec)

mysql>
```

> **NOTE**   *All three trimming functions are standard SQL and are supported in most other widely used databases, including SQL Server, Oracle, and PostgreSQL.*

LPAD() and RPAD() do more or less the opposite of LTRIM() and RTRIM(): they pad out a string to a given length with one or more padding characters. LPAD() and RPAD() have the same syntax:

```
LPAD(string, length, padchars)
RPAD(string, length, padchars)
```

Both functions pad the *string* to *length* using the *padchars*. The difference is that LPAD() adds characters to the left of the original string before returning the padded string, and RPAD() adds the padding characters to the right. The following are some examples using LPAD(); RPAD() works essentially the same way.

```
Command Prompt - mysql -h megalon -u root -p                        _ □ X
mysql> SELECT LPAD('score', 10, '+');
+-----------------------+
| LPAD('score', 10, '+') |
+-----------------------+
| +++++score            |
+-----------------------+
1 row in set (0.01 sec)
mysql> SELECT LPAD('score', 10, '+-');
+------------------------+
| LPAD('score', 10, '+-') |
+------------------------+
| +-+-+score             |
+------------------------+
1 row in set (0.00 sec)
mysql>
```

If *length* is less than the length of *string*, then *string* is truncated to *length* and
returned.

```
Command Prompt - mysql -h megalon -u root -p                        _ □ X
mysql> SELECT LPAD('score', 4, '+-');
+----------------------+
| LPAD('score', 4, '+-') |
+----------------------+
| scor                 |
+----------------------+
1 row in set (0.00 sec)
mysql>
```

NOTE LPAD() *and* RPAD() *are nonstandard, but are also supported
in Oracle. However, unlike with the Oracle versions of these func-
tions, the padchars *argument has no default value and* must *be*
specified.

To replace all occurrences of one substring with another within a given
string, you can use the REPLACE() function, which has the following syntax:

REPLACE(*string, substring_from, substring_to*)

Here's an example:

```
Command Prompt - mysql -h megalon -u root -p                        _ □ X
mysql> SELECT REPLACE('fish-fingers', 'fi', 'mu');
+-------------------------------------+
| REPLACE('fish-fingers', 'fi', 'mu') |
+-------------------------------------+
| mush-mungers                        |
+-------------------------------------+
1 row in set (0.00 sec)
mysql>
```

Finally, here are a few miscellaneous string functions you may find useful from time to time:

QUOTE(*string*): Returns a copy of *string* in which all quotation marks have been escaped.

REPEAT(*string, count*): Returns a new string containing *string* repeated *count* times. (Returns an empty string if *count* is less than 1.)

SPACE(*count*): Returns a string consisting of *count* spaces. (Returns an empty string if *count* is less than 1.)

STRCMP(*string1, string2*): Similar to the C language function of the same name, this returns –1 if *string1* sorts before *string2*, 1 if the reverse is true, and 0 if the two strings are the same. It uses the current character set. This function is case-sensitive before MySQL 4.0; in MySQL 4.0 and later, it is case-insensitive unless at least one of the two strings is binary.

REVERSE(*string*): Returns a string with all of the characters in *string* in reverse order. For example, REVERSE('tram') returns the string 'mart'.

We have not provided an exhaustive listing of all of the string functions supported in MySQL, but instead covered those we feel are likely to be useful in helping you move the processing of strings from your application code into your MySQL queries. For a complete list, see the MySQL Manual.

Pattern-Matching and Regular Expressions

An often-overlooked feature of MySQL is its ability to perform pattern-matching, including the use of using regular expressions. For simple pattern-matching, the LIKE operator is used, with the following syntax:

string LIKE *pattern*

This operator yields either a 1 (**TRUE**) or 0 (**FALSE**), depending on whether or not a match for *pattern* is found in *string*. The *pattern* argument supports two wildcards:

- _ (underscore character), for any single character

- % (percent sign), for any group of characters

These wildcards can be used at the beginning, end, or anywhere inside of *pattern*. Here are some examples:

```
Command Prompt - mysql -h megalon -u root -p                    _ □ ×
mysql> SELECT 'man' LIKE 'm_n', 'moon' LIKE 'm_n', 'mood' LIKE 'm_n';
+---------------------+----------------------+----------------------+
| 'man' LIKE 'm_n'    | 'moon' LIKE 'm_n'    | 'mood' LIKE 'm_n'    |
+---------------------+----------------------+----------------------+
|                  1  |                   0  |                   0  |
+---------------------+----------------------+----------------------+
1 row in set (0.00 sec)
mysql> SELECT 'man' LIKE 'm%n', 'moon' LIKE 'm%n', 'mood' LIKE 'm%n';
+---------------------+----------------------+----------------------+
| 'man' LIKE 'm%n'    | 'moon' LIKE 'm%n'    | 'mood' LIKE 'm%n'    |
+---------------------+----------------------+----------------------+
|                  1  |                   1  |                   0  |
+---------------------+----------------------+----------------------+
1 row in set (0.00 sec)
mysql> _
```

NOTE *Unlike some other databases, MySQL does not support the grouping (*[ ]*) or negation (*^*) operators for use with the* LIKE *operator.*

MySQL also supports full-fledged regular expressions, similar to that implemented in a number of programming languages (using the POSIX 1003.2 standard syntax). A *regular expression* is a sequence of characters and/or special characters (known as *pattern modifiers*) that forms a pattern for which a match is sought in a string. In MySQL, you test for a match using the REGEXP operator and this syntax:

string REGEXP *pattern*

This will evaluate as true if a match is found, and false if it is not.

Regular expressions as used in MySQL accept the pattern modifiers shown in Table 4-2.

Table 4-2. MySQL Regular Expression Pattern Modifiers

MODIFIER*	DESCRIPTION
^	Outside any group, marks the beginning of the string to be searched
	Within a group, negates the pattern; for example, [^a-e] matches any character *except* the letters *a*, *b*, *c*, *d*, or *e*
$	End of the string to be searched
.	Matches any single character
*	Zero or more occurrences of the preceding group (equivalent to {0, })

(Continued)

Table 4-2. MySQL Regular Expression Pattern Modifiers (Continued)

MODIFIER*	DESCRIPTION
+	One or more occurrences of the preceding group (equivalent to {1, })
?	Zero or one occurrence of the preceding group (equivalent to {0, 1})
|	Branch operator (OR); for example, dog|cat matches either *dog* or *cat*
()	Encloses an expression; for example, (aeiou) matches the sequence *aeiou*
[]	Encloses a set or range; for example, [1-4] matches any one of the digits 1, 2, 3, or 4; [c-g] matches any one of the letters *c, d, e, f,* or *g;* [aeiou] matches any one of the letters *a, e, i, o,* or *u.* It is possible to combine sets and ranges in a single group; for example, [0-4g] matches any one of the following: *0g, 1g, 2g, 3g,* or *4g.*
{}	Quantifies the preceding group; {*N*} indicates that the group must be repeated *N* times; {*N, M*} indicates that the group may be repeated from *N* to *M* times

* To match a literal occurrence of any of the characters shown in the Modifier column, escape it with a backslash; for example, [why\?] matches the string "why?" (including the question mark). To match a backslash, use a double backslash: \\.

The following are some examples of regular expressions.

```
mysql> SELECT 'man' REGEXP 'm.n', 'moon' REGEXP 'm.n';
+--------------------+---------------------+
| 'man' REGEXP 'm.n' | 'moon' REGEXP 'm.n' |
+--------------------+---------------------+
|                  1 |                   0 |
+--------------------+---------------------+
1 row in set (0.02 sec)

mysql> SELECT 'man' REGEXP 'm.*n', 'moon' REGEXP 'm.*n';
+---------------------+----------------------+
| 'man' REGEXP 'm.*n' | 'moon' REGEXP 'm.*n' |
+---------------------+----------------------+
|                   1 |                    1 |
+---------------------+----------------------+
1 row in set (0.00 sec)

mysql> SELECT 'man' REGEXP 'm.{2}n', 'moon' REGEXP 'm.{2}n';
+-----------------------+------------------------+
| 'man' REGEXP 'm.{2}n' | 'moon' REGEXP 'm.{2}n' |
+-----------------------+------------------------+
|                     0 |                      1 |
+-----------------------+------------------------+
1 row in set (0.00 sec)

mysql> SELECT 'assess' REGEXP '.*ss$', 'assent' REGEXP '.*ss$';
+-------------------------+-------------------------+
| 'assess' REGEXP '.*ss$' | 'assent' REGEXP '.*ss$' |
+-------------------------+-------------------------+
|                       1 |                       0 |
+-------------------------+-------------------------+
1 row in set (0.01 sec)

mysql>
```

MySQL doesn't provide any direct means to return matched expressions (only that a match was or wasn't found), but it's still possible to use REGEXP in WHERE clauses to achieve the same effect, as in the next example.

```
Command Prompt - mysql -h megalon -u root -p                              _ □ ×
mysql> SELECT firstname, lastname
    -> FROM members
    -> WHERE firstname REGEXP '.*l$' LIMIT 10;
+-----------+-----------+
| firstname | lastname  |
+-----------+-----------+
| Rachel    | Hutton    |
| Rachel    | Kerr      |
| Bill      | Matthews  |
| Rachel    | Roberts   |
| Jill      | Yates     |
| Bill      | Kline     |
| Jill      | Cain      |
| Bill      | Buckman   |
| Jill      | King      |
| Jill      | Cheney    |
+-----------+-----------+
10 rows in set (0.02 sec)

mysql>
```

The RLIKE operator is also supported as an alias to REGEXP, and it works in the same way.

TIP   *For complete details on using regular expressions, see the Unix regexp(7) man page. If you're a Windows user, you can find this on the Web at* http://www.unusualresearch.com/regex/regexmanpage.htm.

Date and Time Functions

In the previous chapter, you saw how MySQL's date and time datatypes can save storage space—50% or more over storing dates as strings—but that's not the only reason for using them. One aspect of applications programming that's often troublesome is working with dates. Different programming languages have radically different ways of representing dates and performing date calculations; users and clients have different requirements for how they're displayed. By leveraging MySQL functions that are associated with DATE, TIME, and DATETIME values, you can minimize and sometimes even eliminate many of these problems.

First, let's look at how to get the current date and time. MySQL supports all of the standard SQL functions for this, as well as several others, as shown in Table 4-3.

Table 4-3. Current Date and Time Functions Supported by MySQL

SQL STANDARD	DESCRIPTION	MYSQL ADDITIONS
CURRENT_DATE	Current date in *YYYY-MM-DD* format (server time)	CURRENT_DATE(), CURDATE()
CURRENT_TIME	Current time in *HH:MM:SS* format (server time)	CURRENT_TIME(), CURTIME()
CURRENT_TIMESTAMP	Current timestamp in *YYYY-MM-DD HH:MM:SS* format (server time)	CURRENT_TIMESTAMP(), NOW(), SYSDATE()*
	Current timestamp in Unix format (seconds elapsed since 1970-01-01 00:00:00) (server time)	UNIX_TIMESTAMP()
	Current UTC date in *YYYY-MM-DD* format	UTC_DATE**, UTC_DATE()**
	Current UTC time in *HH:MM:SS* format	UTC_TIME**, UTC_TIME()**
	Current UTC timestamp in *YYYY-MM-DD HH:MM:SS* format	UTC_TIMESTAMP**, UTC_TIMESTAMP()**

* SYSDATE() is supported to provide compatibility with Oracle.

** The UTC functions were added in MySQL 4.1.1.

Note that functions expecting a TIME value will generally accept DATETIME values while ignoring the date part. Functions that expect a DATE value will generally accept a DATETIME value and ignore the time portion of the value.

It's somewhat customary in MySQL to use NOW(), CURDATE(), and CURTIME(), since these are short and convenient. However, if compatibility with other databases is an issue, you should use the standard SQL functions instead. To convert from a Unix-style timestamp to date/time format, use the FROM_UNIXTIME() function.

If you call any functions returning the current date and/or time in the same query, they will always return the same date and/or time.

```
Command Prompt - mysql -h megalon -u root -p
mysql> SELECT CURRENT_DATE, CURRENT_TIME,
    -> CURRENT_TIMESTAMP, UNIX_TIMESTAMP(),
    -> FROM_UNIXTIME(UNIX_TIMESTAMP())\G
*************************** 1. row ***************************
          CURRENT_DATE: 2004-08-02
          CURRENT_TIME: 23:36:19
     CURRENT_TIMESTAMP: 2004-08-02 23:36:19
      UNIX_TIMESTAMP(): 1091453779
FROM_UNIXTIME(UNIX_TIMESTAMP()): 2004-08-02 23:36:19
1 row in set (0.02 sec)

mysql>
```

Date and Time Formatting and Extraction

If your application doesn't need to support multiple locales or languages, you can perform most, if not all, of your date formatting in your queries using the DATE_FORMAT() function, which takes this form:

DATE_FORMAT(*date, format*)

where *date* is a date, and *format* is a string containing one or more format specifiers and optional additional punctuation marks. Table 4-4 shows a partial listing of the available format specifiers.

Table 4-4. Some Format Specifiers for DATE_FORMAT() and Date Arithmetic Functions

SPECIFIER*	FORMAT
%a	Three-letter day of week (Sun, Mon, Tue, and so on)
%b	Three-letter name of month (Jan, Feb, Mar, and so on)
%c	Month number (0–12)
%D	Day of month with ordinal suffix (0th, 1st, 2nd, 3rd, and so on)
%d	Two-digit day of month (00–31)
%e	Day of month (0–31)
%f	Microseconds (000000–999999)
%H	Two-digit hour (00–23)
%h or %I	Two-digit hour (01–12)
%i	Minutes (00–59)
%j	Day of year (001–366)
%k	Hour (0–23)
%l	Hour (1–12)
%M	Full month name (January, February, March, and so on)
%m	Two-digit month number (00–12)
%p	AM/PM
%r	12-hour time in *HH:MM:SS XM* format
%S or %s	Seconds (00–59)

(Continued)

*Table 4-4. Some Format Specifiers for DATE_FORMAT() and
Date Arithmetic Functions (Continued)*

SPECIFIER*	FORMAT
%T	24-hour time in *HH:MM:SS* format
%U	Week of year (00–53), where Sunday is the first day of the week
%u	Week of year (00–53), where Monday is the first day of the week
%W	Full day of week (Sunday, Monday, Tuesday, and so on)
%w	Day of the week (0–6, where 0=Sunday)
%Y	Four-digit year
%y	Two-digit year

*These specifiers return the names of days and months in English.

The following are a few examples of formatting dates.

```
Command Prompt - mysql -h megalon -u root -p

mysql> SELECT DATE_FORMAT(CURRENT_DATE, '%W, %M %D, %Y');
+-------------------------------------------+
| DATE_FORMAT(CURRENT_DATE, '%W, %M %D, %Y') |
+-------------------------------------------+
| Monday, August 2nd, 2004                  |
+-------------------------------------------+
1 row in set (0.00 sec)

mysql> SELECT DATE_FORMAT(CURRENT_TIMESTAMP, '%a %e-%b-%y %T');
+------------------------------------------------+
| DATE_FORMAT(CURRENT_TIMESTAMP, '%a %e-%b-%y %T') |
+------------------------------------------------+
| Mon 2-Aug-04 23:43:44                          |
+------------------------------------------------+
1 row in set (0.00 sec)

mysql> SELECT
    ->   CONCAT(
    ->          'Day ',
    ->          DATE_FORMAT(CURRENT_DATE, '%j'),
    ->          ' of the year ',
    ->          DATE_FORMAT(CURRENT_DATE, '%Y')
    ->         ) AS today;
+-----------------------+
| today                 |
+-----------------------+
| Day 215 of the year 2004 |
+-----------------------+
1 row in set (0.00 sec)

mysql>
```

TIP   *If you need to return only a formatted time, you can also use
the* TIME_FORMAT() *function. It accepts any of the time-related format
specifiers shown in Table 4-4.*

You can use practically any punctuation you like in formatting dates: commas, dashes, slashes, spaces, and so on. However, you cannot use alphanumeric characters except as part of a format specifier. In addition, you can return a date, time, or date/time value as a number with no formatting whatsoever, simply by forcing it to be evaluated in a numeric context. This will work with any of the functions shown in Table 4-3, as shown in the following example.

```
Command Prompt - mysql -h megalon -u root -p                    _ □ x
mysql> SELECT CURRENT_DATE + 0;
+------------------+
| CURRENT_DATE + 0 |
+------------------+
|         20040802 |
+------------------+
1 row in set (0.00 sec)

mysql>
```

Formatting dates can be even easier in MySQL 4.1.1 and above, using the GET_FORMAT() function. This function returns format strings for a number of locales:

```
GET_FORMAT(DATE|TIME|DATETIME, locale)
```

The *locale* argument can take one of several predefined values: 'EUR', 'USA', 'JIS', 'ISO', and 'INTERNAL'. GET_FORMAT() can be used in place of a format string wherever one is applicable. Here are some examples:

```
Command Prompt - mysql -h megalon -u root -p                    _ □ x
mysql> SELECT
    ->     DATE_FORMAT(
    ->                 CURRENT_DATE,
    ->                 GET_FORMAT(DATE, 'EUR')
    ->                 )\G
*************************** 1. row ***************************
DATE_FORMAT(
            CURRENT_DATE,
            GET_FORMAT(DATE, 'EUR')
            ): 02.08.2004
1 row in set (0.01 sec)

mysql> SELECT
    ->     DATE_FORMAT(
    ->                 SUBDATE('2004-05-25', 45),
    ->                 GET_FORMAT(DATE, 'USA')
    ->                 )\G
*************************** 1. row ***************************
DATE_FORMAT(
            SUBDATE('2004-05-25', 45),
            GET_FORMAT(DATE, 'USA')
            ): 04.10.2004
1 row in set (0.00 sec)

mysql> _
```

The SUBDATE() function employed in the second example is used to subtract dates, as discussed in the "Date Arithmetic" section later in this chapter.

You can also obtain the various parts of a date, time, or datetime as a number using the functions shown in Table 4-5.

CAUTION *The* WEEK() *function exhibits incorrect behavior in MySQL versions previous to 4.0, where the* mode *argument is the default (0). See the MySQL documentation for details. We suggest that you use* WEEKOFYEAR() *instead if it's available to you (MySQL 4.1.1 and above).*

Table 4-5. Functions Returning Portions of Date, Time, or Date/Time Values

FUNCTION	VALUE RETURNED
DAYNAME()	Name of the day of the week (English)
DAYOFMONTH(), DAY()	Day of the month (DAY() was added in MySQL 4.1.1)
DAYOFWEEK()	Number of the day of the week (1=Sunday, 7=Saturday)
DAYOFYEAR()	Day of the year as a number
HOUR()	Hours portion of the time (added in MySQL 4.1.1)
MINUTE()	Minutes portion of the time
MONTH()	Month portion of the date (1=January)
MONTHNAME()	Name of the month (in English); if the date holds a 0 for the month, this function returns NULL
QUARTER()	Quarter of the year (1–4)
SECOND()	Seconds from time
TIME()	Time portion of a date/time (added in MySQL 4..1.1)
WEEK()*	Week of the year (1–53)
WEEKDAY()	Day of the week (0=Monday, 6=Sunday)
WEEKOFYEAR()	Week of the year, the week reckoned as beginning on Monday (added in MySQL 4.1.1)
YEAR()	Four-digit year (1000–9999)

* The WEEK() function takes an optional second *mode* argument. The behavior of this function also changed significantly in MySQL 4.0; see the MySQL Manual for details.

Another means of extracting portions of dates and times is to use the EXTRACT() function, which takes this form:

```
EXTRACT(type FROM date)
```

It returns a number corresponding to the part of the *date* argument specified by *type*. The *type* argument is the name of one of the following units of time: MICROSECOND, SECOND, MINUTE, HOUR, DAY, WEEK, MONTH, QUARTER, or YEAR. MICROSECOND was added in MySQL 4.1.1; WEEK and QUARTER were added in MySQL 5.0.0. (The *date* argument is a date or date/time value in standard format.) Here are some examples:

```
Command Prompt - mysql -h megalon -u root -p                          _ □ ×
mysql> SELECT EXTRACT(HOUR FROM '2004-05-15 15:35:25');
+-----------------------------------------+
| EXTRACT(HOUR FROM '2004-05-15 15:35:25') |
+-----------------------------------------+
|                                       15 |
+-----------------------------------------+
1 row in set (0.00 sec)
mysql> SELECT EXTRACT(MONTH FROM '2004-05-15');
+---------------------------------+
| EXTRACT(MONTH FROM '2004-05-15') |
+---------------------------------+
|                               5 |
+---------------------------------+
1 row in set (0.00 sec)
mysql>
```

If a time value is missing when you use EXTRACT(), it returns 0.

```
Command Prompt - mysql -h megalon -u root -p                          _ □ ×
mysql> SELECT EXTRACT(HOUR FROM '2004-05-15');
+--------------------------------+
| EXTRACT(HOUR FROM '2004-05-15') |
+--------------------------------+
|                              0 |
+--------------------------------+
1 row in set (0.00 sec)
mysql>
```

In addition, the following compound types are permitted: MINUTE_SECOND, HOUR_SECOND, HOUR_MINUTE, DAY_SECOND, DAY_MINUTE, DAY_HOUR, and YEAR_MONTH. Each of these actually specifies a complete set of values; that is, any values that would normally be expected are filled in. For example, if you use HOUR_SECOND for the type, MySQL returns the hours, minutes, and seconds as a number.

```
Command Prompt - mysql -h megalon -u root -p                          _ □ ×
mysql> SELECT EXTRACT(HOUR_SECOND FROM '2004-05-15 15:35:25');
+------------------------------------------------+
| EXTRACT(HOUR_SECOND FROM '2004-05-15 15:35:25') |
+------------------------------------------------+
|                                         153525 |
+------------------------------------------------+
1 row in set (0.00 sec)
mysql>
```

MySQL 4.1.1 and above also supports these compound types, which include microseconds: SECOND_MICROSECOND, MINUTE_MICROSECOND, HOUR_MICROSECOND, and

DAY_MICROSECOND. These also fill in the missing units from the range, as in this example:

```
EXTRACT(DAY_MICROSECOND FROM '2004-05-15 15:35:25.104528')
```

This returns the value 151535250104528.

> **NOTE** *All of the type specifiers mentioned in this section can also be used with date arithmetic functions such as* DATE_ADD(). *See the "Date Arithmetic" section later in this chapter.*

Date and Time Conversion Functions

MySQL also has some handy date and time conversion functions:

FROM_DAYS(*days*): Takes a number of days since 0000-00-00 and returns a date in *YYYY-MM-DD* format. The minimum value accepted by this function is 366, which yields '0001-01-01'; however, you should not use this function for dates preceding the advent of the Gregorian calendar (1582 in Western Europe; 1917 in Russia) in any case, as it does not take the conversion from Julian to Gregorian reckoning into account.

FROM_UNIXTIME(*unix_timestamp[, formatstring]*): Takes a Unix timestamp and returns a date/time formatted according to a *formatstring* using the same format specifiers as the DATE_FORMAT() function (see Table 4-4); the format defaults to standard Unix date/time format.

MAKEDATE(*year, day*): Takes a year and a day of that year and returns a date in Unix format. Note that day may be greater than 366 and MySQL will calculate the year accordingly in the return value; for example, MAKEDATE(2003, 366) returns '2004-01-01'.

MAKETIME(*hours, minutes, seconds*): Returns a time in standard format. Unlike MAKEDATE(), passing out-of-range values to this function will result in a NULL value. (Added in MySQL 4.1.1.)

SEC_TO_TIME(*seconds*): Takes a number of seconds and returns a time in standard Unix (*HH:MM:SS*) format.

STR_TO_DATE(*datestring, formatstring*): The inverse of DATE_FORMAT(); takes a formatted *datestring* and *formatstring* (using the specifiers for DATE_FORMAT()) and returns a date or date/time in standard format. (Added in MySQL 4.1.1.)

`TIME_TO_SEC(hours, minutes, seconds)`: Takes a time in *HH:MM:SS* format and returns a number of seconds. If either the minutes or seconds value is greater than 59, the function returns `NULL`. The upper limit for the *hours* argument is at least 10^{21}.

`TO_DAYS(date)`: The inverse of `FROM_DAYS()`; takes a date string in Unix format and returns the number of days since 0000-00-00. Like `FROM_DAYS()`, this function is not reliable for dates prior to the adoption of the Gregorian calendar in the sixteenth century.

`UNIX_TIMESTAMP(date)`: Returns a Unix timestamp for a `DATE` or `DATETIME` value; can also accept an integer representing a date in *YYYYMMDD* format. Note that the returned value is an unsigned integer. Out-of-range dates will return 0; the year must be between 1970 and 2037 inclusive.

Date Arithmetic

You have two choices when it comes to performing date arithmetic in MySQL:

- Converting dates and times into a common unit before performing the calculation. This isn't that hard to do, and there are times—for instance, when making comparisons in a `WHERE` clause—when it's desirable. However, when you're interested in obtaining a nicely formatted final result, it can be quite cumbersome.

- Using the `INTERVAL` operator alone or in conjunction with the `DATE_ADD()` and `DATE_SUB()` functions. This is generally what you want to do when you need to pass the results of date calculations back to the application. The advantage here is that MySQL automatically returns the results in standard `date`, `time`, or `datetime` format, which can save you a lot of overhead.

Let's look at an example illustrating the first option. Suppose our firm's billing department wants a report of accounts that have unpaid orders that are more than three months old. We need to extract this information from an **orders** table, a partial definition of which might be as follows:

```
CREATE TABLE orders (
  order_id INT AUTO_INCREMENT PRIMARY KEY,
  acct_id  INT UNSIGNED NOT NULL,
  order_date DATE NOT NULL,
  order_amt DECIMAL(8, 2) NOT NULL,
  last_pmt_date DATE NOT NULL,
  order_balance DECIMAL(8, 2) NOT NULL
);
```

For purposes of this set of examples, we'll ignore the possibility that any negative amounts might be stored in the **order_amt** or **order_balance** columns due to refunds or other adjustments. Also, we won't worry about creating any indexes or the fact that this does not represent a fully normalized database schema, since we should really have a separate **payments** table.

NOTE   *In this first example, we also assume that when the order is placed, the last payment date is set to the same value as the order date. The reason for this is that* TO_DAYS('0000-00-00') *returns* NULL.

We need to find all the records for which the last payment date is at least 120 days in the past, and for which there remains an unpaid balance. The unpaid balance part is simple enough—we'll just need a balance > 0 constraint in the WHERE clause. To determine whether a date is more than 120 days in the past, we can use the TO_DAYS() function to convert both the date column and the current date into numbers of days, subtract, and then compare the difference to 120. The resulting query might look something like this:

```
SELECT acct_id, SUM(balance) AS total
FROM orders
WHERE balance > 0
AND TO_DAYS(CURRENT_DATE) - TO_DAYS(last_pmt_date) > 120
GROUP BY acct_id;
```

We've used the SUM() function with a GROUP BY clause in order to produce a listing with one entry per delinquent account, with the total past due for all orders made by that account.

NOTE   *Beginning with MySQL 4.1.1, you can also use the* DATE_DIFF() *function to rewrite* TO_DAYS(CURRENT_DATE) - TO_DAYS(last_pmt_date) > 120 *as* DATE_DIFF(CURRENT_DATE, last_pmt_date) > 120.

Using data from the same **orders** table, we want to do a weekly billing for all new orders from the previous week and in each case show a due date 30 days from the date of the order. We won't worry about whether there's a balance showing on the account, only whether an order was placed in the last seven days. Using the INTERVAL operator makes this much easier than you might think:

```
SELECT acct_id, SUM(balance) AS total,
  MAX(order_date) + INTERVAL 30 DAY AS due_date
```

```
FROM orders
WHERE order_date + INTERVAL 7 DAY >= CURRENT_DATE
GROUP BY acct_id;
```

Alternatively, depending on the exact requirements, we might be able to use this:

```
SELECT acct_id, SUM(balance) AS total,
  MAX(order_date) + INTERVAL 1 MONTH as due_date
FROM orders
WHERE order_date + INTERVAL 1 WEEK >= CURRENT_DATE
GROUP BY acct_id;
```

As we indicated earlier, we can also use INTERVAL in conjunction with MySQL's date arithmetic functions:

```
DATE_ADD(date, INTERVAL expression type)
DATE_SUB(date, INTERVAL expression type)
```

DATE_ADD() returns the date obtained by adding the interval specified by *expression type* to *date*. The *expression* is simply any legal MySQL expression that evaluates to a number. The value used for *date* can be any valid DATE, TIME, or DATETIME value. DATE_SUB() does the same calculation, except that it returns the date obtained by subtracting the specified interval. In all of these cases, the *type* argument is any of the values that can be used with EXTRACT() (see Table 4-5). The following are some examples of using the date arithmetic functions.

Synonymous with these functions are ADDDATE() and SUBDATE(), whose arguments follow the same rules.

```
Command Prompt - mysql -h megalon -u root -p                        _ □ ×
mysql> SELECT ADDDATE('2003-04-14', INTERVAL 11 MONTH);
+-------------------------------------------+
| ADDDATE('2003-04-14', INTERVAL 11 MONTH) |
+-------------------------------------------+
| 2004-03-14                                |
+-------------------------------------------+
1 row in set (0.01 sec)

mysql> SELECT SUBDATE(
    ->                 '2004-03-15 09:25:30',
    ->                 INTERVAL '08:15:15' HOUR_SECOND
    ->               )\G
*************************** 1. row ***************************
SUBDATE(
                '2004-03-15 09:25:30',
                INTERVAL '08:15:15' HOUR_SECOND
              ): 2004-03-15 01:10:15
1 row in set (0.00 sec)

mysql>
```

As you can see from the second query in the preceding examples, there's nothing wrong with using compound *type* specifiers with these functions, as long as you observe the rules explained in our earlier discussion of the EXTRACT() function.

Should you choose ADDDATE() and SUBDATE() over DATE_ADD() and DATE_SUB()? In many cases, it doesn't make any difference; however, beginning with MySQL 4.1.1, ADDDATE() and SUBDATE() have been enhanced somewhat with a simplified alternative syntax when working with numbers of days:

ADDDATE(*date*, *days*)
SUBDATE(*date*, *days*)

Here are a few examples:

```
Command Prompt - mysql -h megalon -u root -p                        _ □ ×
mysql> SELECT ADDDATE('2004-05-25', 12);
+---------------------------+
| ADDDATE('2004-05-25', 12) |
+---------------------------+
| 2004-06-06                |
+---------------------------+
1 row in set (0.00 sec)

mysql> SELECT SUBDATE('2004-05-25', 165);
+----------------------------+
| SUBDATE('2004-05-25', 165) |
+----------------------------+
| 2003-12-12                 |
+----------------------------+
1 row in set (0.00 sec)

mysql> SELECT NOW(), SUBDATE(NOW(), 30);
+---------------------+---------------------+
| NOW()               | SUBDATE(NOW(), 30)  |
+---------------------+---------------------+
| 2004-08-03 00:06:40 | 2004-07-04 00:06:40 |
+---------------------+---------------------+
1 row in set (0.00 sec)

mysql>
```

This shorthand notation is not available with DATE_ADD() and DATE_SUB().

So, as you can see, quite a lot of the work required for date calculations, conversions, and even representations can be handled in queries rather than in application code. Your time spent in learning these and making use of them will generally be well spent.

Other MySQL Functions

In this section, we'll discuss a few miscellaneous functions that don't fit in very well elsewhere, but which you may find useful in your quest to replace program logic with SQL logic for optimization purposes.

How Many Rows Actually Matched?

Sometimes when you've used a LIMIT clause in a SELECT query, it's also handy to know how many rows would have been returned had the LIMIT not been used. In order to do this, first execute the query using the SQL_CALC_FOUND_ROWS option, followed by a SELECT FOUND_ROWS() query. The second query will return the number of *all* rows meeting the conditions set in the query, without the LIMIT clause.

```
Command Prompt - mysql -h megalon -u root -p
mysql> SELECT SQL_CALC_FOUND_ROWS * FROM members
    -> WHERE lastname LIKE 's%' LIMIT 1;
+-----------+----------+------------+
| firstname | lastname | dob        |
+-----------+----------+------------+
| Mary      | Stephens | 1980-05-00 |
+-----------+----------+------------+
1 row in set (0.06 sec)

mysql> SELECT FOUND_ROWS();
+--------------+
| FOUND_ROWS() |
+--------------+
|         1009 |
+--------------+
1 row in set (0.01 sec)

mysql>
```

For example, when displaying a heading such as "Displaying 1 through 10 of 22,052 records," this approach is often faster and less cumbersome than writing a separate query using the COUNT() function.

IP Address Conversion

The INET_ATON() and INET_NTOA() functions convert an IP address string in dotted-quad format to an integer and back again.

```
Command Prompt - mysql -h megalon -u root -p                    _ □ x
mysql> SELECT INET_ATON('192.168.0.120');
+---------------------------+
| INET_ATON('192.168.0.120') |
+---------------------------+
|                3232235640 |
+---------------------------+
1 row in set (0.00 sec)
mysql> SELECT INET_NTOA(3232235640);
+----------------------+
| INET_NTOA(3232235640) |
+----------------------+
| 192.168.0.120        |
+----------------------+
1 row in set (0.00 sec)
mysql>
```

Often, you need to keep IP addresses in logs in your applications. These two functions let you save a bit of space while doing so, since an IP address stored as a string requires *at least* 8 bytes of storage (and as many as 16 bytes), but when converted to an integer, it takes up 8 bytes and 8 bytes only.

What was the Last ID Inserted?

This LAST_INSERT_ID() function returns the last value generated for an AUTO_INCREMENT column for the current connection. It can be useful when inserting records into linked tables. For example, suppose that we've just accepted an order from a new customer, so that we need to insert a new record into a **customers** table and then a related record into an **orders** table. Assuming that the **customerid** column has the AUTO_INCREMENT modifier applied to it in the table definition, we could accomplish this like so:

```
INSERT INTO customers (customerid, lastname, firstname)
  VALUES ('', 'Smith', 'William');
INSERT INTO orders (orderid, customerid, orderdate)
  VALUES ('', LAST_INSERT_ID(), CURRENT_DATE);
```

The value returned by LAST_INSERT_ID() persists for the lifetime of the connection, so we could have done other things between the first INSERT query and the second without altering what was inserted into the **customerid** column of the new record in the **orders** table.

TIP *The value returned by* LAST_INSERT_ID() *is exclusive to each connection, and it's not affected by inserts performed by other connections, even on the same tables. In other words, concurrency is* never *an issue when using this function.*

User Variables

It's a common programming practice to store values returned from queries in the application space for reuse. However, this can often be done within MySQL itself by means of user variables. A *user variable* (identified by a leading @ sign) can contain any scalar value and lasts for the lifetime of the current connection. It can be named using any combination of alphanumeric characters and may include the $ (dollar sign), _ (underscore), and . (period) characters.

You have two options for setting the value of a user variable:

- The SET statement, which simply takes the form SET *@varname* = *value*;. *value* can be any legal MySQL expression that evaluates to a scalar value.

- Within queries, you can use *@varname*:=*value*. In this case, the expression used for *value* can also include one or more column names.

Once the value of a user variable is set, you can use it in any expression. Here is an example that works in MySQL 4.1.1 and newer:

```
Command Prompt - mysql -h megalon -u root -p                    _ □ ×

mysql> SET @three = 3;
Query OK, 0 rows affected (0.01 sec)

mysql> SELECT @days := DATEDIFF(CURRENT_DATE, '2004-01-01');
+-----------------------------------------------+
| @days := DATEDIFF(CURRENT_DATE, '2004-01-01') |
+-----------------------------------------------+
|                                           215 |
+-----------------------------------------------+
1 row in set (0.00 sec)

mysql> SELECT @days + @three;
+----------------+
| @days + @three |
+----------------+
|            218 |
+----------------+
1 row in set (0.00 sec)

mysql>
```

A user variable may hold any scalar type, including integers, floating-point numbers, strings, and dates. You can set a user variable's value using an expression containing other user variables, as well as values derived from other functions.

```
Command Prompt - mysql -h megalon -u root -p                    _ □ X
mysql> SELECT @days + @three;
+----------------+
| @days + @three |
+----------------+
|            218 |
+----------------+
1 row in set (0.00 sec)

mysql> SET @cutoff = '1980-06-01';
Query OK, 0 rows affected (0.00 sec)

mysql> SELECT @triple := @three * COUNT(*) FROM members
    -> WHERE dob > @cutoff;
+------------------------------+
| @triple := @three * COUNT(*) |
+------------------------------+
|                         3480 |
+------------------------------+
1 row in set (0.07 sec)

mysql> SELECT @triple;
+---------+
| @triple |
+---------+
| 3480    |
+---------+
1 row in set (0.00 sec)

mysql>
```

CAUTION   *Never try to set a user variable and then use its value in a* GROUP BY, ORDER BY, *or* HAVING *clause in the same statement. The results of such a query are unpredictable.*

Notice that you're not limited (as is sometimes imagined) to setting user variables in SELECT queries, as you can see in the next example.

```
Command Prompt - mysql -h megalon -u root -p                    _ □ X
mysql> INSERT INTO members
    -> VALUES ('Jim', @lname := 'Smith', '1982-01-25');
Query OK, 1 row affected (0.00 sec)

mysql> SELECT @lname, COUNT(*) FROM members
    -> WHERE lastname = @lname;
+--------+----------+
| @lname | COUNT(*) |
+--------+----------+
| Smith  |      130 |
+--------+----------+
1 row in set (0.06 sec)

mysql>
```

Unfortunately, in web applications, you cannot preserve values between pages by means of MySQL user variables, because each new page load creates its own connection. Even if you use persistent connections, you're almost certain to get the value for a user variable of the same name that was set using a different connection (or a null value in the case where a new connection was established). MySQL won't let you choose a connection identifier, nor can you create or set arbitrary global variables. Even so, user variables can still be useful for multiple queries within the same page and, as you'll see in the example in the next section, for aliasing columns and intermediate results within queries where you can't use real aliases.

Branching: Making Choices in Queries

Branching is obviously an area with a wealth of potential when it comes to replacing programming logic with SQL logic. So, in this section, we present some useful MySQL branching methods with this goal in mind.

No programming or scripting language would be very useful if it didn't provide a way to execute different instructions depending on the outcome of a test condition, such as whether one value is greater than another. MySQL is similar in this regard. It has four flow-control operators that you can use to choose between values based on how one or more conditions are evaluated: IF(), IFNULL(), NULLIF(), and CASE.

True/False Branching with IF()

The IF() operator has the following syntax:

```
IF(test_expression, true_result, false_result)
```

The IF() operator takes three expressions as arguments. If *test_expression* evaluates as true (or 1), than it returns *true_result*; otherwise, *false_result* is returned. Here is a fairly simple example:

Let's look at a slightly more complex scenario. Suppose as part of an e-commerce web site, we have a **products** table defined in part like this:

```
CREATE TABLE products (
  Product_id INT AUTO_INCREMENT PRIMARY KEY,
  product_price DECIMAL(6, 2),
  product_weight DECIMAL(5, 2)
);
```

As part of the checkout process, we need to determine shipping according to the following conditions: if the price of a product is greater than $100 or if the weight of the product is less than 500 grams (0.5 kg), then no charges for shipping are added; otherwise, we add a shipping charge of $4.50 per kilo for any weight in excess of 500 grams.

```
SELECT @p:=product_price AS p, @w:=product_weight AS w,
  @s:=IF(@p > 100.00 OR @w > 0.5, 0, @w * 4.50) AS s, FORMAT(@p + @s, 2) AS t
FROM products
WHERE product_id=productid;
```

When we test this with a bit of sample data, here's the result:

We employed some user variables to get around the problems that arise when trying to use column aliases to define other columns in the same query.

Null-based Branching with IFNULL()

The IFNULL() operator has the following syntax:

```
IFNULL(expression1, expression2)
```

The way the IFNULL() function works may seem a bit counterintuitive: If *expression1* is not NULL, then it is returned; otherwise, *expression2* is returned. You could express the same logic using IF() and NOT IS NULL:

```
IF(NOT IS NULL expression1, expression1, expression2)
```

For example, consider an **orders** table for which a partial definition might be like this:

```
CREATE TABLE orders (
    orderid INT AUTO_INCREMENT PRIMARY KEY,
    acctid INT NOT NULL,
    orderdate DATE NOT NULL,
    shipdate DATE NULL
);
```

To produce a list of recent orders (say within the past 30 days) showing which ones have been and haven't yet been shipped, we could use something like this:

```
SELECT orderid, acctid, IFNULL(shipdate, 'PENDING') AS Shipped
FROM orders
WHERE orderdate >= SUBDATE(CURRENT_DATE, INTERVAL 1 MONTH);
```

Expression Relation-based Branching with NULLIF()

The NULLIF() operator has the following syntax:

```
NULLIF(expression1, expression2)
```

This function tests the relation *expression1 = expression2* and if the result is true (1), then the function returns NULL; otherwise, it returns *expression2*. This could also be written as the following:

```
IF(expression1 = expression2, NULL, expression2)
```

or, as you'll see shortly, like this:

```
CASE WHEN expression1 = expression2 THEN NULL ELSE expression2 END
```

The NULLIF() function may not prove to be as efficient a method as some others in many circumstances. This is because if *expression1* and *expression2* are equal, then *expression2* will actually be evaluated twice.

CASE-based Branching

The CASE structure can be used to test an expression against one or more other expressions in a series and to return one of any number of different values based on the outcome. It works in a manner similar to that of the if ... then ... else ... construct found in most programming and scripting languages.

There are two different versions of CASE.

Multiple Conditions with CASE

One version of CASE is as follows:

```
CASE WHEN condition THEN result
[ELSE else_result | WHEN condition2 THEN result2
[ELSE else_result2 | WHEN...] ]
END
```

In the simplest instance, the *condition* is tested, and if true, then the *result* following the THEN keyword is returned. If *condition* is not true, then NULL is returned. You can override the latter behavior by including an ELSE clause; in this case, if condition is false, then the *else_result* expression value is returned instead of NULL. For example, we could rewrite the example we used for IFNULL() like this:

```
SELECT orderid, acctid,
  CASE
    WHEN shipdate IS NULL
    THEN 'PENDING'
    ELSE shipdate
  END AS Shipped
FROM orders
WHERE orderdate >= SUBDATE(CURRENT_DATE, INTERVAL 1 MONTH);
```

This is a bit more verbose than the IFNULL() version, but it's also easier to read, particularly with the line breaks and indentation we've added here.

We could make the example a bit more selective by introducing additional WHEN ... THEN ... clauses. Using something like the following, we can return "ORDER PENDING" if no shipping date has yet been set, "ORDER SHIPPED ON ..." plus the shipping date if the shipping date is in the past, "FUTURE" if the shipping date is in the future, and "SHIP TODAY" if the shipping date matches today's date:

```
SELECT orderid, acctid, @s := shipdate,
  CASE
    WHEN @s IS NULL THEN 'ORDER PENDING'
    WHEN @s < CURRENT_DATE THEN CONCAT('ORDER SHIPPED ON ', @s)
    WHEN @s > CURRENT_DATE THEN 'FUTURE'
    ELSE 'SHIP TODAY'
  END AS Shipped
FROM orders
WHERE orderdate >= SUBDATE(CURRENT_DATE, INTERVAL 1 MONTH);
```

You'll notice that the result set includes an extra column for the shipping date; very shortly (in the "Our Demonstration Revisited" section), we'll show you how to get rid of this if you don't need it.

> **NOTE**   *A given* CASE *structure may contain any number of* WHEN... THEN... *clauses and a maximum of one* ELSE *clause.*

Comparisons with CASE

The other form of CASE is as follows:

```
CASE expression WHEN value THEN result
[ELSE else_result | WHEN value2 THEN result2
[ELSE else_result2 | WHEN...] ]
END
```

This compares an *expression* to a *value*, both of which can be any valid MySQL expressions, and returns *result* if the two are equal. Otherwise, either NULL or an *else_result* is returned, depending on whether or not an ELSE clause follows.

Here is an example:

```
SELECT
  CASE order_date
    WHEN last_pmt_date
    THEN 'YES'
    ELSE 'NO'
  END AS pmt_status
FROM orders;
```

The CASE block will evaluate to 'YES' if the **order_date** and **last_pmt_date** columns for a given record hold the same value, and 'NO' if they don't.

> **NOTE**   *The syntax for* CASE *varies somewhat from what we've shown in this chapter when it's used inside stored procedures in MySQL 5.0 and later. See Chapter 8 for more information.*

What About Loops?

Given what we've just seen in the way of decision-making capabilities, you might expect that there would be some sort of mechanism for performing iterations as well. However, MySQL does not support loops in (normal) queries. In fact, up until MySQL 5.0, it didn't support any sort of looping constructs at all. Beginning with that version, it's possible to use loops inside stored procedures and user-defined functions. In Chapter 8, we'll examine the constructs used for this purpose.

Our Demonstration Revisited

Let's look again at the query we used at the beginning of this chapter:

```
SELECT
  CONCAT(firstname, ' ', lastname) AS name,
  CASE
    WHEN (@age := YEAR(CURRENT_DATE) - YEAR(dob)) > 65 THEN 'Over 65'
    WHEN @age >= 45 THEN '45-64'
    WHEN @age >= 30 THEN '30-44'
    WHEN @age >= 18 THEN '18-29'
    ELSE 'Under 18'
  END AS age_range
FROM members
ORDER BY lastname, firstname;
```

While it may look complicated, it actually just returns two columns, aliased as **name** and **age_range**. The first of these is relatively simple: we simply concatenate the **firstname** and **lastname** columns with a space in between and return the result as **name**. This is obviously more efficient because we return just one column instead of two.

The **age_range** column appears a bit more complex. Let's look at the first WHEN clause by itself:

```
WHEN (@age := YEAR(CURRENT_DATE) - YEAR(dob)) > 65 THEN 'Over 65'
```

Here's the "trick" that we alluded to earlier: Since we're not interested in the actual age of each member, but only in the age category to which he or she belongs, we set a user variable **@age** in the first WHEN clause, and then use that value in each of the succeeding ones. Since we're not trying to use this value in a GROUP BY, ORDER BY, or HAVING clause, we can do this; the value will remain constant (unless we explicitly set it to another value). Notice that we place the expression in which the value of **@age** is to be set (the difference in years between the year of birth and the current one) inside parentheses. Otherwise, **@age** would be set to the value of the expression YEAR(CURRENT_DATE) - YEAR(dob) > 65; that is, either 1 or 0 (**TRUE** or **FALSE**), and so the column value would always be returned as either 'Over 65' or 'Under 18'.

As for the APIs we used for accessing MySQL from PHP and Python scripts, we'll cover those in the next chapter.

Summary

In this chapter, we basically gave you a crash course in the most common and useful MySQL operators and built-in functions, all the time keeping in mind our central premise of giving you as many opportunities to consider replacing programming logic with SQL logic for optimization purposes.

Why should you go to the trouble of learning and using all of these constructs? The question contains its own answer: so that you can minimize having to do so in your application logic. This makes database interaction faster and more efficient because you generally need to return less data from the database, and because (particularly in the case of web applications) MySQL can usually manipulate the data faster than your programming code can. This is due to the speed at which set processing (operating on a group of records as a single entity) operates as opposed to row processing (working on each record as a separate iteration of a loop).

Maximizing the work done by MySQL also makes migration of your MySQL applications between programming languages and platforms much easier. This may seem trivially self-evident, but as we showed in our demonstration example in this chapter, if your queries already produce the data in the form required for output by your application, your application only needs to output it.

What's Next

Now we've covered just about everything that you need to know in order to create well-structured tables, put data into them, and get that data back out again. In Chapter 5, we'll examine some additional MySQL features that you can employ in your applications. The first of these is the *join*, which is simply a query that selects data from multiple tables. This is obviously more efficient than querying one table, and then using the results to provide parameters for making queries on others. There are several different join types in SQL (and thus MySQL); we'll look at each of these and provide some examples highlighting their use and the differences between them.

Another helpful MySQL feature is the *temporary table*, which can be used to store results of queries and calculations for further use in a manner that's independent of your application. Temporary tables are also convenient in that they only last for the duration of a single session, so there's usually no need to worry about cleanup after you're finished with them.

Both of these features can help you to save time and effort when developing applications. They'll also prove invaluable in getting more work out of MySQL (instead of in your application code) and making more efficient use of MySQL itself.

CHAPTER 5

Joins, Temporary Tables, and Transactions

In this chapter, we'll discuss three additional features you can use to speed up your MySQL applications. While these aren't directly related to one another, each represents an opportunity to decrease the amount of database or code overhead required to perform useful tasks with MySQL by combining queries or operations on the code level into fewer units that perform more work.

- *Joins* allow for the selection of data from multiple tables using a single SQL statement.

- *Temporary tables* provide a way to organize data derived from queries into new tables, which can themselves be queried repeatedly over the lifetime of a MySQL user session.

- *Transactions* allow you to group together related operations into logical units in such a way that all operations either succeed or fail together.

We'll spend some time with each of these features, discussing what it is, how it works, and how you can put it to use in your applications.

The rationale behind joins is relatively simple: it's more efficient to issue a single query than to use a series of them, with the resultset from the first query providing the conditions for one or more additional queries. There are several types of joins, which are distinguished chiefly by how they treat values in one table column that aren't matched in the related column of the other table; we'll cover each of these in turn. In addition, we'll discuss the two basic styles for join notation (theta-style and ANSI-style) and the variations on these that are available in MySQL.

The use of temporary tables is another way to save time and effort, particularly when dealing with several queries that return very large and similar resultsets. When you find yourself dealing with the same subset of table data several times in a single session, it's often faster and more economical to obtain it once and store it in a temporary table, rather than either saving the data in a programming structure (such as an array or hash) or repeating a complex join several times. If you're using several resultsets that contain a large proportion of data in common, it can also make sense to obtain a single resultset that has all the data that's required, store this in a temporary table, and then select from this temporary table as needed. Temporary tables are very convenient to use in MySQL because they are unique to the user session in which they were created. We'll explain just what this means, as well as how to use temporary tables.

Transactions are beneficial because they make it much easier to guarantee data integrity. It's also much more efficient to use transactions than to attempt to perform each query separately in your application logic, testing for its success or failure, and then undoing any previously successful operations in the event that one does fail. By using InnoDB or Berkeley DB (BDB) tables and transactions, you can let MySQL handle this task for you. Using transactions is not necessarily faster in and of itself than not using them; in fact, MyISAM tables (which don't support transactions) are faster than either InnoDB or BDB tables (which do). However, you'll almost certainly save time in development, and your applications will require less code, because you don't need to test and possibly undo each query individually. In this chapter, we'll cover the basic theory of transactions and how they're implemented in MySQL. Later in this book (in Chapter 7), you'll see how these are used in PHP, Python, and Perl.

Joins

A join in MySQL or any other relational database is simply the selection of data from two or more related tables in a single query based on column values common to all of those tables. The cardinal rule for relating tables can be stated as follows: *Tables to be joined must have one or more columns sharing a set of values that allow those tables to be connected in some meaningful way.*

In other words, if we think of tables as modeling real objects, then joins are simply a way of relating objects according to the attributes they hold in common. The column held in common by both tables is usually referred to as the *common key* or *join key*. Of course, it's possible to have more than one common column between two tables, and so it's possible to use more than one join key in any particular join. Most often, the join key will be the primary key of one table and a foreign key in the other.

Before going any further, let's provide a scenario that we'll employ for generating some examples in the rest of this section. This represents a slight modification of the students/classes schema used in Chapter 3. This updated schema is shown in Figure 5-1.

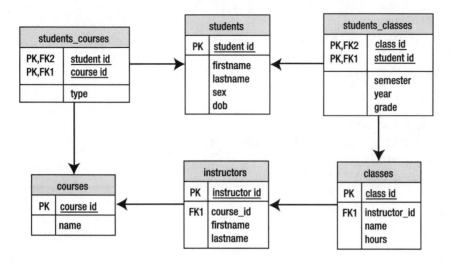

Figure 5-1. Updated students/classes schema

This schema consists of six tables from a database used for tracking students' schedules and grades at a small college. Four of these characterize students, instructors, classes, and courses of study. (Obviously, this is greatly simplified for illustrative purposes.) We also have two lookup tables (**students_classes** and **students_courses**) linking students with classes and students with courses of instruction. In a real-world application, we might do some things differently, but we hope you'll be able to overlook that for the time being.

 NOTE *The students-tables.sql file is included in the ch5 folder of the code accompanying this book (available from the Downloads section of* http://www.apress.com). *Also in that folder you'll find the students-data.sql file, which contains the SQL statements for inserting the test data we'll be referring to in our examples.*

The following is the SQL code for generating the required tables:

```
CREATE TABLE classes (
  class_id int(11) NOT NULL auto_increment,
  instructor_id int(11) NOT NULL default '0',
  name varchar(50) NOT NULL default '',
  hours int(1) NOT NULL default '0',
  PRIMARY KEY  (class_id)
);
```

```
CREATE TABLE courses (
  course_id int(11) NOT NULL auto_increment,
  name varchar(50) NOT NULL default '',
  PRIMARY KEY  (course_id)
);

CREATE TABLE instructors (
  instructor_id int(11) NOT NULL auto_increment,
  course_id int(11) NOT NULL default '0',
  firstname varchar(50) NOT NULL default '',
  lastname varchar(50) NOT NULL default '',
  PRIMARY KEY  (instructor_id)
);

CREATE TABLE students (
  student_id int(11) NOT NULL auto_increment,
  firstname varchar(50) NOT NULL default '',
  lastname varchar(50) NOT NULL default '',
  sex enum('M','F') NOT NULL default 'M',
  dob date NOT NULL default '0000-00-00',
  PRIMARY KEY  (student_id)
);

CREATE TABLE students_classes (
  student_id int(11) NOT NULL default '0',
  class_id int(11) NOT NULL default '0',
  semester enum('FALL','SPRING','SUMMER') NOT NULL default 'FALL',
  year int(4) NOT NULL default '2005',
  grade int(1) default NULL,
  PRIMARY KEY  (student_id,class_id,semester,year)
);

#  Note: For the grade column, we assume that the US system is being used:
#  A = 4, B = 3, C = 2, D = 1, F = 0; for our purposes we'll assume that
#  a value of NULL represents incomplete status (class in progress, etc.)

CREATE TABLE students_courses (
  student_id int(11) NOT NULL default '0',
  course_id int(11) NOT NULL default '0',
  type enum('MAJOR','MINOR') NOT NULL default 'MAJOR',
  PRIMARY KEY  (student_id,course_id)
);
```

NOTE   *We've constructed this in such a way that students may have double majors and/or minors. Limiting students to no more than two of each would need to be done in the application, as MySQL doesn't yet support triggers; we'll discuss this further in Chapter 8.*

While we've shown the foreign key relationships in Figure 5-1, we have not bothered to include them in the table definition statements. However, you should keep them mind, since join keys at least imply a foreign key relationship between the tables being joined, even if it's not made mandatory through the use of constraints.

As for the use of joins, consider the following problem: Suppose we want to know the name of the course area in which a given instructor teaches classes. We could do this by using two separate queries. First, we get the course area number from that instructor's record in the **instructors** table, and then we plug that number into the **courses** table to obtain the name of the corresponding course:

```
SELECT @cnum := course_id FROM instructors
  WHERE firstname = 'Mary' AND lastname = 'Williams';
SELECT name FROM courses WHERE course_id = @cnum;
```

Notice that we employ a user variable in order to preserve the result of the first query and make it available to the second. As you learned in Chapter 4, this frees us from the need to create, set, and refer to an additional application variable in programming code.

Here's what happens when we run these two queries from the MySQL command line:

```
Command Prompt - mysql -h megalon -u root -p                              _ | □ | x |
mysql> SELECT @cnum:=course_id FROM instructors
    -> WHERE firstname='Mary' AND lastname='Williams';
+------------------+
| @cnum:=course_id |
+------------------+
|                1 |
+------------------+
1 row in set (0.11 sec)

mysql> SELECT name FROM courses WHERE course_id=@cnum;
+------------------+
| name             |
+------------------+
| Computer Science |
+------------------+
1 row in set (0.12 sec)

mysql>
```

Since the course number (**course_id** column) is common to both tables, we can write a single query joining both tables using this as the common key for the join. We merely combine any conditions required by each of the original two queries and set the columns common to both tables equal to one another:

```
SELECT c.name
  FROM instructors i, courses c
  WHERE i.firstname = 'Mary' AND i.lastname = 'Williams'
  AND i.course_id = c.course_id;
```

Here's the result:

This result is the same as that obtained by using the two previous queries in succession.

Theta-Style Joins vs. ANSI-Style Joins

There are two accepted styles for writing joins, known as *theta-style joins* and *ANSI-style joins*. Perhaps the best way to explain the difference is to show an example. Let's suppose we want a listing of all instructors that shows the names of the courses of study for which they teach classes. Since the names of the instructors are in one table (**instructors**) and those of the courses are in another (**courses**), we'll need to execute a join on these two tables in order to obtain the desired set of data.

Theta-style join syntax uses commas to separate multiple table names and aliases, just as in the previous example:

```
SELECT c.name
  FROM instructors i, courses c
  WHERE i.firstname = 'Mary' AND i.lastname = 'Williams'
  AND i.course_id = c.course_id;
```

ANSI syntax uses the JOIN and ON keywords instead:

```
SELECT c.name
  FROM instructors i JOIN courses c
  ON i.course_id = c.course_id
  WHERE i.firstname = 'Mary' AND i.lastname = 'Williams';
```

The JOIN keyword is used to separate the names of the tables being joined, and the ON clause contains the equality relation showing which column is being used as the join key. Both varieties of join syntax are permissible in MySQL; however, the ANSI syntax is generally preferable because it's usually easier to read and understand, particularly when writing joins involving three or more tables. There are also some types of joins that can't be written using theta-style notation in MySQL, as you'll see shortly.

In addition, MySQL supports a nonstandard extension of the ANSI syntax that can be used as a sort of shorthand for when the join column has the same name in both tables to be joined:

```
SELECT c.name
  FROM instructors i JOIN courses c
  USING (course_id)
  WHERE i.firstname = 'Mary' AND i.lastname = 'Williams';
```

This has the same result as our earlier example.

The USING keyword is not supported in other database systems; however, if portability isn't an issue, it can be handy for eliminating a bit of typing, as well as for conceptualization purposes.

Join Types

When joining two tables together, MySQL can handle rows that are or aren't matched in one or both tables in several different ways. We'll look briefly at each of these in turn.

Cross Join

Each row from the first table in a *cross join* is joined to all rows from the second. Also known as the *Cartesian product* of two tables, this type of join yields extremely large resultsets, the size of the resultset being the product of the number of rows in each table. Here is an example of a cross join written using theta-style notation:

```
SELECT i.firstname, i.lastname, c.name
FROM instructors i, courses c;
```

Using ANSI-style notation, we would write this as follows:

```
SELECT i.firstname, i.lastname, c.name
  FROM instructors i
  JOIN courses c;
```

or like this:

```
SELECT i.firstname, i.lastname, c.name
  FROM instructors i
  CROSS JOIN courses c;
```

The two ANSI-style forms are equivalent in MySQL.

The reason for this multiplication might be more apparent if you visualize a cross join as shown in Figure 5-2. Very simply, every row in the left-hand table of the join is matched to every row in the table on the right. For the sake of clarity, we've indicated only the matches on the first two rows of the **instructors** table, but you should be able to extrapolate from this and see that there will be 6 X 13 = 78 rows in the resultset. (Don't worry that we're asking you to take this as merely an

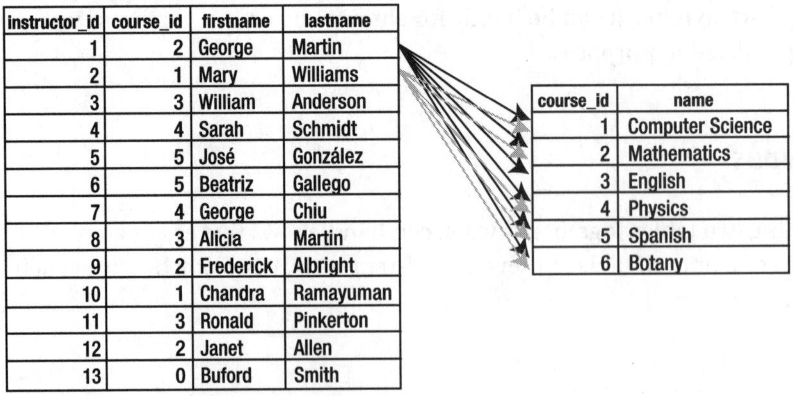

instructor_id	course_id	firstname	lastname
1	2	George	Martin
2	1	Mary	Williams
3	3	William	Anderson
4	4	Sarah	Schmidt
5	5	José	González
6	5	Beatriz	Gallego
7	4	George	Chiu
8	3	Alicia	Martin
9	2	Frederick	Albright
10	1	Chandra	Ramayuman
11	3	Ronald	Pinkerton
12	2	Janet	Allen
13	0	Buford	Smith

course_id	name
1	Computer Science
2	Mathematics
3	English
4	Physics
5	Spanish
6	Botany

Figure 5-2. A cross join matches every row in the tables.

article of faith; we'll offer proof of a more concrete sort very shortly.) Note that the last row in **instructors**, for which there are no records in the **courses** table having the same value in the **course_id** column, is still matched against every row in the right-hand table.

Assuming that we're using the data supplied in students-data.sql, the result-set produced by this query (written in any of the three ways shown) would contain 78 rows (for 13 instructors and 6 course areas). Cross joins are very inefficient due to the sheer size of their resultsets and to the fact that, given *a* equal to the number of rows in the first table and *b* equal to the number of rows in the second, the proportion of redundant data in the result will be:

$$\frac{a(b-1)}{ba} = 1 - \frac{1}{b}$$

In the example shown, approximately 92% (12/13) of the data returned is repetitive and therefore useless to us.

NOTE   *If a join condition is not specified for any other type of join (except a natural join), MySQL will treat it as a cross join. This is true for most other databases as well.*

Inner Join

An *inner join* is defined as a join in which unmatched rows from either table are not to be returned.

Writing inner joins using the theta-style notation is just a matter of adding an appropriate WHERE clause that relates the columns comprising the join key:

```
SELECT i.firstname, i.lastname, c.name
  FROM instructors i, courses c
  WHERE i.course_id = c.course_id;
```

This join will produce a list of all instructors with the names of the course areas in which they teach.

To accomplish the same thing in an ANSI-style join, use an ON or USING clause to define the join key:

```
SELECT i.firstname, i.lastname, c.name
  FROM instructors i
  JOIN courses c
  USING (course_id);
```

The USING keyword is specific to MySQL; the ANSI-standard equivalent to this join is as follows:

```
SELECT i.firstname, i.lastname, c.name
  FROM instructors i
  JOIN courses c
  ON i.course_id = c.course_id;
```

This query is illustrated in Figure 5-3, which shows how just a few of the rows on the left correspond to rows in the table on the right. The last row in the **instructors** table has a **course_id** value of 0; since there are no rows in courses with that value in the **course_id** column, the row from **instructors** isn't included in the resultset. This is indicated by the X over the arrow in the diagram in Figure 5-3.

instructor_id	course_id	firstname	lastname
1	②	George	Martin
2	①	Mary	Williams
3	3	William	Anderson
4	4	Sarah	Schmidt
5	5	José	González
6	5	Beatriz	Gallego
7	4	George	Chiu
8	3	Alicia	Martin
9	2	Frederick	Albright
10	1	Chandra	Ramayuman
11	3	Ronald	Pinkerton
12	2	Janet	Allen
13	0	Buford	Smith

course_id	name
①	Computer Science
②	Mathematics
3	English
4	Physics
5	Spanish
6	Botany

Figure 5-3. An inner join does not return unmatched rows.

CAUTION   *You should never place restrictions on the rows to be returned in a join's* ON *clause; only join conditions of the form* t1.col1 = t2.col2 *(where* t1 *and* t2 *are table aliases) should be placed here. Any restrictions intended to filter the resultset should be placed in a* WHERE *clause.*

You may use the optional INNER keyword as well. However, you should note that using this does *not* by itself make your query into an inner join; in fact, without an ON or USING clause, MySQL will still treat the query as a cross join. Compare the following two queries.

```
Command Prompt - mysql -h megalon -u root -p                          _ □ ×

mysql> SELECT COUNT(*)
    -> FROM instructors INNER JOIN courses
    -> USING (course_id);
+----------+
| COUNT(*) |
+----------+
|       12 |
+----------+
1 row in set (0.04 sec)

mysql> SELECT COUNT(*)
    -> FROM instructors INNER JOIN courses;
+----------+
| COUNT(*) |
+----------+
|       78 |
+----------+
1 row in set (0.01 sec)

mysql>
```

Unless there's an actual need to find rows in one table that aren't matched in another (and sometimes there can be, as you'll see shortly), inner joins are generally the most efficient joins to use. There's no point in returning records you don't need, and you'll save time and effort by not being required to filter out NULL rows from your results.

 NOTE *If a join condition but no join type is specified in an ANSI-style join, MySQL will treat the join as an inner join, just as SQL Server and PostgreSQL will.*

Left (Outer) Join

Outer joins differ from inner joins in that outer joins will return records in one table that aren't matched in another. In a *left outer join* (or more simply, *left-hand join* or even just *left join*), all records from the first (left-hand) table in a join that meet any conditions set in the WHERE clause are returned, whether or not there's a match in the second (right-hand) table.

For example, let's suppose we would like a list of all instructors whose last name begins with the letter *A*, along with any classes that they teach. If we want a list including only those instructors who actually teach any classes, we use an inner join:

```
Command Prompt - mysql -h megalon -u root -p

mysql> SELECT i.firstname, i.lastname, c.name
    -> FROM instructors i
    -> INNER JOIN classes c
    -> USING (instructor_id)
    -> WHERE i.lastname LIKE 'A%';
+-----------+----------+--------------------------------+
| firstname | lastname | name                           |
+-----------+----------+--------------------------------+
| Frederick | Albright | Calculus                       |
| Frederick | Albright | Introduction to Matrices       |
| Frederick | Albright | Modern Geometry                |
| Frederick | Albright | Probability & Statistics       |
| William   | Anderson | English Grammar and Composition|
| William   | Anderson | The Romantic Period            |
| William   | Anderson | Shakespearean Plays and Sonnets|
+-----------+----------+--------------------------------+
7 rows in set (0.07 sec)

mysql>
```

As previously mentioned, the INNER keyword is optional. We could also use theta-style syntax for this query:

```
SELECT i.firstname, i.lastname, c.name
  FROM instructors I, classes c
  WHERE i.instructor_id = c.instructor_id
  AND i.lastname LIKE 'A%';
```

Using a left join, we can obtain a list of all instructors whose last name begins with *A*, whether or not there are any matching entries for those instructors in the **classes** table. As you can see from Figure 5-4, there are three instructors whose last names begin with the letter *A*: William Anderson's instructor ID matches that listed for three classes, and the instructor ID for Frederick Albright is the same as that of four classes. Janet Allen's instructor ID doesn't match with that for any classes at all; since this is a left join, we show an arrow pointing from her record in the **instructors** table to the word *NULL*.

The query and its result are as follows.

```
Command Prompt - mysql -h megalon -u root -p

mysql> SELECT i.firstname, i.lastname, c.name
    -> FROM instructors i
    -> LEFT JOIN classes c
    -> USING (instructor_id)
    -> WHERE i.lastname LIKE 'A%';
+-----------+----------+--------------------------------+
| firstname | lastname | name                           |
+-----------+----------+--------------------------------+
| William   | Anderson | English Grammar and Composition|
| William   | Anderson | The Romantic Period            |
| William   | Anderson | Shakespearean Plays and Sonnets|
| Frederick | Albright | Calculus                       |
| Frederick | Albright | Introduction to Matrices       |
| Frederick | Albright | Modern Geometry                |
| Frederick | Albright | Probability & Statistics       |
| Janet     | Allen    | NULL                           |
+-----------+----------+--------------------------------+
8 rows in set (0.01 sec)

mysql>
```

There are no matching class records for the instructor named Janet Allen, so MySQL dutifully returns a row containing her first and last names in the corresponding columns from **instructors** and a NULL value for the **name** column that was requested from the **classes** table.

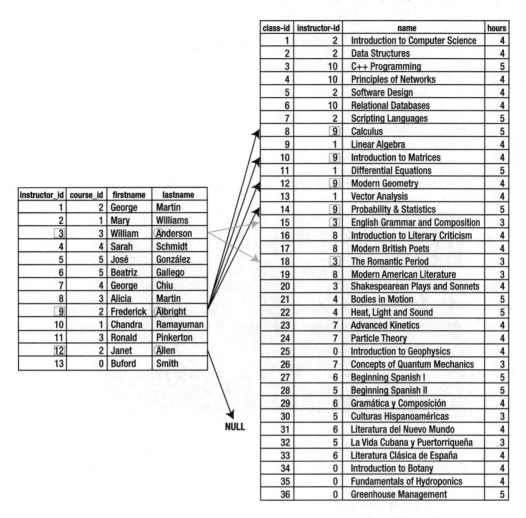

Figure 5-4. A left (outer) join returns all records from the left-hand table that meet any conditions in the WHERE *clause, whether or not there's a match in the right-hand table.*

Let's consider for a minute what happens when we encounter this NULL value in an application. We probably wouldn't want to display the word *NULL*, since it's not very descriptive. Instead, we would likely prefer something a bit more user-friendly, along the lines of "No classes assigned." Rather than test for the NULL value in our application code and make a suitable substitution there, we can use a flow-control operator to accomplish the same thing in the join itself. While we're at it, let's reduce the number of columns in the output to two by using the CONCAT() function on the instructor's first and last names to form a single **instructor** column. We'll also include an ORDER BY clause in the query to alphabetize the results by the instructor's last name.

```
SELECT
  CONCAT(i.firstname, ' ', i.lastname) AS instructor,
  IFNULL(c.name, '[Not currently assigned to any classes.]') AS class
FROM instructors i
LEFT JOIN classes c
USING(instructor_id)
WHERE i.lastname LIKE 'A%'
ORDER BY i.lastname;
```

The result looks like this in the MySQL Monitor:

```
Command Prompt - mysql -h megalon -u root -p                                    _ □ ×

mysql> SELECT
    -> CONCAT(i.firstname, ' ', i.lastname) AS instructor,
    -> IFNULL(c.name, '[Not currently assigned to any classes.]') AS class
    -> FROM instructors i
    -> LEFT JOIN classes c
    -> USING(instructor_id)
    -> WHERE i.lastname LIKE 'A%'
    -> ORDER BY i.lastname;
+--------------------+----------------------------------------------+
| instructor         | class                                        |
+--------------------+----------------------------------------------+
| Frederick Albright | Modern Geometry                              |
| Frederick Albright | Introduction to Matrices                     |
| Frederick Albright | Calculus                                     |
| Frederick Albright | Probability & Statistics                     |
| Janet Allen        | [Not currently assigned to any classes.]     |
| William Anderson   | English Grammar and Composition              |
| William Anderson   | Shakespearean Plays and Sonnets              |
| William Anderson   | The Romantic Period                          |
+--------------------+----------------------------------------------+
8 rows in set (0.00 sec)

mysql>
```

Generally speaking, you can employ any operators, built-in functions, and flow-control operators in multiple-table joins that you could use in SELECT queries from a single table.

NOTE *MySQL does* not *support Oracle-style* (+) = *or* = (+) *theta syntax for outer joins. If you need to specify a left join, you must use ANSI syntax with* LEFT JOIN *or* LEFT OUTER JOIN. *The same is true with respect to right joins: use* RIGHT JOIN *or* RIGHT OUTER JOIN. *Oracle 9 also implements the SQL92 syntax supported by MySQL, as does PostgreSQL 7.1 and later.*

Right (Outer) Join

A *right outer join* (or more, commonly, *right* or *right-hand join*) is similar to a left
join, except that all rows from the second (or right-hand) table in the join that
satisfy any included WHERE clause are returned, whether or not matching rows are
found in the first (left-hand) table. MySQL supports ANSI-style right joins using
either the RIGHT JOIN or RIGHT OUTER JOIN keywords.

As you can see in Figure 5-5, this works as you would expect: in the opposite
fashion from a left join.

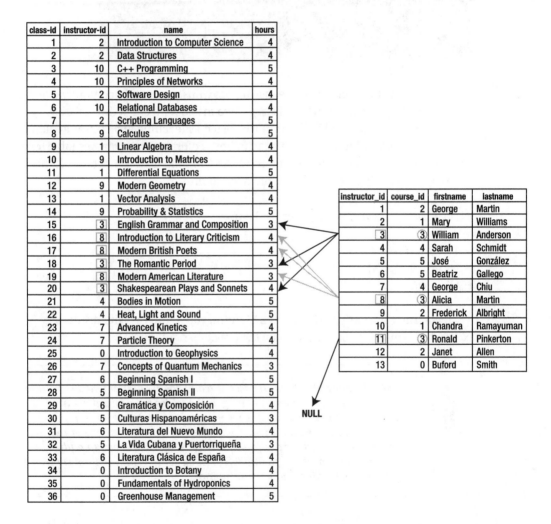

*Figure 5-5. A right (outer) join returns all records from the right-hand table that
meet any conditions in the* WHERE *clause, whether or not there's a match in the
left-hand table.*

The following shows the query represented in Figure 5-5 being run in the MySQL Monitor.

```
Command Prompt - mysql -h megalon -u root -p                              _ □ ×
mysql> SELECT c.name, c.hours, i.firstname, i.lastname
    -> FROM classes c
    -> RIGHT JOIN instructors i
    -> USING (instructor_id)
    -> WHERE i.course_id=3;
+------------------------------------+-------+-----------+-----------+
| name                               | hours | firstname | lastname  |
+------------------------------------+-------+-----------+-----------+
| English Grammar and Composition    |     3 | William   | Anderson  |
| The Romantic Period                |     3 | William   | Anderson  |
| Shakespearean Plays and Sonnets    |     4 | William   | Anderson  |
| Introduction to Literary Criticism |     4 | Alicia    | Martin    |
| Modern British Poets               |     4 | Alicia    | Martin    |
| Modern American Literature         |     3 | Alicia    | Martin    |
| NULL                               |  NULL | Ronald    | Pinkerton |
+------------------------------------+-------+-----------+-----------+
7 rows in set (0.00 sec)

mysql>
```

You can see that there are three instructors whose **course_id** column value is 3 (that is, they all teach English classes). Two instructors teach three classes each, and the third (Ronald Pinkerton) isn't listed as teaching any classes at all.

In this case, NULL values are returned in both columns in the **classes** table for rows that don't match any **instructor_id** values from the instructors table. If this seems a bit confusing, try turning it into a left join:

```
SELECT c.name, c.hours, i.firstname, i.lastname
FROM instructors i
LEFT JOIN classes c
USING(instructor_id)
WHERE i.course_id = 3;
```

If you run this query in the MySQL Monitor, you'll find that the results are exactly the same as those produced by the previous right join.

TIP *Left or right? In most cases, it really doesn't matter whether you use left joins or right joins, as long as the tables to be joined are in the correct order. However, the recommended practice by most professionals is to use left joins whenever possible. Using either one or the other (but not both) is desirable for reasons of consistency. In addition, most people seem to find left joins easier to visualize than right joins when reading and writing queries.*

Full Join

A *full join* returns all rows from both tables being joined that otherwise fulfill any conditions set in a query's WHERE clause. All columns in rows from either table that don't have matches in the other one are filled with NULL values.

MySQL doesn't support explicit full joins; instead we'll offer a couple of alternative ways to simulate a full join later in this chapter, in the "Emulating a Full Join Using a UNION Query" and "Emulating a Full Join Using a Temporary Table" sections.

 CAUTION   *Some references state that the default join type in MySQL is the full join, but this is incorrect usage of the term* full join, *where* cross join *is what's really meant.*

Natural Join

A *natural join* is a MySQL-specific shortcut that performs the same task as an inner or left join in which the ON or USING clause refers to all columns that the tables to be joined have in common. Using this form:

```
SELECT i.firstname, i.lastname, c.name
FROM instructors i
NATURAL JOIN classes c
WHERE i.lastname LIKE 'A%';
```

is the same as using this form:

```
SELECT i.firstname, i.lastname, c.name
FROM instructors i
INNER JOIN classes c
USING(instructor_id)
WHERE i.lastname LIKE 'A%';
```

Similarly, you can make MySQL assume automatically that all same-named columns are to be used as join keys for a left outer join:

```
SELECT i.firstname, i.lastname, c.name
FROM instructors i
NATURAL LEFT JOIN classes c
WHERE i.lastname LIKE 'A%';
```

This yields the same result as the following:

```
SELECT i.firstname, i.lastname, c.name
FROM instructors i
LEFT JOIN classes c
USING(instructor_id)
WHERE i.lastname LIKE 'A%';
```

CAUTION   *You can't use the* INNER *keyword with* NATURAL JOIN. *You'll get a syntax error if you try to do this.*

You can also perform natural right joins, as in the following example.

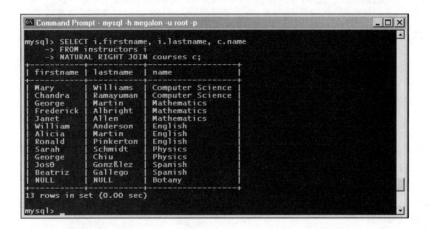

Since there are no instructors in the Botany department, the columns from the left-hand table in the row containing "Botany" from the right-hand table are filled with NULL values.

By using the same name for related columns in different tables and NATURAL [LEFT | RIGHT] JOIN syntax, you can save a lot of typing in your joins. The principal drawback to the USING notation is that this isn't portable from MySQL to other databases. It's also true that someone who is not familiar with your table schemas may need to look them up before being to able to know for certain on which columns the tables in the query are being joined.

TIP   *You can also use* NATURAL LEFT OUTER JOIN *and* NATURAL RIGHT OUTER JOIN, *in addition to what's shown in the examples.*

Self Join

Self joins aren't used often, but they are very handy for one particular purpose: retrieving information that represents a hierarchy. Suppose we want to model the supervisory responsibilities for personnel in an office department, such as that represented by the tree graph in Figure 5-6.

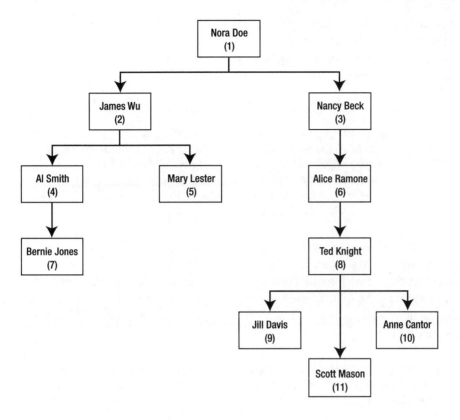

Figure 5-6. A hierarchy of department personnel

As shown here, Nora Doe (Employee #1) supervises James Wu (Employee #2) and Nancy Beck (Employee #3), James Wu supervises Al Smith (Employee #4) and Mary Lester (Employee #5), and so on. It's fairly straightforward to construct a table to hold this data:

```
CREATE TABLE employees (
  employee_id int(11) NOT NULL auto_increment,
  supervisor_id int(11) default NULL,
  firstname varchar(50) NOT NULL default '',
  lastname varchar(50) NOT NULL default '',
  PRIMARY KEY  (employee_id)
);
```

This table contains an **employee_id** column to store the employee's ID number, a **supervisor_id** column to hold the employee ID of the supervisor to whom the employee reports, and **firstname** and **lastname** columns to store the employee's first and last names. We'll allow the **supervisor_id** column of this table to take a NULL value to indicate an employee with no supervisors. The first two statements for inserting the data into this table look like this:

```
INSERT INTO employees (employee_id, supervisor_id, firstname, lastname)
  VALUES (1, NULL, 'Nora', 'Doe');
INSERT INTO employees (employee_id, supervisor_id, firstname, lastname)
  VALUES (2, 1, 'James', 'Wu');
```

NOTE *Writing the remaining* INSERT *statements based on the diagram in Figure 5-6 should be a trivial exercise. Alternatively, you can use the self-join.sql script included in the ch5 directory of the code download for this book (available from the Downloads section of* http://www.apress.com) *to create and populate the **employees** table.*

Data that refers to other data stored in the same table exhibits what's commonly referred to as a *recursive,* or *reflexive, relationship.* A self join is used to extract this data in such a way that this recursive relationship is preserved, and it works by joining the table to itself. Since we can refer to the same table identifier (table name or alias) only once in a given query, we indulge in a couple of bits of alias trickery here:

- We use the same table name twice, but use a different table alias each time. In effect, we're telling MySQL to refer to the same table under two different guises.

- Since the columns which we're retrieving have the same names, we use column aliases to distinguish the columns returned from the table under the first table alias from those returned from the table under the table second alias.

We'll take the additional step of concatenating the first and last names of each employee as well. The resulting query might look like this:

```
mysql> SELECT
    -> CONCAT(e1.firstname, ' ', e1.lastname) AS supervisor,
    -> CONCAT(e2.firstname, ' ', e2.lastname) AS employee
    -> FROM employees e1
    -> JOIN employees e2 ON e1.employee_id = e2.supervisor_id;
+-------------+-------------+
| supervisor  | employee    |
+-------------+-------------+
| Nora Doe    | James Wu    |
| Nora Doe    | Nancy Beck  |
| James Wu    | Al Smith    |
| James Wu    | Mary Lester |
| Nancy Beck  | Alice Ramone|
| Al Smith    | Bernie Jones|
| Alice Ramone| Ted Knight  |
| Ted Knight  | Jill Davis  |
| Ted Knight  | Anne Cantor |
| Ted Knight  | Scott Mason |
+-------------+-------------+
10 rows in set (0.05 sec)

mysql>
```

If we want to include a record showing that Nora Doe is the department head (that she has no immediate supervisor), we can do that using an outer join. Since we're displaying the supervisor column on the left side of the output, we'll need to use a right join:

```
Command Prompt - mysql -h megalon -u root -p                              _ □ ×

mysql> SELECT
    -> IFNULL(CONCAT(e1.firstname, ' ', e1.lastname), "[DEPARTMENT HEAD]")
    ->    AS supervisor,
    -> CONCAT(e2.firstname, ' ', e2.lastname) AS employee
    -> FROM employees e1
    -> RIGHT JOIN employees e2 ON e1.employee_id = e2.supervisor_id;
+-------------------+-----------------+
| supervisor        | employee        |
+-------------------+-----------------+
| [DEPARTMENT HEAD] | Nora Doe        |
| Nora Doe          | James Wu        |
| Nora Doe          | Nancy Beck      |
| James Wu          | Al Smith        |
| James Wu          | Mary Lester     |
| Nancy Beck        | Alice Ramone    |
| Al Smith          | Bernie Jones    |
| Alice Ramone      | Ted Knight      |
| Ted Knight        | Jill Davis      |
| Ted Knight        | Anne Cantor     |
| Ted Knight        | Scott Mason     |
+-------------------+-----------------+
11 rows in set (0.00 sec)

mysql>
```

Notice that we use IFNULL() once again in order to substitute a descriptive message in place of the word *NULL* in Nora's employee record, making use of the fact that the result of concatenating any value to NULL is also NULL. If we wanted to use a left join, we could rewrite this query as follows:

```
SELECT
  IFNULL(CONCAT(e2.firstname, ' ', e2.lastname), "[DEPARTMENT HEAD]")
    AS supervisor,
  CONCAT(e1.firstname, ' ', e1.lastname) AS employee
FROM employees e1
LEFT JOIN employees e2 ON e2.employee_id = e1.supervisor_id;
```

We just switch the aliases used for the columns to be selected and in the ON clause.

Other likely scenarios for using self joins include relating parts of items that themselves are used as parts of other items; department hierarchies in an organization; and sections and subsections of a document, an application, or a web site.

Unions

Beginning with MySQL 4.0, you can use the UNION keyword to combine the results of multiple SELECT queries into a single resultset. This can be very useful in eliminating the need to store resultsets in programming data structures such as arrays or to employ temporary tables (which we'll look at very shortly) in order to preserve intermediate results.

The basic syntax for UNION is as follows:

```
(SELECT ...)
UNION [DISTINCT | ALL]
(SELECT ...)
[UNION
(SELECT ...) [...]]
```

The SELECT statements can be any that are legal in MySQL, as long as each query yields the same number of columns. The parentheses surrounding the individual SELECT statements are required if you want to use an ORDER BY clause that affects the combined resultset. However, it's good practice to use parentheses in any case, to make your queries easier to read.

CAUTION *Prior to MySQL 4.1.1, there's a further restriction in that the values of the columns in the first SELECT query's resultset are used to determine the result types and lengths of the same columns for the combined resultset. This means that column values from the second query and any additional ones might be truncated or otherwise altered in order to match the sizes and types of those resulting from the first SELECT.*

Let's look at a simple example. Suppose we have two tables listing a small firm's salespeople and service technicians. Here's the definition for the **sales** table:

```
CREATE TABLE sales (
    firstname varchar(50) NULL,
    lastname varchar(50) NULL
);
```

NOTE *The table definitions and data for this example are included in the union.sql file in the ch5 directory of this book's downloadable code.*

The structure of the **service_techs** table is identical to this one. In order to obtain a combined listing of all the employees from both tables in a single result, we can do this:

```
Command Prompt - mysql -h megalon -u root -p                          _ □ ×
mysql> (SELECT lastname, firstname FROM sales)
    -> UNION
    -> (SELECT lastname, firstname FROM service_techs)
    -> ORDER BY lastname;
+----------+----------+
| lastname | firstname |
+----------+----------+
| Anderson | Jane     |
| Bridges  | Lucinda  |
| Fields   | Hope     |
| Griffith | George   |
| Miller   | Lisette  |
| Nelson   | Mike     |
| Norton   | Steve    |
| Roberts  | Peter    |
| Roberts  | Denise   |
| Thomas   | Jerry    |
| Williams | Franklin |
| Yates    | Mandy    |
+----------+----------+
12 rows in set (0.11 sec)

mysql>
```

Notice that the ORDER BY clause following the second SELECT (and outside the parentheses surrounding it) controls the sort order for the entire resultset.

By default, MySQL eliminates any duplicated rows from the combined resultset. Beginning with MySQL 4.0.17, you can indicate this behavior using the DISTINCT keyword. While it actually has no effect (since it represents the default behavior), it can serve as a reminder that you're dropping any duplicates. The DISTINCT keyword is also required by the SQL standard, so using it will make your code more portable as well.

If we want *all* rows to be included in the final result, we can use the ALL keyword, like so:

```
Command Prompt - mysql -h megalon -u root -p                          _ □ ×
mysql> (SELECT lastname, firstname FROM sales)
    -> UNION ALL
    -> (SELECT lastname, firstname FROM service_techs)
    -> ORDER BY lastname;
+----------+----------+
| lastname | firstname |
+----------+----------+
| Anderson | Jane     |
| Anderson | Jane     |
| Bridges  | Lucinda  |
| Fields   | Hope     |
| Griffith | George   |
| Griffith | George   |
| Miller   | Lisette  |
| Nelson   | Mike     |
| Norton   | Steve    |
| Roberts  | Denise   |
| Roberts  | Peter    |
| Thomas   | Jerry    |
| Thomas   | Jerry    |
| Williams | Franklin |
| Yates    | Mandy    |
+----------+----------+
15 rows in set (0.00 sec)

mysql>
```

Emulating a Full Join Using a UNION Query

In some cases, you can UNION together a left join and a right join to simulate a full join, as shown in the following example.

```
Command Prompt - mysql -h megalon -u root -p                        _ □ ×
mysql> (
    -> SELECT CONCAT(s.firstname, ' ', s.lastname) AS salesperson,
    -> CONCAT(t.firstname, ' ', t.lastname) AS tech
    -> FROM sales s
    -> LEFT JOIN service_techs t
    -> USING (firstname, lastname)
    -> )
    -> UNION
    -> (
    -> SELECT CONCAT(s.firstname, ' ', s.lastname) AS salesperson,
    -> CONCAT(t.firstname, ' ', t.lastname) AS tech
    -> FROM sales s
    -> RIGHT JOIN service_techs t
    -> USING (firstname, lastname)
    -> );
+-------------------+------------------+
| salesperson       | tech             |
+-------------------+------------------+
| Jane Anderson     | Jane Anderson    |
| Franklin Williams | NULL             |
| Jerry Thomas      | Jerry Thomas     |
| Lisette Miller    | NULL             |
| Peter Roberts     | NULL             |
| Mandy Yates       | NULL             |
| Lucinda Bridges   | NULL             |
| George Griffith   | George Griffith  |
| Hope Fields       | NULL             |
| NULL              | Denise Roberts   |
| NULL              | Steve Norton     |
| NULL              | Mike Nelson      |
+-------------------+------------------+
12 rows in set (0.39 sec)

mysql>
```

In order for this to work, all the columns in the first query's resultset must accept NULL values. (This is true through MySQL 5.0.0.)

As an exercise, try writing a query (using the union.sql tables and data as a basis) whose output looks something like this:

EMPLOYEE	SALES	TECH
Jane Anderson	X	X
Franklin Williams	X	
Jerry Thomas	X	X
[etc. . .		]
Steve Norton		X
Mike Nelson		X

CAUTION *Any column names used in an* ORDER BY *clause applying to an entire union must be common to the resultsets produced by all of the* SELECT *queries making up the union.*

We'll look at another method for simulating full joins using temporary tables a little later in this chapter.

Temporary Tables

Now let's talk about another advanced MySQL feature: *temporary tables*. These allow you to create a short-term storage place within the database itself for a set of data that you need to use several times in a single series of operations. One advantage of this is that you can use SQL to access the data, rather than using programming code, which means that if you need to port your application from, say, PHP to Java, there's that much less code to be translated. There are additional benefits to using temporary tables, as you'll see shortly.

Most often, it's best to obtain a desired set of data in a single SELECT query. However, sometimes this simply isn't possible, or you may want to work with subsets of the same, larger resultset over several successive operations. You can handle intermediate or temporary results for reuse within a single session in two basic ways:

- Using programming constructs such as arrays, hashes, or objects and retrieving data from these when required by the application logic

- Using database tables

The second option is preferable because it tends to be faster, there's less likelihood of bugs in the programming code, and applications are more easily ported (the latter two reasons derive from the simple fact that there's less code to manage). The one drawback to doing this is that you're then required to manage the tables for storing the intermediate results. The solution to this problem is to use temporary tables, which are supported in MySQL 3.23 and later.

NOTE *Beginning with MySQL 5.0.1, views may offer another alternative for handling intermediate or temporary results for reuse. See Chapter 8 for more information about views.*

Creating Temporary Tables

To create a temporary table, simply include the TEMPORARY keyword in a table creation statement. Otherwise, the statements used to create them are no different than those used to create normal tables.

A temporary table can be of type MyISAM, HEAP, MERGE, or InnoDB. (Your MySQL installation must support InnoDB tables in order to use these as temporary tables, of course.) You can also use ISAM as the table type for temporary tables in MySQL versions through the 4.0.*x* series. (Don't forget that ISAM tables are disabled in MySQL 4.1 and removed altogether beginning with MySQL 5.0.0.)

Temporary tables differ from normal tables in that temporary tables exist only for the duration of the current session and are automatically deleted after it ends. (For web applications, this means that temporary tables generally cease to exist upon completion of the current page or script.) The following is a simple example (this particular example was produced on a PC running Windows 2000 Server, but the results will be the same regardless of operating system or platform).

```
C:\>mysql -h megalon -u root -p
Enter password: ******
Welcome to the MySQL monitor.  Commands end with ; or \g.
Your MySQL connection id is 3 to server version: 5.0.0-alpha-max-nt-log

Type 'help;' or '\h' for help. Type '\c' to clear the buffer.

mysql> USE test;
Database changed
mysql> CREATE TEMPORARY TABLE temptable (val INT);
Query OK, 0 rows affected (0.06 sec)

mysql> INSERT INTO temptable (val) VALUES (123);
Query OK, 1 row affected (0.01 sec)

mysql> SELECT * FROM temptable;
+------+
| val  |
+------+
|  123 |
+------+
1 row in set (0.00 sec)

mysql> \q
Bye

C:\>mysql -h megalon -u root -p
Enter password: ******
Welcome to the MySQL monitor.  Commands end with ; or \g.
Your MySQL connection id is 4 to server version: 5.0.0-alpha-max-nt-log

Type 'help;' or '\h' for help. Type '\c' to clear the buffer.

mysql> USE test;
Database changed
mysql> SELECT * FROM temptable;
ERROR 1146 (42S02): Table 'test.temptable' doesn't exist
mysql>
```

Notice that the table was deleted as soon as the session was ended using the \q (or quit) command. You can verify this by logging in again as the same user and trying to query the table you created previously. One interesting and potentially useful side effect of this behavior is that multiple users can employ the same table names for temporary tables without fear of collisions between them. This also means that different users can't access each other's temporary tables. If one user or process needs to access a table created by a different one, you'll need to omit the TEMPORARY keyword from the table definition and take care of maintenance issues (such as deleting the table once there's no further use for it) in your application code.

 CAUTION *In MySQL, you can't refer to the same temporary table more than once in a single query. This means you can't do a self join on a temporary table.*

Emulating a Full Join Using a Temporary Table

We've already looked at one way of duplicating what a full join does by using a
UNION query. Now we'll demonstrate how to simulate a full join with a temporary
table, in the event you're working with a MySQL version earlier than 4.0. This will
be fairly straightforward, but should serve as a good example of the use of a temporary table.

We'll use the same **sales** and **service_techs** tables defined and populated in
the union.sql script, which we used in our earlier example of emulating a full
join. We perform the emulation in four steps:

1. Create the temporary table used to store the intermediate result.

2. Insert the data returned by a left join on the two employees tables.

3. Insert the data from a right join on the same two tables.

4. Select the final data set from the temporary table.

We'll actually combine steps 1 and 2 using CREATE TABLE ... SELECT syntax,
as this is just as valid for temporary tables as it is for normal ones. The left join is
simply the one we used earlier in the first part of the UNION join.

```
mysql> CREATE TEMPORARY TABLE temptable
    -> SELECT
    ->   CONCAT(s.firstname, ' ', s.lastname) AS salesperson,
    ->   CONCAT(t.firstname, ' ', t.lastname ) AS tech
    -> FROM sales s
    -> LEFT JOIN service_techs t
    -> USING (firstname, lastname);
Query OK, 9 rows affected (0.02 sec)
Records: 9  Duplicates: 0  Warnings: 0

mysql>
```

Here is the schema of the temporary table we just created:

```
mysql> DESCRIBE temptable;
+-------------+----------+------+-----+---------+-------+
| Field       | Type     | Null | Key | Default | Extra |
+-------------+----------+------+-----+---------+-------+
| salesperson | char(101)| YES  |     | NULL    |       |
| tech        | char(101)| YES  |     | NULL    |       |
+-------------+----------+------+-----+---------+-------+
2 rows in set (0.00 sec)

mysql>
```

And here's the data that we inserted:

```
Command Prompt - mysql -h megalon -u root -p                          _ □ ×
mysql> SELECT * FROM temptable;
+-------------------+-------------------+
| salesperson       | tech              |
+-------------------+-------------------+
| Jane Anderson     | Jane Anderson     |
| Franklin Williams | NULL              |
| Jerry Thomas      | Jerry Thomas      |
| Lisette Miller    | NULL              |
| Peter Roberts     | NULL              |
| Mandy Yates       | NULL              |
| Lucinda Bridges   | NULL              |
| George Griffith   | George Griffith   |
| Hope Fields       | NULL              |
+-------------------+-------------------+
9 rows in set (0.00 sec)

mysql>
```

Now we need to insert the data from a right join on the same two tables. We already have the necessary SELECT query for this. All we need to do is turn it into an INSERT SELECT, as follows.

```
Command Prompt - mysql -h megalon -u root -p                          _ □ ×
mysql> INSERT INTO temptable (salesperson, tech)
    ->   SELECT
    ->     CONCAT(s.firstname, ' ', s.lastname) AS salesperson,
    ->     CONCAT(t.firstname, ' ', t.lastname) AS tech
    ->   FROM sales s
    ->   RIGHT JOIN service_techs t
    ->   USING (firstname, lastname);
Query OK, 6 rows affected (0.04 sec)
Records: 6  Duplicates: 0  Warnings: 0

mysql>
```

The temporary table now contains the following data:

```
Command Prompt - mysql -h megalon -u root -p                          _ □ ×
mysql> SELECT * FROM temptable;
+-------------------+-------------------+
| salesperson       | tech              |
+-------------------+-------------------+
| Jane Anderson     | Jane Anderson     |
| Franklin Williams | NULL              |
| Jerry Thomas      | Jerry Thomas      |
| Lisette Miller    | NULL              |
| Peter Roberts     | NULL              |
| Mandy Yates       | NULL              |
| Lucinda Bridges   | NULL              |
| George Griffith   | George Griffith   |
| Hope Fields       | NULL              |
| Jane Anderson     | Jane Anderson     |
| NULL              | Denise Roberts    |
| Jerry Thomas      | Jerry Thomas      |
| NULL              | Steve Norton      |
| NULL              | Mike Nelson       |
| George Griffith   | George Griffith   |
+-------------------+-------------------+
15 rows in set (0.00 sec)

mysql>
```

We have some duplicate rows. We can take care of this problem easily enough by using a SELECT DISTINCT instead:

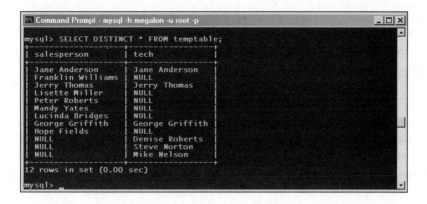

```
Command Prompt - mysql -h megalon -u root -p                    _ □ ×
mysql> SELECT DISTINCT * FROM temptable;
+------------------+------------------+
| salesperson      | tech             |
+------------------+------------------+
| Jane Anderson    | Jane Anderson    |
| Franklin Williams| NULL             |
| Jerry Thomas     | Jerry Thomas     |
| Lisette Miller   | NULL             |
| Peter Roberts    | NULL             |
| Mandy Yates      | NULL             |
| Lucinda Bridges  | NULL             |
| George Griffith  | George Griffith  |
| Hope Fields      | NULL             |
| NULL             | Denise Roberts   |
| NULL             | Steve Norton     |
| NULL             | Mike Nelson      |
+------------------+------------------+
12 rows in set (0.00 sec)

mysql>
```

This is the same data that we obtained using the UNION join earlier.

NOTE *You can also use temporary tables to simulate subselects in older versions of MySQL that don't support these. We'll look at how this can be accomplished when we discuss subqueries in Chapter 8.*

Transactions

Both joins and temporary tables can help reduce the amount of application code needed to get a given amount of work out of MySQL. A third way to streamline your applications that use MySQL is to employ transactions.

A *transaction* is simply a group of related operations that make up a logical or conceptual whole. For example, when you make a purchase using a credit card from a web site, your cardholder account must be debited and the site owner's merchant account must be credited. When problems such as a power outage, a system failure, or loss of a network connection occur, it is possible that all of these necessary operations may not take place, causing data integrity problems. (For example, your card is debited, but the merchant's account doesn't get the credit for the sale.) Transactional features have been added to most popular databases in order to provide a solution to exactly this type of problem. Since version 3.23-max and all 4.0 versions and later, MySQL has provided transactional support using the InnoDB and BDB storage engines.

In MySQL (when using InnoDB or BDB tables) or in any other transactional database, a transaction must follow what are known as the *ACID rules*:

- **Atomicity:** All operations associated with any given transaction must occur as a single unit. If any single operation fails, then the transaction does not take place, and the database is returned to its previous state. This is often stated like this: In the event of the failure of an operation that makes up part of the transaction, the transaction is not *committed*, and the transaction is *rolled back*.

- **Consistency:** The system's state following the transaction must be consistent with its original state. For example, if you're transferring money between two checking accounts, the total of the two accounts must be the same before and after the transfer takes place. If the balance of one account has increased by $100, then the balance of the other account must have decreased by the same amount.

- **Isolation:** Each transaction must appear to be independent of all other actions taking place in the system. In other words (to use our banking example again), the system must behave as though the two accounts between which funds are being transferred have exclusive use of the system while this transaction is taking place. (In practice, true concurrent isolation is fairly difficult to achieve without causing major performance problems, and what usually happens instead is some sort of sequential prioritization.)

- **Durability:** Simply put, once a transaction is completed, it must stay completed. This is achieved in MySQL and other transaction-safe databases by means of a transaction log file, which is updated whenever a transaction is completed.

The main benefit of using transactional tables with your application is that you can ensure data integrity and concurrency in the event that something unexpected may occur. This is very important in the business world, such as for financial institutions.

NOTE   *Both InnoDB and BDB tables support transactions, but there are some problems with BDB tables. They tend to be slow when large numbers of them are simultaneously open; they can't be moved between directories; and you may not be able to delete BDB tables unless you're running in auto-commit mode. Also, BDB tables currently aren't supported on Linux running on other than 32-bit Intel processors, and they aren't supported at all on Mac OS X. For these and other reasons, we recommend that you use InnoDB tables when you need to support transactions in a production environment.*

MySQL Transaction Commands

MySQL has three commands for use in performing transactions:

BEGIN: This command begins a transaction. MySQL supports BEGIN WORK as an alias for this command. Since MySQL 4.0.11, you can also use the standard SQL command START TRANSACTION. Alternatively, you may use SET AUTOCOMMIT = 0;. With all of these commands, changes are not written to disk and logged until a COMMIT statement has been issued. The difference between SET AUTOCOMMIT = 0; and the others is that it disables auto-commit mode until you explicitly turn it back on (by issuing a SET AUTOCOMMIT = 1;); the others merely disable auto-commit mode temporarily, until either a COMMIT or ROLLBACK command has been issued.

ROLLBACK: If there is a failure in any of the queries required for the transaction, you can issue this command to cancel the transaction and return the database to its previous state. Issuing a ROLLBACK requires the "undoing" of each query that was successful prior to the advent of the error condition that necessitated it. Fortunately, thanks to improved versioning techniques, this doesn't take as long as you might think it would.

COMMIT: Once all required queries are completed successfully, this commits the transaction; that is, all changes are saved to the transaction log on disk or in other permanent storage. COMMIT statements execute fairly rapidly, since there is no requirement for any actual additional work in the database to be done, only that operations be recorded.

In MySQL you cannot nest transactions. If you issue a BEGIN statement for a given user while that user has a pending transaction, MySQL will treat it as a COMMIT followed by a BEGIN. In other words, MySQL allows individual users to perform only *sequential* transactions.

NOTE   *MySQL does not support save points as do some other databases. You can only commit or roll back a complete transaction.*

Transaction Processing Considerations

It's best to keep transactions as small as possible. Since MySQL must guarantee that transactions belonging to different users are kept separate, this means that table rows involved in those transactions must be kept locked (and thus not accessible by other others) for the duration of each transaction. In addition, since transactions must be logged as sets of queries, using the minimum number of SQL statements possible per transaction ensures that your application isn't slowed down by the need to log a large number of queries before the next transaction can commence.

You should perform all transactions before and after obtaining user input. Don't write your application in such a way that a transaction is in progress while awaiting user response. Imagine what could happen if a user decided to leave for his lunch break while the database was waiting for one or more of his transactions to finish! Plan your application in such a way that all necessary data is obtained, then the transaction performed, before collecting the next item or set of data.

Summary

In this chapter, we've looked at three features that can help increase the efficiency of your MySQL applications: joins (including UNION joins), temporary tables, and transactions. Each of these can be used in different ways to cut down on the number of queries required to isolate the data you need, reduce or eliminate the need to store data as part of application logic, decrease the number of bugs in programming code, and help guarantee data integrity.

Using joins reduces the number of queries needed to obtain a given set of data by allowing you to combine queries. These also tend to make applications more efficient because they can often eliminate the need to store data in programming constructs so that they can be used in subsequent queries. They make applications less error-prone because less code means less of a chance for bugs to creep into the codebase. We looked at all of the major join types supported by MySQL.

Temporary tables are useful when you want to store the results of queries in tables for reuse several times during a single user or application session, rather than in programming constructs such as arrays or hashes. MySQL's temporary tables are unique to each session, and they are cleaned up for you at the end of each session, which cuts down drastically on table management requirements and worries about issues such as table name collisions. They're also useful in cases where it's unwieldy or even impossible to derive a desired set of data in a single query, such as in our example using a temporary table to simulate a full join, which isn't currently supported in MySQL.

Transactions, supported in MySQL via the InnoDB and BDB storage engines, are useful because they provide a mechanism whereby queries can be grouped together logically and performed as a unit. This is extremely important in scenarios where the state of the database must be preserved; for example, in the case of transferring funds between checking accounts, where the total of the amounts in both accounts must be the same before and after the transfer. Without transactions, you must lock all affected tables and track the success or failure of each single query required to complete the transfer, and in the event of failure, you must be prepared to perform the inverse of each query that succeeded up to that point. (There are also concurrency and other issues involved, but we won't dwell on those here.) Because transactions handle commits and rollbacks for you automatically, you're saved a tremendous amount of code overhead. Many database APIs that are compatible with MySQL provide enhanced support for transactions, including Python's MySQLdb module and `ext/mysqli` in PHP 5, as you'll see in Chapter 7, when we discuss MySQL application programming.

What's Next

In the next chapter, we'll look at additional ways to speed up and improve the efficiency of MySQL-backed applications by identifying bottlenecks in them as they're running. Some of these methods include analysis of log files and status variables, evaluation of table design and queries, caching issues, application bloat, and the configuration of the MySQL server.

CHAPTER 6

Finding the Bottlenecks

SO FAR, WE'VE CONCENTRATED MOSTLY on database design and writing queries through this book, and we'll continue to discuss aspects of those in this chapter. But there are other areas where you can work to improve the performance of MySQL and MySQL-backed applications. This chapter addresses those areas.

For example, many aspects of the MySQL server's operation can be modified by setting configuration variables. Although their default values are often "good enough," sometimes changing these can make a big difference in performance. In addition, you can obtain a lot of information regarding how well MySQL is actually performing by checking the values of system variables.

In the first part of this chapter, we'll look at the commands you need to read configuration and system variables, which ones are likely to be most useful to you (and why), and how to change them when necessary. We'll also take a very brief look at some freely available tools that can help you monitor your server's performance and make changes in its configuration, including mytop (a top clone written in Perl), WinMySqlAdmin, phpMyAdmin, and the new MySQL Administrator, available from MySQL AB. MySQL Administrator promises to become a standard and valuable part of every MySQL database administrator's toolkit.

We'll also look at caching of tables, keys, and queries. MySQL's caches, when used properly, can save a lot of memory and processing overhead. They can speed up your applications considerably by cutting down on the number of times that the server must read and/or write to disk instead of RAM. The query cache, new in MySQL 4.0, is a major resource for improving efficiency. The query cache can have dramatic effects on the speed of frequently repeated queries on tables that are not updated often, particularly if those queries yield large resultsets.

It's also true that the efficiency of your MySQL application is going to be no better than that of your queries. The cardinal rule here is: *Don't do what isn't necessary*. So don't perform unneeded queries. Don't return columns and rows that aren't required by your application. Don't join tables that aren't relevant to the problem you're trying to solve. We'll try to point out the most common errors of these types and what you can do to correct them, or better yet, to avoid making them in the first place. We'll also try to point out some common issues with application logic that affect an application's efficiency, such as repeated queries and connections, unneeded calculations, and the matter of database interoperability layers.

Configuration Issues

In addition to optimizing MySQL databases and applications, you can do a lot toward optimizing the MySQL server itself by way of various configuration settings. The first step is to read the configuration and system variables. Once you've done this, you can take appropriate action if these variables indicate performance could be improved. This action might be one or more of the following:

- Changing a value in the my.cnf (or my.ini) configuration file

- Making changes in the design of one or more tables, or adding or modifying table indexes

- Rewriting the queries that are being used by the application

- Upgrading the server hardware or changing the network configuration

In this section, we'll concentrate on reading configuration and system variables, and changing configuration settings. Later in this chapter, we'll look at some of the other possible solutions.

 NOTE *For more about the MySQL commands for viewing configuration and system variables—how to run them from the system shell, additional information you can get from them, and so on—see Chapter 10 of Martin Kofler's* The Definitive Guide to MySQL, Second Edition, *published by Apress.*

System and Status Variables

In order to understand what's happening with a running MySQL server and to see how well it's performing, you need to be able to read four types of status settings or variables:

- Configuration variables

- System variables

- Running processes

- Table variables

In the following sections, we'll look at the SQL commands you can use to accomplish these tasks and discuss how to interpret the results.

SHOW VARIABLES

The SHOW VARIABLES command is used to read the configuration settings currently in effect for the MySQL server daemon. As there can be in excess of 150 of these (181 on our test server running MySQL 5.0.1-alpha), it's usually a good idea to run this command using a LIKE clause. Here's an example:

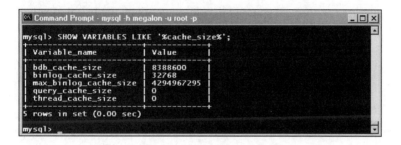

```
mysql> SHOW VARIABLES LIKE '%cache_size%';
+----------------------+------------+
| Variable_name        | Value      |
+----------------------+------------+
| bdb_cache_size       | 8388600    |
| binlog_cache_size    | 32768      |
| max_binlog_cache_size| 4294967295 |
| query_cache_size     | 0          |
| thread_cache_size    | 0          |
+----------------------+------------+
5 rows in set (0.00 sec)

mysql>
```

NOTE *All of the* SHOW *commands discussed in this section support* LIKE *clauses, which can be very useful in narrowing the result to those few variables and values in which you're most interested at any given time. This* LIKE *clause follows the same syntax rules as the* LIKE *clause used with a* SELECT *command (discussed in Chapter 1).*

You can run the equivalent to a SHOW VARIABLES command from a system shell using this command:

```
shell> mysqladmin variables
```

Don't worry—we won't cover *all* of the configuration variables in this chapter. We'll focus on the ones that are most useful to fine-tuning MySQL and MYSQL applications. An alphabetical listing of the 40 or so variables that you're most likely to need to know about when doing so is shown in Table 6-1.

Table 6-1. Some Common MySQL Configuration Variables

VARIABLE	DESCRIPTION/COMMENTS
back_log	Maximum number of outstanding connection requests. If your application requires a great many simultaneous requests (and there's no easy way to avoid that), you may want to increase this value. Note that there are limits on this value imposed by the operating system.
binlog_cache_size	Size of the cache used to store SQL statements during a transaction before they're committed. If your application uses a great many statements per transaction, you can increase this value for better performance.
bulk_insert_buffer_size	Size of the cache used to perform bulk inserts. This affects MyISAM tables only. The default value is 8MB.
concurrent_inserts	When set to ON, this allows inserts to be performed on MyISAM tables while running SELECT queries on them.
connect_timeout	Number of seconds that MySQL will wait for a connection packet before rejecting the connection.
delay_key_write	When this is enabled by being set to ON or ALL, writing to MyISAM tables with keys is faster because the key buffer is flushed to disk only when the table is closed, but tables should be checked frequently with myisamchk –fast –force. ON means that MySQL will honor the DELAY KEY WRITE option when used in a CREATE TABLE statement. OFF means the option will be ignored. ALL means that all tables will be treated as though they were created with this option.
delayed_insert_limit	When using INSERT DELAYED, MySQL will insert this many rows before checking to see if the thread has any SELECT statements to be performed. If your application performs a great many INSERTs and relatively few SELECTs, you may be able to increase performance by raising this number.

Table 6-1. Some Common MySQL Configuration Variables (Continued)

VARIABLE	DESCRIPTION/COMMENTS
delayed_insert_timeout	Number of seconds a DELAYED INSERT thread should wait for INSERT statements.
delayed_queue_size	Number of rows to be queued before performing inserts from a DELAYED INSERT thread.
flush	If this is set to ON, MySQL will free resources after executing each SQL command; this will slow down MySQL and should be used only for troubleshooting crashes.
flush_time	If this is not zero (0), MySQL will stop each flush_time seconds to close all tables in order to free all resources. This will slow down MySQL considerably, and should not be used except on systems with very low memory or disk space.
ft_max_word_length	Maximum length for a word to be included in a full-text index (added in MySQL 4.0).
ft_min_word_length	Minimum length for a word to be included in a full-text index (added in MySQL 4.0).
init_connect	Beginning with MySQL 4.1.2, this can be set to a string containing SQL commands to be executed for each client connecting to MySQL.
interactive_timeout	MySQL waits this many seconds for activity on an interactive connection before closing it.
join_buffer_size	Size of the buffer used for full joins. For large joins where it's not possible to add indexes, you may be able to increase efficiency by increasing this value.
key_buffer_size	Size of the buffer used for index blocks. On a dedicated server, this should usually be about 25% of total RAM. Depending on the operating system, you may be able to increase it beyond this value, but anything above 50% of RAM is liable to be counterproductive due to paging effects caused by the fact that MySQL does not cache data reads from the files, leaving this to be handled by the operating system.

(Continued)

Table 6-1. Some Common MySQL Configuration Variables (Continued)

VARIABLE	DESCRIPTION/COMMENTS
log	Will be ON if logging of all queries is enabled; this will tend to slow down MySQL by a very small amount and the log file will grow extremely rapidly. You may gain some improvement in performance by disabling it, and doing so is recommended if binary logging is enabled. Discontinued as of MySQL 5.0.
log_bin	Will be ON if binary logging is enabled. This is much more efficient than the query log and is recommended instead of it.
log_update	Will be ON if update logging is enabled. As with log, a very small performance increase may be gained by turning this OFF.
long_query_time	If a query takes longer than long_query_time seconds, it will be recorded in the slow query log.
max_allowed_packet	Largest packet allowed. This should be as small as you can make it without impacting your application. You should increase its size only if you need to store and retrieve large BLOB values.
max_connections	Maximum number of simultaneous connections. Increase this only as needed, since doing so incurs filesystem overhead.
max_delayed_threads	Maximum number of threads allowed for DELAY_INSERT operations. Once this number of INSERT DELAYED threads is in use, any additional insertions will be performed as if the DELAYED attribute wasn't specified. This value can be set to 0.
max_join_size	Joins that are likely to read more than max_join_size records will return an error. This can be used to help you catch joins that lack a WHERE clause, that are likely to take a very long time, and that return many excess rows.

Table 6-1. Some Common MySQL Configuration Variables (Continued)

VARIABLE	DESCRIPTION/COMMENTS
max_seeks_for_key	Maximum number of seeks when looking up rows based on a key. By setting this to a low value (try 100 as a starting point), you can force MySQL to prefer keys instead of table scans, which may improve performance if you're using keys to good effect.
max_sort_length	Number of bytes used from TEXT or BLOB values when sorting them. Decreasing this value can increase the speed of ORDER BY queries. However, you should be careful not to make it too small, or you will lose accuracy in performing sorts.
max_user_connections	Maximum number of active connections per user (0 = no limit). This can be used to keep individual users or applications from tying up too many resources.
max_write_lock_count	After this many write locks are in effect, allow some read locks to take place. Normally, update operations take precedence over SELECT queries. Decreasing this value forces MySQL to let some selects to take place after fewer updates have occurred than normal, so that the SELECTs don't get put on hold for so long when large numbers of INSERT and UPDATE queries are taking place.
net_buffer_length	Size to which MySQL's communication buffer is reset between queries. This normally should not be changed; however, to gain a small performance improvement on systems with little memory, it can be can set to the expected length of SQL statements sent by clients.
query_alloc_block_size	Size of memory blocks created for use during processing of queries. It can be increased slightly to help prevent memory fragmentation problems.
query_cache_limit	Query results larger than this are not cached. Default is 1MB.
query_cache_size	Memory used to store results of previous queries. The default is 0 (disabled).

(Continued)

Table 6-1. Some Common MySQL Configuration Variables (Continued)

VARIABLE	DESCRIPTION/COMMENTS
query_cache_type	Used with SELECT NO_CACHE and SELECT_CACHE. Its settings are 0 = OFF; 1 = cache all results except those where SELECT NO_CACHE is used; 2 = cache only result of SELECT CACHE queries.
read_buffer_size	Each thread that does a sequential scan allocates a buffer of this size for each table it scans. If you do many sequential scans, you may want to increase this value.
slow_launch_time	If creation of a thread takes longer than slow_launch_time seconds, it will increment the slow_launch_threads counter.
sort_buffer_size	Size of the sort memory buffer allocated to each thread. This can be increased to speed up ORDER BY and GROUP BY queries. The default is 2MB.
table_cache	Number of open tables for all threads. You can see if this needs to be increased by checking the value of the Open_tables variable (see Table 6-2).
thread_cache_size	Number of threads kept in cache for immediate reuse. New threads are taken from this cache first if any are available. You can sometimes improve performance in cases where there are many new connections by increasing this variable.
tmp_table_size	Temporary tables larger than this are stored on disk. If the server has plenty of memory, this can be increased to improve performance with large resultsets.
transaction_alloc_block_size	Amount of memory allocated for storing queries that are part of a transaction that is to be stored in the binary log when doing a commit.
transaction_prealloc_block_size	Buffer for transaction allocation blocks that are not freed between queries. You can often increase performance by making this large enough to fit all queries in a common transaction.

Memory and cache sizes are in bytes unless otherwise noted.

You will probably need to do some experimenting to get the right "mix" of configuration values for your system, and requirements may (and very likely will) change over time in response to changes in the size and numbers of your databases and tables, number and types of queries being run, number of users, hardware changes, and so forth.

When testing, you can set system variables using the SET command, for example:

```
SET GLOBAL key_buffer_size = 10000000;
```

Once you've determined the best value for your setup, you can force MySQL to use this value from startup by adding the appropriate line to the my.ini file, as shown here:

```
set-variable = key_buffer_size=10000000
```

The following are the most important of these variables in terms of overall performance:

key_buffer_size: This should be about 25% of available system memory. This can be increased somewhat if you have a lot of memory (more than 256MB), but should probably never be more than 45% to 50% of the system's total RAM.

table_cache: If your application requires a lot of tables to be open at the same time, try increasing the size of the table_cache variable. (For more information about caching issues, see the "Caching" section later in this chapter.)

read_buffer_size: If you're doing a lot a sequential scans (see the entry for Handler_read_rnd_next in Table 6-2), you should first try adding table indexes or optimizing existing ones. If that doesn't work or isn't feasible, you may want to increase the size of read_buffer_size.

sort_buffer_size: If you're doing a lot of ORDER BY and/or GROUP BY queries that return large resultsets, you may find that increasing the value of sort_buffer_size helps. You may need to experiment with this. Try increasing it in increments of 5% to 10% of the starting value to see if and by how much this speeds up large queries of this type.

net_buffer_length: In situations where memory is at a premium or you have a very high number of connections, you may be able to improve matters by adjusting the size of net_buffer_length. However, if you set this value to be too small, you'll waste any performance gain you might have otherwise obtained, because MySQL will need to keep resetting this value in order to accommodate queries that are longer than the stated number of bytes.

You can optimize the existing my.cnf configuration file or select one of those supplied with MySQL. These are named my-small.cnf, my-medium.cnf, my-large.cnf, and my-huge.cnf. For serious applications, you'll probably want to use one of the latter two as your starting point.

The best way to optimize these settings is to check the values of a number of MySQL status variables while your application is running, adjust system variables accordingly, and then check the status variables again. To examine status variables, you'll need to use the SHOW STATUS command, which is described in the next section.

SHOW STATUS

The SHOW STATUS command displays information about the status of the running MySQL server. Using this command will show you status information such as how many queries of a given type have been run since MySQL was last restarted, current uptime, caching data, and so on.

As with SHOW VARIABLES, there are about 150 values returned by an unmodified SHOW STATUS command, so it's usually best to use this command with a LIKE clause. Here's an example showing how you might obtain current data about how MySQL is handling threads:

```
Command Prompt - mysql -h megalon -u root -p                      _ □ ×

mysql> SHOW STATUS LIKE '%thread%';
+-----------------------+-------+
| Variable_name         | Value |
+-----------------------+-------+
| Delayed_insert_threads | 0     |
| Slow_launch_threads    | 0     |
| Threads_cached         | 0     |
| Threads_connected      | 2     |
| Threads_created        | 9     |
| Threads_running        | 2     |
+-----------------------+-------+
6 rows in set (0.05 sec)

mysql>
```

You can run the equivalent command from a system shell or DOS prompt as follows:

```
shell> mysqladmin extended-status
```

You can pipe this to a file for later review and analysis using something like this:

```
shell> mysqladmin extended-status > ext-status.txt
```

The file will be created relative to the current directory; you can also specify a system absolute path (such as /home/users/mystuff/ext-status.txt or C:\Documents and Settings\Jon\My Documents\ext-status.txt) if desired. Of course, you can also save the results of a mysqladmin variables command to a file using the same technique.

Table 6-2 shows those status variables that are likely to be of the most use to you when analyzing the performance of your MySQL server. Most of these values are counters; all are reset each time MySQL is restarted.

 NOTE *MySQL configuration variables are displayed in lowercase; status variables are displayed with a leading capital letter.*

Table 6-2. Common MySQL Status Variables

VARIABLE	DESCRIPTION/COMMENTS
Aborted_clients	Number of connections that were aborted without closing the connection properly. If this is a high proportion of the Connections count, there may be problems with your application code (such as waiting too long without activity or failing to close a connection when finished) or networking problems.
Aborted_connects	Number of times that connections to MySQL failed. This could be high compared to the value of Connections for a number of reasons, such as networking problems, failure to employ a correct user/password, incorrect database privileges, or malformed packets. Always investigate the situation when you note a high Aborted_clients / Connections ratio, because this may indicate security problems, such as someone trying to break into your MySQL server! This may also be a sign that the value of max_allowed_packet (see Table 6-1) is set too low. Note that the default value for max_allowed_packet should be large enough for most purposes and probably shouldn't be increased unless you're consistently running queries that return result rows larger than this.
Bytes_received	Number of bytes received from all clients.
Bytes_sent	Number of bytes sent to all clients.
Com_xxx	Number of times each *xxx* command has been executed (For example, Com_insert gives the number of INSERT commands performed; Com_select, Com_show_status, Com_update, and so on work the same way for their associated commands.)

(Continued)

Table 6-2. Common MySQL Status Variables (Continued)

VARIABLE	DESCRIPTION/COMMENTS
Connections	Total number of connection attempts to the MySQL server.
Created_tmp_disk_tables	Number of implicit temporary tables on disk created while executing statements.
Created_tmp_files	How many temporary files have been created by MySQL.
Created_tmp_tables	Number of implicit temporary tables in memory created while executing statements.
Delayed_insert_threads	Number of delayed insert handler threads in use.
Delayed_errors	Number of rows written using INSERT DELAYED for which some error occurred (probably duplicate key).
Delayed_writes	Number of rows written using INSERT DELAYED.
Handler_delete	Number of times a row was deleted from a table. (Com_delete counts the number of actual DELETE commands.)
Handler_read_first	Number of times the first entry was read from an index. If this is high compared to Handler_read_rnd_next, MySQL is probably doing a lot of full-index scans (this is usually a good thing).
Handler_read_key	Number of requests to read a row based on a key. A high Handler_read_key value compared to Handler_read_rnd_next is a good indicator that your queries are optimized and tables are properly indexed.
Handler_read_next	Number of requests to read next row in key order, and is incremented whenever you perform a query on an index column with a range constraint. This count is also incremented when you do an index scan.
Handler_read_prev	Number of requests to read the previous row in key order. This is mainly used to optimize ORDER BY ... DESC.
Handler_read_rnd	Number of requests to read a row based on a fixed position. This will be high if you are doing a lot of queries that require sorting of the result.

Table 6-2. Common MySQL Status Variables (Continued)

VARIABLE	DESCRIPTION/COMMENTS
Handler_read_rnd_next	Number of requests to read the next row in the datafile. This will be high if you are doing a lot of table scans, which usually indicates that tables aren't properly indexed: It can also mean that queries aren't being written to take advantage of existing indexes.
Handler_update	Number of requests to update a row in a table. (Com_update represents the number of actual UPDATE queries.)
Handler_write	Number of requests to insert a row in a table. (Com_insert is the number of actual INSERT commands.)
Key_blocks_used	Number of used blocks in the key cache.
Key_read_requests	Number of requests to read a key block from the cache.
Key_reads	Number of physical reads of a key block from disk. (See the "Key Cache" section later in this chapter.)
Key_write_requests	Number of requests to write a key block to the cache. (See the "Key Cache" section later in this chapter.)
Key_writes	Number of physical writes of a key block to disk.
Max_used_connections	Maximum number of connections that have been in use simultaneously. If this is close to the value of the max_connections configuration variable, it may be time to increase this value, or to look for ways to decrease the number of simultaneous connections required for your purposes.
Not_flushed_delayed_rows	Number of rows waiting to be written in INSERT DELAY queues. If this is very high compared to delayed_insert_limit or delayed_queue_size (see Table 6-1), you may need to increase the value of one or both of these.
Not_flushed_key_blocks	Key blocks in the key cache that have changed but haven't yet been flushed to disk. If this appears persistently high, you may need to increase the value of key_buffer_size (see Table 6-1).
Open_files	Number of files that are currently open.
Open_streams	Number of streams that are currently open (used mainly for logging).

(Continued)

Table 6-2. Common MySQL Status Variables (Continued)

VARIABLE	DESCRIPTION/COMMENTS
Open_tables	Number of tables that are currently open.
Opened_tables	Total number of tables that have been opened.
Questions	Total number of queries that have been sent to the server.
Select_full_join	Number of joins that have been made without using any keys. Ideally, this value should always be 0; if it isn't, you should check all of your table indexes.
Select_full_range_join	Number of joins where a range search was used on a reference table.
Select_range	Number of joins where a range search was used on the first table. (Normally not critical even if quite large.)
Select_range_check	Number of joins without keys where key usage was checked for after each row. Ideally, this value should be 0. If it's not, you should review your tables and joins to see if there are sufficient indexes and if they're being used properly.
Select_scan	Number of joins where a full scan was done on the first table. You should review your joins to see if there are any that could benefit from additional indexing.
Slow_launch_threads	Total number of threads that have taken more than slow_launch_time to create.
Slow_queries	Total number of queries that have taken more than long_query_time seconds to execute. If this number is a very large proportion of the total number of queries, you should check the query log to determine which ones are running slowly and try to remedy this.
Sort_merge_passes	Number of merge passes that MySQL's internal sorting algorithms have needed to perform. If this value is large, you should consider increasing the value of the sort_buffer configuration variable.
Sort_range	Number of sorts that were done with ranges.
Sort_rows	Number of sorted rows.
Sort_scan	Number of sorts that were done by scanning the table. If this isn't 0, you might want to look at indexing the columns used in ORDER BY or GROUP BY queries.

Table 6-2. Common MySQL Status Variables (Continued)

VARIABLE	DESCRIPTION/COMMENTS
Table_locks_immediate	Number of times a table lock was acquired immediately.
Table_locks_waited	Number of times a table lock could not be acquired immediately and a wait was needed. If this is high, and you have performance problems, you should first optimize your queries, and then either split your table or use replication.
Threads_cached	Number of threads in the thread cache.
Threads_connected	Number of currently open connections. This should be fairly close to the value of Threads_running and Threads_created.
Threads_created	Number of threads created to handle connections.
Threads_running	Number of threads that are not sleeping.
Uptime	How many seconds the server has been up.

Of all the variables shown in Table 6-2, the following are probably the most important with regard to index and query optimization:

Handler_read_key, Handler_read_next, **and** Handler_read_rnd_next: The higher that Handler_read_rnd_next is, the more queries there are being run without the use of indexes (the rnd is short for *random*). When taken in relation to each of the first two values, this provides a rough measure of how efficiently you're using indexes. If either of these ratios is greater than a very small fraction, you need to examine your tables and queries for proper use of indexes.

Key_reads **and** Key_read_requests: The ratio of these two values should be a very small fraction. If it isn't, you may need to increase the size of the key_buffer_size configuration variable. If you can't increase this without going past the upper limit value of 50% of system RAM, consider adding more physical memory to the server. See the "Key Cache" section later in this chapter for more information.

Select_full_joins **and** Select_range_check: If either of these numbers is anything other than 0, it means that there are queries being run that don't use any indexes at all. This is the worst possible thing that can happen with regard to efficiency. You should definitely take the time to determine which queries these are, and either add indexes on the appropriate table columns or rewrite the queries to take advantage of existing indexes.

Select_scan: If this number is not 0, you have joins where no indexes are being used for the first table in a join. You should check your joins to see where adding indexes or making use of existing ones can take care of these.

Slow_launch_threads and Slow_queries: These indicate, respectively, the number of threads taking longer than slow_launch_time to begin and the number of queries taking longer than long_query_time (see Table 6-1 for descriptions of these) to run. The default values for these configuration variables are 2 and 10 seconds, respectively. Reasonable values for them under actual usage conditions will vary; we recommend 1 and 3 seconds as a good starting point.

Sort_merge_passes: If you see a large value for this compared with Sort_rows, you likely need to increase the value of the sort_buffer_size configuration variable, as MySQL is needing to make multiple passes to perform sorts required by ORDER BY and GROUP BY queries.

Sort_scan: This many sorts were performed without using any indexes. This can cause a major slowdown of ORDER BY and GROUP BY queries on large tables and large resultsets. You should determine which of these queries is incrementing the Sort_scan count, and add indexes or make use of existing ones.

You can also obtain a short summary of the server status by using the STATUS command (or the abbreviated form \s). As shown in the following example, this command displays basic client and server information, along with an abbreviated version of what you would obtain using the SHOW PROCESSLIST command (described in the next section).

SHOW PROCESSLIST

The SHOW PROCESSLIST command shows the processes currently running on the server, and comes in two versions:

```
SHOW PROCESSLIST
SHOW FULL PROCESSLIST
```

Including the FULL keyword forces the complete display of all SQL commands currently being run; without it, only the first 100 characters of each one is shown.

Here is some sample output from a SHOW PROCESSLIST command (using the \G switch to make it fit nicely within the DOS window):

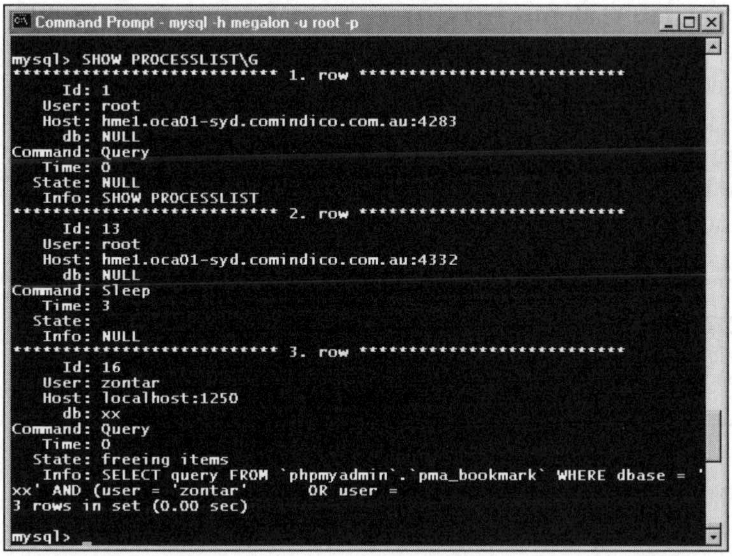

Table 6-3 describes the information displayed by SHOW ProcessLisT.

Table 6-3. SHOW PROCESSLIST Information

COLUMN	DESCRIPTION
Id	Process ID; use with the KILL command to kill a process
User	Database user account name
Host	Host in *hostname:port* format or IP address
db	Name of current database
Command	Type of command; usually either Sleep or Query

(Continued)

Table 6-3. SHOW PROCESSLIST Information (Continued)

COLUMN	DESCRIPTION
Time	Seconds that this command has been running
State	Shows the current state of the process; see Table 6-4
Info	Text of the current SQL command (or NULL for a sleeping thread)

With this command, you can see at a glance what every MySQL user is doing. This is particularly useful if you get a "Too Many Connections" error and need to see what's going on. Unfortunately, there's no simple way to page the results from the MySQL Monitor on Windows systems, but you can pipe the output of the equivalent system shell command mysqladmin processlist to a file. On Linux and other Unix platforms, you can use PAGER less; to page the result. Note that you cannot use a LIKE clause with SHOW PROCESSLIST.

In order to get the most out of SHOW PROCESSLIST, you need to run it as the MySQL root user or as a user with the SUPER privilege. MySQL always reserves one thread for a user with this privilege; for this reason, you should never assign this privilege to an ordinary user. Users with the SUPER privilege can view all threads and kill any thread. Ordinary users can view or kill only their own threads.

 NOTE *The* SUPER *privilege is not supported prior to MySQL 4.0.2. On Win32 platforms, the old* PROCESS *privilege remains in use through MySQL 4.0.10.*

If you observe a process that has been running for an overly long time, you can force it to be terminated using the KILL command:

```
KILL processId;
```

where *processId* is the process ID of the thread.

Generally, any command (other than Sleep, of course) that is taking a very long time to execute has probably run into trouble, so you should investigate to determine the cause of the problem. This may be the result of an incompetent or abusive user or of a "hung" application, and you may need to kill such threads manually. Of course, what constitutes "a very long time" will vary according to your specific situation. If your server is being used in a data warehousing application involving many thousands (or even millions) of records, it may be normal for a single SELECT or SELECT INSERT query to run for 10 or 15 minutes. On the other hand, if the server is supporting a relatively small web site or two, and a single query takes that long to execute, it's a safe bet that something has gone wrong.

Something else to consider is that as systems grow, what may once have been acceptable may no longer be so. For example, programmers may have used SELECT * because tables were small and didn't contain very many rows. As the number of records increases, it may be necessary to fine-tune those queries and retrieve only the columns and rows actually needed by the application. However, this isn't the only possibility for corrective action, as you can see from Table 6-4.

Table 6-4. Common State Values Shown by SHOW PROCESSLIST

STATE VALUE	DESCRIPTION/EXPLANATION
Checking table	The process is examining a table, which is entirely normal.
Closing tables	The thread is saving changed table data to disk and closing the tables used. This should happen very quickly, unless the disk is full, very badly fragmented, or in very heavy use.
Connect out	A replication slave is connecting to the master server. (Used in replication scenarios only.)
Copying to tmp table on disk	A temporary resultset was larger than the value set for the tmp_table_size configuration variable in my.cnf (or possibly my.ini on Windows) that determines the maximum amount of memory in bytes that a resultset may take up; the thread is now copying the temporary table from RAM to disk in order to save memory. If you observe this happening a great deal and your system has sufficient memory, you can safely increase this value and thus the speed at which such large queries are executed.
Creating tmp table	The thread is creating a temporary table to hold the result of a query (or part of the result).
Deleting from main table	The thread is executing the first part of a multiple-table delete (deleting from the first table only).
Deleting from reference tables	The thread is executing the second part of a multiple-table delete (deleting matched rows from other tables).
Flushing tables	The thread is reloading tables and is waiting for all other threads to close their tables before proceeding.
Killed	A KILL command has been issued for this thread, but has not yet taken effect. (Once it has been killed, the thread will no longer be listed.)

(Continued)

Table 6-4. Common State Values Shown by SHOW PROCESSLIST (Continued)

STATE VALUE	DESCRIPTION/EXPLANATION
Sending data	The thread is processing a SELECT statement and sending the resulting rows of data to the user.
Sorting for group	The thread is performing a sort as the result of a GROUP BY query.
Sorting for order	The thread is doing a sort due to an ORDER BY query.
Opening table	The thread is attempting to open a table, which should normally occur very quickly. If this persists, it is likely that a previous ALTER or LOCK command hasn't yet finished.
Removing duplicates	This sometimes occurs when a SELECT DISTINCT can't easily be optimized by MySQL and an extra step must be performed to remove duplicate rows before returning the final result.
Reopen table	This occurs when a thread attempts to obtain a lock for a table, but the table structure changed before the lock was complete; the thread has released the lock, closed the table, and is now trying to reopen it.
Searching rows for update	This happens when an UPDATE query has changed the index that is being used to find rows by the UPDATE query itself. In other words, a query of the form `UPDATE table SET column=newvalue WHERE column=oldvalue;` is being executed, which may take a long time when the table is extremely large, *newvalue* and/or *oldvalue* are the result of a calculation, or the WHERE clause is particularly complex and is comparing a great many values.
Sleep	A connection for this thread is open, but isn't currently executing any commands from the client that opened it.
System lock	The thread is waiting for an external system lock for the table to be released. If you are not using multiple MySQL servers, you can (and probably should) disable system locks by starting the MySQL daemon with `–skip-external-locking`. You can also set `skip_lock=On` in your my.cnf or my.ini file to accomplish this.

Table 6-4. Common State Values Shown by SHOW PROCESSLIST (Continued)

STATE VALUE	DESCRIPTION/EXPLANATION
Upgrading lock	An INSERT DELAYED is waiting to obtain a lock on the table before inserting rows. (INSERT DELAYED causes INSERT statements not to be executed until the table is no longer in use by any threads executing SELECT or DELETE statements on the same table. The server then locks the table and performs all pending INSERT statements for that table before unlocking it again.)
Updating	The thread is performing an UPDATE query on a table.
User Lock	The thread is waiting on a locked table to be released. If this persists, you may have a problem and need to restart the server. In such cases, you should examine the table after the restart to make sure that it hasn't been corrupted. If it has been corrupted, restore it from a backup.
Waiting for tables	The thread was notified that a table that it is trying to open has been changed by another thread. The thread must wait until any other threads using the table have closed it before reopening it, so that it can obtain the updated version of the table.

SHOW TABLE STATUS

It can sometimes be helpful to see how much data has been stored in one or more tables, when they were last accessed, their types, and how much memory has been allocated to them. SHOW TABLE STATUS provides this sort of information. You can use it on a database that is not currently selected by adding a FROM *dbname* clause, and its output can be filtered with a LIKE clause (and wildcards if desired).

The following example shows how to get the status of all tables in the **mdbd** database whose names begin with the string "orders." It also serves to illustrate the columns returned by this command and the type of information displayed in each one.

```
Command Prompt - mysql -h megalon -u root -p                          _ □ ×
mysql> SHOW TABLE STATUS FROM mdbd LIKE 'orders%'\G
*************************** 1. row ***************************
           Name: orders
         Engine: MyISAM
        Version: 9
     Row_format: Dynamic
           Rows: 26
 Avg_row_length: 31
    Data_length: 820
Max_data_length: 4294967295
   Index_length: 2048
      Data_free: 0
 Auto_increment: 27
    Create_time: 2003-11-25 12:59:37
    Update_time: 2004-03-29 13:40:55
     Check_time: 2004-05-30 12:51:03
      Collation: latin1_swedish_ci
       Checksum: NULL
 Create_options:
        Comment: orders table
*************************** 2. row ***************************
           Name: orders2
         Engine: MyISAM
        Version: 9
     Row_format: Fixed
           Rows: 8
 Avg_row_length: 35
    Data_length: 280
Max_data_length: 150323855359
   Index_length: 2048
      Data_free: 0
 Auto_increment: 9
    Create_time: 2004-03-13 00:58:02
    Update_time: 2004-03-14 19:33:30
     Check_time: 2004-05-30 12:51:03
      Collation: latin1_swedish_ci
       Checksum: NULL
 Create_options:
        Comment:
2 rows in set (0.00 sec)

mysql>
```

For InnoDB tables, the **Create_time**, **Update_time**, **Check_time**, and **Max_data_length** columns will be NULL. Available free space will be shown in the Comment column, along with any foreign key constraints defined for the table.

NOTE   *MySQL 4.1.1 adds two new columns: **Collation** and **Checksum**. The **Collation** column shows the table's character set and collation. The **Checksum** column shows the checksum for the table (if there is one). In MySQL 5.0.1, views are also represented in the output of* SHOW TABLES. *If the table is a view, all columns except **Name** and **Comment** will be shown as* NULL, *with the value for **Comment** being* view.

Tools for Monitoring Performance

There are some administration tools available that can make the job of monitoring the MySQL server much simpler and easier. Space does not permit us to go into a great amount of detail concerning these, but we thought it would be a good idea to mention four of the more commonly used ones: mytop, WinMySqlAdmin, MySQL Administrator, and phpMyAdmin.

NOTE *For more information about MySQL administration tools, check the product or project web sites, or consult another reference, such as* Enterprise MySQL *(which will soon be available from Apress).*

mytop

The mytop utility is an Open Source, text-mode tool written in Perl that allows you to monitor server status in real time. This is particularly useful on Unix systems where you want something a little more sophisticated than the output of a SHOW command, but don't want the added overhead of running a GUI on your database server.

However, we've also run this on Windows NT and Windows 2000 systems under ActivePerl from ActiveState.com without any problems. mytop was originally created by Yahoo programmer Jeremy Zawodny and is modeled after the top utility, which is commonly used for monitoring Unix system processes. He continues to develop it and has accepted contributions from several others. The latest release at the time of this writing was version 1.4. You can visit the mytop home page at http://jeremy.zawodny.com/mysql/mytop.

WinMySqlAdmin

WinMySqlAdmin is a Windows-only GUI configuration tool that allows you to read configuration and status data and to update the my.ini file with new configuration variable values using a simple built-in text editor. (One slight drawback is that you can't update a my.cnf file on a Windows machine using this utility.) This program is included with the Win32 distribution of MySQL and should run on all Windows flavors.

This tool is being superseded by MySQL Administrator (described in the next section), but may remain useful with legacy installations of MySQL, versions 3.23 and earlier.

MySQL Administrator

MySQL Administrator is a full-featured GUI tool for configuring and administering a MySQL server and is available for Windows and Linux systems. Still under development at this writing (the latest version was 1.0.9), it is already very powerful and usable and can perform nearly every task that you would otherwise do using the command line and/or a text editor. The interface is extremely intuitive and has a great deal of helpful information built directly into it, such as descriptions of all the configuration variables as part of the appropriate displays. Because MySQL Administrator employs the newer version of the MySQL client programming libraries, it can be used only with servers running MySQL versions 4.0 or newer.

You can probably expect this utility (or one quite similar to it) to become part of the standard MySQL toolkit by the time that MySQL 4.1 is in a production release. In Chapter 8, we'll take a look at another new tool that MySQL AB is developing, the MySQL Query Browser, which provides a graphical interface for working with queries and tables.

phpMyAdmin

phpMyAdmin is an Open Source application written in PHP. It will run on nearly any web server supporting both PHP and MySQL, including both Apache and Internet Information Server (IIS). It can be used with MySQL 3.21 through 4.1 (we have tested releases 2.5.x through 2.6.0 with MySQL 4.1.3-beta and 5.0.1-alpha on servers running PHP 4 and PHP 5; it seems to work fine with these as well), and with PHP 3.0.8–5.0. As of this writing, the latest production release was 2.5.7 and version 2.6.0 was in beta.

 CAUTION   *phpMyAdmin versions previous to 2.6.0 do not employ the new MySQLi library (see Chapter 7). If you wish to use an older version of phpMyAdmin on a web server running PHP 5, you'll need to make sure that the older PHP 4-style* mysql *library is present.*

This tool is very simple to install and configure, and allows users who have the correct privileges to accomplish most MySQL database administration and query-related functions through any relatively recent web browser. For example, you can view processes, check server and table status, and check configuration variables. Although you can't use it to update a my.cnf or my.ini file, you can update configuration variables at least temporarily using the appropriate SET commands.

Administration of multiple MySQL servers is also possible with phpMyAdmin. Another big plus is that phpMyAdmin is internationalized quite well, currently supporting more than 45 languages. For more information about phpMyAdmin and to obtain a copy of the latest version, visit the phpMyAdmin home page at http://www.phpmyadmin.net/ or http://phpmyadmin.sourceforge.net/.

Log Files

MySQL can keep a number of different types of useful records of its activity. Those relating directly to performance issues include the query log, the update log, the binary log, and the slow query log. We'll look briefly at each of these and how to use them in this section.

Before proceeding to descriptions of the individual logs, here's a quick and simple way to see which logs and logging options are enabled on your server:

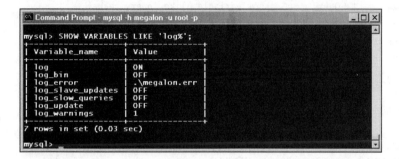

The first three entries show whether the query, update, or binary logs are enabled. The `log_slow_queries` setting indicates whether the slow query log is being kept. The `log_error` setting shows the name of the error log if it's not the default.

Normally, all logs are kept in MySQL's data directory. You can override this behavior by specifying a path in the *=filename* portion of the appropriate lines in your server's my.cnf or my.ini file. For example, to force the binary logs to be saved to the directory /usr/log/mysql, you would need a line that reads like this:

```
-log-bin=/usr/bin/log/mysql
```

General Query Log

The *query log* (sometimes referred to as the *general query log* in order to distinguish it from the slow query log) keeps a record of all connections made to the server and of all queries, the dates and times they were made, and the users (with process IDs) who made them. This log is a plain text file whose format is quite simple, as you can see from this sample:

```
MySql, Version: 5.0.0-alpha-max-nt-log, started with:
TCP Port: 3306, Named Pipe: MySQL
Time              Id Command     Argument
040524 17:59:39   12 Connect     root@localhost on
040524 17:59:43   12 Query       show databases
```

```
040524 18:00:26      12 Quit
040524 18:02:19      34 Connect      pytest@localhost on test
                     34 Query          INSERT INTO employees
                                       (empid, firstname, lastname)
                                       VALUES
                                       ('', 'Joan', 'Newhouse')
                     34 Query          SHOW WARNINGS
                     34 Quit
040525 18:05:11      13 Connect      root@localhost on
040525 18:05:24      13 Query        show variables like 'query_cache'
040525 18:05:28      13 Query        show variables like 'query_cache%'
040525 21:28:58      13 Query        show variables like '%cache%'
040525 21:36:41      13 Query        show variables like '%open%'
040525 21:52:49      13 Query        show status like '%open%'
040525 22:08:44      13 Query        show variables like '%key%'
040526  4:07:45      13 Quit
```

For instance, you can tell that the user **pytest@localhost** logged in to the **test** database at 18:02:19, was given process ID 34, ran an insert query, ran a SHOW WARNINGS command, and then immediately logged out. It's important to note that all SQL commands are logged as they're received, and not necessarily in the order that they're actually executed.

> **NOTE** *Access error messages (caused by trying to use unauthorized privileges) are recorded in the general query log, but query errors and warnings are not logged there. To view those, you need to use a* SHOW ERRORS *or* SHOW WARNINGS *command, or the equivalent API function, such as PHP 4's* mysql_error(), *in your application code.*

Enabling the general query log does slow down MySQL a bit, since it takes time to write a record of each connection and query. In addition, the query log file will very likely grow at a tremendous rate on a busy server! It's usually best to use it only when testing or debugging, and to rely on the update or binary log (preferably the latter) once the server goes into normal production use.

Update Log

In MySQL 3.*x* and 4.*x*, the update log keeps a record of all issued statements that update data. This log can be useful when you're trying to determine whether statements that are supposed to change data are actually doing so.

To enable update logging, use the −log-update=*filename* option in your MySQL configuration file or when running mysqld. The =*filename* portion is optional; the filename defaults to *hostname.###,* where ### is a three-digit numeral, unless you specify a file extension as part of *filename.* If present, this number is incremented for each new update log. A new update log is started whenever the logs are flushed or MySQL is restarted.

> **NOTE** *The update log has been removed in MySQL 5.0, and starting with that version, you must use the binary log instead. In earlier versions, it's still preferable to use the binary log, as it's faster and uses fewer resources. See the "Binary Log" section in this chapter for more information.*

The update log records only statements that actually update data. So an SQL command such as this:

```
UPDATE products SET prodname='Blender' WHERE prodid='147042';
```

does *not* get recorded in the update log if there's no product in the **products** table whose **prodid** is **147042**. An UPDATE statement that sets a column to the same value that column already has also won't be written to the update log.

The update log can also be useful if you need to restore a database following a crash or another severe problem and you have a good known starting point. Note that update queries are logged in the order in which they're actually executed, unlike the case with the general query log.

Binary Log

The binary log, like the update log it's intended to replace, records all statements that update data. Its primary purpose is to make it easy to restore your databases following a critical failure and to assist in replication. However, it can also be useful for debugging purposes, when you need to know whether a particular query, which should have updated a table, has in fact done so. It is faster and less wasteful of space than the update log, and beginning with MySQL 5.0, binary logs replace the update logs entirely.

To enable binary logging, you need to include the following line in the [mysqld] section of a MySQL my.cnf or my.ini configuration file:

```
log-bin[=filename]
```

Alternatively, you can use –log-bin[=*filename*] as a startup option to mysqld. The default name of the binary log file is *hostname*-bin. MySQL automatically supplies a three-digit file extension when it creates a binary log file, so if you try to supply an extension as part of the filename, the extension will be ignored and will *not* be used by MySQL in naming the file.

You can't usefully read a binary log with a text editor, as you can MySQL's other log files. Instead, you must use the `mysqlbinlog` utility, which is supplied as part of all MySQL distributions, as in this example:

```
shell> mysqlbinlog localhost-bin.001
```

You can save the output of `mysqlbinlog` to a text file for later analysis, similar to how you can redirect output from other MySQL utilities. For instance, you might use something like this from a system shell or DOS prompt:

```
shell> mysqlbinlog localhost-bin.001 > binlog1.txt
```

NOTE *For information about the use of* `mysqlbinlog` *with binary logs for replication purposes, run* `mysqlbinlog -help`, *consult the MySQL documentation for* `mysqlbinlog`, *or consult a reference such as the upcoming* Enterprise MySQL *from Apress.*

Slow Query Log

When slow query logging is enabled, MySQL logs all statements taking longer than `long_query_time` (see Table 6-1) seconds to execute. This can be used to find queries that are taking too long to execute, so that they can be optimized.

You can enable the slow query log by adding this line to your MySQL configuration file:

```
log-slow-queries[=filename]
```

Alternatively, you can use `-log-slow-queries[=filename]` as one of the startup options for `mysqld`. By default, the filename is *hostname*-slow.log. In addition, by using `log-long-format` (or `-log-long-format`) in MySQL 4.0 or earlier, you can specify that all queries that don't use any indexes are written to the slow query log, no matter how long those queries take to run. Beginning with MySQL 4.1, you should use `[-]log-queries-not-using-indexes` for this purpose.

NOTE *The time needed by MySQL to acquire table locks is* not *counted as part of the query execution time.*

Caching

MySQL has some caching capabilities that can enhance performance considerably. Here, we will discuss MySQL table, key, and query caching.

Table Cache

It's very important to remember that MySQL tables are actual, discrete files on disk, so that when you run queries, you're causing mysqld to open, read and/or write, and close files for each database table involved. In order to speed up these tasks, MySQL keeps a *table cache*, which is another way of saying that it keeps files open in between queries so that they may be accessed again quickly without the overhead of closing them and then reopening them each time they're needed. The maximum number of files the server keeps open is affected by the table_cache, max_connections, and max_tmp_tables server variables (see Table 6-1).

The optimum value for table_cache is directly related to that of max_connections, as well as to the number of tables that need to be open simultaneously in order to perform multiple-table joins. The table_cache value should be equal to no less than the number of concurrent connections you're expecting to your MySQL server times the largest number tables involved in any one join.

For example, if you know that your server needs to support up 100 simultaneous running connections, and the largest join used by your application involves 5 tables, you should have a table cache size of at least 500. (If you think this implies that each table is opened as many times as there are threads accessing the table, then you're absolutely correct. Three threads running the same three-table join at the same time use nine open tables.) You also need to reserve some extra file descriptors for temporary tables and files as well. This will vary according to how heavily you use temporary tables, but a good rule of thumb is to allow an extra 20%, due to the fact that MySQL also creates temporary tables behind the scenes (whether or not you're creating explicit temporary tables as part of your application). So, in this example, you would want to make sure that table_cache was set to at least 600.

However, there are limits imposed by the operating system on the number of open file descriptors. If you increase the size of the table cache, you need to check your system's documentation and make sure that you're not exceeding this limit; otherwise, MySQL may refuse connections, fail to perform queries, and be very unreliable. It's also necessary to keep in mind that the MyISAM engine uses two file descriptors per open table, so make sure that the value of the open_files_limit configuration variable is high enough to accommodate this. Note that the default value of zero means that MySQL will use as many file descriptors as necessary, up to the maximum allowed by the operating system.

Once opened, a table remains in the table cache until the table cache is full, the table is no longer in use, and a new table needs to be opened. Using a FLUSH TABLES command or the equivalent causes MySQL to attempt to clear the table cache by closing all unused tables. MySQL will, if necessary, temporarily increase the size of the table cache if possible to accommodate all queries being run at the same time.

You should check the Open_tables and Open_files status variables (see Table 6-2) while your application is running, and if these are large compared to table_cache and open_files_limit, you should consider increasing their values. However, don't forget about the operating system limits just mentioned when you do this.

Key Cache

In order to save reading from and writing to MyISAM table index files (.MYI files), MySQL also caches table indexes in a *key cache*. The size of this cache is determined by the value of the key_buffer_size configuration variable. In determining your server's performance with regard to key caching (and thus what the best key buffer size is likely to be), you need to look at two different ratios, which can be derived from status variable values.

The first of these is the cache miss rate, which can be calculated like this:

```
Key_cache_misses = Key_reads / Key_read_requests
```

This figure, which represents the proportion of keys that are being read from disk instead of the key cache, should normally be less than 0.01 for optimum efficiency. If it's much larger than this, you may want to try to increase the value set for key_buffer_size.

The other ratio you need to consider concerns updated keys, which need to be written to disk as quickly as possible. Therefore, you should check this ratio:

```
Key_write_flushes = Key_writes / Key_write_requests
```

You want this to be as close to 1 as possible. Again, if this figure doesn't approach the optimum, you'll want to increase key_buffer_size, if it's possible to do so without interfering with other memory allocations in the MySQL configuration.

Query Cache

Beginning with MySQL version 4.0.1, MySQL also has a *query cache*, which can help increase an application's speed dramatically when performing repetitive queries against your databases.

In order to make effective use of the query cache, you will need to make sure it is active and configured correctly. You can check for this by using show variables. The default values for the variables are shown in this example:

```
Command Prompt - mysql -h megalon -u root -p                          _ □ ×

mysql> SHOW VARIABLES LIKE 'query_cache%';
+-------------------------+---------+
| Variable_name           | Value   |
+-------------------------+---------+
| query_cache_limit       | 1048576 |
| query_cache_min_res_unit | 4096   |
| query_cache_size        | 0       |
| query_cache_type        | ON      |
+-------------------------+---------+
4 rows in set (0.00 sec)

mysql>
```

These variables control the query cache as follows:

query_cache_size: To enable query caching, set this to a nonzero value. This variable holds the total amount of memory (in bytes) set aside for storing cached queries. You might want to try 20MB or 40MB.

query_cache_limit: This is the maximum size for a cached result set. Resultsets larger than this won't be cached.

query_cache_min_res_unit: (MySQL 4.1 and above only) The default value is adequate in most cases. However, if you have a lot of small queries with small results, you may find that decreasing the value to 2048 or even 1024 bytes may improve performance. As you might expect, if you have a lot of very large queries and/or very large resultsets, increasing it to 8192, 16384, or even 32768 may speed up performance a bit.

query_cache_type: This can take one of three values: 0 = OFF (no results are cached), 1 = ON (all queries except those run with SQL_NO_CACHE are cached), and 2 = DEMAND (only queries run with SQL_CACHE are stored and retrieved).

When in use, the query cache stores the text and value of each SELECT statement. When another query is passed later, MySQL will check the cache first to see if a copy of it already exists; if it does, MySQL will return the result of the cache, rather than needing to process the entire query again. This can prove to be very useful and will provide a great speed advantage in an application such as an online catalog, where repetitive queries of products are being issued.

NOTE *The query cache does not return "stale" data. When data is modified, any relevant entries in the query cache are flushed, so that those queries are processed again to produce new resultsets.*

There is some overhead caused by having the query cache enabled. If you use many simple SELECT queries that aren't often repeated, having the query cache enabled may actually impede performance by 5% to 10%. However, using the query cache when your SELECT queries have large resultsets and are often reused, you may see performance increases on the order of 200% or even more.

By careful use and configuration of the query cache and the SQL_CACHE and SQL_NO_CACHE options for SELECT queries, you can cache only those queries that are largest and/or most often repeated, and not bother with those that are small, seldom repeated, or are most likely to return different results each time they're run. In this way, you'll be able to maximize the query cache's efficiency and thus that of your application.

Why Aren't My Queries Being Cached?

If you find that your queries are not being cached, there are two possible sources of problems that you can check. First, checking for cached queries is case-sensitive. Suppose you run this query:

```
SELECT * FROM mytable WHERE id=23;
```

Now let's say that later in the same application you run the same query as:

```
select * from mytable where id=23;
```

The second query will be considered a different query from the first one and rerun, rather than the results being pulled from the query cache. This is because MySQL's matching algorithm uses hashes in its query-matching routines.

Another reason that a query might not be cached is that in order to be cached, a query must begin with the SELECT keyword. It's perfectly legal in MySQL to begin a query with a comment, such as this:

```
/* get data from mytable for record 23 */ SELECT * FROM mytable WHERE id=23;
```

However, this query won't be cached because it doesn't begin with SELECT. Instead, placing your comment at the end of the query:

```
SELECT * FROM mytable WHERE id=23; /* get data from mytable for record 23 */
```

By observing these two rules—using uppercase or lowercase consistently and always beginning select queries with SELECT—you'll save yourself a lot of frustration as you're trying to fine-tune the performance of your MySQL applications.

Application Logic

Many people find that once they build an optimized database scheme for their application, they encounter bottlenecks and performance lags in their applications when trying to perform certain tasks. In this section, we'll discuss some of the causes of these. They include excessive connections, unnecessary or repetitive queries that could be combined into fewer queries, manipulating data in application code that could be handled just as well in a query, and database interoperability or database abstraction layers.

Repetitive Connections

Making repetitive connections to the database from within your application can cause a great amount of server overhead and can drastically reduce the performance of your application. Some people even have the mistaken idea that you must establish a new connection to MySQL each time you send a new query. They don't really understand the concept of a MySQL user session, or they don't realize how much time they have in between queries before MySQL closes the connection. You can easily find out how long a session will last using the appropriate SHOW VARIABLES command:

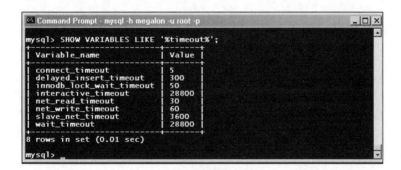

The important values to consider here are those for interactive_timeout and wait_timeout. As you can see, the default value for each of these is quite high: 28,800 seconds, which works out to eight hours. You can also obtain these values using a SELECT query, as shown here:

```
mysql> SELECT @@INTERACTIVE_TIMEOUT, @@WAIT_TIMEOUT;
+-----------------------+----------------+
| @@INTERACTIVE_TIMEOUT | @@WAIT_TIMEOUT |
+-----------------------+----------------+
|                 28800 |          28800 |
+-----------------------+----------------+
1 row in set (0.00 sec)

mysql>
```

For web applications, the story is a bit different: a new connection to MySQL must be made on each new page. Even so, it's almost never necessary to establish a new connection more than once per page, unless you need to interact with more than one database.

We'll discuss connection-related issues and programming strategies in the next two sections.

One Connection, Multiple Queries

If you need to retrieve data in several different places in your application, it is quite unnecessary to make multiple connections to MySQL to perform each query.

Consider the following pseudocode:

```
connect to db
if order form submitted then
  insert order data into db
  if insert is successful
    print success message
  else
    print failure message

close db connection

connect to db

query db for customer info
while recordset is not empty
  get name, address, city, state, zip
  print name, address, city, state, zip

close db connection

connect to db

query db for order info
while recordset is not empty
  get orderID, total, date
  print orderID, total, date

close db connection

connect to db
```

```
query db for order details
while recordset is not empty
  get items from db where orderID is the same as customer
  print items

close db connection
```

By opening (and closing) multiple connections to the database, we are causing our application to perform much more slowly than if we used only one connection to the database, performed all of our needed queries, and then closed the connection.

Here is a better approach than in the previous example, once again using pseudocode, which you should be able to implement easily in your programming or scripting language of choice:

```
if form submitted then
  connect to database
  insert into database
  if insert is successful
    print success message
  else
    print failure message

query database for customer info
while recordset is not empty
  get name, address, city, state, zip
  print name, address, city, state, zip

query database for order info
while recordset is not empty
  get orderID, total, date
  print orderID, total, print date

query database for order details
while recordset is not empty
  get items from database where orderID is the same as customer
  print items

close database connection
```

Here, we made two changes to how the database connection was used that will help improve the performance of the application:

- In the first code section relative to the form submission, we moved the "connect to db" function to inside of the first if block, so that we connect to the database *only* if the form was submitted.

- We removed the repeated openings and closings of connections before and after each query. By doing this, we use only a single connection for all queries, and thus improve the application's overall performance.

In addition, you should note that this simplifies the application code and makes it easier to debug and maintain.

Persistent Connections

The PHP 4 MySQL API provides both persistent and nonpersistent connection options for connecting to MySQL from within your application. There are no set rules that say when you should use either one; however, it is best to sometimes measure the performance of your application with each and determine which works better.

With nonpersistent connections, your application must establish a connection with the MySQL database server, authenticate itself, execute any queries, and, finally, close this connection when all database interaction by the script has been completed. However, with persistent connections, PHP will first check to see if there is already an open database connection using the same username and password, and, if one is found, it will execute the query using the existing connection. The connection will remain available for the next script executed by this user that may try to connect to the database using persistent connections.

PHP 4 uses the mysql_pconnect() function to establish persistent connections. Here's the function prototype:

```
resource mysql_pconnect([string server[,
                         string username[,
                         string password[,
                         int client_flags]]]])
```

This function is employed as follows:

```php
<?php
 // mysql_test_pconnection.php

 if (!mysql_pconnect("localhost", "mysql_user", "mysql_password"))
 {
   printf("Could not connect:  %s\n", mysql_error());
 }
```

```
  else
  {
    print("Connection was successful");
  }
?>
```

The downside to using persistent connections is that connections created by one user or application can persist unused for some time, and thus not be available to other users or applications. The PHP 5 MySQLi API does not support persistent connections for this reason.

Repetitive Queries

Repetitive use of queries in applications can also drastically reduce the performance of your application. Often, multiple SQL queries are written to perform a task that could otherwise be condensed into a single join, or could be better evaluated with your application code.

Consider our pseudocode from earlier; instead of making multiple queries to the database for the customer and order information, it can be condensed into one query that performs all of the given tasks.

```
if form submitted then
  connect to database
  insert into database
  if insert is successful
    print success message
  else
    print failure message

query database for customer info, order info and order details
while recordset is not empty
  get name, address, city, state, zip
  print name,  address, city, state, zip

  get orderID, total, date
  print orderID, total, date

  get items from database where orderID is the same as customer
  print items

close db connection
```

For this example, our SQL query would change from three separate queries that looked like this:

```
# First Query
SELECT name, address, city, state, zip
FROM customers;

# Second Query
SELECT order_id, total, date
FROM orders
WHERE customer_id = '$customer_id';

# Third Query
SELECT items
FROM order_details
WHERE orderID = 'orderID';
```

to one query that looks like this:

```
SELECT c.name, c.address, c.city, c.state, cust.zip,
       o.orderID, o.total, o.date,
       d.items
FROM customers c
JOIN orders o USING (cust_id)
JOIN order_details d USING (order_id)
WHERE o.customer_id = '$customer_id';
```

Although these changes may seem small and insignificant, when used throughout your application, and for large datasets, they can help increase the overall performance of your application.

NOTE   *If you need to repeat queries often, or submit queries that are very similar (differing only in the limiting values used), and you're running MySQL 4.1 or newer, you should look into using prepared statements for these. See Chapter 7 for more information about the MySQL Prepared Statements API, the programming platforms that currently support it, and the requirements for its use.*

Unnecessary Calculations

Frequently, mathematical operations that are done at the application level can be moved into the database level and can help increase the performance of your application. We already discussed this and provided a fairly complex example in Chapter 4, but we wanted to touch on this again in a more general way.

For example, consider the following pseudocode example of a simple calculation:

```
connect to database
query database for var1 and var2
return data array
var3 = var1 * var2
print "The answer is: ", var3
disconnect from database
```

With this example, we must retrieve two variables from the database, load the values into an array for our application, perform the multiplication and assign the value to another variable, and then print it to our users. However, this query and process can be simplified by moving it to the database level. Consider the next example.

```
connect to database
query database for value of the expression (var1 * var2)
return value
print "The answer is: ", value
disconnect from database
```

Now the database performs the calculation and returns only the result. All that we need to accomplish with our application code is printing the answer. This is much simpler, quicker, easier to maintain, and easier to port between programming platforms and even to other databases.

Interoperability and Abstraction Layers

Interoperability and abstraction layers exist for most databases. Although they provide a simple and somewhat standard (to each interoperability layer) approach to connecting your application to multiple brands of databases, they can add a significant performance drop to any database-powered application.

The main reason that interoperability layers can be a performance bottleneck for your application is that they add multiple layers between your application and the database that you are trying to query. For example, most interoperability layers add at least two to three layers between your application and the database. This is illustrated in Figure 6-1.

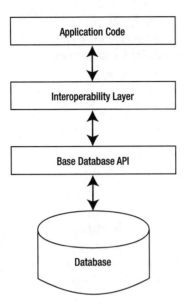

Figure 6-1. Relationships between a database, database interoperability layer, and an application

Generally, when you connect to the interoperability layer, it must translate your application's connection and query code to the correct database API before it can perform the desired operation. Then it must take the database server's response and translate it back into the format used in the application. However, if you don't use the interoperability layer, and you employ a native API for the database instead, the application will connect directly to the database, and then process the response from the database directly. This will eliminate the translation layers between, and thus eliminate the overhead of processing additional code for each of your queries to the database.

A database abstraction layer provides a "wrapper" for native API functions that simplifies working with a database. What we've said here about database interoperability layers also holds true for database abstraction layers: although database abstraction can make things easier for the programmer, there will be a performance penalty imposed by the transformation of abstracted function or method calls to the database's native API.

Summary

In this chapter, we discussed MySQL configuration issues as well as some others that may impact MySQL or MySQL-backed application performance. You can obtain a great deal of information about how well MySQL is operating by reading the values of configuration and status variables using SHOW VARIABLES and SHOW STATUS. We discussed how these and some other useful SHOW commands are employed and what their output represents, concentrating on what they mean in terms of efficiency. Together with some of the log files that can be generated by MySQL, these can provide you with a valuable guide to fine-tuning the server, as well as pinpointing queries that are executing too slowly and other problems that might not be apparent until you've actually starting running your MySQL-backed applications.

We also took a very brief look at four common tools used for monitoring MySQL server performance: mytop, phpMyAdmin, WinMySqlAdmin for Win32 platforms, and the new multiplatform MySQL Administrator currently under development by MySQL AB. Each of these applications simplifies the task of keeping tabs on what and how the server is doing; the last two also provide GUI access for changing the server's configuration.

Another way in which MySQL allows you to improve performance is by taking advantage of its caching capabilities. By doing so, you can cut down dramatically on the number of times the server must read or write to disk instead of RAM, and this can speed up things considerably. MySQL has had good table and key caching for quite some time, and beginning with version 4.0, it also has query caching capabilities that, when understood and used properly, can dramatically reduce the time needed to perform repetitive queries—sometimes 200% or more.

We also looked at some application-oriented issues. Many of these we've touched on throughout this book, but we wanted to restate them as simply and clearly as possible. For instance, it probably can't be said enough times that it's silly and wasteful to send several queries separately from application code when these can be combined into a single query with a single resultset to be returned to the client. Another common source of inefficiency occurs when you perform calculations in application code that could be done as part of your queries. Doing the latter is almost always faster and means that there are fewer elements to return in query results. This also helps to make application code more compact and easier to maintain.

Finally, we talked a bit about database interoperability and abstraction layers, which are very popular among some application developers. While these can make it easy to write and port database-enabled applications, they can also incur a serious performance penalty because they interpose additional layers between the client and the database. It is always more efficient to write directly to the database's native API, such as the MySQL C API, or as close to it as the programming environment will allow. If portability is a concern, it's much better to design standards-compliant tables and queries than it is to rely on database-specific features and depend on an interoperability or abstraction layer to smooth out the differences for you.

What's Next

With a few exceptions, what we've discussed in this book so far can be accomplished from the command line. However, it's not very practical to type in queries and read them from a shell or DOS window every time you wish to use MySQL. You need to be able to connect your applications with MySQL, and to send data back and forth between the database and your applications' users. In Chapter 7, we'll look at some of the more common APIs available for use with MySQL, such as PHP 4's `mysql` extension, the new `ext/mysqli` for PHP 5, and Python's `MySQLdb` module. While we'll concentrate on Open Source programming languages in our discussion, it's also true that, no matter which language or platform your applications run on, chances are very good that an interface to MySQL is available.

Some of these APIs have extra functions or methods for making it easier to work with MySQL features such as transactions, and we'll discuss these and show you examples. In addition, MySQL 4.1 and higher can provide enhanced functionality for programmers when using newer programming libraries or modules that take advantage of it. We'll also talk about the new Prepared Statements API, which allows for greater efficiency through the reuse of precompiled queries, and the Multiple Statements API, which permits you to transmit more than one SQL statement in a single query string and receive the results for all the queries sent in a single response.

CHAPTER 7

MySQL Programming

WE'VE SEEN IN PREVIOUS CHAPTERS that we can subsume a great deal of programming functionality and logic into our queries. This is very useful when running queries from the command line in the MySQL Monitor, but what about writing *programs* that work with MySQL? In order to develop applications that interact effectively with MySQL, we need to know how to submit queries to MySQL from client applications and retrieve the results so that we can use the result data in the program code. This is provided by a MySQL *Application Programming Interface* (API).

In this chapter, we'll start off by discussing what an API is in general, and more specifically, what you can expect for a MySQL API to provide you in terms of writing programs that make use of MySQL for data storage and retrieval. We'll conduct a brief survey of a number of these APIs, including the official MySQL C language API, which acts as a blueprint for many of the other APIs. We'll also talk about some database-agnostic APIs that can be used with MySQL. However, as this is a book primarily about MySQL rather than databases in general, our major focus will be on APIs that have been created specifically for working with MySQL.

Once we've looked at the range of APIs that are available for MySQL programming, we're going to devote the remainder of this chapter—the bulk of it—to investigating in greater depth what we feel are the four APIs most likely to be of interest to those involved with MySQL client programming, particularly in the Open Source arena:

- The `mysql` extension for PHP 3 and PHP 4, which is still available for use in PHP 5 when working with MySQL versions below 4.1. This library of functions allows you to accomplish almost anything you need for using versions of MySQL through 4.0 in your PHP scripts. It's a good example of a "classic" or general-purpose function-oriented database programming library.

- The new `mysqli` extension ("mysqli" stands for "MySQL Improved") introduced in PHP 5. This extension provides access to new programming capabilities in MySQL 4.1 and above, including prepared statements and multiple statements. It also makes it possible to program with MySQL in an object-oriented fashion in PHP without the need for extra libraries, and simplifies working with transactions as well.

- The **Perl-DBI** module with DBD::mysql, used for Perl programming with MySQL. Perl-DBI is object-oriented, is compatible with several common databases, and provides a fairly representative example of a database-agnostic database API. However, in this chapter, we'll discuss only how it's used with MySQL.

- The MySQLdb module, also known as mysql-python, which provides a very nice high-level object-oriented interface for working with MySQL as well as a low-level set of functions similar to those found in PHP's mysql library and the MySQL C API.

As there are a great many books and other resources out there covering MySQL programming with the older PHP mysql extension, we'll favor covering in greater detail the new mysqli extension for PHP 5. In addition to offering support for new programming functionality available beginning in MySQL 4.1, there's another aspect of mysqli of great interest to PHP programmers—a new object-oriented interface. While mysqli can be used in a procedural manner, we'll concentrate primarily on the object-oriented way to use this extension.

Overview of MySQL APIs

In this section, we'll begin by talking a bit about APIs in general, what they're good for, and what we might expect from a good database API used to work with MySQL. Then we'll move on to offer you a brief survey of available MySQL APIs as well as some other database APIs that aren't specific to any one RDBMS but are compatible with MySQL.

What's an API?

An API provides a programming language an additional "vocabulary" for working with things that aren't part of the core language. For example, a graphics library might provide a Polygon class or set of functions that allows the programmer to describe a polygonal shape, and gives the programmer a set of "hooks" for accomplishing common tasks easily—in this case, for creating a polygon, determining how many sides it has, how long each side is, filling in the polygon with a color or pattern, positioning the polygon on the screen, and so on.

A database API needs to provide the following capabilities to client applications and the programmers writing them:

- Establishing a database connection

- Transmitting a query so that MySQL can execute it

- Obtaining a response to the query: if executing a SELECT, retrieving a result set from the database; in the case of an INSERT, UPDATE, or DELETE query, verifying that it was successful

- Recognizing when an error has occurred, identifying its type, and knowing where it was likely to have occurred

- Disconnecting from the database when the connection's no longer needed by the client

In the case of an API for MySQL, this allows programmers working in PHP, C, Python, Perl, and other languages to communicate with MySQL from their application code. That is, a MySQL API adds a new module, library, or extension to the language; this API contains functions or objects that are specific to working with MySQL. For example, the MySQL C language API and the PHP mysql extension provide a function named mysql_query(), which can be used to transmit a query (in the form of a string of SQL) to the MySQL server.

In addition, each API has ways to determine the structure of result set data sent by MySQL and to translate it into data structures, such as arrays or objects, that are native to the programming language being used. APIs also are able to understand MySQL's error and warning conditions and codes, and understand how to obtain information about how queries were performed, such as determining how many rows were returned by a SELECT or how many records were affected by an UPDATE query.

Requirements for a MySQL API

Whatever language you're programming in, and whatever the environment, you'll need to be able to execute each of these tasks in order to use MySQL with your application. Let's examine in turn each of the five steps listed in the previous section.

Connecting to MySQL

For purposes of authentication and access, MySQL regards applications no differently than it does human users. Just as you must log into a MySQL server as a particular user with a specific password, so must an application send a connection request, transmitting a username and password, as shown in Figure 7-1.

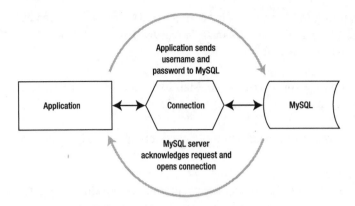

Figure 7-1. A client application establishing a connection with MySQL

In addition, most if not all MySQL APIs require a hostname parameter to be provided when calling connection functions or methods, even if the application is running on the same machine as MySQL, in which case the hostname can be given as either localhost or the loopback IP address 127.0.0.1. They generally also have an optional port parameter that can be supplied in case the MySQL server has been configured to listen for requests on some port other than 3306, and often include a database name as well.

TIP *If your application is accessing MySQL over a network, you can often achieve faster transmission times using the host's IP address rather than the hostname. This is particularly true on networks with slow DNS and/or a great many hosts.*

Whether you're using an object-oriented API or a procedural one, the basic idea is that you use a programming construct such as a function, object method, or object constructor to transmit login and connection information to MySQL. The MySQL server then signals back to the application that the connection request is approved with a connection identifier; just as when you log in using the MySQL Monitor, your MySQL connection ID is displayed, as shown here:

```
Command Prompt - mysql -h gojira -u root -p                          _ □ ×

C:\>mysql -h gojira -u root -p
Enter password: ******
Welcome to the MySQL monitor.  Commands end with ; or \g.
Your MySQL connection id is 3 to server version: 4.1.4-gamma-nt-max-log

Type 'help;' or '\h' for help. Type '\c' to clear the buffer.

mysql>
```

The application stores this value and uses it in subsequent requests to MySQL during that session.

The precise details vary according to API, but connecting to MySQL from an application is usually done in one of two ways. Object-oriented APIs tend to use a connection class whose constructor is called with the necessary values, and once this object is instantiated, further work is accomplished by calling methods of this object. The MySQLdb module for Python is a bit different in this respect, as we'll see later in this chapter, using the connect() method of the MySQLdb class to return a Connection object, but the idea is the same.

Procedural APIs generally have a connection function that returns a value identifying the connection. Depending on the API, this value can be known as a connection, resource identifier, or handle. Whatever the nomenclature, this value is then employed as a parameter to functions that accomplish other tasks making use of that connection.

Executing Queries

Once a connection has been established by your application, it's ready to obtain data from MySQL in much the same way that you yourself would do so—by running queries. In fact, when you sit at the keyboard and run queries by typing them in, you're not actually using the MySQL server directly. What you're really doing is making use of the client application known as the MySQL Monitor, which transmits your keyboard input to the MySQL server via TCP/IP, as shown in Figure 7-2.

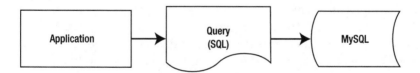

Figure 7-2. An application transmitting a query to the MySQL server

NOTE   *If you connect using* localhost *as the host name, MySQL will normally try to use a Unix socket, or a named pipe on Windows platforms, rather than TCP/IP.*

The precise mechanics of transmitting queries vary between the different MySQL APIs: when using an object-oriented API such as mysqli or MySQLdb, you call a method of the object that models a database connection instantiated in the previous step; when using a procedural API, you'll call a function that accomplishes the same task. In either case, your application transmits the text of an SQL statement to MySQL.

CAUTION *A MySQL client application is subject to the MySQL privileges system just like any other MySQL user. If you're having trouble getting your application to connect to MySQL, make sure the application is connecting to MySQL with a valid username and password, and that you're using the correct hostname or IP address for the server. If certain types of queries repeatedly fail, make certain that the account being used has the privileges needed to perform the desired queries.*

Beginning in the MySQL 4.1.*x* series, the picture can become a bit more complicated with the introduction of the Multiple Statements and Prepared Statements APIs. The Multiple Statements interface allows for more than one query to be sent at a time by the client, and for MySQL to send more than one result set in response, one per query (see the upcoming "Retrieving Results" section). This can help speed up your MySQL applications where you need to run several queries at once (or close together in sequence), since these can be sent in a single request rather than several.

The Prepared Statements API also promises performance gains for MySQL client applications. This API allows you to preprocess queries that are frequently repeated by the application. This means that the query is parsed only once, when it's first executed, and thereafter the prepared query can be reused. An additional performance benefit comes from the fact that such queries can be sent to the server in a binary format rather than as text, meaning that fewer bytes must be transmitted per request.

We'll talk about both of these newer APIs in more detail when we discuss the `mysqli` extension for PHP 5 later in this chapter, and we'll also see how multiple statements can be emulated in some libraries such as Perl-DBI.

CAUTION *In order to take advantage of the MySQL Multiple Statements and Prepared Statements APIs, two things are necessary. First, the server must be running MySQL version 4.1.2 or greater. Second, your application must use a client library that supports the MySQL Client API version 4.1.2 or greater. (For PHP programmers, this means you must be using the PHP 5 mysqli extension.) Older versions of the client library will not provide access to either interface. In addition, they aren't capable of sending passwords encrypted by the method used in versions 4.1 and newer of the MySQL server.*

Retrieving Results

When you submit a query to the MySQL Monitor using the keyboard, you receive in response a tabular representation of the result of that query, which (just to refresh your memory) will look something like this:

```
Command Prompt - mysql -h megalon -u root -p                          _ □ ×

mysql> SELECT p.name AS product, c.name AS category, p.price AS price
    -> FROM products p
    -> JOIN categories c
    -> ON c.id = p.category_id
    -> ORDER BY p.name;
+-----------------------------+----------------------+---------+
| product                     | category             | price   |
+-----------------------------+----------------------+---------+
| Ants Ants Revolution        | Entertainment        | 16.95   |
| Bass Blaster Fishing Mortar | Sporting Equipment   | 79.95   |
| Churn-O-Bill Butter Churn   | Kitchen and Cookware | 18.00   |
| Congeal-O-Meal              | Kitchen and Cookware | 22.50   |
| Gas-Powered Turnip Slicer   | Kitchen and Cookware | 22.95   |
| INTERCAL Home Study Course  | Home Study           | 39.95   |
| Personal Breathalyser       | Entertainment        | 68.95   |
| Souper Soup Dehydrator      | Kitchen and Cookware | 24.95   |
| Thrash-O-Matic Plus         | Sporting Equipment   | 49.95   |
+-----------------------------+----------------------+---------+
9 rows in set (0.02 sec)

mysql>
```

This is acceptable and even convenient in some situations, like when you're just running a query for yourself and you don't really care exactly how the output is formatted, just so long as you can read and understand it. If you need to remember that the price for the INTERCAL Home Study Course is $39.95, you can always jot it down on a bit of paper. Unfortunately, if you're writing a piece of software, and you'd like your application to retain this information, it's not quite so simple. You need to be able to retrieve column values in a predictable fashion, manipulate them, and store them into variables.

In any case, MySQL sends back results to the client application as shown in Figure 7-3. However, the form in which these are transmitted is that of a low-level binary structure that isn't readily understood by most programming languages. Part of the purpose of a MySQL client API is to translate this data into structures that can readily be worked with. Most often the result set is presented to the programmer as a set or series of arrays, one array per row in the result set, one array element per column. In most cases, the developer can specify whether these are to be presented (or "fetched") as indexed or associative arrays. For example, consider a result row represented by an indexed array $row from the following query:

```
SELECT e.id AS empid, CONCAT(e.fname, ' ', e.lname) AS name, d.name AS dept
FROM employees e
JOIN departments d
ON e.departement_id = d.id;
```

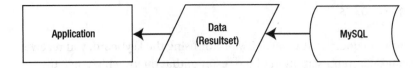

Figure 7-3. MySQL sends a result set back to the application.

This row might be output by the programmer like this (using PHP syntax):

```
printf("Employee Number: %s; Name: %s; Department: %s",
       $row[0], $row[1], $row[2]);
```

When using an indexed array, the array elements are numbered in the same order as the columns were specified in the query.

When using an associative array, the same output statement might be written like this:

```
printf("Employee Number: %s; Name: %s; Department: %s",
       $row["eid"], $row["name"], $row["dept"]);
```

In this case, the column names are used as the keys of the associative array. If aliases are specified, then these are used instead.

TIP *Using numeric indices to refer to columns is generally much faster than using associative arrays or objects. However, it's not nearly as convenient as using column names or aliases, either.*

In some APIs, the programmer can also choose to have the results returned as a set of objects, where each row in the result set is obtained as an object, and the object's members correspond to the result's columns. When fetching the same result set as a set of objects, you might write the same output routine as shown here (again using PHP syntax for the sake of example):

```
printf("Employee Number: %s; Name: %s; Department: %s",
       $row->eid, $row->name, $row->dept);
```

NOTE *For more information about the underlying structure of MySQL result sets, result rows, and fields, see the "C API Data Types" section of the MySQL Manual. This can be viewed online at* http://dev.mysql.com/doc/mysql/en/C_API_datatypes.html.

Detecting and Handling Errors

Programmers need to be able to find out when something has gone wrong with their applications, and when working with an autonomous entity such as a database server, the problem of tracking down the source of an error grows more complex: Did the error occur in the application code, or did the problem occur with MySQL? This isn't a terribly challenging concept to grasp—there's a problem with your query or with the table or tables you're trying to work with, and MySQL tells you that a problem has arisen, as shown in Figure 7-4.

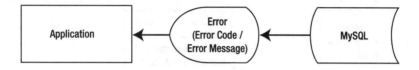

Figure 7-4. MySQL encounters an error and sends an error message to the application.

As you've seen earlier in this book, that isn't difficult when working from the command line:

When writing an application, however, it's more of a problem, particularly when your code is expecting a result set to be passed back to it from MySQL in response to a query. To take care of these situations, many if not most MySQL (and other database) API functions return **FALSE** or the equivalent, such as a null or undefined value (depending on the language), upon failure. This gives you the opportunity to test whether or not the attempted action was successful. If it wasn't, then you can use error functions or variables to return an error code and/or message. In most if not all cases, these automatically give you information about the last error generated by MySQL during your session (that is, since your application has been connected to MySQL). The typical sequence of events can be mapped out as shown in Figure 7-5.

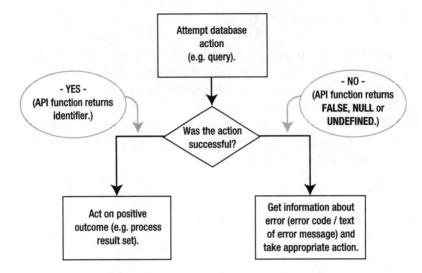

Figure 7-5. Determining whether a query or other database action was successful

Of course, the simplest course of action to take when something goes wrong is simply to exit the program after displaying the text of the error message returned by MySQL. Here's how we'd do that in Perl using the DBI interface to connect to MySQL:

```
$dsn = "dbi:mysql:mydb@localhost:3306";
$dbh = DBI->connect($dsn, $user, $pass)
            or die $DBI::errstr;
```

In ordinary language, what this says is, "Try to connect to the database identified by the data source name $dsn using the user name $user and password $pass. If this succeeds, assign the connection ID returned by MySQL to the variable $dbh. Otherwise, print the error message output by MySQL and then bail out." (The data source name is a string containing the database type, the name of the server, the port that it's running on, and the name of the database. We'll discuss this further later in this chapter—see the "Perl-DBI" section.) Of course, simply exiting the application is fine for development and debugging purposes. However, in a production application, you'll likely want to do more than that, rather than leaving the user looking at a blank screen or a potentially cryptic error code or message, but this is the basic logic involved.

You can generally test any type of action you want to make with regard to MySQL in a similar fashion, as we'll see when we discuss individual APIs in more depth later in this chapter. All MySQL APIs (that we know of, at least) provide ways of obtaining both error codes and error message text, so that in your applications you can do something like this (using the PHP mysql extension this time):

```
# attempt to connect
if($link = mysql_connect($server, "$user@$host", $password))
{
  printf("Connected to %s as user \"%s\"", $server, "$user@$host");
  $dbs = mysql_list_dbs($link);
  if(count($dbs) == 0)
    print ", but there are no databases for you to view.\n";
  else
  {
    $i = 0;
    print "; please a select a database from the following list:\n\n";
    while($db = mysql_result($result, $i++))
      printf("%s\n", $db);


    #  and so on...
  }
}
else
{
  switch( mysql_error() )  #  set error message according to error code
  {
    case 1043:  #  ER_HANDSHAKE_ERROR
    case 2001:  #  CR_SOCKET_CREATE_ERROR
      $msg = "Possible networking error; if the problem persists,
              contact Tech Support";
    break;

    case 1130:  #  ER_HOST_NOT_PRIVILEGED
      $msg = "Server \"$server\" does not accept logins from \"$host\"";
    break;

    case 1045:  #  ER_ACCESS_DENIED_ERROR
    case 1132:  #  ER_PASSWORD_NOT_ALLOWED
    case 1133:  #  ER_PASSWORD_NO_MATCH
      $msg = "Access denied to \"$user@$host\"; please check
              your username and password, then try again";
    break;
```

```
case 1203:  #  ER_TOO_MANY_USER_CONNECTIONS
  $msg = "Maximum number of users logged into server \"$server\"";
break;


case 2005:  #  CR_UNKNOWN_HOST
case 2006:  #  CR_SERVER_GONE_ERROR
  $msg = "There is no server named \"$server\" on this network";
break;


case 2049  #  CR_SECURE_AUTH
  $msg = "You must use a secure connection to access server \"$server\"";
break;


#  and so on...


case 2001:  #  CR_UNKNOWN_ERROR
default:
  $msg = "Undetermined error; if this condition persists,
          contact Tech Support";
break;
}
printf("LOGIN ERROR: %s.\n\n", $msg);
#  ...
}
```

The exact text of error messages can and does change between different MySQL versions. It also may be slightly different for the same version of MySQL running on different platforms. For these reasons, it's generally best to use error codes rather than the error messages themselves when writing applications. Code relying on the latter is not very portable and is liable to break in deployment.

 CAUTION *Error codes have changed significantly between MySQL 3.23 and MySQL 4.0. Be sure your application uses the correct ones for your MySQL version. In addition, beginning with MySQL 4.1, MySQL also returns industry-standard* SQLSTATE *error codes as well as its own.*

Since new error codes are being added all the time, the best places to find these are in the following files of the MySQL distribution (file paths are relative to your MySQL installation directory, which is usually /usr/local/ on Unix systems including Linux and C:\mysql on Windows platforms):

- include/mysqld_error.h: MySQL-specific error codes (server).

- include/errmsg.h: MySQL-specific error codes (client).

- include/sql_state.h: SQLSTATE error codes for MySQL 4.1 and newer. (This file isn't included with all binary distributions, but it can found in the include directory in the source code.)

- share/*language*/errmsg.txt: Language-specific text of error messages where language is the name of the language; for example, English-language error messages are found in include/english/errmsg.txt.

- Docs/mysqld_error.txt: Combined listing of server error codes and error messages.

TIP *In MySQL 4.0 and above, error codes are four digits long. Those beginning with 1 are server errors, and those beginning with 2 are client errors.*

Disconnecting from MySQL

Once your application has finished running, it should be able to disconnect from MySQL (see Figure 7-6). The MySQL server will eventually disconnect clients on its own after a set period of inactivity; by default this is eight hours, but can be altered by making the proper changes in the configuration files. However, connections take up system and network resources, and there are a maximum number of connections permitted to be open at any particular time. (The default is 100 simultaneous connections; this can also be changed, but is a finite number in any case.)

Figure 7-6. Either the client application or the MySQL server can disconnect.

All MySQL APIs include some type of disconnection method or function that breaks the link between the client application and the MySQL server; its precise name varies, of course, but it is usually similar to `close()` or `disconnect()`, and generally either takes as a parameter the connection resource identifier returned by MySQL when the connection was established or is called as a method of the object instantiated or invoked to begin the session. Calling this method or function is the equivalent of typing `quit` or `\q` in the MySQL Monitor.

No matter which language you might be programming in, you need its MySQL API to perform certain tasks for you—connecting to MySQL, submitting queries to MySQL, fetching results from MySQL, cutting the connection to MySQL when you've finished, and letting you know if and when there are problems encountered at any point in this process. The nuts and bolts of how each language and API implements these steps vary, but the results are the same.

MySQL APIs

Before we begin the in-depth discussion and examples of our four "target" APIs, let's take a brief survey of what's available for different programming languages and platforms. We'll also tell you where you can obtain each of these APIs.

MySQL C API

The MySQL C Language API was created by MySQL AB for the purpose of writing their own MySQL client software applications in C. These include the MySQL Monitor (`mysql`), and `mysqladmin` command-line clients, as well as the GUI-based MySQL Administrator, Control Center, and Query Browser applications. In fact, nearly all of the client programs available from MySQL AB were created using MySQL AB's own library implementing this API, known simply as `mysqlclient`.

The C Language API can be considered the core MySQL client API, as most other MySQL-specific database APIs use this as their model and provide wrappers for the C API functions. This is especially true of both the `mysql` and `mysqli` extensions for PHP, which follow the C API very closely in terms of function names and purposes. However, the C API—like anything else having to do with C programming—is very low-level and requires an enormous amount of attention to detail, which is why higher-level scripting languages like PHP and Python were invented and MySQL APIs implemented for those languages.

Our later discussion in this chapter will focus on the APIs available for PHP 4 and 5, Perl, and Python, but it's a good idea to be aware of the C API, especially if you plan to develop using MySQL with multiple programming languages or you want to develop a MySQL module for a language that doesn't yet have one of its own. For more information about the MySQL C API, see the corresponding section of the MySQL Manual, which includes complete descriptions of all available functions, their input and return types, their uses, and possible errors that they can generate.

For coding examples making use of the MySQL C API, one of the best places to look is the source code for MySQL clients available from MySQL AB. You can find these in the MySQL source code distribution in the `clients` directory.

mysql

The `mysql` extension is the standard function library provided with PHP 3, 4, and 5 for use with MySQL 3–4.0. It can be used with later versions of MySQL, but does not offer access to any of the programming capabilities that became available for applications using version 4.1 or newer of the MySQL client libraries, such as multiple statements and prepared statements.

This function-oriented extension, as we've mentioned, does a good job of modeling and making accessible the basic requirements for working with MySQL: with it, you can connect to MySQL, send queries, and receive results in a form that's compatible with structures already familiar to you if you've any experience programming in PHP.

The `mysql` extension comes as part of the PHP 4 and PHP 5 binary and source distributions, available from `http://www.php.net`.

mysqli

The `mysqli` extension (short for "MySQL Improved") is new in PHP 5 and is intended specifically for use with MySQL versions 4.1 and above. It provides a number of advances over the older `mysql` extension, including

- Support for the MySQL Multiple Statements API

- Support for the Prepared Statements API

- Access to `SQLSTATE` error messages

- Better access to MySQL warnings

- Support for improved client authentication protocol

- New convenience functions/methods for working with transactions

In addition to a function API similar in many ways to that provided by the `mysql` extension, `mysqli` provides a new object-oriented interface for MySQL programming in PHP. We'll cover both ways of using `mysqli`, but, given that in version 5 PHP and PHP programming are both moving to a much more solidly object-oriented paradigm than was inherent in either PHP 3 or PHP 4, we'll focus more closely and in depth on the OOP style.

> **NOTE**   *It is possible to use the older* `mysql` *extension with PHP 5—in fact, you should use it for working with MySQL versions previous to 4.1 in PHP 5. It is not possible to use* `mysqli` *with PHP 4, at least not as of this writing.*

The other major difference between `mysqli` and the old `mysql` extension is that `mysqli` does not allow the use of persistent connections. This was a design decision on the part of the PHP development team due to the fact that persistent connections don't really improve the efficiency of PHP/MySQL applications, and that permitting them tends to lead to a large number of open connections, which causes unnecessary server load.

> **NOTE**   *You can run both* ext/mysql *and* ext/mysqli *on the same installation of PHP 5; however, you'll have to use the older version of the MySQL client libraries. This means that you won't have access to Prepared Statements or Multiple Statements in* `mysqli`, *and you'll be using pre-MySQL-4.1 password encryption in both extensions. For information on how to set up PHP 5 in this manner, see the "Installation" section of the PHP Manual.*

`mysqli` is included with the release version of PHP 5 and can be obtained as part of the PHP 5 source or binary package from the downloads page at `http://www.php.net`.

MySQLdb

`MySQLdb` is a module for Python 1.5.2 and later that works with all versions of MySQL beginning with 3.22. It is also partially compatible with MySQL 4.1 and MySQL 5.0; however, it does not support the MySQL Multiple Statements or Prepared Statements APIs. We've used it successfully with Python 2.2 and 2.3 on Windows and Linux, and it should work on any platform that supports both Python and MySQL.

MySQLdb consists of two object-oriented modules:

- _mysql: This is a lower-level interface to MySQL that follows the MySQL C API fairly closely, and also resembles the PHP mysql and mysqli extensions in many ways.

- MySQLdb: This module implements the Python DB API Interface, version 2. While it does not support MySQL 5.0's cursors, it does implement its own cursors; in fact, you must use these in order to obtain results from a query. MySQLdb also implements convenience methods for working with transactional tables.

We'll cover MySQLdb in some detail later in this chapter, concentrating on the MySQLdb module proper (as opposed to _mysql). At the time this book was written, the most recent version of MySQLdb was version 1.0; you can download the latest version from the MySQLdb SourceForge project page at http://sourceforge.net/projects/mysql-python/.

Using Older Clients with MySQL 4.1 and 5.0

It's possible to use older client libraries written for use with MySQL 3.22, 3.23, and 4.0 with MySQL versions 4.1 and 5.0. However, there are a couple of issues that you'll need to be aware of.

Inaccessible APIs: As we've mentioned elsewhere, pre-4.1 clients cannot use the MySQL Multiple Statements or Prepared Statements APIs. Such clients don't "speak" the protocol required to let MySQL 4.1 or higher know that what's being sent is supposed to be using one of these APIs. In these cases, you'll likely have to issue each query separately and in its entirety.

Some pre-4.1 client APIs may offer their own equivalents of these features. This is true of both Perl-DBI, which emulates prepared statements, and Python's MySQLdb, which emulates multiple statements (see the discussions of these APIs later in this chapter for details). However, these won't be as efficient as true support for the MySQL-native versions.

Password encryption: The password encryption scheme used by the MySQL server changed beginning with MySQL 4.1. Previously, passwords were hashed to produce strings that were 16 bytes long. Beginning with MySQL 4.1, password hashing was strengthened considerably, and encrypted passwords became 41 bytes long. Clients and client modules that were written using the older MySQL client libraries aren't able to encrypt passwords according to the new algorithm. (In other words, they can't produce the longer 41-byte password hashes.)

If you've upgraded from an older version of MySQL to version 4.1 or newer, part of the upgrade process is to run the `mysql_fix_privilege_tables` script that updates the privilege tables in a number of ways, the most important of which for purposes of our discussion here is that it changes the length of the **Password** column in the **mysql.user** table from 16 to 41. However, it does not update the passwords of existing users. This in and of itself isn't a problem, as MySQL will automatically try to use the old password algorithm to authenticate a user when it finds a 16-bit hash in the **Password** column for that user.

However, if you try to connect to MySQL 4.1 or 5.0 using an older client to access an account whose password was set *since* the upgrade, you'll get an error message that looks like this:

```
Client does not support authentication protocol requested
by server; consider upgrading MySQL client
```

In other words, pre-4.1 clients can lock themselves out of a newer MySQL server simply by changing their own passwords. This is because using `PASSWORD()`, `GRANT`, or `SET PASSWORD` will use the newer encryption algorithm and generate a 41-byte password hash on the server that the client can't generate the next time it tries to authenticate.

There are basically two ways in which you can get around this problem. One of them is to start the MySQL server with the –old-passwords option, or, alternatively, change the width of the **mysql.user.Password** column back to 16. Either of these things will cause the server to generate the old-style, 16-byte password hashes when setting passwords. However, doing either of these things also causes *all* clients to connect to MySQL using the older password-hashing algorithm, and so it isn't as secure as upgrading your clients to use the newer libraries that support 41-byte password hashes.

The other solution is to use the backwards-compatible `OLD_PASSWORD()` function for setting the passwords of older clients. For example:

```
SET PASSWORD FOR 'jon'@'localhost' = OLD_PASSWORD('newpassword');
```

This scenario allows newer clients to use full-strength 41-byte hashing for passwords. The one disadvantage is that you must be careful to use `OLD_PASSWORD()` for any pre-4.1 client any time you take any action that would change its MySQL password.

Note that authentication is *not* a problem for a 4.1 or higher client attempting to log in to a server running MySQL 4.0 or earlier. In this case, the client knows that it's communicating with an older server and uses 16-byte password hashing automatically.

Other Language-Specific MySQL APIs

The APIs we've discussed so far aren't the only ones available for working with MySQL. Here are some of the other APIs that are available for working directly with MySQL in a single programming language:

- **MySQL++**: This is an object-oriented library for use in C++ applications accessing MySQL. The most recent version is 1.7.9. You can find out more about MySQL++ by reading the online manual at http://dev.mysql.com/doc/plusplus/en/index.html.

- **mysqltcl**: This is a MySQL library for use with the Tcl scripting language, version 8.1 and higher. The latest version (2.50 as of this writing) is thread-safe and subinterpreter safe. The mysqltcl home page, where you can download the library and documentation, is at http://www.xdobry.de/mysqltcl/.

- **MySQL:elj**: This is an interface for working with MySQL in the Eiffel programming language. You can download it from http://elj.sourceforge.net/projects/db/mysql/.

- **Ruby MySQL**: This library is for Ruby 1.6.8 and higher working with MySQL 3.23.54 and above, and should run on all platforms for which these are supported. It is an almost exact reimplementation of the MySQL C API in Ruby. Downloads and documentation are available from http://www.tmtm.org/en/mysql/ruby/.

MySQL-Compatible APIs

In addition to language-specific APIs, MySQL is compatible with a number of database and language-agnostic interoperability or abstraction layers. We won't be going into detail about any of these (with the exception of Perl-DBI) in this chapter, but they are available for languages without native MySQL APIs and for cases where you want to write applications that are more easily ported to other databases.

ODBC: iODBC, UnixODBC, and MyODBC

ODBC stands for *Open Database Connectivity*. Microsoft originally devised this interface for database interoperability in 1992, and it quickly became an industry-wide standard. Most databases are or can be made compatible with ODBC, and MySQL is no exception. There are several ways in which you can access MySQL using ODBC:

- **iODBC** and **UnixODBC**: These libraries provide ODBC services on Unix platforms, and are compatible with most widely used databases, including Oracle, SQL Server, PostgreSQL, DB2, and (of course) MySQL. Both of these are Open Source projects from which source code is freely available. For more information about iODBC and iODBC downloads, see `http://www.iodbc.org/`; for UnixODBC, the best starting point is `http://www.unixodbc.org/`.

- **MyODBC**: Also known as Connector/ODBC, this is MySQL's own ODBC driver, which is available for a number of platforms, including Windows, Linux, Solaris, AIX, and Mac OS X. See `http://www.mysql.com/products/connector/odbc/` for more information and downloads.

JDBC

Java Database Connectivity (JDBC) is the Java standard for interaction with relational databases. Using a JDBC driver for MySQL, it's possible for any Java programmer familiar with JDBC to write client applications that interface with a MySQL server. The two most widely used JDBC drivers for MySQL are

- **Connector/J**: MySQL's own JDBC driver, available at `http://www.mysql.com/products/connector/j/`. This driver can be used with most Java tools and applications, including most Apache Jakarta projects such as Tomcat, as well as JBoss, BEA WebLogic, Forte, NetBeans, and IBM's VisualAge and WebSphere products.

- **JDBC-MySQL**: This is an Open Source JDBC driver for MySQL for Resin 2.0 and above. You can obtain the latest JAR files and documentation from `http://www.caucho.com/projects/jdbc-mysql/index.xtp`.

Perl-DBI (DBD::mysql)

`DBI` is the Database Interface for the Perl programming language, with drivers for most common databases including MySQL, and will serve as our in-depth example of a database-agnostic API for MySQL later in this chapter. Both compiled C and "Pure Perl" versions of the MySQL driver (`DBD::mysql`) are available.

If you're using Perl and need to install or upgrade DBI or the MySQL driver, you can do so easily using CPAN, or, if you use ActiveState's ActivePerl distribution, you can use their PPM package manager. More information about Perl-DBI can be found via the DBI home page at http://dbi.perl.org/.

PHP–PEAR::DB and PEAR::DB_DataObject

One widely used database interoperability library for PHP is PEAR::DB. This is part of the PHP Extension and Application Repository, which you can find online at http://pear.php.net/. It provides a unified object-oriented interface to most of the databases that can be used with PHP 4 and 5 and any version of MySQL 3.23 or newer. PEAR::DB_DataObject is a another PEAR library that extends PEAR::DB in some interesting ways, by mapping each database table to an object and creating "get" and "set" methods for all of the table's columns. For example, tables named **product** and **category** might be queried as follows:

```
$product =& new Product();
$category =& new Category();
$product->addCondition("Price", "<", "50.00");
$product->addLinkedObject($category, "CategoryId:Id");

$product->find();

while( $product->fetch() )
  printf("Name: %s; Price: \$%s; Category: %s",
         $product->getName(), $product->getPrice(), $category->getName());
```

This would be roughly equivalent to writing the following query:

```
SELECT p.name, p.price, c.name
FROM product p
JOIN category c
ON p.category_id = c.id
WHERE p.price < 50.00;
```

You could then use a standard fetch_*() methods from the mysql or mysqli extension to retrieve the rows in the result.

Using such an interface can speed up development a great deal, since it abstracts the writing of queries to a significant degree. However, as with any database interoperability layer, there is a performance penalty. As we discussed in Chapter 6, you'll get the most speed when you write as closely to the native API for your platform as is possible.

NOTE *If you're a Rexx programmer, you might be interested to know that RexxSQL is compatible with MySQL. See the RexxSQL project page at SourceForge (*http://rexxsql.sourceforge.net/*) for more information.*

PHP and the mysql Extension

The combination of PHP and MySQL using PHP's mysql extension has in recent years become one of the mainstays of web site development. As such, there have been dozens if not hundreds of books written about it that go into much greater depth than we can hope to in the limited amount space we have available to us here (you can find the titles of one or two good ones on the back cover of the book you're reading right now). We'll cover the fundamentals of the mysql extension in this section, but bear in mind that we'll only be scratching the surface, and this is an area that definitely merits further study if you're not familiar with it already.

Even if you don't use PHP for development, there are a number of reasons why you should at least become acquainted with it:

- **Market penetration**: Roughly a third of all web sites today—belonging to owners ranging from local sports clubs to large multinational corporations—use PHP. Not only is PHP a runaway favorite on sites hosted on servers using Linux as their operating system, but recent statistics suggest that it may also be in wider use on Windows servers than any other non-Microsoft technology. It's difficult to know exactly how many sites are using which database, but it's a safe bet that a large proportion of those running PHP use MySQL. The chances are very good that, if you're a MySQL administrator or developer, you're going to work on MySQL databases used to store data for web sites running PHP at some point during your career.

- **Knowing the internals of your abstraction or compatibility library**: If you're a PHP developer working on MySQL-driven web sites but using a library such as PEAR::DB or Metabase (http://freshmeat.net/projects/metabase/), you need to be aware that such libraries serve as "wrappers" for this extension. If you're at all interested in what's happening under the hood, so to speak, then you'll find the ensuing material particularly useful. And well you should: what happens if you should encounter a choke point in your application or a bug in the library that you're using and you need to fix it, work around it, or at least be able to file an effective report with the library's maintainers? You'll need a deeper understanding of what's going on behind the scenes in order to be able to handle both types of problem.

- **Similarity to the MySQL C (and other) APIs**: As we've mentioned previously, the mysql extension closely parallels the MySQL C API, which forms the basis for most other MySQL APIs. If you're new to programming with MySQL, learning the PHP mysql extension is an excellent place to get started, and will provide you with a leg up on learning other MySQL APIs, including the PHP 5 mysqli extension, which we'll also cover later in this chapter.

As you can see, there are some very good reasons indeed for being familiar with the PHP mysql extension. While we can't cover every facet of it here, we will make sure that by the time you finish reading this section, you'll be able to accomplish the most common and necessary tasks—getting connected to the database, transmitting queries to it, and retrieving result data from it—that will be required of you in building and maintaining a PHP-powered web site backed by a MySQL database.

Fundamentals

The mysql extension consists of a large family of functions whose usage follows quite closely the basic paradigm for database interaction that we outlined earlier in this chapter. In this section, we'll list the most important of these functions, grouped according to their purpose and use, and then in the next section, we'll provide a couple of examples showing you how to put them together.

Before we talk about the mysql functions, you should note that there are several PHP configuration variables that can affect how this extension behaves, as shown in Table 7-1.

Table 7-1. Configuration Variables for mysql Extension

NAME	DEFAULT VALUE	DESCRIPTION
mysql.allow_persistent	On	Whether or not to allow persistent connections.
mysql.max_persistent	−1	Maximum number of persistent connections (if permitted); −1 = unlimited.
mysql.max_links	−1	Maximum number of all connections; −1 = unlimited.
mysql.default_port*	NULL	Port that will be used if not specified in mysql_connect(); used only if not NULL, otherwise defaults to 3306.

(Continued)

Table 7-1. Configuration Variables for mysql *Extension (Continued)*

NAME	DEFAULT VALUE	DESCRIPTION
mysql.default_socket*	NULL	Socket to be used if none specified.
mysql.default_host*	NULL	Host to which PHP will try to connect if not specified in mysql_connect(); used only if not NULL; otherwise the default is "localhost".
mysql.default_user*	NULL	Default username to use if not specified in mysql_connect(); for security reasons, this is best left empty.
mysql.default_password*	NULL	Default password to use if not specified in mysql_connect(); this is best left blank for reasons of security.
mysql.connect_timeout	0	Number of seconds without activity before the connection will be closed. 0 = infinite.

Notes: 1. All of these values can be overridden by the equivalent configuration variables being set in the MySQL my.cnf or my.ini file. 2. Those values that can be changed by PHP scripts are marked with an asterisk (*); the remainder can be only be set in php.ini.

Connecting to a MySQL Database

To connect to a MySQL server, we can use the mysql_connect() function, whose complete prototype is shown here:

```
linkID mysql_connect([string server[, string username[, string password[,
              bool newlink[, int flags]]]]])
```

The return value of this function is a resource identifier that can be used as an argument to database selection and query functions, as we'll see shortly. The input parameters of this function are as follows:

- *server*: This is the name or the IP address of the MySQL server. If MySQL is running on a nonstandard port, the port number can be specified by writing this value in the format *server:port*. The default value is localhost:3306 unless a different value has been set for one or both of the configuration variables mysqldefault_host and mysql.default_port. It is also possible to use the path to a Unix socket or Windows named pipe for this argument.

- *user*: The MySQL user account name to log in to. If this isn't specified in mysql_connect(), it will default to the name of the current system user, unless a default username has been set for mysql.default_user.

- *password*: The password for the MySQL user account to log in to. Unless mysql.default_password has been set, this defaults to an empty string.

- *newlink*: The default is 0/**FALSE**. Normally, if mysql_connect() is called twice in the same script with the same parameter values, a new connection will not be created the second time it's called; instead, the identifier for the existing connection will be returned. If this is set to 1 or **TRUE**, this behavior will be overridden and a second connection established. (Added in PHP 4.2.0.)

- *flags*: Added in PHP 4.3.0, this allows you to use one or more of the connection option constants MYSQL_CLIENT_COMPRESS (allows compression), MYSQL_CLIENT_IGNORE_SPACE (allows spaces after MySQL function names used in queries), and MYSQL_CLIENT_INTERACTIVE (will cause the server to wait interactive_timeout instead of wait_timeout seconds before closing the connection due to inactivity). Multiple flags used together are separated with the | (binary "OR") character.

 NOTE *For security reasons, it is best to leave the values for* mysql.default_user *and* mysql.default_password *blank in the php.ini configuration file.*

A call to this function using all parameters might look something like this:

```
$link
   = mysql_connect("somehost:10000", "me", "mypassword", FALSE,
                   MYSQL_CLIENT_COMPRESS|MYSQL_CLIENT_INTERACTIVE);
```

Most often, only the hostname, username, and password need to be specified:

```
$link = mysql_connect("myhost", "me", "mypassword");
```

Generally, unless you need to connect to more than one server, it's only necessary to call this function once in a single given script. However, you must bear in mind that when using PHP, each page requires a new connection, so you'll need to use this function at or near the start of any page that requires interaction with MySQL.

You can also use the function mysql_pconnect() instead of mysql_connect(), the difference between the two being that mysql_pconnect() uses persistent connections. This means that PHP will try to find an existing connection using the same parameters as used in the current call to mysql_pconnect() and will open a new connection only if no such existing connection is found. It also means that the connection will not be closed when the script terminates. We recommend against using persistent connections, particularly in a scenario (such as a busy web host with a number of different sites) where many different clients are accessing MySQL, as you're liable to have a pool of unused connections taking up resources that could be used by other MySQL clients.

NOTE *The new PHP 5* mysqli *extension does* not *support persistent connections, the reasons for this being much the same as those we give in the text for not using them. This being the case, we definitely recommend that you begin no new PHP/MySQL development with the* mysql *extension using* mysql_pconnect() *to initiate database connections, since when you upgrade to PHP 5 and MySQL 4.1 or higher and start using the* mysqli *extension, you won't be able to use persistent connections in any case.*

Once you've connected to the server, you'll need to select a database before you can start running queries. This is accomplished by means of the function mysql_select_db(), whose prototype is shown here:

```
bool mysql_select_db(string dbname[, linkID link])
```

This function performs the equivalent of issuing a USE command in the MySQL Monitor; it tells MySQL which database you want to use. It returns **TRUE** on success and **FALSE** on failure. The *dbname* argument is the name of the database; the *link* argument is optional and defaults to the value of the identifier for the link most recently opened by the current connection. If no connection is open, PHP will try to open a new one, just as though you'd called mysql_connect() with all of its default values.

A typical call to this function might look like this:

```
if( mysql_select_db("mydb", $link) )
{
  /* query tables in database "mydb"... */
}
else
  print "<p>Couldn't access database mydb.</p>\n";
```

TIP *If your application is able to connect to MySQL but can't select a particular database, make sure that the account being used has privileges on that database.*

Sending Queries

After connecting to the server and selecting a database, you're ready to submit queries. There are two functions you can employ for this purpose—mysql_query() and mysql_unbuffered_query(). It's much more common, especially in a web setting, to use the first of these, so we'll look at mysql_query() first. The prototype for this function is shown here:

```
resultID mysql_query(string query[, linkID link])
```

The *query* parameter for this function is simply the quoted text of an SQL statement. Any type of statement—SELECT, UPDATE, DELETE, SHOW TABLES, and so on—can be used for this purpose, so long as the statement follows the rules for SQL syntax in MySQL. The optional *link* parameter is the connection identifier returned by a call to mysql_connect(). If this argument is omitted, then it's assumed that you want to use the connection ID for the most recently opened connection. Technically, this argument is required only if you've multiple database connections open at the same time and you need to use one other than the one last opened, but it's good practice to specify it anyway. If there is no open connection, then PHP will try to open one, just as if you had called mysql_connect() with all of its default parameters. mysql_query() returns a result identifier which is then used by one of the mysql_fetch_*() functions to retrieve result rows—see the following section for an explanation of these.

A typical call to this function might look like this:

```
$link = mysql_connect("somehost", "me", "mypassword");
$product_id = $_POST["pid"];
$query = "SELECT p.name, p.price, c.name
          FROM product p
          JOIN category c
          ON p.category_id = c.id
          WHERE p.id = '$pid'";
$result = mysql_query($query, $link);
```

Of course, there's no reason why you have to store the query in a variable, particularly if the query is a short one, and it's perfectly acceptable to write something like this:

```
$result = mysql_query("SELECT * FROM products LIMIT 75, 100", $link);
```

Your primary consideration should be that the code is easy to read, understand, and update if and when necessary.

NOTE *When sending a query to MySQL using the* mysql *extension, it's not necessary to use a terminating semicolon for the query. Use* $query = "SELECT * FROM products"; *and not* $query = "SELECT * FROM products;";.

The mysql_unbuffered_query() function (introduced in PHP 4.0.6) takes the same parameters as mysql_query(), and is used in much the same fashion. The difference is that mysql_query() receives the entire result set from the server in one go, and the result set is stored in memory. When mysql_unbuffered_query() has been used, the result set is kept on the database server and individual rows are retrieved from the server, one at a time.

There can be some advantages to using mysql_unbuffered_query(), particularly when your query returns a very large result set: you can begin processing rows almost immediately, instead of waiting for the entire result set to be sent from the database, and not storing the entire result set can save memory on the web server. There are also some disadvantages: you can't seek a particular row (you must go through the result rows in the order in which they're returned), and you must fetch all the rows in the result set (whether your application actually needs them or not) before you can submit another query.

TIP *Most often, especially for PHP scripts that generate web pages, you'll want to use* mysql_query() *rather than* mysql_unbuffered_query().

In the event that a query fails, for whatever reason, either one of the functions mysql_query() and mysql_unbuffered_query() will return **FALSE**. Thus you can test for the success of a query using syntax of the type shown here:

```
if($result = mysql_query($query, $link))
{
  /* process results... */
}
```

```
else
{
  /*  handle error...  */
}
```

Note that this technique works with any sort of query, and not just SELECT queries. See the section "Catching and Reporting Errors with mysql" later in this chapter to find out how you can obtain MySQL error codes and messages using mysql when you need to determine for what reason a particular query has failed.

 NOTE *If you're using this extension with PHP 5, you may want to write a wrapper class or two that express some of the* mysql *functions as methods, so that you can take advantage of PHP 5's exception-handling capabilities. In fact, we'll do something similar (overriding some of the* mysqli *object's methods) in order to accomplish this using* ext/mysqli *for PHP 5. See the Multiple Statements examples in the "PHP 5 and mysqli" section for some ideas on how to do this.*

Retrieving Result Rows and Result Set Data

Once you've submitted a query and retrieved a result from MySQL using mysql_query(), your next task is to access the data contained in that result in a meaningful way so that you can actually use it in your PHP script. Depending on your preferences and requirements, there are several different ways in which you can do this, and we'll look at all of these in this section. In addition, the mysql extension also has some very useful functions for obtaining result set meta-data—that is, information about the result set itself and about the columns into which it's organized—which we'll also demonstrate for you.

Fetching Result Rows

As we alluded earlier in this chapter (see "Retrieving Results" under "Requirements for a MySQL API"), it's possible to get result rows from MySQL in several different forms, and the mysql extension has a number of functions that can be used for this purpose. All of these functions work in the same general fashion: the function is called with the result set identifier as a parameter, and the function either returns the next available row from the result set, or **FALSE** if there are no more rows to be fetched.

We list the prototypes of these functions along with a brief description of each function here:

- `mysql_fetch_row(resultID)`: This returns the row as an indexed array; the value in the first column is indexed as 0, the second as 1, and so on.

- `mysql_fetch_assoc(resultID)`: Returns each row as an associative array. The names of the columns serve as the keys. If column aliases were specified in the query, then these are used instead.

- `mysql_fetch_array(resultID[, type])`: This function can return the rows as indexed or associative arrays (or both), depending upon the `type` argument. `type` can take one of three values, which are defined as PHP constants by the `mysql` extension: `MYSQL_ASSOC` causes this function to return associative arrays like `mysql_fetch_assoc()`, `MYSQL_NUM` makes it return indexed arrays like `mysql_fetch_row()`, and `MYSQL_BOTH` causes this function to return arrays whose elements can be accessed either by index *or* key at the programmer's discretion. The default value is `MYSQL_BOTH`.

- `mysql_fetch_object(resultID)`: This function returns result rows as objects whose properties have the names of the columns (or their aliases, if used) as names.

- `mysql_result(resultID, int row[, mixed field])`: This function returns a single cell from a result set. The rows are indexed beginning with 0. If there is more than one column in the result, you must specify which column you wish to have returned by using the `field` argument, which can be either a numeric index (starting with 0 for the first column) or the column name or alias. Unless you've selected just one column from a table in your query, you'll find that using one of the other fetch functions is generally faster than using this function to fetch one column at a time.

The simplest way to use one of these functions to retrieve a set of result rows is in a `while` loop. Suppose that we've already established a connection with MySQL, and submitted the query `SELECT id, name, price FROM products ORDER BY name;`, and obtained a result identifier as the variable $result. We can then retrieve and output all the rows from this result as shown here:

```
while($row = mysql_fetch_assoc($result))
{
  extract($row);
  printf("<p>Name: %s; Price: %s; Product ID: %s</p>\n", $name, $price, $id);
}
```

Notice here how we used the PHP `extract()` function on $row to add its associative array keys as variable names and so save ourselves a bit of typing.

TIP   *You can use* `table_name.column_name` *syntax for the array keys of result rows with all of the* `mysql_fetch-*()` *functions that return associative arrays. For example, you could use* `$row["products.price"]` *to refer to the* `price` *column of the* `products` *table after setting* `$row = mysql_fetch_array(MYSQL_ASSOC);`. *This can be handy when processing joins where column aliases weren't assigned.*

Obtaining Data About Result Sets and Columns

There are some additional functions in the `mysql` extension that can be very useful in obtaining information about result sets. Among these are `mysql_num_rows()`, `mysql_affected_rows()`, `mysql_num_fields()`, and `mysql_fetch_fields()`. `mysql_num_rows()` takes a result identifier as its sole argument, and returns the number of rows in that result. Here's an example, in which we assume that a connection's been established and we've already selected the database we want to use:

```php
<?php
  $letter = "S";
  $query = "SELECT id, name, price
            FROM products
            WHERE name LIKE '$letter%'";
  $result = mysql_query($query);
  printf("<p>There are %d products whose names
            begin with the letter \"%s\".</p>\n",
         mysql_num_rows($result), $letter);
?>
```

CAUTION   *If you obtain a result set using* `mysql_unbuffered_query()`, *you must retrieve all of the rows in the result before you can call* `mysql_num_rows()` *and expect to obtain the correct value. Otherwise, it will return only the number of rows that you've fetched so far.*

The `mysql_num_rows()` function is valid only for obtaining the number of rows returned by a `SELECT` query. For queries that modify data, you can use `mysql_afffected_rows()`, as shown here:

```php
<?php
  $link = mysql_connect("myhost", "me", "mypassword");
  mysql_select_db("mydb", $link);
```

```
$query = "DELETE FROM products WHERE price > 100.00";
mysql_query($query);
printf("<p>%d records were deleted from the table.</p>\n",
        mysql_affected_rows($link));
?>
```

This function accepts a link resource identifier as its argument, and returns the number of rows affected by the last INSERT, UPDATE, or DELETE statement made using the connection represented by that resource ID. If none is specified, then mysql_affected_rows() will assume the most recently established connection.

 CAUTION *When you submit an* UPDATE *query, MySQL reports only the number of rows that were actually changed. If you need to know how many records match the* WHERE *condition after the update is performed, you'll need to submit a query using the SQL* COUNT() *function.*

There may be occasions on which you select from a table without knowing ahead of time how many columns there are in it or what their names are. You can find out how many columns are in a result set using the mysql_num_fields() function, which takes a result identifier as its argument. For additional information about the fields, you can use mysql_fetch_field(), which can be best illustrated by means of the example in Listing 7-1.

Listing 7-1. mysql-fetch-field.php: Retrieving Column Data from a Table with mysql_fetch_field()

```
<!DOCTYPE HTML PUBLIC "-//W3C//DTD HTML 4.01 Transitional//EN"
    "http://www.w3.org/TR/html4/loose.dtd">
<html>
<head>
<meta http-equiv="Content-Type" content="text/html; charset=iso-8859-1">
<title>Getting Column Data From a Table (PHP4 / mysql)</title>
</head>
<body bgcolor="#DEDEDE">
<table cellpadding="3" cellspacing=\"1\" frame="box" rules="rows"
        bgcolor="#ABABAB" align="center">
<?php
  #  names of database and table
  $database = "mdbd";
  $table = "orders";

  #  connect to MySQL, select DB
```

```
$connection = mysql_connect("localhost", "jon", "eleanor");
mysql_select_db($database, $connection);

#  select all columns from the table
$result = mysql_query("SELECT * FROM $table LIMIT 1")
  or die( mysql_error() );

#  get the number of columns in the result
$num_fields = mysql_num_fields($result);

#  HTML table heading with name of a database and table, number of columns
printf("<tr><th bgcolor=\"#FFFFFF\" colspan=\"%d\">
        Columns in table <em>%s</em>:</th></tr>\n<tr>",
        $num_fields, $table);

#  counter to track columns
$i = 0;

# for each column...
do
{
  #  start a new nested HTML table in which to display this column
  printf("<td><table border=\"1\" cellspacing=\"0\"
                    cellpadding=\"2\" bgcolor=\"#FFFFFF\">\n
          <tr><th colspan=\"2\">Column %d</th></tr>\n", $i);

  #  get an object corresponding to the column
  $col = mysql_fetch_field($result, $i);

  #  get a copy of this object as an associative array
  #  (in other words, we'll turn each $col->property_name into a
  #  $col_array["property_name"] to make it easier to loop through all
  #  of the object's properties)
  $col_array = get_object_vars($col);

  #  for each element in the associative array, display the key and value
  #  the name of the key is a property of the column
  foreach($col_array as $property => $value)
    printf("<tr><td>%s</td><td>%s</td></tr>\n", $property, $value);

  #  close the nested HTML table
  print "</table>\n</td>\n";
} while(++$i < $num_fields);  #  get the next column if there is one
?>
```

```
    </tr>
  </table>
  </body>
</html>
```

TIP   *If you're not familiar with* get_object_vars(), *which converts objects into associative arrays, see the PHP Manual page for this very useful function at* http://www.php.net/get_object_vars.

The output of this PHP 4 page in a web browser is shown here:

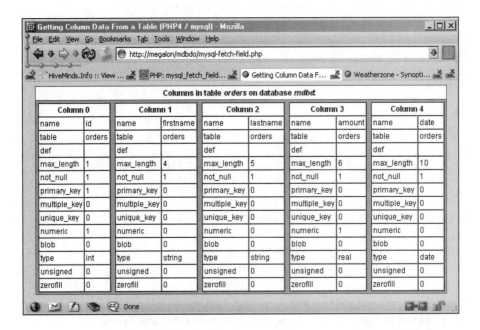

You can see a complete listing of the properties exposed by the field object returned by mysql_fetch_field() in the screenshot. The name, table, and type properties are strings, and the max_length property is an integer showing the size of the column. The remaining properties are integers where 1 stands for **TRUE** and 0 for **FALSE**. For example, looking at the first column, we can see that its name is id, it's a column in the orders table, and its datatype is INT. Oddly enough, its max_length is reported as 1, but this is because it's an AUTO_INCREMENT column, as we can see by running a SHOW CREATE TABLE command on the same table in the MySQL Monitor:

```
Command Prompt - mysql -h megalon -u root -p                    _ □ x
mysql> SHOW CREATE TABLE orders\G
*************************** 1. row ***************************
       Table: orders
Create Table: CREATE TABLE `orders` (
  `id` int(11) NOT NULL auto_increment,
  `firstname` varchar(25) NOT NULL default '',
  `lastname` varchar(25) NOT NULL default '',
  `amount` decimal(6,2) NOT NULL default '0.00',
  `date` date NOT NULL default '0000-00-00',
  PRIMARY KEY (`id`)
) ENGINE=MyISAM DEFAULT CHARSET=latin1 COMMENT='orders table'
1 row in set (0.23 sec)

mysql>
```

We can also tell that the **id** column is the table's primary key, that it doesn't
accept null values, and that it's a numeric type. The information returned by
mysql_fetch_field() is also available via a number of separate functions:
mysql_field_name(), mysql_field_table(), mysql_field_len(), mysql_field_type(),
and mysql_field_flags(). All of these functions take two arguments—a result
identifier, and a column offset (starting with 0). You should be able to tell from
the function names what all but the last of them do. The mysql_field_flags()
function returns a string consisting of zero or more of the words not_null,
primary_key, unique_key, multiple_key, blob, unsigned, zerofill, binary, enum,
auto_increment, and timestamp, separated by spaces. You can use PHP's explode()
function to separate the string into separate words or strpos() to test for the
presence or absence of one or more of the words in the string.

NOTE   *You'll find the source code for* mysql-fetch-field.php *and the
other examples in this chapter that use the* mysql *extension under
PHP4 in the* /ch7/mysql *directory of this book's code download
package, which is freely available from the publisher's web site at*
http://www.apress.com.

Although you may not need to use it every time you interact with MySQL,
one other function of which you should be aware is mysql_free_result(). This
function takes a result identifier as its parameter and returns either **TRUE** or
FALSE depending on whether or not it's successful in freeing all the memory
associated with the result set indicated by the ID. Given that the mysql extension
is most often used in conjunction with fairly short web scripts and result sets of
small to moderate size, and that resources are freed up at the end of a PHP
script, you can usually omit any calls to this function. However, if you're dealing
with long, complex scripts using a lot of different result sets, or a query that
returns a particularly large result, you may find that using mysql_free_result()
when you've finished with a given result set may improve PHP's performance.

> **NOTE** *While it's not an absolute requirement to do so, it is considered good coding practice to free all result set and connection memory by using* mysql_free_result() *and* mysql_close() *as soon as you've finished with them.*

Catching and Reporting Errors with mysql

When something goes wrong with a MySQL interaction such as an attempt to connect to a server, selecting a database, or sending a query, you'll need to find why this happened so that you can take corrective action in your PHP script. We discussed this more generally earlier in this chapter. The mysql extension offers two error-reporting functions that can help in this regard. Let's look at both of these and see how they can be useful to you in managing errors that may occur.

The mysql_error() function takes an optional connection identifier as its sole argument; if none is used, then PHP assumes that you meant the most recently opened connection (or in some cases, the most recently attempted connection). The function returns the text of the last error message that was generated by MySQL. Its sibling is mysql_errno(), which takes the same (optional) argument and returns a MySQL error code. For example, to find out what goes wrong should an attempt to establish a new connection fails, you can use something like this in your PHP scripts:

```
$link = mysql_connect("myhost", "me", "mypassword")
   or die("Failed to connect. MySQL said: " . mysql_error()
        . ". (Error code was " . mysql_errno() . ".)\n");
```

In this context, it doesn't make sense to use a connection identifier, since mysql_connect() returns **FALSE** if it fails. Otherwise, it's good practice to use the connection ID, even if you're only working with one open connection.

For more information about MySQL error messages and error codes, see the section "Detecting and Handling Errors" earlier in this chapter.

Disconnecting from the Server

Connections to MySQL made using mysql_connect() are automatically terminated at the end of PHP scripts. (If mysql_pconnect() is used to establish persistent connections, then the programmer has no way to close them manually and must wait for PHP and MySQL to do it.) Most of the time, closing database connections isn't a big issue: most PHP scripts are used to generate web pages dynamically, and this normally doesn't take a great deal of time or (provided you're following reasonable practices) system resources.

However, there can be occasions when you're using PHP for other things, such as importing large amounts of data into multiple databases or updating them, or using a GUI application built with a library such as PHP-GTK (which is becoming increasingly common these days). In such cases, a PHP script might run for a considerable length of time, connecting to several different databases during the course of its run. In these situations, you can use `mysql_close()` to close a connection. This function takes an optional single argument, a connection identifier, and returns **TRUE** on success or **FALSE** upon failure. This has the same result as typing /q or `quit` at the command prompt in the MySQL Monitor; the session is ended, and the user (in this case, the application) must reconnect in order to interact any further with MySQL.

PHP 5 and mysqli

In July of 2004, PHP programming entered a new era with the initial production release of PHP 5.0. The feature of greatest general interest is probably the new Zend 2.0 engine which forms the core of PHP 5; it supports a new object model that provides for improved inheritance, supports interfaces and object overloading, adds exception handling as in C++ and Java, and includes many other additions and enhancements to objects and classes in PHP. PHP 5 also has greatly improved XML processing, enhanced support for web services (including a new SOAP extension), and of particular interest to us, a brand-new extension for working with MySQL, named `mysqli` (for "MySQL Improved").

In the following sections, we'll discuss the rationale behind creating this new extension, what exactly is "new" about it, and why it promises to change how PHP programmers work with MySQL. Then we'll dig into the nuts and bolts of this new MySQL API and provide working examples that will show you some of the ways in which it can be used.

Why a New Extension?

So what's wrong with the `mysql` extension, anyway? In and of itself there's nothing terribly "wrong" with it, really. It's enjoyed a long and highly successful career as an integral part of Open Source web development, and has helped power millions—yes, *millions*—of web sites. However, since this extension first appeared in 1997 as part of PHP 3, both PHP and MySQL have changed considerably, and MySQL is about to undergo even greater changes as version 4.1 and then version 5.0 reach "gold" release status.

We've already mentioned one change, beginning in MySQL 4.1, concerning how the manner in which MySQL client applications authenticate to a MySQL server is much more secure than previously was the case. We've also hinted at some powerful new API functionality for applications using the version 4.1 and higher MySQL client libraries, which we'll discuss in much greater detail shortly. One feature that we've not previously mentioned is that applications using the new client protocols to communicate with MySQL 4.1 and above can perform much more quickly than clients using the old protocols.

It's also true that there are several characteristics of the mysql extension that can be considered "misfeatures." For example, some mysql extension functions will, in the absence of a connection to MySQL, try to establish one for you (see the previous section of this chapter). This is not the case with ext/mysqli.

In addition, as more and more developers are using PHP for larger and more complex projects, more of them are turning to an object-oriented methodology, and mysqli helps to address this.

What's New in mysqli

First of all, mysqli, unlike the old mysql extension, presents an object-oriented programming interface. While it retains a procedural API similar to that of mysql in some ways, we think that a great many programmers will prefer the object-oriented API, as the syntax is less error-prone and in many cases much terser. The method names are shorter than the equivalent function names, and in some instances, they take fewer arguments because data passed by function parameters in the procedural API can, in the object-oriented API, be held in objects representing connections and result sets instead.

The mysqli extension also simplifies working with transactions. In ext/mysql (a common PHP programmers' abbreviation for "mysql extension," a reference to the directory in the PHP distribution where the extension library file is found), you had to send explicit queries to toggle autocommit mode, and to begin and to commit transactions. ext/mysqli introduces new functions and methods that streamline this process considerably.

ext/mysqli also supports two new MySQL APIs, introduced in MySQL 4.1. The Multiple Statements API allows your application to send multiple SQL statements in a single function or method call and to receive multiple result sets in a single response. The Prepared Statements API supports the optimization of oft-repeated queries by using placeholders for limiting values and preparsing or compiling the queries themselves so that after the first time a particular query is submitted, only the new limiting values need to be sent to MySQL.

mysqli Procedural API Basics

As we've mentioned already, mysqli can be used in one of two ways: either as a library of functions similar in some ways to those found in the older ext/mysql, or as an object-oriented API. In the next few sections, we'll cover the procedural or function-oriented version of this extension.

If you've used the PHP4 mysql extension, you'll find that many of the familiar functions are still present, but have slightly different names, substituting *mysqli_* for the familiar *mysql_* prefix. Porting a PHP application from using the mysql extension to mysqli isn't always as simple as running a search-and-replace on the source code, but many of the mysqli functions do work in much the same way as their older counterparts. Of course, there are also some "false friends" as well; we'll try to help you look out for these.

We'll not cover all of the mysqli functions in this chapter, as there are about 75 of them, but we will cover the most important ones. These are listed in Table 7-2.

Table 7-2. mysqli Function API—Partial Listing

FUNCTION	DESCRIPTION
mysqli_init()	Initializes a link object for use with mysqli_real_connect()
mysqli_options()*	Sets connection options prior to opening connection with mysqli_real_connect()
mysqli_connect()	Opens a new connection to the MySQL server
mysqli_real_connect()	Opens a connection to the MySQL server, using a resource link generated by mysqli_init() (preferred)
mysqli_select_db()	Selects the default database for subsequent database queries
mysqli_close()	Closes a previously opened database connection
mysqli_errno()	Returns the error code for the most recent function call
mysqli_error()	Returns a string description of the last error
mysqli_warning_count()	Returns the number of warnings from the last query for the given link
mysqli_real_escape_string()	Escapes special characters in a string for use in an SQL statement, taking into account the current character set of the connection
mysqli_prepare()*	Prepares an SQL statement for execution
mysqli_execute()*	Executes a prepared statement
mysqli_stmt_close()*	Closes a prepared statement
mysqli_query()	Performs a query on the database

(Continued)

Table 7-2. mysqli Function API—Partial Listing (Continued)

FUNCTION	DESCRIPTION
mysqli_real_query()	Executes an SQL query
mysqli_num_rows()	Gets the number of rows in a result set
mysqli_fetch_array()	Fetches a result row as an associative, a numeric array, or both (see text)
mysqli_fetch_assoc()	Fetches a result row as an associative array
mysqli_fetch_object()	Returns the current row of a result set as an object
mysqli_fetch_row()	Gets a result row as an enumerated array
mysqli_bind_param()*	Binds variables to a prepared statement as parameters
mysqli_bind_result()*	Binds variables to a prepared statement for result storage
mysqli_fetch()*	Fetches results from a prepared statement into the bound variables
mysqli_free_result()	Frees the memory associated with a result
mysqli_insert_id()	Returns the last ID generated for an **AUTO_INCREMENT** column during this session
mysqli_autocommit()*	Turns on or off auto-committing database modifications
mysqli_commit()*	Commits the current transaction
mysqli_rollback()*	Rolls back a transaction

Functions that are new in mysqli that have no analogue under the old mysql extension are marked with an asterisk in Table 7-2. The remainder should look familiar to users of the older MySQL API for PHP, and work in a similar fashion. There are also three resource types, as follows:

- mysqli_link: A link resource; represents a connection by PHP to the MySQL server.

- mysql_result: A result resource; represents a result set returned from a query.

- mysqli_stmt: A statement resource; represents a prepared statement.

The first two of these should also be familiar to users of the MySQL extension in PHP4; the statement resource type is new in PHP5 and is supported when using MySQL 4.1 and higher. This is used only when working with prepared statements, which we'll look at later on in our discussion.

Procedural Example

Listing 7-2 presents a simple example showing how to use mysqli to connect to a database, send a SELECT query, and then retrieve and display the results, using the procedural style.

Listing 7-2. mysqli-procedural-select.php: SELECT Query Using the mysqli Function API

```
<!DOCTYPE HTML PUBLIC "-//W3C//DTD HTML 4.01 Transitional//EN"
    "http://www.w3.org/TR/html4/loose.dtd">
<html>
<head>
<meta http-equiv="Content-Type" content="text/html; charset=iso-8859-1">
<title>SIMPLE mysqli SELECT :: PROCEDURAL STYLE</title>
<!- Filename: procedural-select.php ->
</head>
<body>
<?php
  # establish connection
  $link = mysqli_init();
  mysqli_real_connect($link, 'localhost', 'user', 'pass', 'db');

  # if connection fails, tell us why
  if( mysqli_connect_errno() )
    die("Connect failed: " . mysqli_connect_error());

  $query =
    "SELECT empid, firstname, lastname
    FROM employees
    ORDER BY lastname";

  # submit query
  mysqli_real_query($link, $query);

  # get result
  if($result = mysqli_store_result($link))
  {
?>
```

```
<table border="1" width="30%">
<tr>
  <th width="10%">Employee #</th>
  <th>First Name</th>
  <th>Last Name</th>
</tr>
<?
    //  fetch rows from result set
    while($row = mysqli_fetch_assoc($result))
    {
      //  extract column values and
      //  display them
      extract($row);
      printf("<tr>
                <td align=\"center\">%s</td>
                <td>%s</td>
                <td>%s/td>
              </tr>\n",
              $empid, $firstname, $lastname;
    }
?>
</table>
<?
  }
  else
    #  if the query fails, tell us why
    echo mysqli_error();

  #  free resources used by result set
  mysqli_free_result($result);

  #  terminate the connection
  mysqli_close($link);
?>
</body>
</html>
```

NOTE *Source code for the previous example and other examples in this section that make use of PHP 5 with the* mysqli *extension may be found in the* /ch7/mysqli *directory of the code download for this book.*

Procedural Version of mysqli vs. the Old mysql Extension

The example that we looked at in the previous section should be very familiar to you if you've worked with the mysql extension in PHP4 or earlier versions of PHP, but there are some differences to consider when using the procedural style for mysqli as contrasted with the old MySQL extension. These differences extend to all phases of interacting with MySQL—connection, transmission of queries, fetching of results, and handling of errors—and can trip you up if you're not mindful of them. Let's look at each of these areas in turn.

Making the Connection

To establish a connection, you'll first need to call mysqli_init() to create a new link object, and then use this object as one of the parameters of mysqli_real_connect(). Both of these steps are required. It's important to remember that, unlike the case with the older mysql extension, you *must* refer to the link when you make the connection and send queries.

NOTE *Another difference between* mysqli_real_connect() *and* mysql_connect() *is that the former can include the database name, which saves you a step—unlike the case with the* mysql *extension, where you must select the database in a separate call to* mysql_select_db().

Another feature new to mysqli is that you can set connection options using the function mysqli_options(). While it's also possible to establish a connection using the function mysqli_connect() (and using this function doesn't require a call to mysqli_init() beforehand), we recommend using mysqli_init() and mysqli_real_connect() instead because you can't set options without making a call to mysqli_init() first. The function prototype for mysqli_options() is

```
bool mysqli_options(object link, int option, string value)
```

The options and their uses are shown in Table 7-3.

Table 7-3. Connection Options for Use with mysqli_options()

OPTION	DESCRIPTION
MYSQLI_OPT_CONNECT_TIMEOUT	Connection timeout (in seconds)
MYSQLI_OPT_LOCAL_INFILE	Enables or disables use of LOAD LOCAL INFILE

(Continued)

Table 7-3. Connection Options for Use with mysqli_options() (Continued)

OPTION	DESCRIPTION
MYSQLI_INIT_CMD	An SQL command to execute when first connecting to the MySQL server
MYSQLI_READ_DEFAULT_FILE	Tells MySQL to read options from the named option file instead of my.cnf (or my.ini on Windows)
MYSQLI_READ_DEFAULT_GROUP	Tells MySQL to read options from the named group in my.cnf or the file specified with MYSQL_READ_DEFAULT_FILE

For example, to establish a connection while setting the connection timeout to 5 minutes (300 seconds), you'd use something like this:

```php
<?php
  $link = mysqli_init();

  mysqli_options($link, MYSQLI_CONNECT_TIMEOUT, "300")
    or die("Failed to set connection options.");

  mysqli_real_connect($link, 'localhost', 'user', 'pass', 'db');
?>
```

You can set multiple connection options by making additional calls to mysqli_options() before using mysqli_real_connect(). Conversely, if you don't need to set any connection options, then there's no requirement that you call mysqli_options() at all. If you use mysqli_init() and mysqli_real_connect(), then you're prepared in the event that your requirements change.

Submitting Queries and Obtaining a Result

To send a query to MySQL, you have two choices. You can use either of the following:

- mysqli_real_query() followed by mysqli_use_result() or mysqli_store_result().

- The shorter mysqli_query(). This function takes two parameters— a link object, and either of the constants MYSQLI_USE_RESULT or MYSQLI_STORE_RESULT.

There are two modes for returning a result set: you can employ either storage mode or usage mode. Using storage mode—that is, mysqli_real_query() and mysqli_store_result(), or mysqli_query() with MYSQLI_STORE_RESULT—is usually preferable, since this returns the entire result set. Otherwise, you must call mysqli_free_result() before submitting the next query. In addition, usage mode (using mysqli_use result() or using mysqli_query() with MYSQLI_USE_RESULT) tends to be more efficient than storage mode. This is because storage mode can tie up the server and prevent other threads from updating any tables until the result set is freed.

NOTE *If no result type is specified for* mysqli_query(), *the type defaults to* MYSQLI_STORE_RESULT.

Fetching Rows from a Result Set

Just like the mysql extension, the mysqli extension provides several convenience functions for fetching rows from a result set. These are exact analogues of the equivalent mysql extension functions, and differ only in their names: mysqli_fetch_array(), mysqli_fetch_assoc(), mysqli_fetch_object(), and mysqli_fetch_row(). The first three of these act upon a result resource and return the next row from it as, respectively, an indexed (enumerated) array, an associative array, and an object. The last function returns an array that is indexed, associative, or both, depending upon the value of its optional second parameter, which can be MYSQLI_NUM, MYSQLI_ASSOC, or MYSQLI_BOTH. MYSQLI_BOTH is the default value.

CAUTION *While testing our* mysqli *examples, we encountered what appears to be a bug in PHP 5.0.1 whereby the result type argument for* mysqli_fetch_row() *actually defaults to* MYSQLI_ASSOC, *even though the PHP documentation says differently. Practice safe coding, and always specify such arguments.*

However, error reporting when using mysqli is considerably different. In the procedural version of mysqli, connection errors are reported using two new functions specific to this purpose. mysqli_connect_errno() returns a MySQL error code, and mysqli_connect_error() returns the corresponding error message text from MySQL. For query errors, use the functions mysqli_error() and mysqli_errno().

You can also check for warnings and obtain the text of these if any are returned. To retrieve any warnings generated by a query, simply send a SHOW WARNINGS; command to the database immediately following the query. We'll show you an example of this in the next section.

The Object-Oriented Style for mysqli

When using the object-oriented version of mysqli, the three resource types listed previously are represented by predefined classes that are instantiated by the programmer. Work is accomplished by calling various methods of the class instances. To create a new connection to MySQL, one calls the mysqli class constructor, which instantiates a new link object. To send a query, we call this object's query() method, which yields a result resource object. The resource object's fetch_*() methods are used to return the rows. This should become clearer if we take the previous example and rewrite it in object-oriented style, as shown in Listing 7-3.

Listing 7-3. mysqli-oop-select.php: A Simple SELECT Query Using the Object-Oriented Style for mysqli

```
<!DOCTYPE HTML PUBLIC "-//W3C//DTD HTML 4.01 Transitional//EN"
    "http://www.w3.org/TR/html4/loose.dtd">
<html>
<head>
<meta http-equiv="Content-Type" content="text/html; charset=iso-8859-1">
<title>SIMPLE MySQLI SELECT :: OBJECT_ORIENTED STYLE</title>
</head>
<body>
<?php
  // connect to MySQL
  $link = new mysqli('localhost', 'jon', 'eleanor', 'test');

  // notify us in the event of a connection error
  if( mysqli_connect_errno() )
    die("Connect failed: " . mysqli_connect_error());

  $query = "SELECT empid, firstname, lastname
            FROM employees
            ORDER BY lastname";
```

```
  //  submit query
  if($result = $link->query($query))
  {
?>
<table border="1" width="30%">
<tr>
  <th width="10%">Employee #</th>
  <th>First Name</th>
  <th>Last Name</th>
</tr>
<?
    while($row = $result->fetch_object())
    {
      //  display the rows
      printf("<tr>\n<td>%s</td><td>%s</td>\n<td>%s</td>\n</tr>",
              $row->empid, $row->firstname, $row->lastname);
    }
?>
</table>
<?
    printf("<p>Number of rows returned: %s.</p>\n", $link->num_rows);
  }
  else  //  notify us if the query failed
    printf("<p>Error #%s: %s.</p>", mysqli_errno(), mysqli_error());

  //  free result memory, and close the connection
  $result->close();
  $link->close();
?>
</body>
</html>
```

Unlike the case when using the procedural style, there's no need to call `mysqli_init()`; we merely call the `mysqli` class constructor. The resulting output is the same as for the procedural version of this example: it appears in a web browser, and should look something like what's shown here:

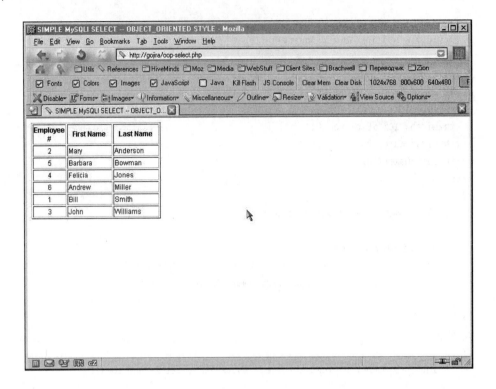

mysqli's Object-Oriented API (Links and Result Sets)

As we've already mentioned, `mysqli` provides three classes for working with database connections (links), result resources, and prepared statements. We'll defer talking about prepared statements for just a little while yet, but we'll go ahead and sum up the most important and useful methods and properties of the first two classes. First, let's look at the `mysqli` class constructor:

```
mysqli([string hostname [, string username [, string password [,
  string databasename [, int port [, string socket]]]]]])
```

You should note that all of the arguments for this constructor are optional, and `mysqli` will supply the following default values for those that you omit:

hostname	`mysqli.default_host` or `'localhost'` if none specified
username	`mysqli.default_user` or empty string
password	`mysqli.default_pw` or empty string
databasename	None

(Continued)

| *port* | `mysqli.default_port` or 3306 |
| *socket* | `mysqli.default_socket` (empty string) |

The values prefixed by `mysqli.` are those set in the php.ini configuration file. You can obtain and set these values using the `ini_get()` and `ini_set()` functions, respectively. You can also see what these values are in the output of `phpinfo()`, as shown in Figure 7-7.

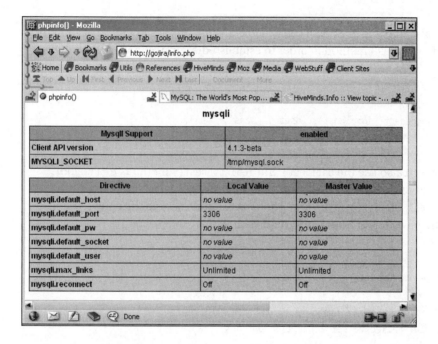

Figure 7-7. mysqli-phpinfo: Output of phpinfo() showing default values for mysqli configuration variables

CAUTION *Since it's so easy to find out what the default values are for the username and password, we strongly urge you never to set default username and password values in the php.ini file, nor to rely on them in your PHP scripts, especially in a production environment. Always leave the* `mysqli.default_user` *and* `mysqli.default_pw` *entries in the php.ini file blank.*

Generally speaking, you'll most often want to call the constructor with the first three or four arguments, for example

```
$link = new mysqli('localhost', 'user', 'pass');
```

or

```
$link = new mysqli('localhost', 'user', 'pass', 'test');
```

In the first case, you can always select a database after creating a new mysqli object using its select_db() method, which takes the database name as its sole argument, like so:

```
$link->select_db('test');
```

It's also possible to call the constructor without any arguments at all, and then to call its connect() method in order to establish the connection, as shown here:

```
<?php
  $link = new mysqli();
  $link->connect('localhost', 'user', 'pass', 'db');
?>
```

You can also use the options() and real_connect() methods in a fashion analogous to that shown earlier for the functions mysqli_options() and mysqli_real_connect(). Here's our previous example setting the connection timeout, rewritten in object-oriented fashion:

```
<?php
  $link = new mysqli();

  $link->options(MYSQLI_CONNECT_TIMEOUT, '300')
    or die("Failed to set connection options.");

  $link->real_connect('localhost', 'user', 'pass', 'db');
?>
```

Notice that since we're calling methods of the link object, it's not necessary to pass it as a parameter when using mysqli in the object-oriented style.

Table 7-4 provides a summary of the other mysqli class methods and properties that you're mostly likely to need.

Table 7-4. mysqli Class Methods and Properties

METHOD NAME	DESCRIPTION
change_user(string dbname)	Changes the database user.
close()	Closes the current connection.

(Continued)

Table 7-4. mysqli Class Methods and Properties (Continued)

METHOD NAME	DESCRIPTION
connect(args)	Opens a new connection to MySQL; takes the same arguments as the class constructor.
query(string query)	Performs a query, and returns a result resource object.
real_connect(args)	Attempts to open a connection to MySQL database server; takes the same arguments as the class constructor.
escape_string(string string)	Escapes special characters in a string for use in an SQL statement.
store_result()	Transfers a result set from the last query to PHP; as explained in the text, you should use this method rather than use_result() unless you have a good reason for doing so.
use_result()	Transfers an unbuffered result set from the last query.
select_db(string dbname)	Selects a database.

PROPERTY NAME	DESCRIPTION
affected_rows	Number of affected rows in a previous MySQL operation.
errno	Error code for the most recent function call.
error	Error string for the most recent function call.
info	Retrieves information about the most recently executed query.
field_count	Number of columns in the most recently returned result set.
insert_id	Most recently generated ID for an **AUTO_INCREMENT** column by an INSERT operation.
warning_count	Number of warnings generated by the previous SQL statement; you can display the warnings themselves using the result of a SHOW WARNINGS query. (Available only when using MySQL 4.1 or newer.)

NOTE *When using the procedural style for* mysqli, *the **affected row count, error number, error message, field count, last inserted ID,** and **warning count** are all retrieved using functions. When using the object-oriented style, these values are obtained as* properties, *and not methods, of a* mysqli *object. Similarly, the number of fields and the number of rows in a result set are found as properties of a* mysqli_result *object, not as methods, even though we use functions for these when employing the procedural style.*

Whether you use store_result() or use_result() to obtain a result set, the value returned is a mysqli_result object. To obtain rows from the result set or other information about it, you'll need to use the proper methods and properties associated with this class, as shown in Table 7-5.

Table 7-5. mysqli_result Class Methods and Properties

METHOD NAME	DESCRIPTION
close()	Frees result memory; closes result set
fetch_array(const array_type)	Gets a result row as an associative array (by using the supplied constant MYSQLI_ASSOC as the argument), a numeric array (MYSQLI_NUM), or both (MYSQLI_BOTH—the default value)
fetch_assoc()	Gets a result row as an associative array (column names act as keys)
fetch_object()	Gets a result row as an object (column names used as properties)
fetch_row()	Gets a result row as an enumerated array
fetch_field(int column_index)	Gets information about the indicated column from a result set
fetch_fields()	Gets information for all columns from a result set
PROPERTY NAME	**DESCRIPTION**
field_count	Number of fields or columns in result set
num_rows	Number of rows in result set

You shouldn't have any difficulties in using these to obtain result rows and basic information about the result set itself.

NOTE *Additional methods and properties are available for more complex operations such as navigating directly to a given row in a result set; see the PHP 5 online manual at* http://www.php.net/ manual/en/ *for more information about these.*

Getting Warning Messages with mysqli

As we've already mentioned, when using mysqli you can also check to see if there were any warnings issued in response to a query and retrieve the text of them by sending a SHOW WARNINGS; to MySQL. Listing 7-4 gives an example illustrating how you'd do this using the object-oriented mysqli API.

Listing 7-4. oop-insert-warnings.php: Retrieving Warning Messages from MySQL

```
<!DOCTYPE HTML PUBLIC "-//W3C//DTD HTML 4.01 Transitional//EN"
    "http://www.w3.org/TR/html4/loose.dtd">
<html>
<head>
<meta http-equiv="Content-Type" content="text/html; charset=iso-8859-1">
<title>MySQLI INSERT WARNINGS :: OBJECT-ORIENTED STYLE</title>
</head>
<body>
<?php
  # establish connection
  $link = new mysqli("localhost", "jon", "eleanor", "test");

  if( mysqli_connect_errno() )
    die("Connect failed: " . mysqli_connect_error());

  $query = "INSERT INTO employees
              (empid, firstname, lastname)
            VALUES
              ('', 'Peter', 'Parker'),
              ('', 'Bruce', 'Wayne'),
              ('', 'Clark', 'Kent')";

  # submit query
  if($result = $link->query($query))
  {
    $num_warnings = $link->mysql_warning_count;
    if($num_warnings > 0)  # were there any warnings issued?
    { # if so, send a SHOW WARNINGS query and output the results
```

```
        if($result = $link->query("SHOW WARNINGS"))
        {
          printf("<table border=\"1\" width=\"30%\">
                  <tr><th>Warnings: %s</th></tr>
                  <tr><th>Level</th><th>Code</th><th>Message</th></tr>",
                  $num_warnings);

          while($row = $result->fetch_object())
            printf("<tr>\n<td>%s</td><td>%s</td>\n<td>%s</td>\n</tr>",
                    $row->Level, $row->Code, $row->Message);
          print "</table>\n";
        }
        else  #  if for some reason we couldn't retrieve the warnings...
          printf("<p>Unable to retrieve warnings.<br>
                  Error number #%s: %s.</p>",
                  $link->mysqli_errno, $link->mysqli_error);
      }
      else
        printf("<p>No warnings issued.</p>\n");
    }
    else
      printf("<p>Error number #%s: %s.</p>",
              $link->mysqli_errno, $link->mysqli_error);

    #  if the INSERT was successful, show how many rows were inserted
    printf("<p>Affected rows: %s</p>\n", $link->affected_rows);
    #  free result set memory
    $result->close();
  }
  else  #  if the INSERT failed, let us know why it did
    printf("<p>Error number #%s: %s.</p>",
            $link->mysqli_errno, $link->mysqli_error);
  #  close the connection
  $link->close();
  #  signal that we're done
  print "<p>Script completed.</p>";
?>
</body>
</html>
```

You can see the results here:

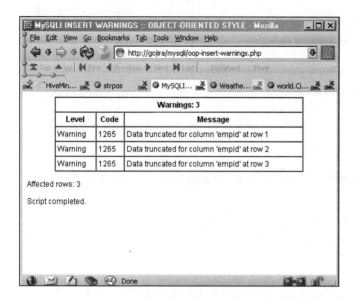

The result set returned by MySQL in response to a SHOW WARNINGS; command has three columns, which are named Level, Code, and Message. In this example, we hard-coded these names, but of course it's also possible to get them using the array returned by the result set object's fetch_fields() method. (See the "Working with Multiple Statements in mysqli" section later in this chapter for an example in which this method is used.)

NOTE *When using* ext/mysqli *in the object-oriented way,* mysqli_warning_count *is a* property *of the* mysqli *object. When using the procedural style, this warning count is obtained by calling* mysqli_warning_count() *as a* function *that takes a link object as a parameter.*

Working with Transactions in mysqli

There are three built-in methods of the mysqli class that simplify working with transactions. (Note that these work only with InnoDB and Berkeley DB tables as of this writing.)

- autocommit(): Toggles auto-commit mode (**FALSE** or 0 for "off," **TRUE** or 1 for "on"). Calling this method with the argument **FALSE** is equivalent to issuing the BEGIN command. You can obtain the current auto-commit status using SELECT @@autocommit, and test it if you wish, but it won't hurt anything to call this method whether or not auto-commit mode is already disabled.

- commit(): Commits the pending transaction. Equivalent to issuing a MySQL COMMIT command.

- rollback(): Rolls back the current transaction. Equivalent to issuing a MySQL ROLLBACK command.

Listing 7-5 shows an example illustrating the transfer of a sum of money between two checking accounts:

Listing 7-5. simple-transaction.php: Using Transactions with mysqli (Object-Oriented Style)

```
<!DOCTYPE HTML PUBLIC "-//W3C//DTD HTML 4.01 Transitional//EN"
  "http://www.w3.org/TR/html4/loose.dtd">
<html>
<head>
<meta http-equiv="Content-Type" content="text/html; charset=iso-8859-1">
<title>mysqli Transaction Example (OO Style)</title>
</head>
<body>

<?php
  #  Simple transactions example assumes the accounts table supports transactions
  #  Filename: simple-transaction.php

  #  amount to be transferred
  $amt = 50.00;

  #  account numbers
  $acct1 = '14532';
  $acct2 = '30041';

  #  connect and verify connection...
  $link = new mysqli('localhost', 'me', 'password', 'accounts');

  if( mysqli_connect_errno() )
    die("Connect failed: " .
       mysqli_connect_error());

  #  display beginning balances
  $bal_query = "SELECT acctid, balance
                FROM checking
                ORDER BY acctid";

  if($result = $link->query($bal_query))
```

```
        {
    ?>
    <table>
      <tr><th colpsan=\"2\">Starting Balances:</th></tr>
      <tr><td>Acct #:</td><td>Balance:</td></tr>
    <?php
        while($row = $result->fetch_object())
          printf("<tr><td>%s</td><td align=\"right\">\$%f.2</td></tr>\n",
                  $row->acctid, $row->balance);
      }
    ?>
    </table>
    <?php
      #  turn off auto-commit, and begin the transaction
      $link->autocommit(FALSE);

      #  subtract sum from first account
      $subtract_query = "UPDATE checking
                          SET balance = balance - $amt
                          WHERE acctid = $acct1";
      if($result = $link->query($subtract_query))
      {
        printf("<p>Subtracting \$%f.2 from account #%s...</p>\n", $amt, $acct1);
        #  if subtraction is successful,
        #  add amount to second account
        $add_query =
          "UPDATE checking
           SET balance = balance - $amt
           WHERE acctid = $acct2";

        #  if subtraction is also successful,
        #  commit the transaction;
        #  otherwise do a rollback
        if($result = $link->query($add_query))
        {
          printf("<p>Adding \$%f.2 to account #%s...</p>\n", $amt, $acct2);
          $link->commit();
        }
        else
        {
          print "<p>Error - rolling back transaction.</p>\n";
          $link->rollback();
        }
      }
```

```
  #  display ending balances
  if($result = $link->query($bal_query))
  {
?>
<table>
  <tr><th colpsan="2">Ending Balances:</th></tr>
  <tr><td>Acct #:</td><td>Balance:</td></tr>
<?php
    while($row = $result->fetch_object())
      printf("<tr><td>%s</td><td align=\"right\">\$%f.2</td></tr>\n",
             $row->acctid, $row->balance);
  }
?>
</table>
<?php
  #  clean up...
  $result->close();
  $link->close();

  print "<p>Script complete.</p>\n";
?>
</body>
</html>
```

The output of this PHP 5 script can be seen in Figure 7-8.

 TIP *PHP 5 also offers advanced exception-handling capabilities using Java-style* try... catch... *syntax that can be especially useful when working with transactions.*

We've covered the basics of using mysqli in an object-oriented fashion for connecting to MySQL, sending queries, retrieving results, and where necessary, obtaining error and warning messages. In the next two sections of this chapter, we'll turn our attention to some enhancements to MySQL programming with PHP that have become available only with the arrival of PHP 5, the mysqli extension, and versions 4.1 and later of MySQL—prepared statements and multiple statements.

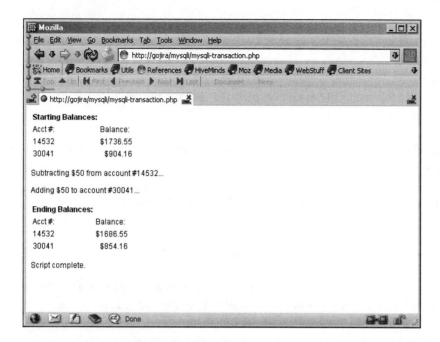

Mozilla

File Edit View Go Bookmarks Tab Tools Window Help

http://gojira/mysqli/mysqli-transaction.php

Home Bookmarks Utils References HiveMinds Moz Media WebStuff Client Sites

Top Up First Previous Next Last Document More

http://gojira/mysqli/mysqli-transaction.php

Starting Balances:

Acct #:   Balance:
14532 $1736.55
30041 $904.16

Subtracting $50 from account #14532...

Adding $50 to account #30041...

Ending Balances:

Acct #:   Balance:
14532 $1686.55
30041 $854.16

Script complete.

Done

Figure 7-8. Output of the mysqli transaction example in a web browser

Working with Prepared Statements in mysqli

PHP 5's mysqli extension supports two new programming features for MySQL 4.1
and above, which we talked about in a general way at the beginning of this
chapter. One of these is *prepared statements*. (We'll discuss the other API
enhancement—multiple statements—in the next section of this chapter.) These
allow you to reuse queries with placeholders in order to increase their efficiency.
A prepared statement is simply one that's been parsed and stored so that it can
be referred to and executed again immediately rather than having to be reparsed
each time it's run. This is particularly useful when connecting to MySQL over a
network, due to the fact that after the query has been parsed the first time, only
parameter data need be sent over the network connection for subsequent execu-
tions of the same statement.

The mysqli_stmt Class

The mysqli extension uses a mysqli_stmt class to represent a prepared statement,
and an object of this class is created by calling the prepare() method of the
mysqli class. This method takes as its sole argument a string representing a query
in which any values to be passed into the query (such as we would do by variable interpolation in PHP) are replaced by question marks.

The `mysqli_stmt` class has the following methods:

- `mysqli_bind_param()`: Binds values to a prepared statement; it's simpler to demonstrate how to pass parameters to this function than to offer a lengthy explanation; see the examples in the following section, which should make the basics clear.

- `mysqli_execute()`: Executes the prepared statement once any necessary parameters are bound to it.

- `mysqli_bind_result()`: Fetches results from a prepared statement into bound variables.

- `mysqli_stmt_close()`: Closes the prepared statement.

The `mysql_stmt` object also has some properties that are useful for detecting error conditions and getting other information. These include the following:

- `error`: Text of the last error message generated by this statement

- `errno`: MySQL error code last generated by this statement

- `sqlstate`: SQLSTATE code last generated by this statement

- `affected_rows`: Number of rows affected the last time the statement was executed

These are analogous to the same-named properties of the `mysqli` class and can be used in much the same fashion.

Prepared Statement Examples and Discussion

In Listing 7-6, we use a prepared statement to run a SELECT query twice with a different limiting value each time.

Listing 7-6. oop-prepared-statements.php: mysqli Prepared Statements Example (Object Oriented)

```
<!DOCTYPE HTML PUBLIC "-//W3C//DTD HTML 4.01 Transitional//EN"
    "http://www.w3.org/TR/html4/loose.dtd">
<html>
<head>
<meta http-equiv="Content-Type" content="text/html; charset=iso-8859-1">
<title>mysqli Prepared Statement Example</title>
```

```
</head>
<body>
<?php
  #  Filename: oop-prep-statements.php

  #  Example of selecting records
  #  using prepared statements

  #  connect to database
  $link = new mysqli("localhost", "jon", "eleanor", "test");

  if( mysqli_connect_errno() )
    die("Could not connect: " . mysqli_connect_error());

  #  the question mark acts as a placeholder for a variable;
  #  we'll determine the variable after preparing the statement
  $query = "SELECT firstname, lastname
            FROM employees
            WHERE empid < ?";

  #  string containing parameter
  #  datatype characters
  $types = 'i';

  #  Note: Valid datatypes are
  #  i = INTEGER
  #  d = DOUBLE
  #  s = STRING
  #  b = BLOB

  #  prepare statement
  #  (instantiate mysqli_stmt object)
  $stmt = $link->prepare($query)
    or die("ERROR: " . $stmt->error);

  #  bind parameters to prepared
  #  statement (arguments to this
  #  function are: an array of
  #  datatypes and the variables to be
  #  bound as parameters)
  $stmt->bind_param($types, $empid);

  #  set values for bound parameter
```

```
$empid = 4;

# execute prepared statement
$stmt->execute()
  or die("Execution failed: "
            . $stmt->error);

#   there are two columns in the result
#   here we determine what variables will
#   be used to represent each column
$stmt->bind_result($fname, $lname);

#   retrieve rows from the result set, until there are no more
while( $stmt->fetch() )
  printf("<p>Name: %s %s</p>", $fname, $lname);

#   set values for bound parameter

$empid = 2;

# execute prepared statement
$stmt->execute()
  or die("Execution failed: " .
         $stmt->error);

$stmt->bind_result($fname, $lname);

while( $stmt->fetch() )
  printf("<p>Name: %s %s</p>", $fname, $lname);

#   close prepared statement
$stmt->close();

#   close database connection
$link->close();

#   signal that we're done
print "Script completed.\n";
?>
</body>
</html>
```

In our example, we've used a simple SELECT query, but there's no reason that prepared statements can't be used for repeated queries of any type. The steps involved are as follows:

- Create a connection object (instance of mysqli class).

- Write the query, and then replace with question marks any values to be bound later.

- Prepare the query using the prepare() method; this creates a mysqli_stmt prepared statement object.

- Bind variables to the statement using the prepared statement's bind_param() method. This method takes as its parameter a string of characters. The characters in this string correspond, in order, to the datatypes of each of the variables to be bound. See the comments in the code example for the characters to be used for each type.

- Assign values to the variables.

- Execute the query using the mysqli_stmt object's execute() method.

- Use the prepared statement object's bind_result() method to bind output variables to the columns of the result set.

- Get the result set's rows using the prepared statement object's fetch() method. The values of the columns will be available as the variables to which they bound.

- Don't forget to clean up afterwards by closing the prepared statement object, as well as any other objects that are no longer needed.

We think prepared statements can be shown to be even more useful with the example in Listing 7-7, which performs several inserts in succession:

Listing 7-7. oop-prep-insert.php: Inserting Successive Records with a Prepared Statement

```php
<?php
  #  FILE: oop-prep-insert.php
  # insert records using prepared statement

  #  connect to database
  $link = new mysqli("localhost", "jon", "eleanor", "test")
    or die("Could not connect: " . mysqli_connect_error());
```

```
#  display original contents of table
$result = $link->query("SELECT * FROM employees");

print "<table border=\"1\">
        <tr><th colspan=\"3\">BEFORE...</th></tr>
        <tr>
          <th>Employee #</th>
          <th>First Name</th>
          <th>Last Name</th>
        </tr>\n";

while($row = $result->fetch_object())
  printf("<tr><td>%s</td><td>%s</td><td>%s</td></tr>\n",
          $row->empid, $row->firstname, $row->lastname);

print "</table>\n";
$result->close();

#  template for insert query
#  the query will insert two values
$query = "INSERT INTO employees (firstname, lastname) VALUES (?, ?)";

#  parameter datatype string
#  (two parameters, each a string value)
$types = 'ss';

#  prepare statement
$stmt = $link->prepare($query)
  or die("ERROR: " . $stmt->error);

#  values to be inserted

$names = array(
                array("first" => "Jane", "last" => "Jetson"),
                array("first" => "Wilma", "last" => "Flintstone"),
                array("first" => "Betty", "last" => "Rubble")
              );

#  initialize count of inserted rows
$rows = 0;

#  for each of the sets of values...
foreach($names as $name)
```

```
{
   #  bind parameters to prepared statement
   #  $name["first"] takes the place of the first placeholder,
   #  and $name["last"] takes the place of the second one
   $stmt->bind_param($types, $name["first"], $name["last"]);

   #  execute the statement
   $stmt->execute();

   #  update inserted row count
   $rows += $stmt->affected_rows;

   #  show that the row was inserted
   printf("<p>Rows inserted: %d</p>\n", $rows);
} #  (end of foreach loop)

#  close prepared statement
$stmt->close();

#  display updated contents of table
$result = $link->query("SELECT * FROM employees");

print "<table border=\"1\">
        <tr><th colspan=\"3\">AFTER...</th></tr>
        <tr>
          <th>Employee #</th>
          <th>First Name</th>
          <th>Last Name</th>
        </tr>\n";

while($row = $result->fetch_object())
   printf("<tr><td>%s</td><td>%s</td><td>%s</td></tr>\n",
          $row->empid, $row->firstname, $row->lastname);

print "</table>\n";
$result->close();

# close database connection
$link->close();

print "Script completed.\n";
?>
```

You can see the resulting output here:

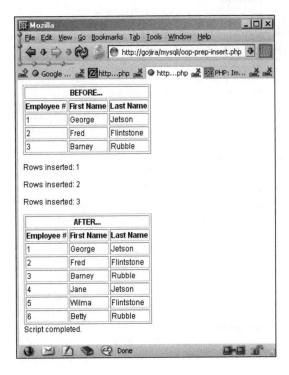

Working with Multiple Statements in mysqli

Using the `mysqli` extension with PHP 5 and MySQL 4.1 or above also makes it possible to send multiple queries in the same request, and to retrieve multiple result sets from MySQL's response. The basic requirements for using the Multiple Statements API are the same as for any other `mysqli` functionality: you must be using PHP 5 along with MySQL 4.1 or higher. The concept of multiple statements isn't too difficult to understand, and we'll show you a couple of examples shortly, complete with inline comments in the code that ought to help make things clear.

Sample Database and Queries

For the next two examples, we'll use the **world** database available from MySQL AB's web site at `http://dev.mysql.com/doc/`. This sample database consists of three tables, defined as shown here, along with a few rows of sample data from each table (as the database takes up about 375 kilobytes, we obviously can't reproduce it in its entirety here):

```
CREATE TABLE City (
  ID INT(11) NOT NULL AUTO_INCREMENT,
  Name CHAR(35) NOT NULL,
  CountryCode CHAR(3) NOT NULL,
  District CHAR(20) NOT NULL,
  Population INT(11) NOT NULL,
  PRIMARY KEY  (ID)
);

INSERT INTO City VALUES (1, 'Kabul', 'AFG', 'Kabol', 1780000);
INSERT INTO City VALUES (2, 'Qandahar', 'AFG', 'Qandahar', 237500);
INSERT INTO City VALUES (3, 'Herat', 'AFG', 'Herat', 186800);
INSERT INTO City VALUES (4, 'Mazar-e-Sharif', 'AFG', 'Balkh', 127800);
INSERT INTO City VALUES (5, 'Amsterdam', 'NLD', 'Noord-Holland', 731200);
INSERT INTO City VALUES (6, 'Rotterdam', 'NLD', 'Zuid-Holland', 593321);
INSERT INTO City VALUES (7, 'Haag', 'NLD', 'Zuid-Holland', 440900);
# etc.

CREATE TABLE Country (
  Code CHAR(3) NOT NULL,
  Name CHAR(52) NOT NULL,
  Continent ENUM('Asia','Europe','North America','Africa','Oceania',
                 'Antarctica','South America') NOT NULL,
  Region CHAR(26) NOT NULL,
  SurfaceArea FLOAT(10,2) NOT NULL,
  IndepYear SMALLINT(6),
  Population INT(11) NOT NULL,
  LifeExpectancy FLOAT(3,1),
  GNP FLOAT(10,2),
  GNPOld FLOAT(10,2),
  LocalName CHAR(45) NOT NULL,
  GovernmentForm CHAR(45) NOT NULL,
  HeadOfState CHAR(60) NULL,
  Capital INT(11) NULL,
  Code2 CHAR(2) NOT NULL,
  PRIMARY KEY  (Code)
);

INSERT INTO Country VALUES ('AFG', 'Afghanistan', 'Asia',
  'Southern and Central Asia', 652090.00, 1919, 22720000, 45.9,
  5976.00, NULL, 'Afganistan/Afqanestan', 'Islamic Emirate',
  'Mohammad Omar', 1, 'AF');
INSERT INTO Country VALUES ('NLD', 'Netherlands', 'Europe',
  'Western Europe', 41526.00, 1581, 15864000, 78.3, 371362.00, 360478.00,
```

```
  'Nederland', 'Constitutional Monarchy', 'Beatrix', 5, 'NL');
INSERT INTO Country VALUES ('ANT', 'Netherlands Antilles', 'North America',
  'Caribbean', 800.00, 0, 217000, 74.7, 1941.00, NULL,
  'Nederlandse Antillen', 'Nonmetropolitan Territory of The Netherlands',
  'Beatrix', 33, 'AN');
INSERT INTO Country VALUES ('ALB', 'Albania', 'Europe', 'Southern Europe',
  28748.00, 1912, 3401200, 71.6, 3205.00, 2500.00, 'Shqipëria', 'Republic',
  'Rexhep Mejdani', 34, 'AL');
#  etc.

CREATE TABLE CountryLanguage (
  CountryCode CHAR(3) NOT NULL,
  Language CHAR(30) NOT NULL,
  IsOfficial ENUM('T','F') NOT NULL DEFAULT 'F',
  Percentage FLOAT(3,1) NOT NULL,
  PRIMARY KEY  (CountryCode,Language)
);

INSERT INTO CountryLanguage VALUES ('AFG', 'Pashto', 'T', 52.4);
INSERT INTO CountryLanguage VALUES ('NLD', 'Dutch', 'T', 95.6);
INSERT INTO CountryLanguage VALUES ('ANT', 'Papiamento', 'T', 86.2);
INSERT INTO CountryLanguage VALUES ('ALB', 'Albaniana', 'T', 97.9);
INSERT INTO CountryLanguage VALUES ('DZA', 'Arabic', 'T', 86.0);
INSERT INTO CountryLanguage VALUES ('ASM', 'Samoan', 'T', 90.6);
INSERT INTO CountryLanguage VALUES ('AND', 'Spanish', 'F', 44.6);
#  etc.
```

The next example is a bit longer and more involved than the previous `mysqli` examples. Part of the reason for this is that we'll be using three queries instead of just one—after all, that's what the Multiple Statements interface is all about. Because we'll be reusing the same queries in our final PHP 5 example with `mysqli` as well as this one, we've broken them out into a separate include file in Listing 7-8.

Listing 7-8. queries.inc.php: Queries Used in the Two mysqli Multiple Statements Examples

```
<?php
  $queries = array();

  # array containing each query and its title/heading for display
  # the title element is the title/heading, the text element is
  # the text of the query
  # (note: $limit is defined in the calling file)
  $queries[]
```

```
    = array(
            "title" => "$limit Most Populous Countries",
            "text" => "SELECT Name AS name, Continent AS continent,
                        Population AS population
                    FROM Country
                    ORDER BY population DESC LIMIT $limit"
        );

$queries[]
    = array(
            "title" => "$limit Most Populous Cities",
            "text" =>  "SELECT ci.Name AS city, co.Name AS country,
                        ci.Population AS population
                    FROM City ci
                    JOIN Country co
                    ON ci.CountryCode = co.Code
                    ORDER BY population DESC LIMIT $limit"
        );

$queries[]
    = array(
            "title" => "$limit Most Widely-Spoken Languages",
            "text" => "SELECT cl.Language AS language,
                        FLOOR( SUM(co.Population * cl.Percentage * .01) )
                        AS speakers
                    FROM CountryLanguage cl
                    JOIN Country co
                    ON cl.CountryCode = co.Code
                    GROUP BY language
                    ORDER BY speakers DESC LIMIT $limit"
        );

# make an array of just the queries
$sql = array();
foreach($queries as $query)
    $sql[] = $query["text"];
?>
```

This include file (queries.inc.php) contains the text of three queries, each accompanied by a descriptive title for display purposes. The SQL and description are stored together as an associative array within a larger indexed array named $queries. For convenience in the calling file, we also define an array variable named $sql that contains just the text of each query as elements.

Multiple Statements Example #1 (Conventional Error Handling)

This first multiple statements example is fairly basic. We'll submit three queries to MySQL in a single request, MySQL will return three result sets in a single response, and we'll iterate through each result set in turn, displaying the data it contains in a neat HTML table layout.

Before we begin, let's look at the steps involved in an interaction making use of the multiple statements:

1. Establish a connection with the MySQL server.

2. Join the SQL text of the queries together into a single string, interposing semicolons between what were separate queries.

3. Transmit the string to MySQL as the argument to either the function mysqli_multi_query() (procedural style) or the multi_query() method of the mysqli class (object-oriented style)—we'll use the latter.

4. Fetch a result set from the response returned by MySQL.

5. Process this result set as you would normally, manipulating and displaying the data extracted from it as required by your application. This result set can be handled in exactly the same way as one returned from a single query.

6. When you've finished with this result set, close it, and then check to see if any additional result sets have been returned by MySQL. This is done using the more_results() method of the mysqli class (if you're using the procedural style, you make a call to the function mysqli_more_results()). If a value of **TRUE** is returned, call the next_result() method (function equivalent: mysqli_next_result()) to fetch the next result set, and then repeat the previous steps beginning with Step 3.

7. When there are no more result sets to be processed—that is, when the method or function called in Step 6 returns **FALSE**—you're finished. You can then send more queries, or close the connection if your PHP script doesn't need to interact with MySQL any further.

Unlike the case with prepared statements, no special objects are required to prepare multiple statements. Provided you're using the mysqli extension to access a MySQL server running version 4.1.2 or later, you simply combine the desired queries into a single string, send it to MySQL using the multi_query() method of the mysqli class (or the mysqli_multi_query() function if you're coding in the procedural style), and then iterate through the result sets using the more_results() and next_result() methods (or the functions mysqli_more_results() and mysqli_next_result()), treating each result set individually just as you would the result returned from a single query.

Listing 7-9 presents the source code of the example; like the other PHP 5/mysqli examples in this portion of the chapter, it can be found in the ch7/mysqli directory of the download package that accompanies this book. Additional explanatory material can be found in the code comments, which, as you will see, are profuse. You can obtain the download package by visiting the publisher's web site at http://www.apress.com/.

Listing 7-9. oop-multi-select.php: PHP5/mysqli Multiple Statements Example #1

```
<!DOCTYPE HTML PUBLIC "-#W3C//DTD HTML 4.01 Transitional//EN"
        "http://www.w3.org/TR/html4/loose.dtd">
<html>
<head>
<meta http-equiv="Content-Type" content="text/html; charset=iso-8859-1">
<title>MYSQLI MULTIPLE STATEMENTS #1 :: OBJECT-ORIENTED STYLE</title>
</head>
<body>
<?php
  #  contains definitions for $queries and $sql arrays (text of queries)
  require('queries.inc.php');

  #  connect to MySQL
  $link = new mysqli('localhost', 'root', '', 'world');

  #  notify us of connection error, and exit
  if( mysqli_connect_errno() )
    die("Connect failed: " . mysqli_connect_error());

  #  limit for number of rows returned from each query
  $limit = 5;

  #  join queries together using semicolon as delimiter
  #  character and send as a multiple query
  if( $link->multi_query( implode(";", $sql) ) )
  {
    $n = 0;  #  counter for table headings

    do
    {
      #  fetch result of first query
      if($result = $link->store_result())
```

```
{
  #  get number and names of the columns in the result set
  $c = $link->field_count;
  $fields = $result->fetch_fields();

  #  start output HTML table with heading
  printf("<table border=\"1\" cellpadding=\"3\" cellspacing=\"0\"
              align=\"center\" width=\"275\">\n
          <tr><th colspan=\"%s\">%s</th></tr>\n",
            $c, $queries[$n++]["title"]);

  #  second row of table contains column names
  print "<tr>";

  for($i = 0; $i < $c; $i++)
    printf("<th>%s</th>", ucwords($fields[$i]->name));

  print "</tr>\n";

  #  for each row in result set...
  while($row = $result->fetch_row())
  {
    print "<tr>"; #  start a new HTML table row

    #  for each column in this row...
    for($j = 0; $j < $c; $j++)
    {
      $val = $row[$j];  #  column value

      #  queries are arranged so that last column
      #  contains numeric output: if this is last
      #  column then add commas, e.g. 1000000 gets displayed
      #  as 1,000,000; also right-align table cell
      if($j == $c - 1)
      {
        $val = number_format($val);
        $align = " align=\"right\"";
      }
      else
      { #  take care of any special characters in value
        $val = htmlentities($val);
        $align = "";
      }
```

```
        #  output column value in HTML table cell
        printf("<td%s>%s</td>", $align, $val);
      }

      print "</tr>\n";  #  close HTML table row
    }

    #  when all rows are retrieved, close the result object...
    $result->close();
  }

  #  ...and close HTML table
  print "</table>\n";

  #  if there's another result set, write HTML
  #  horizontal rule to separate next HTML table
  if( $link->more_results() )
    print "<hr width=\"200\">\n";
  }

  #  get next result set, if there is one
  while( $link->next_result() );
}

#  when there are no more result sets, close the connection
$link->close();

#  let user know we're done
print "<p>Script completed.</p>\n";
?>
</body>
</html>
```

This example and the one that follows in the next section were tested using PHP 5.0.1 and MySQL 4.1.4-gamma.

Multiple Statements Example #2 (Object-Oriented Setting with Exceptions)

In an effort to write cleaner, more object-oriented code, we've rewritten the example from the previous section using two additional features that are new in PHP 5: exception handling, which models that of Java very closely, and the new dom extension, which does a very good job of implementing the W3C's Document Object Model Level 2 Core API. This is not a short example—in fact, it's the longest that you'll see in this book—but we wanted to give you a taste of what it's like to use mysqli in a genuine object-oriented setting along with at least one other object-oriented extension (ext/dom).

We'll present the code for this example mostly of a piece, but with plenty of inline comments to show you what's going on. Note that this example uses the same queries.inc.php include file as in the previous example, defining the queries used.

You'll also notice that there's a second require() statement in this example. This file contains the definitions of the class files that we need in order to be able to make use of exception handling. First, let's look at the code for these two classes, shown in Listing 7-10, and then we'll discuss the reasons why we wrote them.

Listing 7-10. Mysqli_classes.inc.php: mysqli Extension and Exception Classes Include File

```php
<?php
class AP_Mysqli extends mysqli
{
  public function connect($host = NULL, $user = NULL, $pass = NULL,
                          $db = NULL, $port = NULL, $socket = NULL)
  {
    #  call the parent method of the same name
    $link = parent::connect($host, $user, $pass, $db, $port, $socket);

    #  if an error results, throw an exception, passing the
    #  error message and SQLSTATE code to the Exception subclass
    #  constructor
    if( mysqli_connect_errno() )
      throw new AP_MysqliException(mysqli_connect_error(), $this->sqlstate);

    return $link;
  }

  #  repeat for additional methods we need to call
  public function multi_query($sql)
  {
    $result = parent::multi_query($sql);

    if($this->errno)
      throw new AP_MysqliException($this->error, $this->sqlstate);

    return $result;
  }
```

```php
  public function store_result()
  {
    $result = parent::store_result();

    if($this->errno)
      throw new AP_MysqliException($this->error, $this->sqlstate);

    return $result;
  }

  public function more_results()
  {
    $result = parent::more_results();

    if($this->errno)
      throw new AP_MysqliException($this->error, $this->sqlstate);

    return $result;
  }

  public function next_result()
  {
    $result = parent::next_result();

    if($this->errno)
      throw new AP_MysqliException($this->error, $this->sqlstate);

    return $result;
  }
}

# Exception subclass
class AP_MysqliException extends Exception
{
  public function __construct($message, $sqlstate)
  {
    parent::__construct($message, $sqlstate);
  }
}
?>
```

NOTE *In the interest of brevity, we've reproduced only those class methods that are required for our example. Additional methods are provided in the actual include file, and you can write more of your own that override existing* mysqli *methods using these as a model. You might also want to write* AP_MysqliResult *and* AP_MysqliStmt *classes to override* mysqli_result *and* mysqli_stmt *class methods so that you can use these to throw exceptions as well.*

Exceptions represent a very clean methodology for dealing with errors arising from programs. Rather than writing a separate check for each function or method call for an error and branching at that point, methods are defined to "throw" exceptions that are instances of a well-formed Exception class or a subclass of it. PHP 5's support for exceptions makes it possible to test a block of code as a unit, then follow this block up with separate error-handling blocks for different sorts of errors. For example, with conventional error-testing, you might write a simple database interaction like this (using pseudocode):

```
if connection is established
  send query
  if result obtained
    for each row in result
      if row fetched
        for each column in row
          if column value obtained
            process and output value
          else determine why column value not obtained
      else determine why row fetch failed and act accordingly
    else determine why result not obtained and act accordingly
else determine why connection failed and act accordingly
```

Here we have four nested if ... else blocks—and of course these check only for possible errors encountered in working with the database. There are liable to be more in the block we've labeled simply as process and output values: if the string doesn't contain invalid characters..., if this value is not zero..., and so on. Using exceptions, we can rewrite the pseudocode for this routine as

```
try to execute following statements:
  establish connection
  send query
  obtain result
  for each row in result
    fetch row
    for each column in row
      process and output value
```

```
end try block
catch exceptions due to database error (e.g. failed connection)
catch exceptions due to string-handling errors (e.g. illegal characters)
catch expections due to math errors (e.g. division by zero)
#  and so on
```

This code is much easier to read and maintain without four (or more) levels of nested if ... then blocks that really don't contribute to the application's processing of data.

mysqli and related classes don't throw exceptions automatically (at least, not as of PHP 5.0.1), so we write wrapper classes for these that override the methods of the original classes in order to throw exceptions when errors are encountered. We also define an AP_MysqliException class that subclasses PHP 5's own built-in Exception class. In this way, we can segregate those exceptions thrown by our database interaction classes from other sorts of exceptions that might be triggered elsewhere in the code. By the way, there's nothing stopping you from subclassing even further, and writing exception classes called (for example) AP_MysqliConnectionException, AP_MysqliLoginException, and AP_MysqliInvalidAggregateFunctionException to handle, respectively, failure to connect at all (due to network or hardware failure), use of a bad username/password, or attempting to execute a query containing an aggregate function without a GROUP BY clause. You can be just as general or fine-grained in your exception handling as you want or need to be.

TIP *If you need to know more than is shown in the PHP Manual about how a PHP 5 class is constructed, you can reverse-engineer any class by using the PHP 5 Reflection API. For information on how to do this, see the documentation at* http://www.php.net/manual/en/language.oop5.reflection.php.

Now let's look at the main file for this example, presented in Listing 7-11. As in the previous example, we've commented nearly every line of code to guide you along and help you understand what's taking place at each point. To provide some relief from what may seem like a limitless number of pages of code, we've chosen to discuss the PHP 5 dom extension in a sidebar, which you'll find about halfway through this listing.

Listing 7-11. oop-multi-select-with-dom.php: Multiple Statements Example #2— with Exception Handling and the ext/dom Extension

```
<!DOCTYPE HTML PUBLIC "-//W3C//DTD HTML 4.01 Transitional//EN"
        "http://www.w3.org/TR/html4/loose.dtd">
<?php
  # contains class definitions for AP_Mysqli,
```

```php
# AP_MysqliResult, and AP_MysqliException classes
require('AP_Mysqli_classes.inc.php');
# contains definitions for $queries and $sql arrays (text of queries)
require('queries.inc.php')

# throws an exception when a user error is encountered
function ErrorsToExceptions($code, $message)
{
  throw new Exception($message, $code);
}

# sets the ErrorsToExceptions function as the error handler
set_error_handler("ErrorsToExceptions");

# we place all code likely to throw an exception into a try block
try
{
  # connect to MySQL...
  # we can't override the mysqli class constructor,
  # but we can override its connect() method, so we call
  # the AP_Mysqli class constructor and then its connect()
  # method, which overrides the parent class connect()
  # so we can throw an exception in case of failure
  $link = new AP_Mysqli();

  # no if() block here... the try/catch blocks
  # take care of handling any errors/exceptions
  $link->connect('localhost', 'root', '', 'world');

  # set LIMIT value for all queries
  $limit = 5;

  # create a new DOMDocument object (this is the
  # the basis for the HTML document that we'll display
  # to the user when we're done)
  $doc = new DOMDocument;

  # create new DOMElement objects
  # corresponding to <html> and <head> tags
  $html = $doc->createElement("html");
  $head = $doc->createElement("head");

  # create new DOMElement (tag name: meta) and set
  # its http_equiv and content attributes
  $meta = $doc->createElement("meta");
```

```
$meta->setAttribute("http-equiv", "Content-Type");
$meta->setAttribute("content", "text/html; charset=iso-8859-15");

# append the <meta> to the <head>
$head->appendChild($meta);

# create DOMElement object for the <title> tag, a DOMText (text node)
# object containing the <title> tag text, and insert the text into
# the <title>
$title = $doc->createElement("title");
$title_text = "MYSQLI MULTIPLE STATEMENTS #2 :: O-O
                STYLE W/ EXCEPTIONS AND DOM";
$title->appendChild( $doc->createTextNode($title_text) );
# now append the <title> to the <head>, and the <head> to the <html>
$head->appendChild($title);
$html->appendChild($head);

# create a <body> element for this page
$body = $doc->createElement("body");

# the $sql array contains as its elements the text of each
# of the queries we want to execute; defined in queries.inc.php

# join all the queries together into a single string, using
# the semicolon character as the delimiter
$link->multi_query( implode(";", $sql) );

# counter used for tracking the table headings
# associated with each query's results
$n = 0;

# do{ ... } while( $link->next_result() ) -
# run the code inside the do block so long as there is
# another result set to be retrieved from the
# multiple result set sent back by MySQL in response
# to the multiple query
do
{
  # get the result set
  $result = $link->store_result();

  # since each result set may have a different
  # number of fields/columns, we need to get
  # the number of fields in this result set
  $c = $link->field_count;
```

```
# get the fields array associated with this result set
# note: we could also have used the following...
#        $fields = $result->fetch_fields();
#        $c = count($fields);
# ... to obtain this information
$fields = $result->fetch_fields();

# we display the data from each result set
# in a separate table; here we start the table
# by creating a DOMElement object corresponding
# to a HTML <table> tag, then set its align, width,
# border, cellpadding, and cellspacing attributes to
# the desire values - this is the equivalent of writing
# <table align="center" width="475" border="1"
#        cellpadding="3" cellspacing="0">
$table = $doc->createElement("table");
$table->setAttribute("align", "center");
$table->setAttribute("width", "475");
$table->setAttribute("border", "1");
$table->setAttribute("cellpadding", "3");
$table->setAttribute("cellspacing", "0");
```

Generating Markup Without Using Strings: A Brief Look at ext/dom

One recurring problem in web development is the dynamic generation of error-free HTML, which is usually accomplished by assembling long quoted strings of markup and outputting them to the page. This is a tedious process requiring the escaping of quotes and special characters, as well as the constant battle against typographical errors—forget so much as a single angle bracket or quotation mark, and you've turned a web page into a disaster area. Even after you've tracked down the error in the HTML itself, you still have to hunt through your code to find what's generating the malformed markup and fix it. Then there's the matter of setting attributes—you write a routine that generates a table layout, and then find out that you need to make alternating rows have different background colors. That means you've got to root through a mass of string handling code, break strings, insert new pieces into them, and so on.

Wouldn't it be nice if there were an object-oriented way to handle this problem—if, say, you could just create a Table object, and call a few methods to set its attributes? Wouldn't it be even nicer if you could assemble a Table, complete with Row, Cell, and Content members, then write a loop to change the background of every second row to a contrasting color before displaying it? Since 1998, the W3C has had a standard in place for accomplishing just these kinds of tasks: the Document Object Model, which provides a set of interfaces for reading, creating, altering, and deleting pieces of markup in an object-oriented fashion. The dom extension in PHP 5 is a very good implementation of this API, which in its entirety is complex, but conceptually can be boiled down to a few simple concepts:

- A markup document (XML, HTML, WML, and so on) can be represented by a collection of objects, each representing a tag such as <head>, <body>, or <p>.

- Tag attributes are represented by object properties.

- Content of tags is also represented by objects.

- The parent-child relationships between tags are represented by object properties.

The most basic interface is a DOMNode, and there are four types of these that we need be concerned with:

- DOMDocument: Corresponds to a complete markup document

- DOMElement: Corresponds to a markup tag

- DOMText: Corresponds to the textual content of a markup tag

- DOMEntityNode: Corresponds to an entity representing a character that can't be expressed by ASCII codes 0–255

To create a new markup document, call the DOMDocument constructor. To create new markup elements, call the createElement() method of the DOMDocument instance, with the tag name (a string value) as its argument; this returns an instance of DOMElement. To set the element's attributes, call the DOMElement instance's setAttribute() method; this takes two arguments (both strings): the name of the attribute, and the value it's to be set to. To add text content to an element, call the DOMDocument's createTextNode() method, then the DOMText returned by this method to the desired element by calling the element's appendChild() method. This method can also be used to nest one markup element inside another. If text contains one or more special characters that would require the use of a character entity to display in a HTML page, then you must call the createEntityReference() method of the DOMDocument class for each such character.

Here's a short example, in which we'll create the HTML representation of a paragraph containing the sentence "My name is **José**":

```
<p id="myP">My name is <b>Jos&eacute;</b>.</p>
```

and then display it to the client:

```
$doc = new DOMDocument();
$p = doc->createElement("p");
$p->appendChild( doc->createTextNode("My name is ") );
$b = doc->createElement("b");
$b->appendChild( $doc->createTextNode("Jos") );
#   the character entity for "é" is "&eacute;" -- we drop the "&" and ";"
#   and pass the remainder to createEntityReference()
$b->appendChild( $doc->createEntityReference("eacute") );
$p->appendChild($b);
$p->appendChild( $doc->createTextNode(".") );
$doc->appendChild($p);
#   oops -- we forgot to set the id attribute... but no need to back up:
$p->setAttribute("id", "myP");
#   output as HTML markup
print $doc->saveHTML();
```

For handling errors, the W3C DOM specifications include a DOMException class and ext/dom implements this; no special effort is required to make use of it. All that's necessary is this:

```
try
{
   #   code using DOM classes
}
catch(DOMException $e)
{
   #   code to handle DOM-related exceptions
}
```

Of course, there's a lot more to the DOM API than what we've discussed here, but this will be sufficient for this example. For more information, see the appropriate PHP Manual page at http://www.php.net/dom and the W3C DOM pages at http://www.w3.org/DOM/.

```
# now we'll create the HTML table row containing the table title
# first a DOMElement for the <tr>
$tr = $doc->createElement("tr");

# create a table heading cell (<th>), setting its colspan attribute
# equal to the number of columns in the result (so that it spans all
```

```
# the columns in the table), and then inserting
# a DOMText node containing the title text describing the query
$th = $doc->createElement("th");
$th->setAttribute("colspan", $c);
$th->appendChild( $doc->createTextNode($queries[$n++]["title"]) );

# append the heading cell to the row, and the row to the table
$tr->appendChild($th);
$table->appendChild($tr);

# next row: contains HTML table column headings; the text for
# these will be the field names or aliases from the result set
$tr = $doc->createElement("tr");

# for each result set column...
for($i = 0; $i < $c; $i++)
{
  # create a new heading cell...
  $th = $doc->createElement("th");
  # ...into which we insert the name of the field
  $th->appendChild(
          $doc->createTextNode( ucwords($fields[$i]->name) )
                );

  # insert the heading cell into the row
  $tr->appendChild($th);
}

# after all the column headings have been created,
# append the row containing them to the table
$table->appendChild($tr);

# now display the result set data
# for each row in the result set...
while($row = $result->fetch_row())
{
  # start a new HTML table row
  $tr = $doc->createElement("tr");

  # for each column in the result set...
  for($j = 0; $j < $c; $j++)
  {
    # get the value stored in this column
    $value = $row[$j];
```

```
# create a HTML table cell in which to display this value
$td = $doc->createElement("td");

# if the value's a number, format it nicely and
# right-align it in the table cell
if( is_numeric($value) )
{
  $value = number_format($value);

  $td->setAttribute("align", "right");
  $td->appendChild( $doc->createTextNode($value) );
}
else  # if the value consists of text, we have
{     # to handle things a bit differently...
  # convert any special characters in the value to
  # their HTML entity equivalents, because you can't
  # create a DOMText node containing any special
  # characters; instead you must create a DOMEntityReference
  $value = htmlentities($value);

  # $matches will contain all bits of text coming between
  # a pair of "&" and ";" characters are used to delimit a
  # HTML character entity
  preg_match_all("/&([^;]*);/", $value, $matches);

  # $parts will contain all bits of text in the original string
  # separated by a "&" or ";"
  $parts = preg_split("/&|;/", $value, -1, PREG_SPLIT_NO_EMPTY);

  # now check each substring in $parts
  foreach($parts as $part)
    $td->appendChild( # is there a match in $matches?
                      in_array($part, $matches[1])
                      # yes: create an entity reference node
                      ? $doc->createEntityReference($part)
                      # no: create a text node
                      : $doc->createTextNode($part)
                      # append the correct type of node
                    );

}
# once all the content nodes have been created and appended
# to the table cell, append the cell to the table row
$tr->appendChild($td);
```

```
    }
    # append the row to the HTML table
    $table->appendChild($tr);
  }
  # free the memory used for this result set
  $result->close();


  # append the <table> to the <body>
  $body->appendChild($table);


  # if there's another result set to be processed,
  # create a <hr>, set its width, and then append
  # it to be body of the document
  if( $link->more_results() )
  {
    $hr = $doc->createElement("hr");
    $hr->setAttribute("width", "350");


    $body->appendChild($hr);
  }
} while( $link->next_result() ); # end of the do loop


# no more result sets: close the connection
$link->close();


# append the <body> to the <html>
# append the <html> to the DOMDocument
$html->appendChild($body);
$doc->appendChild($html);


# call the saveHTML() to convert the DOM objects to
# a string of HTML, and output this to the client
print $doc->saveHTML();
} # ends the try block, now to handle errors/exceptions
catch(AP_MysqliException $e)
{ # exception thrown by mysqli or mysql_result
  # AP_MysqliException is defined in AP_Mysqli_classes.inc.php
  print "<b>- MYSQLI ERROR -</b><br>";
  printf("SQLSTATE %s - %s", $e->getCode(), $e->getMessage());
}
catch(DOMException $e)
{ # exception thrown by a DOM object - defined as part of ext/dom
  # (also in the W3C DOM specifications)
  print "<b>- DOM ERROR -</b><br>";
```

```
      printf("DOM Error #%s — %s", $e->getCode(), $e->getMessage());
   }
   catch(Exception $e)
   { # any other exceptions
     print "<b>- GENERAL ERROR -</b> ";
     printf("PHP Error #%s — %s", $e->getCode(), $e->getMessage());
   }
?>
```

Why use the dom extension here? We wanted to demonstrate that it is possible in PHP 5 to work with MySQL, utilizing it as part of a sophisticated and multifaceted object-oriented methodology. To accomplish this end, we need an object-oriented means for generating HTML, rather than simply assembling and printing strings to the page using procedural code. The output of either version of the Multiple Statements example script looks exactly the same, as is shown here:

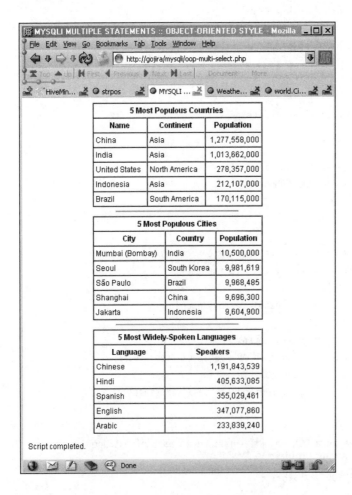

PHP 5 and mysqli—Some Concluding Remarks

The `mysqli` extension in PHP 5, when used with MySQL version 4.1.2 or later, fulfills not only the basic requirements for a useful database API, but goes beyond to provide a great deal of functionality previously unavailable to PHP developers working with MySQL. PHP is emerging as a viable object-oriented development platform and has the potential to move beyond the web and into the realms of systems programming (PHP-CLI) and GUI application development (PHP-GTK) as well; the new object-oriented interface provided by this extension is part of this maturation process and helps guarantee that, as PHP and MySQL grow, the combination PHP+MySQL platform will be able to grow with it.

Another noteworthy aspect of `ext/mysqli` is that it's the first widely used programming library to implement the new Prepared Statements and Multiple Statements APIs. Prepared statements can make for faster interaction with MySQL when many of your queries follow similar patterns, differing only in their limiting values; this API extension allows you to compile your queries so that, after the first time such a query is sent, only the new values need be transmitted to MySQL. Use of the Multiple Statements API will also make your MySQL programming with PHP 5 more efficient because you can combine several queries into one, and thus several requests and responses into a single request and a single response. This is particularly helpful in a scenario where your application is accessing MySQL over a network.

`mysqli` represents a logical progression of the `mysql` extension that made its initial appearance in PHP 3, and it seems reasonable to assume that MySQL APIs for other programming languages will follow suit in adopting the enhancements that it has already implemented.

We've devoted a great deal of space in this chapter to MySQL programming with PHP, but it is true that there are other popular Open Source languages that can be used to work with MySQL, and we'd be remiss if we didn't examine one or two of them. In the following sections, we'll look at MySQL programming with Perl using the Perl-DBI library—which will also serve as an example of a database-agnostic API—and Python's `MySQLdb` module, which provides both a high-level object-oriented interface and a lower-level interface that resembles `ext/mysql` and `ext/mysqli` quite closely in many respects.

Perl-DBI

If there's any Open Source programming language whose popularity and usage rival that of PHP, it's Perl. In fact—as any Perl programmer worth his or her salt will be quick to tell you—PHP is a relative upstart, as Perl's inception (1987) predates that of PHP (1995) by several years. Like PHP and most other modern programming and scripting languages, Perl itself provides a basic core or "grammar" and specialized, task-specific capabilities are implemented in libraries or modules. Perl-DBI is Perl's standard database interface module and is used to interact with different databases. Conceptually it is similar to OBDC, JDBC, or ADO in that it presents an object-oriented set of methods, variables, and conventions which provide a consistent programming interface across multiple database platforms. To interact with a database, we call various methods of a database connection object (the DBI object) in order to connect with the database, submit queries, and retrieve the results.

Perl DBI already comes with most Perl distributions; if you need to acquire it or update your current installation, this is a relatively painless and straightforward process. If you're using ActivePerl from ActiveState, you can employ ActiveState's PPM (Perl Package Manager); otherwise, you can obtain the necessary modules via CPAN. If you require information on how to install or update Perl modules, see the documentation supplied with your Perl distribution.

CAUTION *As of this writing, the dbd::mysql driver for Perl-DBI did not yet support the improved authentication protocol used in MySQL 4.1 and above as discussed earlier in this chapter in the sidebar "Using Older Clients with MySQL 4.1 and 5.0." Be sure to check for updated versions of the module frequently, which you should do in any case.*

Here's an example that will show you how to establish a database connection with MySQL, send a query, and retrieve and display the results using Perl-DBI:

```perl
#!/usr/bin/perl -w
# mysql_test.pl
use strict;
use DBI;  #  include the DBI module

my $db = "mdbd_ch8";  # database name
my $host = "gojira";  # hostname (default is "localhost")
my $port = "3306";  # MySQL port (default is 3306)
my $user = "jon";  # username (default is current system user)
my $pass = "eleanor";  # password
my $dsn = "DBI:mysql:database=$db;$host:$port";
# $dsn = connection string; default is the DBI_DSN environment variable
my $sth;  # SQL statement handle

# make connection
my $dbh = DBI->connect($dsn, $user, $pass) or die("Cannot Connect");
# prepare and execute query
my $query = "SELECT id, name FROM tbl";
```

```
$sth = $dbh->prepare($query);  # get a statement handle object
$sth->execute();  # submit the query

# declare variables
my $id;
my $name;

# assign fields to variables
$sth->bind_columns(undef, \$id, \$name);
# the fetch() method retrieves the next row from the result set
# until there are no more rows to return
while( $sth->fetch() )
{
  print "ID: ";
  print "$id \r\n";
  print "Name: ";
  print "$name \r\n";
}

$sth->finish();  # free resources used by the query handle
$dbh->disconnect();  # disconnect from database
# end mysql_test.pl
```

The output of this script is shown here:

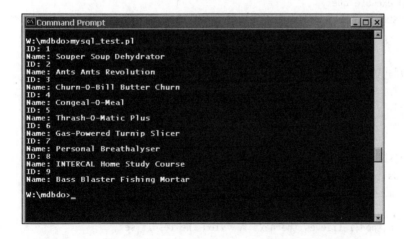

NOTE   *The code for the previous example and the other examples in this section using Perl-DBI can be found in the /ch7/perl-dbi directory of the code download for this book.*

DBI also has built-in support for prepared statements. While these are not the same precompiled prepared statements supported in MySQL 4.1 and newer, they may still save you some time and help streamline your code. Here's a simple of example of a SELECT query that's prepared using a placeholder and then sent to MySQL using different limiting values:

```perl
#!/usr/bin/perl -w
# mysql_prep_test.pl - select query and output,
# using a prepared statement
# NOTE: this is not the same as the Prepared Statements API in MySQL 4.1+!
use strict;
use DBI;  # include the DBI module

my $db = "mdbd_ch8";  # database name
my $host = "gojira";  # hostname (default is "localhost")
my $port = "3306";  # MySQL port (default is 3306)
my $user = "jon";  # username (default is current system user)
my $pass = "eleanor";  # password
my $dsn = "DBI:mysql:database=$db;$host:$port";
# $dsn = connection string; default is the DBI_DSN environment variable
my $sth;  # SQL statement handle

# make connection
my $dbh = DBI->connect($dsn, $user, $pass) or die("Cannot Connect");
# Prepare and execute query
my $query = "SELECT name FROM products WHERE id=?";
$sth = $dbh->prepare($query);  # get a statement handle object

# declare variables
my $id;
my $name;

$id = 3;
$sth->execute($id);  # submit the query
# assign fields to variables
$sth->bind_columns(undef, \$name);

# the fetch() method retrieves the next row from the result set
# until there are no more rows to return
$sth->fetch();

print "ID: $id \r\nName: $name \r\n";
```

```
$id = 5;
$sth->execute($id);   # submit the query

$sth->fetch();
print "ID: $id \r\nName: $name \r\n";

$id = 8;
$sth->execute($id);   # submit the query

$sth->fetch();
print "ID: $id \r\nName: $name \r\n";

$sth->finish();  # free resources used by the query handle
$dbh->disconnect();  # disconnect from database
# end mysql_prep_test.pl
```

We show the output of this example here:

In addition to the fetch() method, the statement handler object has the following methods for retrieving rows from a result set:

- fetchrow_array(): Returns the next row as an array

- fetchrow_arrayref(): Returns the next row as a reference to an array

- fetchrow_hashref(): Returns the next row as a reference to a hash

- fetchall_arrayref(): Returns all rows in a single two-dimensional array (that is, an array of rows, each of which is an array of values)

Like fetch(), each of the first three of these four methods returns a null or false value when there are no more rows to be returned.

For queries that don't return a result, we can use the database connection object's do() method:

```perl
#!/usr/bin/perl -w
# FILE: simple-insert.pl -- Shows how to use the do() method to
# perform an INSERT query
use strict;
use CGI qw(:standard);
use DBI;

my $db = "mdbd_ch8";
my $host = "gojira";
my $port = "3306";
my $user = "jon";
my $pass = "eleanor";
my $dsn = "DBI:mysql:database=$db;$host:$port";

# make connection
my $dbh = DBI->connect($dsn, $user, $pass)
  or die("Cannot Connect");
my $rows = $dbh->do(
                        qq{
      INSERT INTO members
      (firstname, lastname, dob)
      VALUES
      ('Janet', 'Sloan', '1978-12-05'),
      ('Steven', 'Jones', '1981-08-16'),
      ('Alison', 'Kassel', '1977-10-22')
                        }
                    );

$dbh->disconnect();
# end simple-insert.pl
```

The DBI module also provides error-logging capabilities using the trace() method of the DBI and statement handler objects. This method can be used to set the error-reporting level (0 = disabled to 9 = extremely verbose; generally a level of 2 to 4 will provide sufficient debugging information but not too much) and direct its output to a file or standard filehandle such as STDERR (the default) or STDOUT. For example, to set error reporting to level 2 (the default) and to save all debugging information to a file named dbi_err.log, you can call the following command at the beginning of your script:

```perl
DBI->trace(2, 'dbi_err.log');
```

You can also call this method for a specific statement handler prior to calling its execute() method if you wish to trap debugging output for a specific query. Once the statement has executed, error tracing will revert to its previous behavior.

 TIP *If you do a lot of database programming with Perl, it would be well worth your while to investigate **dbish**, the DBI shell. This is a command-line environment similar in some ways to the MySQL Monitor; however **dbish** is database independent. See the DBI documentation for more information.*

Python and MySQLdb

For our final example of an Open Source language API for use with MySQL, we've chosen Python's MySQLdb module. You've already had an introduction of sorts to this library in Chapter 4, where we showed you a fairly complete Python CGI script that used it. MySQLdb is not supplied with either the base Python distribution from http://www.python.org or ActivePython from http://www.activestate.com; you'll need to obtain it from the project's home page at http://sourceforge.net/projects/mysql-python.

As of this writing, the latest version of the library was 1.0 (released in June 2004); it should work with version 1.5.2 of Python or any later version, and is compatible with MySQL versions 3.22, 3.23, and 4.0. MySQLdb is definitely compatible with these Python and MySQL versions on both Unix and Windows platforms, and should work with them on any platform that supports them both.

We've also used this module successfully with MySQL 4.1 and 5.0, but you should be aware that MySQLdb 1.0 does not yet support the new password encryption that was implemented in MySQL version 4.1 (see the sidebar "Using Old Clients with MySQL 4.1 and 5.0" earlier in this chapter). MySQLdb's lead developer, Andy Dustman, is at work on adding support for the Prepared Statements API and other new functionality supported in MySQL 4.1 and newer, so be sure to check the SourceForge project page periodically for updates. Installation of MySQLdb is accomplished using a setup script provided with the module; see the provided documentation for details.

MySQLdb is actually a wrapper for a low-level API (known as _mysql) similar in many ways to the C API, but it should be more than sufficient for your needs in most circumstances. It supports the Python Database API Specification, which can be found at http://www.python.org/topics/database/DatabaseAPI-2.0.html. All interactions with the database are mediated by the MySQLdb class.

A database interaction using this library can be accomplished as follows:

- To access the MySQLdb module, simply import it by name; you'll be able to call any desired methods of the MySQLdb class after doing so.

- To create a new connection to MySQL, we use the connect() method, which returns a Connection object. This method's parameters are the same as those for the C API mysql_real_connect() function, with similar default values.

- Create an instance of the Cursor object by calling the Connection object's cursor() method; the cursor type and thus the structure of the rows returned in the result set is determined by the argument passed to this method. The default is MySQLdb.cursors.cursor, in which case the columns in the result set are accessible using numeric indexes (i.e., as Python tuples). To make the columns accessible by name (that is, to return the rows as dictionaries), use MySQLdb.cursors.DictCursor as the parameter to the cursor() method. (Refer to the Python CGI script in Chapter 4 for an example.)

- Once the connection is established and a cursor instantiated, the next step is to transmit a query. The text of an SQL query is sent to MySQL using the Cursor object's execute() method. This is used no matter what type of query is to be submitted. Alternatively, where multiple queries are to be executed at once, you can use the executemany() method.

- The result set can be obtained using one of the Cursor object's fetch*() methods: fetchone() returns a single row; fetchmany(n) returns up to n rows of the result set (the default value is 100); and fetchall() returns all of the rows. In each case, the method returns **None** if there are no further rows in the result. Generally speaking, you should use fetchone() when you need or expect only one row in the result, fetchall() when you know that there will be several (but not a huge number of) rows, and fetchmany() when you know that there will be a very large number of rows in the result, or you wish to limit the number of rows to be handled at one time in your application to a specific number. You can also use fetch_row() (defined in the _mysql module in lieu of fetchone()).

NOTE *Of course, MySQL doesn't actually support cursors prior to version 5.0.0, but the Python DB API specifies them, and so MySQLdb has been written to provide emulation of them.*

Here's a simple example that executes a single SELECT query and displays the result:

```
#!user/bin/local/python
# FILE: simple-select.py -- simple MySQL script

import MySQLdb
db = MySQLdb.connect(host="localhost", user="user", passwd="pass", db="mydb")
cursor = db.cursor()  # create a new cursor

date = "1980-06-15"
query = "SELECT firstname, lastname, dob FROM members WHERE dob < %s"
cursor.execute(query, (date,))  # parameters must be passed as a sequence

result = cursor.fetchall()  # obtain the result

# the result set is just a tuple of tuples:
print "%s columns in result set..." % len(result[0])
print "%s records were returned..." % len(result)

# now output the column values from each row, one row per line
for row in result:
  print "NAME: %s %s; DOB: %s" % (row[0], row[1], row[2])

cursor.close()
#  end
```

NOTE *The code for the examples in this section using Python and MySQLdb can be found in the directory named /ch7/python-mysqldb in the code archive for this book. You can download this archive at no charge from* http://www.apress.com.

Note that we used the close() method to close the cursor. This isn't actually necessary unless we're using serverside cursors, but it's still good practice to use it in all of our MySQLdb code in case we decide to use them at some future point.

> **NOTE** *When using serverside cursors, the result set is stored on the server until the rows are fetched from it by the client; when using clientside cursors, the entire result set is sent to the client, and it's from there that the rows are fetched. The Python cursor types that we use in our examples are all clientside cursors, as these are generally more efficient than serverside cursors. For information about using serverside cursors, see the MySQLdb documentation.*

Alternatively, if we wanted to fetch and process the rows one at a time, we could do something like this:

```
#!user/bin/local/python
# FILE: simple-select-2.py -- fetching one row at a time

import MySQLdb

db = MySQLdb.connect(host="localhost", user="jon", passwd="*****", db="mdbd")

# create a new cursor; use it to execute the query
cursor = db.cursor()
date = "1980-06-15"
query = "SELECT firstname, lastname, dob FROM members WHERE dob < %s"
cursor.execute(query, (date,))

# fetch successive rows from the cursor, display them until none is returned
while 1:
    row = cursor.fetchone()
    if row is None: break
    print "NAME: %s %s; DOB: %s" % (row[0], row[1], row[2])

cursor.close()
#  end
```

While the Multiple Statements API isn't yet supported in MySQLdb, we can still submit multiple queries in one go by means of the Cursor object's executemany() method. We can use this method to perform a series of INSERT queries in a single operation, as shown here:

```
#!user/bin/local/python
# FILE: multi-insert.py--performing multiple inserts using executemany()

import MySQLdb
```

```
db = MySQLdb.connect(host="localhost", user="user", passwd="pass", db="mydb")
cursor = db.cursor()

query = "INSERT INTO orders (firstname, lastname, amount, date) \
        VALUES (%s, %s, %s, %s)"
values =  (
              ("Jim", "Williams", 125.55, "2004-03-15"), \
              ("Rachel", "Lewis", 227.80, "2004-03-18"), \
              ("John", "Lee", 72.05, "2004-03-12") \
          )

cursor.executemany(query, values)
last = cursor.insert_id()
num = db.affected_rows()

print "Last inserted id: %s; number of rows inserted: %s" % (last, num)
cursor.close()
#  end
```

This doesn't actually send all queries to MySQL in a single request, nor does it retrieve all result sets in a single response as it would with the Multiple Statements API in MySQL 4.1 or higher. However, as you can see, it can help to streamline your Python application code.

We've used a couple of Python analogues to ext/mysql functions in this last example; these Python functions can be found in the _mysql module. The Cursor object's insert_id() method works just like the PHP ext/mysql (or C) API function mysql_insert_id(), and the Connection object's affected_rows() method performs the same task as mysql_affected_rows() does in PHP using the mysql extension (or in the MySQL C API).

 NOTE *If you're accustomed to working with either of the two PHP MySQL APIs (covered earlier in this chapter), you should have little if any trouble at all relating that experience to the _mysql module—provided you know how to program in Python, of course. The low-level Python API implements connection and result objects similar to what's found in the object-oriented version of PHP 5's ext/mysqli; many of the methods have similar or even the same names.*

This API also provides convenience methods for working with transactions, as you can see by reading the comments in the following example:

```
#!user/bin/local/python
# FILE: simple-transaction.py
# demonstrates a simple transaction using MySQLdb
# (assumes that the accounts table is an InnoDB table)

# import the MySQLdb library
import MySQLdb

# the account numbers for the accounts we'll be transferring funds between
account1 = "6557"
account2 = "8510"
accounts = [account1, account2]

# the amount to be transferred
amount = "75.00"

# query to obtain account balances
balance_query = "SELECT CONCAT(firstname, ' ', lastname), balance \
                    from accounts WHERE account_number = %s"

# queries to transfer funds
add_query = "UPDATE accounts SET balance = balance + %s \
            WHERE account_number=%s"
subtract_query = "UPDATE accounts SET balance = balance - %s \
                    WHERE account_number=%s"
transfer_queries = [add_query, subtract_query]

# connect to the database and select the accounts table
db = MySQLdb.connect(host="localhost", user="zontar", passwd="", db="mdbd")

# check to see if AUTOCOMMIT is turned on; if it is, disable it for
# the duration of the transaction
cursor = db.cursor()
cursor.execute("SELECT @@AUTOCOMMIT", )
row = cursor.fetchone()
if row[0] == 1:
  db.begin()

# get the starting balances
print "-STARTING BALANCES-\n"
for account in accounts:
  cursor.execute(balance_query, (account,))
  row = cursor.fetchone()
  print "ACCOUNT #:%s\tNAME: %s\tBALANCE:%s" % (account, row[0], row[1])
```

```
print

# now perform the transfer
# if all goes well, do a commit and display the new balances;
# if any exception is raised, report it and do a rollback instead
try:
  for transfer_query, account in zip(transfer_queries, accounts):
    cursor.execute(transfer_query, (amount, account))
except Exception, e:
  print "Database error - transfer cancelled due to ", e
  db.rollback()
else:
  print "Transfer of %s was successful" % amount
  db.commit()
  print "-ENDING BALANCES-\n"
  for account in accounts:
    cursor.execute(balance_query, (account,))
    row = cursor.fetchone()
    print "ACCOUNT #:%s\tNAME: %s\tBALANCE:%s" % (account, row[0], row[1])

# close the cursor
cursor.close()
```

As you can see from these examples, if you know Python and can write queries, you can use the MySQLdb and _mysql modules to write MySQL-backed Python scripts and applications.

Summary

MySQL applications programming is a topic that could easily fill a large book of its own, as we found out firsthand over the course of writing this one. In fact, when we sat down to plan this book originally, this chapter wasn't even in our outline. Instead, what was intended to be a relatively short section of an altogether different chapter has turned out to be one of the longest in the book—and this was after we had cut from it about half the material that we wanted to cover.

There are at least as many APIs giving you ways to use MySQL in your application programs as there are programming languages and platforms, but each must perform a certain minimum set of tasks. In presenting this chapter to you in its present form, we've tried to accomplish a number of goals. One of these was to provide you with an overview of what's required in MySQL applications programming—that is, of the steps needed to connect your application to a MySQL database, submit queries, retrieve results, and disconnect again when the program has finished its interaction with the MySQL server. There are many variations on this theme, but all MySQL APIs must and do accomplish these things. Some APIs have enhanced functionality, such as special functions or methods for signaling the beginning and end of transactions, but all fulfill these basic requirements.

We also surveyed some of the most common MySQL APIs, telling you which languages they can be used with, what they're capable of, and how and where you can obtain them for your own use. Some of these, such as PHP's mysql and mysqli or Python's MySQLdb, are specific to MySQL. Others, like ODBC and Perl's DBI, are database-agnostic and provide access to a number of different databases utilizing the same functions or methods for working with each one. While we wanted to emphasize *MySQL* programming (as opposed to database programming that just happens to use MySQL), we wanted to make you aware of what's available in the realm of database interoperability APIs because there are languages for which MySQL libraries don't exist, and there are situations in which you may need to deploy your application with more than one database.

We also provided you with a more comprehensive examination of MySQL APIs used with Open Source programming languages—PHP 4, PHP 5, Perl, and Python—complete with detailed discussions of their features, and working examples of each. We emphasized the mysql extension used in PHP 4 and 5, and the mysqli extension in PHP 5, due to the fact that PHP is used so widely with MySQL, especially in web development.

We've paid especially close attention to mysqli—more so than we did mysql— because mysqli is relatively new (as is PHP 5 itself) and not yet extensively covered in the literature. In addition, when used with MySQL 4.1 and above, it offers increased functionality not available with the older mysql extension in the form of the Prepared Statements and Multiple Statements APIs. ext/mysqli also offers for the first time to PHP developers a native MySQL interface that is object-oriented, allowing them to use it with other object-oriented libraries in conjunction with PHP 5's new exception handling capabilities, and we provided a fairly involved example showing how this can be accomplished, demonstrating how to extend the mysqli class to allow for object-oriented exception handling as well as integration with another object-oriented extension, PHP 5's ext/dom library.

In addition, we looked at Perl's DBI module as an example of an Open Source database interoperability library that works quite well with MySQL. Finally, we also examined the MySQLdb library for Python, which, like mysqli and Perl-DBI, provides an object-oriented interface for accessing MySQL.

Throughout this discussion, we've tried to emphasize the core requirements that a MySQL programming interface must meet in order to be viable. We showed you how the APIs that we examined in detail fulfill these needs, as well as how each of them can offer functional "extras" while still delivering on all of those requirements.

What's Next

In Chapter 8, we'll discuss some coming attractions in the world of MySQL, and with one new major version (4.1) nearing release and another major version (5.0) in development as this book went to press, there will be plenty to talk about. MySQL 4.1 was almost certain to be ready for production use before the end of 2004, and it now appears that MySQL 5.0 will be ready sometime in late 2005 or early 2006.

We've already discussed in this chapter and previous ones some of the new features that will be making an appearance in MySQL 4.1 when it's released for production use. One of these that we haven't yet talked much about will definitely help you to write more efficient queries and fewer of them—subqueries and derived tables. Subqueries can be defined as queries within queries, and can be used to combine queries. Derived tables are subqueries that return sets, and are an important step on the road to implementing database views (we'll come back to these very shortly). In some cases, they make it possible to return results in a single query that would otherwise require two or more queries to obtain.

We'll look at some other new features in MySQL 4.1 such as index caching, the new `GROUP_CONCAT()` function, a new enhancement to column definitions that will save you the trouble of checking for duplicate keys before inserting new records into a table (`ON DUPLICATE KEY UPDATE`). We'll also examine and provide some examples showing you how to use the new behavior of the `TIMESTAMP` column type in MySQL 4.1 and above.

At the time that this book was being written, serious development of MySQL 5.0 was already well underway, with two prerelease alphas already being available for testing. The first of these (MySQL 5.0.0-alpha) has already implemented stored procedures and stored functions; these represent a key feature that MySQL users have long awaited. Stored procedures and stored functions enable you to save blocks of SQL code for reuse, just as functions in programming languages such as PHP, C, Perl, and other languages make it possible to group a batch of program statements together to be called as a group when needed. We'll describe how stored procedures and stored functions are created, altered, and dropped in MySQL 5.0, show you the new flow-control syntax that's been added for use within these stored entities, and provide numerous working examples of them.

MySQL 5.0.1-alpha, made available just before this book was published, adds another major enhancement that's long been on users' wish lists—views. Views can be thought of as tables that are defined in terms of existing tables and used to encapsulate complex queries. This often allows you to use simple selects to get the data that you're after in a particular situation. Of course, this isn't the only thing they're good for, and we'll provide a complete examination of view syntax and usage as implemented in MySQL 5.0.1, again with numerous examples that we've developed and tested for this book, and which you'll be able to try out for yourself using the alpha prerelease from MySQL AB.

Finally, we'll look ahead to other improvements expected in MySQL beyond the 5.0 series of releases, including a description of triggers and our best guess as to how these will be implemented.

By the time you finish reading Chapter 8, you'll have a good idea of what to expect as future versions of MySQL become present versions, and you'll be prepared to take advantage of what these have to offer you in terms of making your databases and database-enabled applications faster, more accessible, and more efficient.

CHAPTER 8

Looking Ahead

MYSQL IS CONSTANTLY EVOLVING, AND THANKS to the Open Source paradigm of "Release early and often," improvements can be seen in nearly every single release. As with most software, however, significant changes and additions most often occur in major releases.

As we write, MySQL 4.1 has reached "gamma" status with the recent release of version 4.1.4, and a production version is very likely to be available not long after this book has gone to press. While there are other features worth mentioning—and we will mention them!—we'll focus primarily on subqueries (queries within queries), their different types, and the ways in which they can be used.

5.0-alpha versions of MySQL have been available for testing and feedback since the beginning of 2004. In this chapter, we'll discuss what will become available in these upcoming versions of MySQL, including a detailed look at what may be the most eagerly anticipated new feature of all in the 5.0.X series: stored procedures and stored functions. These will provide a way to store, combine, and reuse oft-repeated queries and pieces of SQL logic and functionality, and thereby promise great advances for database developers and administrators in terms of both efficiency and security for MySQL and the applications that use it. We'll also devote a good deal of space to views, which have been implemented in MySQL 5.0.1. Views provide a means of abstracting sets of data derived by complex queries and making them available in much simpler tabular form. As we'll see, views will have a positive impact on usability and security for MySQL database administrators and developers.

We'll also discuss what you're likely to be seeing in MySQL 5.1 when it becomes available. Triggers are another frequent entry on MySQL users' wish lists, as are views. An implementation of triggers in MySQL will allow you to set stored procedures to be triggered automatically (hence the term "trigger") when certain events take place within a database. We'll also try to provide some ideas as to what triggers will be like when they're implemented.

MySQL 4.1

We've already talked about some of the features that are new in MySQL 4.1, such as prepared statements and multiple statements and the SHOW WARNINGS command, in previous chapters. In this section we'll discuss what are probably the two most important new additions in MySQL 4.1 because of the increased speed, flexibility, and power they lend to SELECT queries. These are subqueries (also known as nested queries or subselects) and derived tables. In addition, as we'll see later in this chapter, they mark an important stage in MySQL's evolution, as they pave the way for enterprise-level features such as stored procedures, triggers, and views.

Subqueries and Derived Tables

Try as we might to combine queries using the various types of joins, SQL functions, and operators that we've looked at previously in this book, sometimes it's necessary to use more than one query to derive the exact data that we require. Even in cases where we can use a single query to obtain a desired result, we find that what seems conceptually very simple often requires very complex joins or unions. In MySQL 4.1, these problems can often be overcome through the use of *subqueries*, that is, queries within other queries. Being able to use subqueries can ease matters greatly, and they can allow us to combine queries or simplify them considerably. They also provide for *structured* queries, in which the different parts of a query can be considered apart from the others. This tends to make them much more easily read and understood than the more complex statements that they can be used to replace.

Subqueries can be used in several places within queries and in several ways. In the next few examples, we'll use two tables, representing products and categories of products. (You may recognize some of the **products** table data from the QA Testing example in Chapter 2.) These tables are structured as shown in the following two CREATE TABLE statements:

```
CREATE TABLE products (
   id INT(11) NOT NULL AUTO_INCREMENT PRIMARY KEY,
   category_id INT(11) NOT NULL,
   name VARCHAR(30) NOT NULL,
   price DECIMAL(6,2) NOT NULL
);

CREATE TABLE categories (
   id INT NOT NULL AUTO_INCREMENT PRIMARY KEY,
   name VARCHAR(30) NOT NULL
);
```

Each product has a name and a price. Each product belongs to a category (and only one category); this relationship is indicated by the **category_id** column in the **products** table, which serves as a foreign key linking to the **categories** table.

The table creation statements and some statements to insert sample data are included in the *ch8* directory of the code download for this book (available from the Downloads section of http://www.apress.com).

Subqueries can be used in any of the SELECT, INSERT, UPDATE, DELETE, or SET statements. (They can also be used with the DO statement, which we'll see when we discuss stored procedures later in this chapter.) Subqueries can include any of the constructs found in any other SELECT query, including FROM and WHERE clauses, joins, LIMIT clauses, unions, function calls, and so forth.

Subqueries As Scalar Values

The simplest use of a subquery is one in which it produces a single scalar value, as in this example:

```
Command Prompt - mysql -h megalon -u root -p                              _ □ ×
mysql> SELECT (SELECT name FROM categories WHERE id = 4)
    -> FROM products
    -> WHERE id = 2;
+------------------------------------------+
| (SELECT name FROM categories WHERE id = 4) |
+------------------------------------------+
| Entertainment                            |
+------------------------------------------+
1 row in set (0.00 sec)

mysql>
```

The subquery, sometimes also referred to as an inner query, is written inside parentheses to distinguish it from the outer query.

This particular example may seem trivial, but it forms the basis for some more useful possibilities, as we'll see shortly. You should note that a subquery used in this manner (with = or any other relational operator that compares scalar values) must return a *single* value; otherwise an error will result, as shown here:

```
Command Prompt - mysql -h megalon -u root -p                              _ □ ×
mysql> SELECT (SELECT name FROM categories)
    -> FROM products
    -> WHERE id = 2;
ERROR 1241 (21000): Subquery returns more than 1 row
mysql>
```

If the categories table contained only one row, no error would result from dropping the WHERE clause of the subquery.

Subqueries can also be used in expressions and with SQL functions, as shown in the three examples in the next illustration. In the third of these example queries, you can see that they may also be aliased.

```
Command Prompt - mysql -h megalon -u root -p                                          _ □ ×
mysql> SELECT
    ->    (SELECT id = 4 FROM categories
    ->     WHERE name LIKE 'ent%')
    -> FROM products WHERE id = 1\G
*************************** 1. row ***************************
(SELECT id = 4 FROM categories
    WHERE name LIKE 'ent%'): 1
1 row in set (0.00 sec)

mysql> SELECT
    ->    (SELECT name FROM categories
    ->     WHERE name LIKE 'ent%')
    -> FROM products WHERE id = 1\G
*************************** 1. row ***************************
(SELECT name FROM categories
    WHERE name LIKE 'ent%'): Entertainment
1 row in set (0.00 sec)

mysql> SELECT
    ->    (SELECT LENGTH(name) FROM categories
    ->     WHERE name LIKE 'ent%') AS len
    -> FROM products WHERE id = 1\G
*************************** 1. row ***************************
len: 13
1 row in set (0.00 sec)

mysql>
```

The real power of subqueries begins to become more apparent when we start using them in WHERE clauses. Here's a simple instance that illustrates a very common scenario:

```
Command Prompt - mysql -h megalon -u root -p                                          _ □ ×
mysql> SELECT category_id, name, price
    -> FROM products
    -> WHERE price = (SELECT MAX(price) FROM products);
+-------------+----------------------------+-------+
| category_id | name                       | price |
+-------------+----------------------------+-------+
|           3 | Bass Blaster Fishing Mortar | 79.95 |
+-------------+----------------------------+-------+
1 row in set (0.00 sec)

mysql> SELECT c.name AS category, p.name AS product, p.price
    -> FROM products p
    -> JOIN categories c
    -> ON c.id = p.category_id
    -> WHERE p.price = (SELECT MAX(price) FROM products);
+--------------------+----------------------------+-------+
| category           | product                    | price |
+--------------------+----------------------------+-------+
| Sporting Equipment | Bass Blaster Fishing Mortar | 79.95 |
+--------------------+----------------------------+-------+
1 row in set (0.01 sec)

mysql>
```

In the second of the two example queries just shown, we do a join on the **categories** table in order to obtain the category name. You should notice that the inner query doesn't require the use of the table aliases from the outer query; it's autonomous in that respect, as the outer query is concerned only with the value returned by the inner query, and not with any of the tables or columns referenced by the inner query.

It's also possible in MySQL to reverse the order of the subquery yielding the scalar value and the value you're comparing it to:

```
Command Prompt - mysql -h megalon -u root -p                          _ □ x
mysql> SELECT c.name AS category, p.name AS product, p.price
    -> FROM products p
    -> JOIN categories c
    -> ON c.id = p.category_id
    -> WHERE (SELECT MAX(price) FROM products) = price;
+--------------------+-----------------------------+---------+
| category           | product                     | price   |
+--------------------+-----------------------------+---------+
| Sporting Equipment | Bass Blaster Fishing Mortar | 79.95   |
+--------------------+-----------------------------+---------+
1 row in set (0.01 sec)

mysql>
```

However, you should be aware that this isn't part of the SQL standards and may not work in other databases, so if portability is a concern, use the value or column name first, followed by the subquery.

There are other ways to accomplish this particular task without the use of the subquery. One of these is to store an intermediate result in application code or to employ a MySQL user variable for the same purpose, like so:

```
SELECT @pmax := MAX(price) FROM products;
SELECT c.name AS category, p.name AS product, p.price
FROM products p
JOIN categories c
ON c.id = p.category_id
WHERE id = @pmax;
```

Alternatively, you could write something like this:

```
SELECT c.name AS category, p.name AS product, p.price
FROM products p
JOIN categories c
ON c.id = p.category_id
ORDER BY p.price DESC LIMIT 1;
```

This at least has the advantage of being a single query. However, neither of these methods is as easy to read and understand as when we use the subquery. There's also the problem of what happens when more than one product has the maximum price.

You're not limited to testing for equality in such cases; you can use any comparison that's appropriate to the type of data returned by the subquery. Suppose you want to promote those products having greater than the average price of all products, and you'd like a list with the names and IDs of the products and their prices. It would also be helpful to have the product categories listed as well. This will require another join on the **products** and **categories** tables, with a nested subquery in the WHERE clause, as shown here:

```
Command Prompt - mysql -h megalon -u root -p                                    _ □ X
mysql> SELECT p.id, c.name AS category, p.name AS product, p.price
    -> FROM products p
    -> JOIN categories c
    -> ON c.id = p.category_id
    -> WHERE p.price < (SELECT AVG(price) FROM products);
+----+----------------------+---------------------------+--------+
| id | category             | product                   | price  |
+----+----------------------+---------------------------+--------+
|  1 | Kitchen and Cookware | Souper Soup Dehydrator    | 24.95  |
|  3 | Kitchen and Cookware | Churn-O-Bill Butter Churn | 18.00  |
|  4 | Kitchen and Cookware | Congeal-O-Meal            | 22.50  |
|  6 | Kitchen and Cookware | Gas-Powered Turnip Slicer | 22.95  |
|  2 | Entertainment        | Ants Ants Revolution      | 16.95  |
+----+----------------------+---------------------------+--------+
5 rows in set (0.00 sec)

mysql>
```

In this example, we did a greater-than test, and the value returned by the subquery was obtained by using the AVG() function within the subquery.

Subqueries That Return Sets

In the last example from the previous section, you may notice that we were still testing against a single scalar value. In the current scenario, this is helpful when we want to compare prices of products against the average price for all products or the price of the largest product overall. How about finding the most expensive product in each category? It turns out that you can also make comparisons against subqueries that return *sets* of values using the IN, ANY, and SOME operators. In previous versions of MySQL, these operators were useful only with a set of values that you supplied directly. Beginning in MySQL 4.1, the set can be the result of another query.

NOTE *Remember that the operator* IN *is equivalent to* = ANY *or* = SOME. *We discussed this in Chapter 4; see the "Operators for Working with Sets" section of that chapter if you need to refresh your memory.*

For example, you can use a subquery in the WHERE clause of a query, like so:

```
Command Prompt - mysql -h megalon -u root -p                                    _ □ X
mysql> SELECT p.name AS product, c.name AS category, p.price
    -> FROM products p
    -> JOIN categories c ON c.id = p.category_id
    -> WHERE p.price IN
    ->    (SELECT MAX(price) FROM products GROUP BY category_id);
+----------------------------+----------------------+--------+
| product                    | category             | price  |
+----------------------------+----------------------+--------+
| INTERCAL Home Study Course | Home Study           | 39.95  |
| Souper Soup Dehydrator     | Kitchen and Cookware | 24.95  |
| Bass Blaster Fishing Mortar| Sporting Equipment   | 79.95  |
| Personal Breathalyser      | Entertainment        | 68.95  |
+----------------------------+----------------------+--------+
4 rows in set (0.01 sec)

mysql>
```

When using IN or its synonyms, you can put GROUP BY and HAVING clauses in the subquery, unlike the case with equality and other operators that make direct comparisons between scalar values. Notice that the set must still be one-dimensional; that is, it can return results only from a single column.

Benefits of Subqueries

So what are the advantages of using subqueries? For one thing, the syntax is often much closer to natural language and human thinking processes. Look again at the WHERE clause of the last query we showed you:

```
WHERE price IN (SELECT MAX(price) FROM products GROUP BY category_id)
```

This is remarkably similar to saying in ordinary language ". . . where the price is in the set of maximum prices obtained when we group together the products according to their categories."

Another reason to use subqueries even when you don't have to is because they tend to be easier to break down into their logical components. This makes them relatively simple to modify, which can be very handy when you're working with dynamically generated queries, for example.

In addition, there are situations in which it's either extremely difficult or even impossible to accomplish a desired task in a single query without using a subquery. You saw such a case in the last example: Without subqueries, obtaining information of this sort (maximum or minimum by category) becomes much more difficult, and requires either the use of a temporary table or a dodge known as the "Max-Concat Trick," which in this case would look something like this:

```
SELECT
  SUBSTRING( MAX( CONCAT(LPAD(p.price, 6, '0'), p.name) ), 7) AS name,
  c.name AS category,
  0.00 + LEFT( MAX( CONCAT(LPAD(p.price, 6, '0'), p.name) ), 6) AS price
FROM products p
JOIN categories c
ON c.id = p.category_id
GROUP BY p.category_id;
```

We'll leave it as an exercise for you to work out the details, but the basic idea here is that you concatenate each product name with its corresponding price, get the maximum of the resulting set of strings within each category, then split that string back into its parts again. This is highly inefficient, and not a recommended practice.

Subqueries That Return Rows—Derived Tables

We've talked about subqueries that return single values and those that return one-dimensional sets or lists of values. The progression doesn't end there. Beginning with version 4.1, MySQL also supports subqueries that return two-dimensional sets of values that can be identified by column and row—in other words, just as you would access items of data in a table. This type of subquery is known as a *derived table* and can be used in the FROM clause of the outer query. Its columns may be referenced along with the rest of those used in the outer query, provided we give the derived table an alias.

NOTE *Understanding the concept of a derived table is an important step on the road to understanding what an SQL view is and does, as we'll see later in this chapter when we look at features being implemented in MySQL 5.0.*

Perhaps an example will serve to make this clearer, so let's see how we can use a derived table to tell us how many categories contain more than one product.

NOTE *In this particular case, you could also obtain this information by means of a* HAVING *clause:* SELECT category_id, COUNT(category_id) AS number FROM products GROUP BY category_id HAVING number > 1;.

To obtain the number of products in each category, along with the ID of the category, you'd use a GROUP BY query, like so:

```
SELECT category_id, COUNT(category_id)
FROM products
GROUP BY category_id;
```

You can't test any of the values returned by this in the WHERE clause of an outer query because this query returns neither a single value nor a list of values, but a result set. What you can do is to assign it an alias and then use it in the FROM clause; when you do this, MySQL 4.1 versions and above let you treat it just like any other table in that you can refer to its columns using table_name.column_name syntax (or "dot" notation if you prefer to call it that). You can think of this as something like creating a temporary table, except that you do it inside the query at one go and the table disappears as soon as the query has been executed. You can also use aliases on the columns in the derived table as well.

You can see how this works here:

```
Command Prompt - mysql -h megalon -u root -p                        _□×
mysql> SELECT c.cid FROM
    -> (SELECT category_id AS cid, COUNT( category_id ) AS ct
    ->  FROM products
    ->  GROUP BY category_id
    -> ) AS c
    -> WHERE c.ct > 1;
+-----+
| cid |
+-----+
|   2 |
|   3 |
|   4 |
+-----+
3 rows in set (0.00 sec)

mysql>
```

Once you grasp the concept, this is not difficult to understand and modify if and when necessary. For instance, we can now get a set of the categories for which there are more than two products, just by changing the test in the WHERE clause of the outer query:

```
SELECT c.cid FROM
( SELECT category_id AS cid, COUNT(category_id) AS ct
  FROM products
  GROUP BY category_id ) AS c
WHERE c.ct > 2;
```

We can also use this derived table in a join, like so:

```
Command Prompt - mysql -h megalon -u root -p                        _□×
mysql> SELECT c1.cid, c2.name AS category FROM
    -> ( SELECT category_id AS cid, COUNT(category_id) AS ct
    -> FROM products
    -> GROUP BY category_id ) AS c1
    -> JOIN categories c2
    -> ON c1.cid = c2.id
    -> WHERE c1.ct > 2;
+-----+---------------------+
| cid | category            |
+-----+---------------------+
|   2 | Kitchen and Cookware |
+-----+---------------------+
1 row in set (0.00 sec)

mysql>
```

If this seems confusing, perhaps you'll be able to see better just what's happening here if we break it down by means of a temporary table, as shown here:

```
Command Prompt - mysql -h megalon -u root -p                    _ □ X
mysql> CREATE TEMPORARY TABLE tempcat
    -> SELECT category_id AS cid, COUNT(category_id) AS ccount
    -> FROM products GROUP BY category_id;
Query OK, 4 rows affected (0.02 sec)
Records: 4  Duplicates: 0  Warnings: 0

mysql> SELECT * FROM tempcat;
+-----+--------+
| cid | ccount |
+-----+--------+
|  1  |   1    |
|  2  |   4    |
|  3  |   2    |
|  4  |   2    |
+-----+--------+
4 rows in set (0.01 sec)

mysql> SELECT c1.cid, c2.name AS category
    -> FROM tempcat c1
    -> JOIN categories c2
    -> ON c1.cid = c2.id
    -> WHERE c1.ccount > 2;
+-----+--------------------+
| cid | category           |
+-----+--------------------+
|  2  | Kitchen and Cookware |
+-----+--------------------+
1 row in set (0.00 sec)

mysql> _
```

First we create the temporary table using a CREATE ... SELECT statement to extract the necessary data from **products**. The contents of this temporary table (named **tempcat** in the preceding example) are shown next—this is exactly what's contained in the derived table in the query that used the subquery. Next, we do a join on the temporary and **categories** tables. The end result is the same as that obtained from the single query we used before.

Other New Features in MySQL 4.1

While subqueries are the principal new attraction in MySQL 4.1, there are some additional new features that you should be aware of.

INSERT ON DUPLICATE KEY UPDATE: Using this new option for INSERT statements, it's possible to cause an insert that would duplicate a primary key to update the row matching that key instead. This means it's no longer necessary for you to check in your application code to see if a given key exists; MySQL will handle this for you.

New GROUP_CONCAT() function: This function returns all the concatenated values from a group. The syntax is

```
GROUP_CONCAT([DISTINCT] expr [order-by-clause] [SEPARATOR separator-string])
```

Here, *expr* is a column name or expression. Multiple expressions or columns (separated by commas) may be used. The optional *order-by-clause* follows the same rules for ORDER BY as used in a SELECT query. Also, an optional *separator-string* to be used in concatenating the values may be specified using the SEPARATOR keyword. Note that all of these arguments must be placed inside the parentheses following GROUP_CONCAT.

For example, referring to the same **products** table that we've been using in the previous sections, we could generate a list of prices of products for each product category as a single string, in which the names are separated by a colon with a space on either side of it as shown here:

```
Command Prompt - mysql -h megalon -u root -p
mysql> SELECT category_id,
    ->     GROUP_CONCAT(price ORDER BY price SEPARATOR ' : ') AS pgroup
    -> FROM products
    -> GROUP BY category_id;
+-------------+--------------------------------------+
| category_id | pgroup                               |
+-------------+--------------------------------------+
|           1 | 39.95                                |
|           2 | 18.00 : 22.50 : 22.95 : 24.95        |
|           3 | 49.95 : 79.95                        |
|           4 | 16.95 : 68.95                        |
+-------------+--------------------------------------+
4 rows in set (0.01 sec)

mysql>
```

Another enhancement from the viewpoint of efficiency is the addition of a new key cache system for MyISAM tables in MySQL 4.1.1 and a new command, CACHE INDEX, whose syntax is shown here:

```
CACHE INDEX table_name IN key_cache_name;
```

Prior to assigning indexes to a key cache, you must first create the key cache, as shown here:

```
SET GLOBAL key_cache_name.key_buffer_size = size;
```

This can also be done in the my.ini or my.cnf configuration file. The *size* parameter is an integer that is usually specified as a multiple of 1024 and some power of 8. Currently, all indexes from a table are assigned to a given key cache; eventually, it will be possible to assign only specified indexes to a cache.

By assigning table indexes to separate key caches, it's possible to fine-tune MySQL's performance by providing extra cache space for table indexes requiring it. The rationale behind this is more or less as follows: Tables normally "compete" for key cache space, and normally, this is a good thing. Tables that experience heavy usage will normally have their indexes kept in memory, and so MySQL will not have to retrieve their indexes from disk. However, you may have a table that is not used very often, but when it is queried, it's very important that the query executes as quickly as possible. Using a key cache, you can guarantee that this table's indexes will always be in memory and that MySQL won't be slowed down by being required to read them in again from disk.

Finally, we should mention that the behavior for TIMESTAMP columns changes in MySQL 4.1.2 and above. From this release, it's possible to create TIMESTAMP columns that default to the current date/time value and update this value whenever a record is updated. To illustrate this, let's create a table named **ts_test**, as shown here:

```
Command Prompt - mysql -h megalon -u root -p                    _ □ ×
mysql> CREATE TABLE ts_test (
    -> id INT NOT NULL AUTO_INCREMENT PRIMARY KEY,
    -> name VARCHAR(20),
    -> last_modified TIMESTAMP NOT NULL DEFAULT CURRENT_TIMESTAMP
    ->    ON UPDATE CURRENT_TIMESTAMP
    -> );
Query OK, 0 rows affected (0.02 sec)

mysql>
```

In order to take advantage of the **last_modified** column's properties in this regard, we must insert a null value into the column—using any other value, including 0 (zero) or the empty string, won't work. Let's insert a few rows into **ts_test** and see what happens:

```
Command Prompt - mysql -h megalon -u root -p                    _ □ ×
mysql> INSERT INTO ts_test (id, name, last_modified) VALUES
    -> ('', 'mary', NULL),
    -> ('', 'bill', ''),
    -> ('', 'joanne', 0),
    -> ('', 'richard', NULL);
Query OK, 4 rows affected, 5 warnings (0.01 sec)
Records: 4  Duplicates: 0  Warnings: 5

mysql> SHOW WARNINGS;
+---------+------+-------------------------------------------------------+
| Level   | Code | Message                                               |
+---------+------+-------------------------------------------------------+
| Warning | 1265 | Data truncated for column 'id' at row 1               |
| Warning | 1265 | Data truncated for column 'id' at row 2               |
| Warning | 1265 | Data truncated for column 'last_modified' at row 2    |
| Warning | 1265 | Data truncated for column 'id' at row 3               |
| Warning | 1265 | Data truncated for column 'id' at row 4               |
+---------+------+-------------------------------------------------------+
5 rows in set (0.00 sec)

mysql>
```

When we select all the values in the table, this is what we see: Only the rows into which we inserted **NULL** actually stored the current date/time. Furthermore, we received no warning about the row into which we inserted a zero. Now let's try updating three of the rows in **ts_test**:

```
Command Prompt - mysql -h megalon -u root -p                    _ □ ×
mysql> UPDATE ts_test SET name = 'william' WHERE name = 'bill';
Query OK, 1 row affected (0.00 sec)
Rows matched: 1  Changed: 1  Warnings: 0

mysql> UPDATE ts_test SET name = 'joan' WHERE name = 'joanne';
Query OK, 1 row affected (0.00 sec)
Rows matched: 1  Changed: 1  Warnings: 0

mysql> UPDATE ts_test SET name = 'ricky' WHERE name = 'richard';
Query OK, 1 row affected (0.00 sec)
Rows matched: 1  Changed: 1  Warnings: 0

mysql> SELECT * FROM ts_test;
+----+---------+---------------------+
| id | name    | last_modified       |
+----+---------+---------------------+
|  1 | mary    | 2004-08-29 10:56:48 |
|  2 | william | 2004-08-29 11:02:55 |
|  3 | joan    | 2004-08-29 11:03:29 |
|  4 | ricky   | 2004-08-29 11:03:44 |
+----+---------+---------------------+
4 rows in set (0.00 sec)

mysql>
```

Because of the ON UPDATE clause in the column definition, the **last_modified** column for any record in **ts_test** will be updated to the current date and time whenever that record is updated. However, if you set a timestamp column to an explicit value as part of an INSERT or UPDATE query, that value will be used instead:

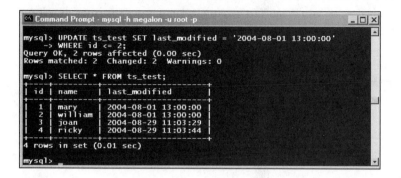

```
Command Prompt - mysql -h megalon -u root -p

mysql> UPDATE ts_test SET last_modified = '2004-08-01 13:00:00'
    -> WHERE id <= 2;
Query OK, 2 rows affected (0.00 sec)
Rows matched: 2  Changed: 2  Warnings: 0

mysql> SELECT * FROM ts_test;
+----+---------+---------------------+
| id | name    | last_modified       |
+----+---------+---------------------+
|  1 | mary    | 2004-08-01 13:00:00 |
|  2 | william | 2004-08-01 13:00:00 |
|  3 | joan    | 2004-08-29 11:03:29 |
|  4 | ricky   | 2004-08-29 11:03:44 |
+----+---------+---------------------+
4 rows in set (0.01 sec)

mysql>
```

NOTE *This auto-updating behavior for* TIMESTAMP *columns is effective only with tables created in MySQL 4.1.2 and above. If you've upgraded MySQL from a previous version and wish to take advantage of this feature for an existing table (created using the previous version of MySQL), you'll need to drop the table, re-create it, and reinsert any records that were present in the original.*

MySQL 5.0

It's difficult to say which is the greater source of excitement surrounding MySQL 5.0—the arrival of stored procedures in MySQL, or the appearance of views. In this section, we'll discuss both of these features in detail. We'll define and explain the concepts behind both stored procedures and views, and show you some working examples of each. (Of course, when we say "working," we mean that these examples will work if you try them on an installation of MySQL 5.0.1 or newer.) We'll also talk about how these features will help to improve your MySQL applications in terms of both efficiency and security.

Stored Procedures and Stored Functions

A database stored procedure or stored function acts much like a function or method does in programming languages such as PHP, C, Java, or Perl: It's a way to group together a series of statements and to identify this grouping so that we can later refer to it by name instead of repeating all the statements again. The following is a comparison of stored procedures and stored functions in MySQL 5.0:

- In MySQL 5.0.0 and 5.0.1, a stored procedure could refer to tables, but a stored function could not do so. This restriction is expected to be lifted in later 5.*X* releases, so you'll want to be sure to keep abreast of new developments in this area.

- A stored function actually returns a value, whereas the output of a procedure must be assigned to a user variable. Because of this, stored functions don't have output parameters, only input parameters.

- Both stored procedures and stored functions may use existing MySQL functions as well as other stored procedures and stored functions.

It's very important not to confuse stored functions with the user-defined functions (UDFs) that have been supported in MySQL since version 3.23.*XX*. (This is why we refer to them here as "*stored* functions" rather than simply "functions.") A UDF must be written in C, then compiled as a shared object file and installed on the same system where the MySQL server is being run. A stored function is written in SQL as part of a CREATE FUNCTION statement, just as a stored procedure is written using SQL within a CREATE PROCEDURE statement.

 CAUTION *UDFs continue to be supported in MySQL 5.0, and stored functions and UDFs share the same namespace. This means that if you're already using a UDF with a given name, you may encounter problems if you try to create a stored function with the same name that acts within the same database.*

It's very possible that MySQL will be extended in some fashion to allow stored procedures and stored functions to be written in other languages, but in any case no compilation is necessary to use stored procedures or stored functions, nor do we expect it to become this way in the future.

Benefits

- Stored procedures and stored functions allow you to execute queries and other blocks of SQL code that are frequently repeated much more quickly because they're precompiled. This means that MySQL doesn't have to try to optimize them again—they've already been stored in optimized form.

- Queries made by means of stored procedures are very portable between applications written in different languages or running on different platforms. Minimal application logic is required to execute a stored procedure (as we'll see shortly), and the same is true of tasks like string manipulation in order to insert limiting values into queries and other SQL code—instead, we can pass those values as parameters to the stored procedure or stored function.

- Stored procedures and stored functions allow us to encapsulate and modularize our queries—that is, just as we can do with functions, objects, and methods in programming languages like C, Java, PHP, and so on, we can treat stored procedures as "black box" entities with input and output parameters that are known to us, but whose internals needn't concern us when we use them, so long as they perform as specified. This keeps application code cleaner and easier to maintain because we're no longer mixing it with SQL. It also makes it easier to construct larger, more complex queries using the results of smaller and simpler ones, because you can call an existing stored procedure or stored function that supplies some of the data or functionality that you require in the new stored procedure or stored function that you're currently writing.

- Because database internals such as database and table names, passwords, and so forth aren't readily visible to the application or the end user, using stored procedures is more secure. Applications have access only to the functionality they require to accomplish their tasks; there's no direct access to stored data, only to procedures that return just what's required. By means of stored procedures, we can allow application writers to manipulate data without giving them direct access to the data itself. (As we'll see a bit later in this chapter, even in cases where it is desirable to give programmers and other users access to some but not all data, you'll be able in MySQL 5.0 to employ views to accomplish this.) Banking and other financial entities make heavy use of stored procedures (and views) for these reasons.

Syntax

As we mentioned already, to create a new stored procedure or stored function, you use the CREATE PROCEDURE or CREATE FUNCTION command, respectively. Let's examine the syntax for these commands.

```
CREATE PROCEDURE | FUNCTION procedure_name (parameter1[, parameter2,...])
[RETURNS type]
[ LANGUAGE SQL | [NOT] DETERMINISTIC |
  SQL SECURITY {DEFINER | INVOKER} | COMMENT string]
BEGIN
sql_statement(s)
END
delimiter
```

The CREATE keyword is followed by PROCEDURE or FUNCTION depending on which one you want to create. The *procedure_name* is simply the name by which you wish to refer to the stored procedure or stored function, and can be any legal MySQL identifier. This is followed by a list of zero or more parameters—even if there are none, the parentheses are required (think of a PHP or JavaScript function declaration here). For stored procedures, each parameter takes the form

```
[ IN | OUT | INOUT ] parameter_name type
```

where IN, OUT, or INOUT specifies whether the parameter is input, output, or both (IN is the default value). This is followed by the name of the parameter and its type, which may be any valid MySQL datatype, just as you'd use as part of a column definition in a CREATE TABLE statement. The IN, OUT, and INOUT keywords are not used with stored functions, as stored functions can have input parameters only.

TIP *If you've had experience in programming in languages that make use of them, then you can think of* INOUT *parameters as being somewhat like passing values by reference or using pointers; the variable itself is changed by the procedure. We'll provide an example of a stored procedure using* INOUT *parameters a bit later (see the "IF ... ELSEIF ... ELSE" section).*

If you're defining a stored function, you can specify a return type using RETURNS. Remember that only a stored function may return a value, and the body of the function must contain a RETURN statement. It's important to remember that the parentheses are still required even in cases where your procedure doesn't have any input or output parameters at all; this lets MySQL know not to expect any.

NOTE *From this point on in our discussion, we'll use the term "procedure" to mean either a stored procedure or a stored function, and we'll make it clear if what we're saying applies only to one or the other.*

Each of the next set of clauses, also known as the procedure's "characteristics," is optional. In MySQL 5.0.0 and 5.0.1, the LANGUAGE clause accepts only SQL as its argument, although this will probably change in the future, as there are plans to introduce support for additional languages in stored procedures and stored functions. PHP is a very strong candidate in this regard, and it's likely to be the first external language to be supported. The DETERMINISTIC keyword means that the stored procedure or stored function is always supposed to produce the same result for the same input parameters, and so NOT DETERMINISTIC means that the result may be different for different invocations of the procedure (or function), even if the input is the same. This clause is accepted but not actually supported in MySQL 5.0.0.

In addition, the SQL SECURITY clause can be used to determine whether the privileges of the procedure's creator or user should be in effect when the procedure is invoked. In the current MySQL 5.0 alpha versions, in order to access tables referenced in the procedure, the user calling the procedure must have the appropriate permissions on those tables. This is almost certain to be fixed by the time MySQL 5.0 is released for production use. MySQL also supports comments for procedures.

Once created, stored procedures and stored functions are stored in the **mysql.proc** table indefinitely. In order to delete a procedure, you can use DROP PROCEDURE and DROP FUNCTION along with the name of the procedure; for example, in order to delete a stored procedure named **myproc**, you would execute the statement

```
DROP PROCEDURE myproc;
```

To view the statement used to create a procedure, use the SHOW CREATE PROCEDURE or SHOW CREATE FUNCTION statement. To see the definition of a function named **myfunc**, you'd use

```
SHOW CREATE FUNCTION myfunc;
```

You can also alter some characteristics of a procedure using the ALTER PROCEDURE or ALTER FUNCTION command:

```
ALTER PROCEDURE | FUNCTION procname
  NAME newname | SQL SECURITY {DEFINER | INVOKER} | COMMENT comment
```

CAUTION CREATE PROCEDURE, SHOW CREATE PROCEDURE, DROP PROCEDURE, *and* ALTER PROCEDURE *work only with stored procedures.* CREATE FUNCTION, SHOW CREATE FUNCTION, DROP FUNCTION, *and* ALTER FUNCTION *work only with stored functions. For example, you can't use* DROP PROCEDURE *to drop a stored function.*

The body of the stored procedure or stored function comes between the BEGIN and END keywords, and may contain nearly any valid SQL statements, subject only to the limitation that in MySQL 5.0, only stored procedures (but not stored functions) may refer to tables. They may also contain some flow-control, looping, and variable-declaration constructs that are specific to stored procedures and stored functions. See the sections "Flow Control in Stored Procedures," "Looping in Procedures," and the sidebar "Declaring Variables Within Procedures" for more about these.

TIP *While some databases don't permit you to create, alter, or drop tables within a stored procedure, MySQL does allow you to do so. You'll see an example of creating a table inside a stored procedure when we discuss cursors later in this section.*

Stored Procedure Examples

If you've not worked with stored procedures before, it may seem like we've just thrown lot of information at you, so let's look at a couple of examples that may help to clear things up a bit. A very simple one would be a stored procedure like the one shown here, which has only a single output parameter:

```
Command Prompt - mysql -h megalon -u root -p

mysql> DELIMITER | ;
mysql> CREATE PROCEDURE simple_query(OUT prodid INT)
    -> BEGIN
    ->   SELECT p.id INTO prodid
    ->   FROM mdbd_ch8.products p
    ->   WHERE p.name = 'Thrash-O-Matic';
    -> END
    -> |
Query OK, 0 rows affected (0.00 sec)

mysql> DELIMITER ; |
mysql> CALL simple_query(@id);
Query OK, 0 rows affected (0.00 sec)

mysql> SELECT @id;
+------+
| @id  |
+------+
| 5    |
+------+
1 row in set (0.00 sec)

mysql>
```

You'll notice that before we entered the definition for the stored procedure, we used the DELIMITER command to change the character used to terminate a query from a semicolon to a pipe character. This is because MySQL needs some way to distinguish the semicolon used to end SQL statements inside the body of the procedure from what's used to terminate the CREATE PROCEDURE statement itself. Once we've done so, we simply use DELIMITER again like so:

```
DELIMITER ; |
```

This tells MySQL that we want to use the semicolon to terminate commands once again. You don't necessarily have to use the pipe character as your delimiter in such cases, but since it's not often used in queries, it's a good choice.

NOTE *Logging out of MySQL and then back in again resets the delimiter character to the semicolon. However, if you lose the connection for some reason, or even if the MySQL server crashes, the delimiter will remain the same, so long as the client continues to run; this information is stored in the client, and not on the server.*

The procedure itself consists of the bare minimum that's required following the output parameter—the BEGIN keyword followed by an SQL block containing just one statement followed by END and the delimiter character we specified before writing the CREATE PROCEDURE command.

Once a procedure has been created, it's invoked using the CALL command followed by the number of parameters required in the procedure's definition. When the procedure is called, it sets values for any output parameters by means of the SELECT ... INTO ... statement. Just as with the parameters for a function or method in programming languages such as PHP, Perl, and so on, we don't have to use the same variable names as used in the procedure definition; we can use whatever names we like, and we can use these just like we would any other user variables. In other words, which values get inserted into the variables we use in the CALL statement depends on their order in the procedure definition.

We just showed a simple SELECT query, but we're not limited in what sort of query we use this value in:

```
Command Prompt - mysql -h megalon -u root -p
mysql> UPDATE products SET name = CONCAT(name, " Plus")
    -> WHERE id = @id;
Query OK, 1 row affected (0.00 sec)
Rows matched: 1  Changed: 1  Warnings: 0

mysql> SELECT * FROM products WHERE id = @id;
+----+-------------+------------------+-------+
| id | category_id | name             | price |
+----+-------------+------------------+-------+
| 5  |           3 | Thrash-O-Matic Plus | 49.95 |
+----+-------------+------------------+-------+
1 row in set (0.00 sec)

mysql>
```

One other point we need to mention before we continue concerns how the procedures are associated with databases. Normally, a procedure is associated with the database selected at the time the CREATE PROCEDURE or CREATE FUNCTION statement is executed. If we wish to refer to this procedure later after selecting a different database, it's necessary to qualify its name with the name of the database to which it belongs, using *dbname.procedurename* notation. In addition, any tables referred to within a procedure are assumed to be in the current database. The USE statement normally employed for selecting a particular database isn't permitted inside procedures, and since a procedure might be called at any time, no matter which database (if any) is currently selected, MySQL must "know" which database to use. However, this tends to make procedures much more flexible as a result.

In other words, suppose we have selected the database named **mydb**, and we create a procedure named **myproc,** which selects records from a table named **mytable**. Unless you use *dbname.tablename* notation to specify that **mytable** is part of some other database, MySQL assumes that it should try to find **mytable** in **mydb**, and an error will result if it can't find a table by that name in that database. In addition, if you select a different database and then try to call **myproc** using CALL myproc();, an error will result; in that case, you must fully qualify the name of the procedure:

```
CALL mydb.myproc();
```

Let's turn now to an example of a stored procedure that uses several parameters. First, as before, let's change the statement delimiter to the pipe character and then define the stored procedure **get_prod_info**, as shown here:

```
Command Prompt - mysql -h megalon -u root -p                        _ □ ×
mysql> DELIMITER | ;
mysql> CREATE PROCEDURE get_product_info
    -> (
    ->    IN prodid INT,
    ->    OUT prodname VARCHAR(50),
    ->    OUT catname VARCHAR(50),
    ->    OUT prodprice DECIMAL(5,2)
    -> )
    -> BEGIN
    ->    SELECT p.name, c.name, p.price
    ->      INTO prodname, catname, prodprice
    ->    FROM products p
    ->    JOIN categories c
    ->    ON c.id = p.category_id
    ->    WHERE p.id = prodid;
    -> END
    -> |
Query OK, 0 rows affected (0.00 sec)

mysql>
```

This procedure takes the ID for a product and returns the name of the product, the name of the category to which it belongs, and the price of the product. It has one input parameter and three output parameters having the names and datatypes shown here:

```
CREATE PROCEDURE get_product_info
(
   IN catid INT,
   OUT catname VARCHAR(50),
   OUT prodname VARCHAR(50),
   OUT prodprice DECIMAL(5,2)
)
```

The body of this procedure consists of a single SELECT query, with an INTO clause that stores the three column values in the output parameters, and that uses the **prodid** parameter value in the WHERE clause:

```
SELECT c.name, p.name, p.price
   INTO catname, prodname, prodprice
FROM products p
JOIN categories c
ON c.id = p.category_id
WHERE p.id = prodid;
```

Now we reset the semicolon as the delimiter character, then call the procedure using an integer value for **prodid** and user variable names for the output parameters. Then we can select these three user variables in order to view the result:

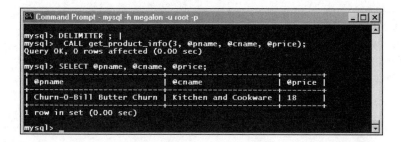

> **NOTE** *In the rest of the examples covering stored procedures and stored functions, we'll assume that the delimiter character has been set to "|" (pipe character) and left that way for the duration of the session, rather than taking up space by showing you a continuous switching back and forth when it's not really necessary.*

Although output parameters can contain only scalar values, you can still obtain result sets using stored procedures, simply by not using output parameters for the result of the SELECT. Here's a simple example, which also shows you what the output of a SHOW CREATE PROCEDURE statement looks like:

```
Command Prompt - mysql -h megalon -u root -p                              _ | □ | X
mysql> SHOW CREATE PROCEDURE get_product_rows\G
*************************** 1. row ***************************
           Procedure: get_product_rows
            sql_mode:
    Create Procedure: CREATE PROCEDURE `mdbd_ch8`.`get_product_rows`()
BEGIN
    SELECT p.id, p.name, p.price, c.name
    FROM products p
    JOIN categories c
    ON c.id = p.category_id
    ORDER BY c.name, p.name;
END
1 row in set (0.00 sec)

mysql> CALL get_product_rows()|
+----+--------------------------+-------+-----------------------+
| id | name                     | price | name                  |
+----+--------------------------+-------+-----------------------+
|  2 | Ants Ants Revolution     | 16.95 | Entertainment         |
|  7 | Personal Breathalyser    | 68.95 | Entertainment         |
|  8 | INTERCAL Home Study Course| 39.95 | Home Study           |
|  3 | Churn-O-Bill Butter Churn| 18.00 | Kitchen and Cookware  |
|  4 | Congeal-O-Meal           | 22.50 | Kitchen and Cookware  |
|  6 | Gas-Powered Turnip Slicer| 22.95 | Kitchen and Cookware  |
|  1 | Souper Soup Dehydrator   | 24.95 | Kitchen and Cookware  |
|  9 | Bass Blaster Fishing Mortar| 79.95 | Sporting Equipment  |
|  5 | Thrash-O-Matic           | 49.95 | Sporting Equipment    |
+----+--------------------------+-------+-----------------------+
9 rows in set (0.00 sec)

Query OK, 0 rows affected (0.14 sec)

mysql>
```

As we've already said, you're not limited to using SELECT queries in stored procedures. Let's create a stored procedure for transferring money between two bank accounts, using the same **accounts** table and initial data as we used for the Python transactions example in Chapter 5:

```
CREATE TABLE accounts (
    account_number int(11) NOT NULL default '0',
    firstname varchar(50) NOT NULL default '',
    lastname varchar(50) NOT NULL default '',
    balance decimal(8,2) NOT NULL default '0.00',
    PRIMARY KEY  (account_number)
);

INSERT INTO accounts VALUES (6557, 'Gerald', 'Roberts', '1602.92');
INSERT INTO accounts VALUES (8510, 'Morris', 'Johnson', '2176.21');
```

In this example, we'll assume that we're using a MyISAM table and therefore not enforcing transaction compliance. However, you should note that you'll want to use START TRANSACTION rather than BEGIN or BEGIN WORK inside a stored procedure in order to avoid clashing with the BEGIN keyword as used to demarcate the procedure's body. We'll commence by defining a stored procedure named **transfer_funds** as shown here:

```
Command Prompt - mysql -h megalon -u root -p                    _ □ X

mysql> CREATE PROCEDURE transfer_funds
    -> (
    ->    IN amt DECIMAL(6,2),
    ->    IN from_acct INT,
    ->    IN to_acct INT
    -> )
    -> BEGIN
    ->    UPDATE accounts SET balance = balance - amt
    ->    WHERE account_number = from_acct;
    ->
    ->    UPDATE accounts SET balance = balance + amt
    ->    WHERE account_number = to_acct;
    -> END
    -> |
Query OK, 0 rows affected (0.01 sec)

mysql>
```

The procedure has three input parameters and no output parameters.
The parameters **amt**, **from_acct**, and **to_acct** are intended to pass (in order) the
amount to be transferred, the ID number of the account from which the funds
are to be taken, and the number of the account that will receive the transferred
funds. We'll check the initial state of the data with a simple select query, then call
the stored procedure and verify the result with another SELECT * FROM accounts;:

```
Command Prompt - mysql -h megalon -u root -p                    _ □ X

mysql> SELECT * FROM accounts|
+----------------+-----------+----------+---------+
| account_number | firstname | lastname | balance |
+----------------+-----------+----------+---------+
|           6557 | Gerald    | Roberts  | 1602.92 |
|           8510 | Morris    | Johnson  | 2176.21 |
+----------------+-----------+----------+---------+
2 rows in set (0.01 sec)

mysql> CALL transfer_funds(125.50, 6557, 8510)|
Query OK, 1 row affected (0.01 sec)

mysql> SELECT * FROM accounts|
+----------------+-----------+----------+---------+
| account_number | firstname | lastname | balance |
+----------------+-----------+----------+---------+
|           6557 | Gerald    | Roberts  | 1477.42 |
|           8510 | Morris    | Johnson  | 2301.71 |
+----------------+-----------+----------+---------+
2 rows in set (0.00 sec)

mysql>
```

As you can see, stored procedures will have a lot to offer users of MySQL
when they're finally available in a production release.

NOTE   *Stored procedures and stored functions in MySQL 5.0+ require
the **proc** table to be present in the **mysql** database, and will not work
without it. If you're upgrading an existing installation, be sure to run
the **mysql_fix_privilege_tables** script included with the MySQL distribution files in order to add the **proc** table to your grant tables. (An
early [alpha] version did not add this table, so make sure that you
obtain and install the latest version from* http://dev.mysql.com/.)
We also recommend that you take a look at the output of a
SHOW CREATE TABLE mysql.proc; *command—you should find it
most instructive.*

Stored Function Examples

Stored functions are similar to stored procedures in that both allow you to save predefined blocks of code for reuse. As we've already noted, stored functions differ from stored procedures in that stored functions actually return a value. For this reason, stored functions have only input parameters (if any parameters at all), so the IN, OUT, and INOUT keywords aren't used. Stored functions have no output parameters; instead, you use a RETURN statement to return a value whose type is determined by the RETURNS *type* statement, which precedes the body of the function. Here's an example of a relatively simple function named **get_volume** that takes the radius of a sphere as input, and returns its volume:

```
Command Prompt - mysql -h megalon -u root -p
mysql> CREATE FUNCTION get_volume(radius FLOAT)
    -> RETURNS FLOAT
    -> BEGIN
    ->   DECLARE volume FLOAT;
    ->
    ->   SET volume = (4 / 3) * PI() * POW(radius, 3);
    ->
    ->   return volume;
    -> END
    -> |
Query OK, 0 rows affected (0.01 sec)

mysql>
```

To invoke the function, you don't use CALL as you would with a stored procedure; instead, you merely use the name of the procedure along with any parameters that are required by it. This can be done as part of a SELECT statement, as shown here:

```
Command Prompt - mysql -h megalon -u root -p
mysql> SELECT get_volume(5.5)|
+-----------------+
| get_volume(5.5) |
+-----------------+
| 696.90997314453 |
+-----------------+
1 row in set (0.00 sec)

mysql>
```

You can also refer to functions directly in expressions, and you're not limited to working with numbers, as you'll see in the next example.

Stored functions and stored procedures can invoke other stored functions and stored procedures. In this example, we create a new function named **get_volume_in_words** that makes use of the **get_volume** function from the previous example:

```
Command Prompt - mysql -h megalon -u root -p                          _ □ ×

mysql> CREATE FUNCTION get_volume_in_words(radius FLOAT)
    -> RETURNS VARCHAR(100)
    -> BEGIN
    ->   RETURN CONCAT(
    ->                 'If the radius of the sphere is ',
    ->                 radius,
    ->                 ', then its volume is ',
    ->                 get_volume(radius),
    ->                 '.'
    ->                );
    -> END
    -> |
Query OK, 0 rows affected (0.00 sec)

mysql>
```

Rather than just spitting out a number without any context, this function tells us exactly what information **get_volume** is providing, in a plain English sentence. Let's try it out:

```
Command Prompt - mysql -h megalon -u root -p                          _ □ ×

mysql> SELECT get_volume_in_words(10)|
+-------------------------------------------------------------------+
| get_volume_in_words(10)                                           |
+-------------------------------------------------------------------+
| If the radius of the sphere is 10, then its volume is 4188.790205.|
+-------------------------------------------------------------------+
1 row in set (0.00 sec)

mysql>
```

These two functions may be trivial in and of themselves, but they serve to illustrate the potential for managing and organizing complex tasks by breaking them down into smaller ones. Remember that you're not limited to calling only functions from other functions—you can use stored procedures from within stored functions, and the reverse is true as well.

Flow Control in Stored Procedures

Stored procedure and function syntax in MySQL 5.0 and above includes a number of flow-control constructs that may look familiar to you, particularly if you've read Chapter 4. However, the syntax for some of these differs when used in a stored procedure or stored function, so you'll want to look at the descriptions and examples that follow, in order to be aware of these. In addition, MySQL 5.0 and above support some looping constructs that aren't available outside stored procedures and functions—for information on these and some examples, see the sections on LOOP, REPEAT, and WHILE later in this chapter.

IF ... ELSEIF ... ELSE

This construct is much like the if... elseif... else... found in such program-
ming languages as PHP and Perl, and should not be confused with the IF(),
IFNULL(), and NULLIF() functions we introduced earlier in this book (see
Chapter 4). Its syntax is

```
IF condition THEN statement-block
[ELSEIF condition THEN statement-block]
[ELSE statement-block]
END IF;
```

The condition following IF may be any expression that evaluates to Boolean
TRUE or **FALSE**. Should this condition evaluate as **TRUE**, then the statement or
statements immediately following THEN are executed; otherwise, control passes to
the next ELSEIF (if there is one) and its condition is evaluated—if that expression
is true, the statement block following the next THEN executes. There can be any
number of ELSEIF clauses in an IF block. If there is an ELSE clause and no condition has tested as **TRUE** up to that point, then the statement (or block of
statements) following ELSE is executed.

This example creates a stored function that compares two integer values. If
the first value is greater than the second, a 1 is returned; if the second value is
larger, a –1 is returned; and if the two values are the same, the function returns a 0:

```
Command Prompt - mysql -h megalon -u root -p

mysql> delimiter | ;
mysql> CREATE FUNCTION compare(value1 INT, value2 INT)
    -> RETURNS INT
    -> BEGIN
    ->   DECLARE temp INT;
    ->
    ->   IF value1 > value2
    ->     THEN SET temp = 1;
    ->     ELSEIF value2 > value1
    ->     THEN SET temp = -1;
    ->     ELSE SET temp = 0;
    ->   END IF;
    ->
    ->   RETURN temp;
    -> END
    -> |
Query OK, 0 rows affected (0.00 sec)

mysql>
```

Here you can see the **compare** function being used:

```
Command Prompt - mysql -h megalon -u root -p

mysql> delimiter ; |
mysql> SELECT compare(10, 2), compare(4,8), compare(6, 6);
+----------------+--------------+---------------+
| compare(10, 2) | compare(4,8) | compare(6, 6) |
+----------------+--------------+---------------+
|              1 |           -1 |             0 |
+----------------+--------------+---------------+
1 row in set (0.01 sec)

mysql>
```

Note that a complete IF block must be terminated by an END IF and a semicolon.

Here's an example of a stored procedure that also uses IF ... THEN ... ELSE logic. This procedure, named **get_running_total**, also makes use of two INOUT parameters:

```
Command Prompt - mysql -h megalon -u root -p
mysql> CREATE PROCEDURE get_running_total
    -> (
    ->   IN prodid INT,
    ->   INOUT total DECIMAL(5,2),
    ->   INOUT names VARCHAR(255)
    -> )
    -> BEGIN
    ->   DECLARE prodprice DECIMAL(5,2);
    ->   DECLARE prodname varchar(50);
    ->
    ->   SELECT price, name INTO prodprice, prodname
    ->   FROM products
    ->   WHERE id = prodid;
    ->
    ->   SET total = total + prodprice;
    ->
    ->   IF LENGTH(names) = 0 THEN
    ->     SET names = prodname;
    ->   ELSE
    ->     SET names = CONCAT(names, ', ', prodname);
    ->   END IF;
    -> END
    -> |
Query OK, 0 rows affected (0.00 sec)

mysql>
```

As we mentioned earlier, an INOUT parameter is actually modified by the procedure it's used in, similar to passing a parameter by reference in some programming languages. In this procedure, we use two INOUT parameters: one to store a cumulative total of the prices of the products identified by the **id** parameter each time the procedure is called, and one to store a comma-delimited list of the names of those products. A couple of calls to this procedure with intervening SELECT queries to read the values of the variables passed should help to demonstrate just how these work:

```
Command Prompt - mysql -h megalon -u root -p
mysql> SET @accumtotal = 0|
Query OK, 0 rows affected (0.01 sec)

mysql> SET @accumitems = ''|
Query OK, 0 rows affected (0.00 sec)

mysql> CALL get_running_total(3, @accumtotal, @accumitems)|
Query OK, 0 rows affected (0.01 sec)

mysql> SELECT @accumtotal, @accumitems|
+-------------+-------------------------+
| @accumtotal | @accumitems             |
+-------------+-------------------------+
| 18          | Churn-O-Bill Butter Churn |
+-------------+-------------------------+
1 row in set (0.00 sec)

mysql> CALL get_running_total(7, @accumtotal, @accumitems)|
Query OK, 0 rows affected (0.00 sec)

mysql> SELECT @accumtotal, @accumitems|
+-------------+---------------------------------------------------+
| @accumtotal | @accumitems                                       |
+-------------+---------------------------------------------------+
| 86.95       | Churn-O-Bill Butter Churn, Personal Breathalyser |
+-------------+---------------------------------------------------+
1 row in set (0.01 sec)

mysql>
```

Declaring Variables Within Procedures

The DECLARE statement is used to create variables for use within a stored procedure or stored function. These can serve as counters or iterators, to provide temporary storage of intermediate values used in calculating a result, or for any other purpose. Such variables are local to the procedure; in order to pass their values back to a calling routine or query, you must RETURN the value in the case of a stored function, or assign the value to an output parameter of a stored procedure. The local variable itself cannot be referenced from outside the stored procedure or function.

Any DECLARE statements that are used in a stored procedure or function must come first in the body, immediately following the BEGIN keyword, and before any other statements. The variable's type must be included in the declaration, as shown here, where *name* is the name of the variable and *type* is its datatype:

```
DECLARE name type;
```

Each local variable may be of any datatype supported by MySQL.

It's also possible to save a bit of time and typing by providing a default value for the variable, using the DEFAULT keyword followed by the desired initial value. For example, you can replace these four statements (two DECLARE and two SET statements):

```
DECLARE myvar INT;
DECLARE yourvar VARCHAR(40);

SET myvar = 1;
SET yourvar = '';
```

with these two DECLARE statements using DEFAULT:

```
DECLARE myvar INT DEFAULT 1;
DECLARE yourvar VARCHAR(40) DEFAULT '';
```

You can declare as many local variables as you require in a stored procedure or stored function, using as many DECLARE statements as necessary, so long as all of them precede any other statements following the BEGIN keyword that starts the body of the procedure.

CASE

The CASE block provides a somewhat cleaner way of providing multiple responses to conditions than does IF... ELSEIF... ELSE, and comes in two varieties. The first of these allows for different actions to be taken depending upon the value of a single expression that follows the opening CASE keyword. Each value to be tested against resides in its own WHEN clause, of which there can be one or more, and is followed by THEN. The statement or statements to be executed should the expression match the value follow the THEN keyword. Finally, an optional ELSE prefaces one or more statements to be executed if the expression fails to match any of the WHEN values.

NOTE *When used inside a stored procedure or stored function, a* CASE *block terminates with* END CASE *instead of* END.

The syntax for the first form of CASE can be summed up as shown here:

```
CASE expression
WHEN value THEN statement-block
[ELSE statement-block]
END CASE;
```

We provide an example in the stored function **letter**, which takes a single character as input, and tells us which of the first three letters of the alphabet it is, or if it isn't any of these:

```
Command Prompt - mysql -h megalon -u root -p

mysql> delimiter | ;
mysql> CREATE FUNCTION letter(aletter VARCHAR(1))
    -> RETURNS VARCHAR(50)
    -> BEGIN
    ->   DECLARE msg VARCHAR(50);
    ->   DECLARE temp VARCHAR(1);
    ->
    ->   SET temp = LCASE(aletter);
    ->
    ->   CASE temp
    ->     WHEN 'a' THEN SET msg = 'First letter.';
    ->     WHEN 'b' THEN SET msg = 'Second letter.';
    ->     WHEN 'c' THEN SET msg = 'Third letter.';
    ->     ELSE SET msg = 'Some other letter.';
    ->   END CASE;
    ->
    ->   RETURN msg;
    -> END
    -> |
Query OK, 0 rows affected (0.04 sec)

mysql> SELECT letter('a')|
+---------------+
| letter('a')   |
+---------------+
| First letter. |
+---------------+
1 row in set (0.00 sec)

mysql> SELECT letter('C'), letter('q')|
+---------------+--------------------+
| letter('C')   | letter('q')        |
+---------------+--------------------+
| Third letter. | Some other letter. |
+---------------+--------------------+
1 row in set (0.00 sec)

mysql>
```

Alternatively, we could have written this function using IF... ELSEIF... ELSE:

```
CREATE FUNCTION letter(aletter VARCHAR(1))
RETURNS VARCHAR(50)
BEGIN
  DECLARE msg VARCHAR(50);
  DECLARE temp VARCHAR(1);

  SET temp = LCASE(aletter);

  IF temp = 'a' THEN SET msg = 'First letter.';
    ELSEIF temp = 'b' THEN SET msg = 'Second letter.'';
    ELSEIF temp = 'c' THEN SET msg = 'Third letter.';
    ELSE SET msg = 'Some other letter.';
  END IF;

  RETURN msg;
END
```

Since we're testing against the same value in every branch of this SQL block, it's shorter and simpler just to use CASE.

The other version of CASE takes a separate expression in each WHILE clause, evaluates it, and if it is true, it executes any statements following the accompanying THEN keyword. The syntax for this form is shown here:

```
CASE
WHEN condition THEN statement
[ELSE statement]
END CASE;
```

Here's an example of a stored procedure named **divisors** that finds the lowest divisor of a number if it's 2, 3, or 5, and lets us know if the number supplied as input isn't divisible by any of these three values:

```
Command Prompt - mysql -h megalon -u root -p                              _ □ X
mysql> CREATE PROCEDURE divisors
    -> (
    ->   IN val INT,
    ->   OUT msg VARCHAR(50)
    -> )
    -> BEGIN
    ->   SET msg = CONCAT_WS(' ', val, 'is...');
    ->
    ->   CASE
    ->     WHEN val MOD 2 = 0
    ->       THEN
    ->         SET msg = CONCAT_WS(msg, ' ', 'divisible by 2...');
    ->     WHEN val MOD 3 = 0
    ->       THEN
    ->         SET msg = CONCAT_WS(msg, ' ', 'divisible by 3...');
    ->     WHEN val MOD 5 = 0
    ->       THEN
    ->         SET msg = CONCAT_WS(msg, ' ', 'divisible by 5...');
    ->     ELSE
    ->       SET
    ->         msg =
    ->           CONCAT_WS(msg, ' ', 'not divisible by 2, 3, or 5.');
    ->   END CASE;
    -> END
    -> |
Query OK, 0 rows affected (0.00 sec)

mysql>
```

Let's examine the output of this procedure for some different input values
and see what we can discern about the behavior of this second form of CASE from
the results:

```
Command Prompt - mysql -h megalon -u root -p                              _ □ X
mysql> CALL divisors(9, @output)|
Query OK, 0 rows affected (0.00 sec)

mysql> SELECT @output|
+--------------------------+
| @output                  |
+--------------------------+
| 9 is...divisible by 3... |
+--------------------------+
1 row in set (0.00 sec)

mysql> CALL divisors(13, @output)|
Query OK, 0 rows affected (0.00 sec)

mysql> SELECT @output|
+-----------------------------------+
| @output                           |
+-----------------------------------+
| 13 is...not divisible by 2, 3, or 5. |
+-----------------------------------+
1 row in set (0.00 sec)

mysql> CALL divisors(6, @output)|
Query OK, 0 rows affected (0.00 sec)

mysql> SELECT @output|
+--------------------------+
| @output                  |
+--------------------------+
| 6 is...divisible by 2... |
+--------------------------+
1 row in set (0.00 sec)

mysql>
```

For an input value of 9, we get back "9 is . . . divisible by 3." For 13, we get the message, "13 is . . . not divisible by 2, 3, or 5." So far, so good. But what about a number that has *two* divisors among the set against which we're testing? When we test 6 as a value, we get only the first of these: "6 is . . . divisible by 3." This tells you that the WHEN branches of a CASE block are mutually exclusive: Once one of the conditions for which you're testing is found to be true, *only* the statements following the corresponding THEN are executed, any remaining WHEN clauses are skipped, and program flow exits the CASE block immediately thereafter.

CAUTION   *Programmers used to working in languages such as PHP, Perl, JavaScript, and so on, should take special note that SQL has no statement analogous to* break *for CASE structures. Every WHEN branch of a CASE behaves as though it were terminated with a* break *(or, in SQL terms, a* LEAVE *statement). In other words, you can't "fall through" from one branch of a CASE block to the next one.*

Before we move on, you should also note that the conditions being tested in the WHEN clauses of this form of CASE don't have to involve the same variables. For example, consider a CASE block such as this one:

```
CASE
   WHEN x > 10 THEN output = output / 2;
   WHEN y < 5 THEN output = output + 10;
   WHEN z = 0 THEN output = -1;
END CASE;
```

This is perfectly legitimate and may in some instances prove to be useful, just so long as you bear in mind that (in this particular case) if x is greater than 10, then the values of y and z will never be tested.

Looping in Procedures

One major enhancement that stored procedures and stored functions provide to you in your SQL programming is that they give you the ability to execute code in loops. MySQL 5.0 supports three looping constructs: LOOP, REPEAT, and WHILE. They are largely equivalent, and which one you use depends on both the situation you're in and your own style or preferences. Each looping construct allows you to perform an action or set of actions a specified number of times, while a condition is true, or until a desired condition has been met. We'll examine these and provide you with some working examples in the next three sections of this chapter.

NOTE *While there is no FOR or FOREACH loop in MySQL procedures, controlling loops by means of a counter is not difficult to accomplish using any of the three looping constructs that are available, as you'll see from some of the examples in the following sections.*

LOOP, LEAVE, ITERATE

The most basic looping construct of the three offered in MySQL 5.0 and newer is LOOP, which, together with a set of labels, identifies a block of SQL code that is to be repeated one or more times. The labels must appear at both the beginning and end of the loop, and must match. A beginning label must be followed with a colon (:) and precedes the LOOP keyword; an ending label follows the END LOOP keywords but precedes the final semicolon (;) marking the end of the loop. A label can be any valid MySQL identifier.

TIP *A LEAVE statement (see the text that follows) won't function without a label. Therefore, you should label every LOOP construct that you use in a stored procedure or stored function. Labels aren't quite so necessary with REPEAT and WHILE (see the next two sections), but using them in longer procedures will help make your code easier to read and maintain.*

The syntax for a loop with a label is shown here:

```
label: LOOP
END LOOP label;
```

Once begun, a LOOP will repeat indefinitely until something happens to cause execution to pass out of it. In order for it to be useful, MySQL provides a statement for doing just that: the LEAVE statement:

```
LEAVE label;
```

If you're familiar with the break keyword in programming languages such as Java, Perl, C, or PHP, then you'll find that LEAVE works in much the same fashion; it terminates the loop at the point where LEAVE is encountered.

There's also a statement that causes execution to pass back to the beginning of a loop. This is the ITERATE statement, which, like LEAVE, also uses a label:

```
ITERATE label;
```

In this example, we create a stored function using LOOP, LEAVE, and ITERATE. This function, which we've named **loop_example**, is basically a reimplementation of the integer division (DIV) operator that became available in MySQL 4.1; it takes two integers as arguments, and returns the number of times that the first one will go into the second without regard to any fraction or remainder:

```
Command Prompt - mysql -h megalon -u root -p                          _ □ ×

mysql> CREATE FUNCTION loop_example(start INT, finish INT)
    -> RETURNS INT
    -> BEGIN
    ->   DECLARE counter INT DEFAULT 0;
    ->   DECLARE temp INT;
    ->
    ->   SET temp = finish;
    ->
    ->   myloop:
    ->     LOOP
    ->       SET temp = temp - start;
    ->       SET counter = counter + 1;
    ->
    ->       IF temp >= start
    ->         THEN ITERATE myloop;
    ->       END IF;
    ->
    ->       LEAVE myloop;
    ->     END LOOP myloop;
    ->
    ->   RETURN counter;
    -> END
    -> |
Query OK, 0 rows affected (0.01 sec)

mysql>
```

Here's the **loop_example** function in use:

```
Command Prompt - mysql -h megalon -u root -p                          _ □ ×

mysql> SELECT loop_example(2, 10)|
+---------------------+
| loop_example(2, 10) |
+---------------------+
|                   5 |
+---------------------+
1 row in set (0.00 sec)

mysql>
```

Let's look more closely at how the LOOP construct in this function works, by repeating the code for it with some comments:

```
myloop:    #  marks the beginning of the loop "myloop"
LOOP
  SET temp = temp - start;    #  perform subtraction
  SET counter = counter + 1;  #  increment counter

  IF temp >= start  #  is the new value greater than the input value?
    THEN ITERATE myloop;  #  if it is, go back to the "myloop" label
  END IF;

  LEAVE myloop;  #  (otherwise) break out of the loop
END LOOP myloop; #  marks the end of the loop "myloop"
```

We could also have written this loop as

```
myloop:
LOOP
  SET temp = temp - start;
  SET counter = counter + 1;

  IF temp < start
    THEN LEAVE myloop;
  END IF;
END LOOP myloop;
```

In this instance, the ITERATE wasn't really necessary; however, in more complex loops, you may want to return to the beginning of the loop from one of several different points, depending on the circumstances; ITERATE makes this possible.

REPEAT

REPEAT is another useful looping construct. It's somewhat easier to use in some circumstances than LOOP, because it has a terminating condition built into its syntax, as shown here:

```
[label:] REPEAT
statement-block
UNTIL condition
END REPEAT [label];
```

The block of statements appearing between the REPEAT and UNTIL keywords is executed repeatedly until the condition indicated by UNTIL is met. Here's an example of a stored procedure (named **repeat_sum**) that gets the sum of an integer and all positive integers less than itself using a REPEAT ... UNTIL loop:

```
Command Prompt - mysql -h megalon -u root -p

mysql> CREATE PROCEDURE repeat_sum
    -> (
    ->   IN val INT,
    ->   OUT output INT
    -> )
    -> BEGIN
    ->   DECLARE counter INT DEFAULT 0;
    ->
    ->   SET output = 0;
    ->
    ->   REPEAT
    ->     SET counter = counter + 1;
    ->     SET output = output + counter;
    ->   UNTIL counter = val
    ->   END REPEAT;
    -> END
    -> |
Query OK, 0 rows affected (0.01 sec)

mysql>
```

In this procedure, we start by declaring a counter equal to 0, then, each time we go through the REPEAT loop, we increment it, adding it to the output parameter **output**, and then checking to see if it's yet equal to the original **value**. When counter and value are equal, we exit the loop. We can test it as shown here:

```
Command Prompt - mysql -h megalon -u root -p                    _ |□| x|
mysql> CALL repeat_sum(10, @mysum)|
Query OK, 0 rows affected (0.00 sec)

mysql> SELECT @mysum|
+--------+
| @mysum |
+--------+
| 55     |
+--------+
1 row in set (0.00 sec)

mysql>
```

 CAUTION *When writing* REPEAT *loops, make sure that the condition following* UNTIL *will be met at some point. Otherwise you'll have an endless loop, which means you'll quite likely have to kill the thread and start over.*

WHILE

The WHILE loop in some ways can be regarded as the inverse of a REPEAT loop. With a REPEAT loop, statements are executed until some condition is met. In a WHILE loop, execution of the statement block following the DO keyword continues only so long as the specified condition is true.

Here's the formal syntax for WHILE:

```
[label:] WHILE condition DO
statement-block
END WHILE [label];
```

In the next example, we use a WHILE loop in a stored function to obtain the factorial of an integer:

```
Command Prompt - mysql -h megalon -u root -p                    _ □ X
mysql> CREATE FUNCTION factorial(value INT)
    -> RETURNS INT
    -> BEGIN
    ->   DECLARE temp INT;
    ->   DECLARE output INT DEFAULT 1;
    ->
    ->   SET temp = value;
    ->
    ->   WHILE temp > 1 DO
    ->     SET output = output * temp;
    ->     SET temp = temp - 1;
    ->   END WHILE;
    ->
    ->   RETURN output;
    -> END
    -> |
Query OK, 0 rows affected (0.00 sec)

mysql> SELECT factorial(3), factorial(5), factorial(10)|
+--------------+--------------+---------------+
| factorial(3) | factorial(5) | factorial(10) |
+--------------+--------------+---------------+
|            6 |          120 |       3628800 |
+--------------+--------------+---------------+
1 row in set (0.00 sec)

mysql> _
```

The factorial of an integer is defined as the product of that integer and all
the positive integers less than itself and greater than 1, so the factorial of 5 (often
written as 5!) is $5 \times 4 \times 3 \times 2 = 120$, as you can see from our test of the **factorial**
function above. 0! (zero factorial) is defined as 1 and the factorial of a negative
number is undefined. With these additional conditions in mind, you could write
a somewhat improved version of the stored function. This **better_factorial** function uses a CASE block to distinguish the cases where the input value is equal to
or less than zero, and to act accordingly as shown here:

```
CREATE FUNCTION better_factorial(value INT)
RETURNS INT
BEGIN
  DECLARE temp INT;
  DECLARE output INT DEFAULT 1;

  SET temp = value;
  CASE
    WHEN value < 0 THEN SET output = 0;
    WHEN value = 0 OR value = 1 THEN SET output = 1;
    ELSE
      WHILE temp > 1 DO
        SET output = output * temp;
        SET temp = temp - 1;
      END WHILE;
  END CASE;

  RETURN output;
END
```

This example also illustrates how you can nest multiple flow-control constructs inside one another within a single stored function or stored procedure.

Cursors

Stored procedures using SELECT INTO are somewhat limited in that they can't be used to retrieve more than one row from a table in a single query, because you can't store more than one value in a single variable.

A cursor can be thought of as an entity that points a SELECT statement at a particular row of a table. In MySQL 5.0, cursors are fairly simple. They're read-only, forward-only, meaning that they can be used only for the following:

- To read data from a table row, but not update it or insert new rows into the table.

- To move through the rows of a table in the order returned by MySQL; they can't be programmed to skip rows, iterate through rows in reverse order, and so on.

Cursors are expected to be enhanced in MySQL 5.1 and subsequent versions to include the capabilities excluded here (and possibly others). However, even with the limited implementation available in MySQL 5.0, they make it possible using a stored procedure to fetch query results into another table where they can be processed further.

Cursor Statements: Syntax

In order to create and use cursors in MySQL 5.0, we need to make use of the commands DECLARE, OPEN, FETCH, and CLOSE. Let's look at each of these in turn, and then in the next section, we'll put them together in a working example.

First, we must declare a cursor in a manner similar to that in which we declare a local variable for a stored procedure, using the DECLARE CURSOR command, whose syntax is

```
DECLARE name CURSOR FOR statement;
```

In this command, *name* stands for the name of the cursor and *statement* for a SELECT statement. For instance, one of the cursor declaration statements you'll see in the next section is

```
DECLARE prodrecord CURSOR FOR SELECT name, price FROM products;
```

In ordinary language, this statement says, "The cursor named **prodrecord** will be used to work with rows returned by the query `SELECT name, price FROM products;`." A cursor can be declared only once, and used with only one query in any given procedure. It's possible and frequently desirable to declare and use multiple cursors in a single procedure, but each cursor must be uniquely named. The cursor name must follow the rules for MySQL identifiers (see Chapter 1), and all `DECLARE CURSOR` statements must come at the beginning of the body of a stored procedure, just as with `DECLARE` statements used to create local variables.

Before we can actually begin using the cursor, it must be opened. The `OPEN` command tells MySQL to prepare the cursor for use with the result set of the query to which it is bound by the `DECLARE CURSOR` statement. The syntax for the `OPEN` command is simply

```
OPEN cursor-name;
```

where `cursor-name` is the name of the cursor. The cursor must previously have been declared before it can be opened.

In order to point this cursor to successive rows in the result set, we use the `FETCH` command, shown here:

```
FETCH cursor-name INTO var1[, var2[, var3[, ...]]];
```

This command tells MySQL to store the column values for the next row of the result set into one or more variables for subsequent use in the stored procedure. There must be as many variables as there are columns in the result set, and the variables must previously have been declared using `DECLARE`. `FETCH` is generally only useful if used in some sort of a loop; and we'll see in the next section how this is done, and how to tell when there are no more rows left to retrieve.

Finally, when you're finished with the cursor, you need to close it using the `CLOSE` command as shown here. Once again, `cursor-name` is the name of the cursor:

```
CLOSE cursor-name;
```

MySQL will automatically close the cursor upon completion of the stored procedure in which the cursor was declared, but it's always good practice to do so explicitly, and free up the resources used by the cursor as soon as they're no longer needed.

NOTE   *A cursor is actually a special SQL datatype that corresponds to a row from a result set.*

There's one other matter we need to take care of before we can proceed to a
working example. When processing a SELECT query that was entered from the
command line, MySQL just gives us the entire result set in one go, and, as you
saw in Chapter 7, when you're writing MySQL applications in a language such as
PHP or Python, you're provided with a means to tell when you've reached the
end of the result set. For example, in PHP 5 using ext/mysqli, you'll use a while
loop with one of the fetch_*() methods of the mysqli class, which conveniently
returns a Boolean **FALSE** when you've reached the end, like so:

```php
<?php
    while($row = $result->fetch_object())
    {
      // display the rows
      printf("<tr>\n  <td align=\"center\">%s</td>\n
              <td>%s</td>\n  <td>%std>\n</tr>",
              $row->empid, $row->firstname, $row->lastname);
    }
?>
```

As with a programming language's MySQL API, we obtain a result set by
retrieving successive rows of it, one at a time, inside a loop (such as WHILE ... DO
or REPEAT ... UNTIL). However, when you're working with cursors inside a stored
procedure and you reach the end, you're likely to see something like this:

Unlike the case with a high-level API such as PHP 5's ext/mysqli or Python's
MySQLdb, there's no handy built-in function or method that behaves in the desired
fashion. Instead, you must do a bit of error handling. This is accomplished by
declaring an error handler in the procedure using the DECLARE HANDLER command.
Here's a simplified version of its syntax:

```
DECLARE [CONTINUE | EXIT] HANDLER FOR condition statement;
```

This statement tells MySQL what to do in the event that an error or warning
is generated while executing a stored procedure or stored function. In MySQL 5.0,

you have two choices: `CONTINUE` or `EXIT` (which is the default). By using `CONTINUE`, you can tell MySQL to execute the *statement* that follows, which can be any statement that's valid inside a stored procedure. Using `EXIT` will cause MySQL to terminate execution of the stored procedure at the point where the error is encountered.

NOTE *In future versions of MySQL beyond 5.0, an* `UNDO` *option is also expected to be supported in addition to* `CONTINUE` *and* `EXIT`. *This will allow you to undo the last action performed in the stored procedure or stored function, that is, to undo the action that gave rise to the error or warning.*

The *condition* to be handled can be expressed in a number of ways including MySQL error codes and `SQLSTATE` values for error conditions. (When signaling an error, MySQL 5.0 and above will provide both sorts of error codes, with the MySQL error code first, followed by the `SQLSTATE` error code in parentheses.) It is possible to set a single handler for multiple conditions in one `DECLARE HANDLER` statement by separating them with commas.

TIP *You can find an up-to-date listing of MySQL and* `SQLSTATE` *error codes supported by MySQL in the online version of the MySQL Manual at* `http://dev.mysql.com/doc/mysql/en/Error-handling.html`.

In the next section, we'll put all of this together in a simple working example.

Cursor Example

In this example we'll use a cursor within a stored procedure named **cursor1** in order to copy data from certain records found in one table (**products**) into a different table (**curtest**). We'll be referring once again to the **products** table that we've used throughout this chapter. Let's begin by examining the `CREATE PROCEDURE` statement:

```
Command Prompt - mysql -h megalon -u root -p                          _ □ ×
mysql> CREATE PROCEDURE cursor1()
    -> BEGIN
    -> DECLARE prodrecord
    ->   CURSOR FOR
    ->     SELECT name, price
    ->     FROM products
    ->     ORDER BY name;
    ->
    -> DECLARE done INT DEFAULT 0;
    -> DECLARE CONTINUE HANDLER FOR SQLSTATE '02000' SET done = 1;
    ->
    -> DECLARE prodname VARCHAR(30);
    -> DECLARE prodprice DECIMAL(6, 2);
    ->
    -> CREATE TABLE curtest(
    ->    name VARCHAR(30),
    ->    price DECIMAL(6, 2)
    -> );
    ->
    -> OPEN prodrecord;
    ->
    -> WHILE NOT done DO
    ->   FETCH prodrecord INTO prodname, prodprice;
    ->
    ->   IF prodprice > 50.00 THEN
    ->     INSERT INTO curtest
    ->     VALUES (prodname, prodprice);
    ->   END IF;
    -> END WHILE;
    ->
    -> CLOSE prodrecord;
    ->
    -> END
    -> |
Query OK, 0 rows affected (0.00 sec)

mysql>
```

(Once again, we've already used the DELIMITER command to set the pipe character as the statement delimiter.)

This procedure has no input or output parameters. It does have a number of variable and other declarations. Let's repeat those here with some comments. First of all, we declare the cursor that we'll use to fetch records from the **products** table:

```
DECLARE prodrecord
  CURSOR FOR
    SELECT name, price
    FROM products
    ORDER BY name;
```

This cursor is named **prodrecord**, and we indicate in the declaration's FOR clause that it will be used for a query that selects the **name** and **price** columns for all rows in the **products** table, and that the results of this query will be ordered by the **name** column. It's important that we get the declaration right, because this cursor can't be used for any other query, not even one that's only slightly different from this one. In other words, if we change the query as it's actually used in the procedure, then we must change the query in the cursor declaration so that it matches it exactly.

Next, we declare an integer local variable named **done**, which we'll use as a flag to let us know when the procedure has finished executing. We set its default value to 0 (**FALSE**). Then we declare a CONTINUE handler for SQLSTATE '02000', which, as you saw in the last section, is the SQLSTATE error that results when

MySQL can't find any more records from a table. (Note that the error code needs to be set off in single quotation marks.) The handler tells MySQL that when this condition is encountered, it should set the value of **done** to 1 (**TRUE**) and then continue execution of the procedure.

```
DECLARE done INT DEFAULT 0;
DECLARE CONTINUE HANDLER FOR SQLSTATE '02000' SET done = 1;
```

For the error-handler declaration we could also have used this:

```
DECLARE CONTINUE HANDLER FOR NOT FOUND SET done = 1;
```

Before getting into the procedure itself, we declare two additional variables, which we'll use for temporary storage of column values from the rows to be fetched from the **products** table.

```
DECLARE prodname VARCHAR(30);
DECLARE prodprice DECIMAL(6, 2);
```

Notice that these are the same datatypes as those used in the original **products** table for the **name** and **price** columns. They're also the same types as the **name** and **price** columns in the table named **curtest**, which we define next using a normal CREATE TABLE statement:

```
CREATE TABLE curtest(
  name VARCHAR(30),
  price DECIMAL(6, 2)
);
```

It isn't necessary for you to use the same column names in both tables. We've done so here only as a matter of convenience. However, it *is* necessary that you use compatible datatypes for any variables or table columns that will be holding the same data. For example, if we used INT for either the **prodprice** local variable or the **price** column in the new **curtest** table that we're storing the data in, we'd be very likely to truncate the values being retrieved from the **price** column of the **products** table.

Now we open the **prodrecord** cursor:

```
OPEN prodrecord;
```

The OPEN statement, as noted previously, prepares the cursor to receive rows returned by a FETCH operation. Trying to use a cursor prior to opening it will result in a fatal error, and the procedure will not execute past the point where this occurs—unless, of course, you've prepared for this eventuality by having declared the proper handler beforehand.

The remainder of this procedure consists of a WHILE loop in which we fetch successive records from **products** and store the column values in the variables **prodname** and **prodprice**. This is accomplished for each row selected by means of a single FETCH ... INTO statement. Next we test the value of **prodprice** to see if it's greater than 50.00; if it is, then we store both column values in **curtest** using an INSERT command:

```
WHILE NOT done DO
    FETCH prodrecord INTO prodname, prodprice;

    IF prodprice > 50.00 THEN
        INSERT INTO curtest
        VALUES (prodname, prodprice);
    END IF;
END WHILE;
```

The statements inside the WHILE loop continue to execute so long as the value of **done** is **FALSE** (0). After the last row in the result set matching the query is retrieved, MySQL will return an SQLSTATE error condition (error code 02000) the next time that an attempt is made to fetch a row from that result set. When this occurs, the handler we declared previously will set the value of **done** to 1 and execution will continue: Here, the next point in program flow is the beginning of the WHILE loop, where **done** is tested again. Its value is now found to be **TRUE**, so the condition NOT done evaluates to **FALSE**, and the procedure exits the loop. We're not going to use the **prodrecord** cursor anymore, so as a matter of good housekeeping we close the cursor with the statement

```
CLOSE prodrecord;
```

We can now run **cursor1** using a CALL command, and then view the result by selecting all data from the **curtest** table, as shown here:

Let's test this result by comparing it with the data that's still in the **products** table:

```
Command Prompt - mysql -h megalon -u root -p                    _ □ ×
mysql> SELECT name, price FROM products
    -> WHERE price > 50.00|
+-----------------------------+---------+
| name                        | price   |
+-----------------------------+---------+
| Personal Breathalyser       | 68.95   |
| Bass Blaster Fishing Mortar | 79.95   |
+-----------------------------+---------+
2 rows in set (0.01 sec)

mysql>
```

You're not limited to inserting data into just one table. For example, you could easily rewrite the WHILE loop in this example as something like this:

```
WHILE NOT done DO
  FETCH prodrecord INTO prodname, prodprice;

  IF prodprice > 50.00 THEN
    INSERT INTO curtest
    VALUES (prodname, prodprice);
  ELSE
    INSERT INTO curtest2
    VALUES (prodname.prodprice)
  END IF;

END WHILE;
```

Or even as this:

```
WHILE NOT done DO
  FETCH prodrecord INTO prodname, prodprice;

  CASE
    WHEN prodprice > 50.00 THEN
      INSERT INTO curtest
      VALUES (prodname, prodprice);
    WHEN prodprice > 25.00 THEN
      INSERT INTO curtest2
      VALUES (prodname, prodprice);
    ELSE
      INSERT INTO curtest3
      VALUES (prodname.prodprice)
  END CASE;

END WHILE;
```

Assuming that the tables **curtest2** and **curtest3** exist—because either they're already present in the database or you've created them as part of the stored procedure—the first of these two loops will cause data for all products costing more than 50 dollars to be inserted into **curtest** and that for all products costing 50 dollars or less to be inserted into **curtest2**. The second loop would cause data for all products costing more than 50 dollars to be inserted into **curtest**, data for products costing more than 25 but less than or equal to 50 dollars to be inserted into **curtest2**, and data for products costing 25 dollars or less into **curtest3**. And so on: You can use any logical or other operators found in MySQL as well as any flow-control or looping constructs supported in MySQL stored procedures in testing or manipulating the data that you've extracted from table rows retrieved using FETCH.

You can also use most of the variations on CREATE TABLE supported by MySQL, such as CREATE TABLE IF NOT EXISTS and CREATE TEMPORARY TABLE, in a stored procedure.

Taking Derived Tables to the Next Level—Views

Unnamed views became possible in MySQL 4.1 with the inclusion of subselects that allow for the use of derived tables. Beginning with version 5.0.1, MySQL includes support for named views, usually referred to simply as "views." Before we demonstrate how these are implemented in MySQL, let's talk first a little bit about exactly what views are and how they will prove useful to MySQL database administrators and developers when it's possible to deploy MySQL 5.0 in a production setting.

Views are also sometimes known as *virtual tables*, because they're defined in terms of (other) tables through the use of queries. (We'll see exactly how a view is defined in the upcoming "Syntax—Creating, Altering, and Dropping Views" section.) A view can be thought of as a "window" into a table, or perhaps a viewport that shows us a selected portion of a table at any given time, not unlike what's shown in Figure 8-1.

However, a view is not merely a convenient container for a subset of records from a table. For one thing, a view is a "live" or dynamic snapshot of table data; when the data in the underlying table changes, so does that in the view. For another, we can construct views that aren't merely subsets of table data; for example, we can perform calculations on the data, or obtain aggregate information for analysis purposes.

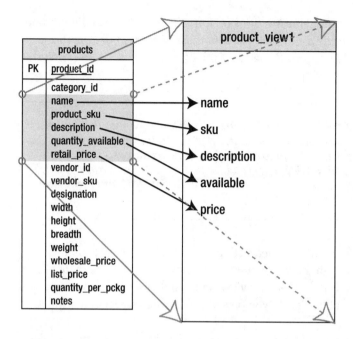

Figure 8-1. A view can be thought of as a "window" into a table.

Finally, in some cases, a view can be active as well as passive—in other words, when the view is updated, so is the data in the table upon which the view is based. It's possible for this to happen so long as the SELECT statement used in defining the view meets the following conditions:

- Data is selected from one and only one table (in other words, you can't perform an update on a view that was defined using a join).

- The statement is not a SELECT DISTINCT query.

- The statement does not contain any GROUP BY or HAVING clauses, and does not use any aggregate functions.

- No UNION operators are used in the query.

 CAUTION *A bug in MySQL 5.0.1 prevents the use of UNION queries in view definitions. According to* bugs.mysql.com, *this will be fixed in the next release.*

There are some additional restrictions on how views may be used to update data in underlying tables. We'll discuss some of these shortly, in the "Syntax— Creating, Altering, and Dropping Views" section, which follows the one you're reading right now.

NOTE *If the definition of the underlying table changes, the change may not carry over to views derived from that table. For example, if we add a new column to a table that serves as the basis for a view, the new column does not get added to the view. This is true not only of MySQL (at least in version 5.0.1), but also with many other databases, including Oracle.*

Conversely, if we're not concerned with using views to update data, then there are few restrictions on how they may be defined. You can use practically any legal SELECT query as the basis for a view, and you're not confined to selecting data from a single table. Nor do you necessarily have to select data from any tables at all.

It's also quite possible to select data from one view in defining another view; generally this isn't a recommended practice, but it can be and is done with databases that support views, the most notable exception to this being PostgreSQL. (MySQL *does* support nested views, as we'll see shortly.) The only major prohibition in the ANSI standard is that SELECT statements used to define views may not contain an ORDER BY clause, but, we'll see, MySQL ignores this restriction.

CAUTION *Don't confuse the terms "virtual tables" and "derived tables." Both are defined using queries (subqueries in the case of derived tables) and both depend upon database tables for their existence. However, a derived table has no name and is transitory; it exists only for the lifetime of a query, and there is no way to recall it once the query has been completed, save by rerunning the query. A virtual table (or view) is a named entity that, once created, persists until it's dropped, and that can be accessed at any time following its creation.*

Syntax—Creating, Altering, and Dropping Views

As we've already mentioned, a view is based on a SELECT query, and this query usually makes up most of the view's definition. To define a new view, we use the CREATE VIEW statement, whose standard syntax is shown here. While most databases offer extensions to it, nearly all of them that feature views support the basic form shown here. As you can see, it's relatively straightforward and shouldn't be too difficult for you to understand just by looking at it:

```
CREATE [OR REPLACE] VIEW view (columns) AS
select-query
(WITH CHECK OPTION);
```

The optional OR REPLACE clause following the CREATE keyword is used to tell MySQL to re-create the view even if it already exists. Otherwise you'll get an error if you try to create a view with the same name as an existing one.

In the preceding definition, *view* is the name of the view, which is covered by the same rules that govern other MySQL identifiers. This may be followed optionally by a list of *columns*—note that these are simply column names, as the types and sizes of the columns are already defined either in the table from which they're being retrieved or in the SELECT statement. Next comes the AS keyword, which marks the beginning of the *select-query* used to obtain the data that will serve as the view's contents.

The optional WITH CHECK OPTION clause following the query is defined in the SQL standard for use in creating a view that permits updates of its underlying table. (Recall that such a view may refer to only one table, as explained in the previous section.) In MySQL, this option doesn't do anything; it is simply ignored by the command parser.

In addition to CREATE OR REPLACE VIEW, MySQL allows you to update an existing view with an ALTER VIEW command, although this isn't part of the SQL standard. (Oracle and SQL Server also support this command.) MySQL's ALTER VIEW replaces the SELECT query currently used in defining the view with a new query. The syntax is as shown here:

```
ALTER VIEW view (columns) AS
new-select-query
(WITH CHECK OPTION);
```

As is the case with CREATE VIEW, the WITH CHECK OPTION clause is ignored in an ALTER VIEW; it is permitted for compatibility with other databases and the SQL standard but doesn't actually do anything in MySQL.

In order to retrieve the query that was used to define a view, we use a new variation on the SHOW CREATE command, as shown here:

```
SHOW CREATE VIEW view;
```

Dropping a view is also very simple:

```
DROP VIEW view;
```

The DROP VIEW statement is supported by all major databases that implement views. *view* stands for the name of the view to be dropped.

These few statements are all that are required to work with views. We'll provide some demonstrations showing how to use them in the next section.

Examples

Because views look and act very much like tables do, they allow us to abstract complex queries and present users or application writers with the sets of data they want or need in a manner that appears direct to them while allowing us to preserve a highly normalized database schema. Let's create and use some views employing MySQL 5.0.1 or newer to illustrate this. For our first few examples, we'll once again use the **world** database available from the MySQL AB web site, which we also employed in some of the programming examples in Chapter 7. You can refer back to that chapter if you need to see once again how the tables are defined.

Here's a fairly basic example in which we create a view based on the **City** table. This view, which we've named **big_cities**, contains data only for those cities with a population in excess of 7,500,000, as shown here:

```
Command Prompt - mysql -h megalon -u root -p

mysql> CREATE VIEW big_cities AS
    -> SELECT * FROM City
    -> WHERE Population > 7500000;
Query OK, 0 rows affected (0.00 sec)

mysql>
```

Once we've created the view, we can select data from it just as we would a table. Since we used SELECT * to create **big_cities**, this view has the same columns, with the same names and datatypes, as in the original table. We can use any sort of SELECT query to retrieve data from this view that would be legal to use with the equivalent table. For example, we can select just a couple of the columns, and use an ORDER BY clause to sort the result. We show two examples here:

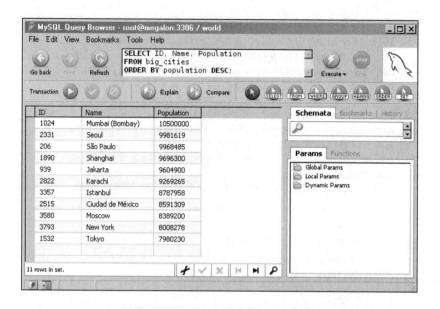

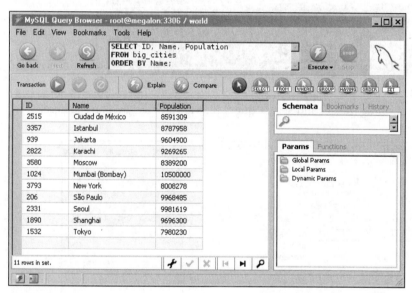

So far, you might say, we've not really accomplished anything that we couldn't have done using a CREATE SELECT statement such as this one:

```
CREATE TABLE big_cities
  SELECT * FROM City
  WHERE Population > 7500000;
```

NOTE *For many of the illustrations in this section showing* SELECT *query output, we're using the MySQL Query Browser, which MySQL AB began developing in early 2004. (The version used for this book was 1.0.7-beta.) This graphical tool provides a GUI interface (comparable in many ways to SQL Server's Query Analyzer) for testing and viewing the results of queries and stored procedures, as well as for administering tables. This application also provides some nice "extras" such as syntax highlighting and quick access to documentation on MySQL functions. You can download source code and compiled binaries for Linux and win32 platforms from* http://dev.mysql.com/downloads/query-browser/index.html.

However, as we said earlier, a view isn't just a static "slice" of a table—it's a dynamic subset of the table that updates in real time. This can be demonstrated by altering a row in the base table like this:

```
mysql> UPDATE City
    -> SET Name = 'Mexico City'
    -> WHERE Name = 'Ciudad de México';
Query OK, 1 row affected (0.02 sec)
Rows matched: 1  Changed: 1  Warnings: 0

mysql>
```

and then running the second SELECT query on the view, as you can see here:

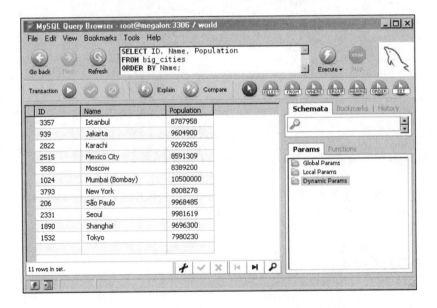

We also told you earlier that this dynamism isn't always limited to going in one direction. Let's prove this right now by updating the view and then seeing what happens when we perform a SELECT query on the base table. First we'll select some data from **City**:

```
mysql> SELECT ID, Name, Population
    -> FROM City
    -> WHERE Population > 7500000
    -> ORDER BY Name;
+------+----------------+------------+
| ID   | Name           | Population |
+------+----------------+------------+
| 3357 | Istanbul       |   8787958  |
|  939 | Jakarta        |   9604900  |
| 2822 | Karachi        |   9269265  |
| 2515 | Mexico City    |   8591309  |
| 3580 | Moscow         |   8389200  |
| 1024 | Mumbai (Bombay)|  10500000  |
| 3793 | New York       |   8008278  |
|  206 | Sao Paulo      |   9968485  |
| 2331 | Seoul          |   9981619  |
| 1890 | Shanghai       |   9696300  |
| 1532 | Tokyo          |   7980230  |
+------+----------------+------------+
11 rows in set (0.02 sec)

mysql>
```

Now we'll update the view using the command line in the MySQL Monitor:

```
mysql> UPDATE big_cities
    -> SET Name = 'Bombay'
    -> WHERE Name LIKE 'Mumbai%';
Query OK, 1 row affected (0.05 sec)
Rows matched: 1  Changed: 1  Warnings: 0

mysql>
```

When we run the SELECT again, we can see that the base table has indeed been updated:

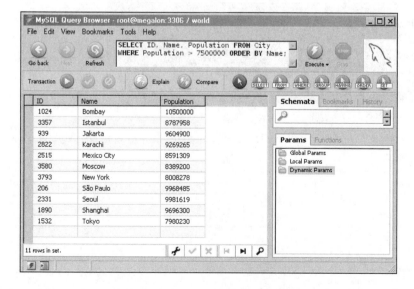

Before we continue, let's pause to answer a question that you're likely to be asking by now: *How do I list the views that I've created?* If you're thinking that you'd use a SHOW VIEWS command, that's a good guess, but the way that this is done in MySQL is through the use of a SHOW TABLES query. Beginning with MySQL 5.0.1, the output of SHOW TABLES contains two columns rather than one as in earlier versions:

```
Command Prompt - mysql -h megalon -u root -p                          _ □ x

mysql> SHOW TABLES FROM world;
+-----------------+------------+
| Tables_in_world | table_type |
+-----------------+------------+
| big_cities      | VIEW       |
| city            | BASE TABLE |
| country         | BASE TABLE |
| countrylanguage | BASE TABLE |
+-----------------+------------+
4 rows in set (0.04 sec)

mysql>
```

Now let's create a new view based on the **City** table. The data in this view is intended for direct display to end users (perhaps some young geography students) who don't really need to see the city ID, so you should probably just omit that from the definition for the new view. The data will also be more user-friendly if it shows the full names of the countries in which the world's largest cities are located, rather than the three-letter codes from the **City** table. To accomplish these goals, you'll need to join the **CountryCode** column in **City** on the **Code** column in the **Country** table so that you can obtain the corresponding value from the **Country.Name** column. However, **City** also has a **Name** column. To help avoid confusion, you can employ a list of column names following the name of the view in the CREATE VIEW statement. Putting this all together, we might arrive at a view definition that looks something like this:

```
Command Prompt - mysql -h megalon -u root -p                          _ □ x

mysql> CREATE VIEW big_cities_students (city, country, inhabitants)
    ->   AS
    ->     SELECT ci.Name, co.Name, ci.Population
    ->     FROM City ci
    ->     JOIN Country co
    ->     ON(co.Code = ci.CountryCode)
    ->     WHERE ci.Population > 5000000;
Query OK, 0 rows affected (0.03 sec)

mysql>
```

Let's see what happens when we try selecting from this view in the MySQL Query Browser:

Notice that because this view is defined in terms of a join, you can't update it directly. Here's what happens when you try:

However, you can update either or both of the base tables of the view—
City and **Country**—and any matching rows in **big_cities_students** will also be updated.

The ALTER VIEW command allows you to change the definition of an existing view, as previously discussed. We use this command here to modify the **big_cities_students** view in order to include a larger subset of data from the **City** table:

```
Command Prompt - mysql -h megalon -u root -p                          _ □ ×

mysql> ALTER VIEW big_cities_students (city, country, inhabitants)
    ->    AS
    ->       SELECT ci.Name, co.Name, ci.Population
    ->       FROM City ci
    ->       JOIN Country co
    ->       ON(co.Code = ci.CountryCode)
    ->       WHERE ci.Population > 1000000;
Query OK, 0 rows affected (0.02 sec)

mysql> SELECT COUNT(*) FROM big_cities_students;
+----------+
| COUNT(*) |
+----------+
|      237 |
+----------+
1 row in set (0.07 sec)

mysql>
```

As you can see from the result of the COUNT() query, we've increased the number of cities in this view from 24 to 237.

We could have accomplished the same thing by using

```
CREATE OR REPLACE VIEW big_cities_students (city, country, inhabitants)
  AS
    SELECT ci.Name, co.Name, ci.Population
    FROM City ci
    JOIN Country co
    ON(co.Code = ci.CountryCode)
    WHERE ci.Population > 1000000
    ORDER BY Name;
```

Both of these methods are really just shorthand for DROP VIEW big_cities; followed by CREATE VIEW big_cities AS...;.

Now that we've explored the mechanics of views in MySQL 5.0.1, we'll talk about some of the advantages that views offer MySQL database administrators and developers in the following section. We'll also address some security and related concerns.

Benefits

At least some of the advantages of using views should be apparent. For instance, suppose you have a user who is interested in seeing which product categories have the most products and by which departments these products are sold. Without bogging down the discussion with an additional schema at this point, let's just suppose that you can create a view fulfilling these requirements as follows:

```
CREATE VIEW product_view (catid, catname, catcount, deptname) AS
SELECT c1.cid, c2.name, c1.ct, d.name AS category
FROM
    ( SELECT
```

```
            category_id AS cid,
            department.id AS did,
            COUNT(category_id) AS ct
        FROM products
        GROUP BY category_id
    ) AS c1
JOIN categories c2
ON c1.cid = c2.id
JOIN departments d
ON d.id = c2.department_id
WHERE c1.ct > 1
GROUP BY d.id;
```

Once this is done, your user can obtain the current listing by running a simple SELECT query on the view, like so:

```
SELECT * FROM product_view;
```

The view acts in all respects like any other table, except that your user does not need to worry about doing a join on three tables in order to obtain the data that he or she actually wants to see. Your user can order or filter the rows of this view:

```
SELECT * FROM product_view ORDER BY deptname, catname;
```

Or even use it in a join on another table:

```
SELECT DISTINCT(p.deptname), CONCAT(m.firstname, ' ', m.lastname) AS manager
FROM product_view p
JOIN departments d
ON p.deptname = d.deptname
JOIN managers m
ON d.manager_id = managers.id
ORDER BY m.lastname ASC;
```

Of course, this join could very likely be done more efficiently by writing a new query against the original tables involved rather than using the view, and if the data were needed often enough in this form, you might want to define a new view that does so. If you're in doubt, you can always compare the two methods using the EXPLAIN command to see how much of an efficiency boost you would gain from doing so.

Security and privacy protection are another issue that views can help to address. Let's look at a scenario involving employee records. Suppose we want to build an address book application for our company intranet allowing employees to obtain name, department, and internal contact information for other employees, but not giving access to confidential data such as salary history or home address and phone. We could define a view such as

```
CREATE VIEW address_book_view (fname, laname, dept, title, email, ext) AS
SELECT e.firstname, e.lastname, d.name, j.jobtitle, e.email, e.workphone
FROM jobs j
JOIN employees e
ON e.job_id = j.id
JOIN departments d
ON e.department_id = d.id;
```

The address book application could then query this view as desired:

```
#  List of mail room employees
SELECT * FROM address_book_view WHERE deptname = 'Mail Room';
#  List all receptionists
SELECT * FROM address_book_view WHERE title LIKE '%receptionist%';
#  Get the number of receptionists in each department
SELECT deptname, COUNT(deptname) AS num
  FROM address_book_view
  WHERE title LIKE '%receptionist%'
  GROUP BY deptname;
# etc., etc. ...
```

These queries can include whatever sorting, filtering, and grouping criteria that are needed.

You don't have to worry about address book users obtaining confidential information like home telephone numbers, rates of pay, marital status, and so on, because that data is never available to them—or even to the programmers writing the address book application.

On the other hand, for the payroll department, a view such as this one would be more applicable:

```
CREATE VIEW payroll_view
  (fname, minitial, lname, addr1, addr2, city, state, postcode, title, rate,
    mstatus, numdependents, taxid)
AS
  SELECT e.firstname, e.lastname, e.address1, e.address2, e.city, e.state,
    e.postcode, j.jobtitle, j.rate, e.mstatus, e.numdependents, e.taxid
  FROM employees e
  JOIN jobs j
  ON e.job_id = j.id
  WHERE e.startdate <= NOW()
    AND e.enddate >= DATE_SUB(NOW(), INTERVAL 30 DAY);
```

By now, you're probably getting the idea, but there's more to keeping data secure than this. Not only do we sometimes need to prevent unauthorized parties from reading certain types of information, but we must also be able to protect data from being overwritten when it shouldn't be. If you look back for a moment at the views that we created in the previous section, you'll recall that it's sometimes possible to update a view and thus update the data in the base table from which it derives. However, there are often times when we don't want this to happen. Some databases, like Oracle, allow you to deal with this type of situation by declaring a view to be read-only. MySQL doesn't afford this option.

So how do we accomplish this task? The answer lies in leveraging the MySQL privileges system, which applies to views in much the same way as it does to tables. For instance, we can use table-level permissions in such a way that users may access views but not their base tables. Still referring to the examples in the previous section, suppose we want to create a user named **student** who can access either of the **big_cities** or **big_cities_students** views, but not any of the base tables in the world database. You can create such a user using standard GRANT commands, as shown here:

```
mysql> GRANT SELECT ON world.big_cities_students to 'student'@'%'
    -> IDENTIFIED BY 'geography';
Query OK, 0 rows affected (0.03 sec)

mysql> GRANT SELECT ON world.big_cities to 'student'@'%'
    -> ;
Query OK, 0 rows affected (0.00 sec)

mysql>
```

This user then logs in using the MySQL Monitor, and runs a SELECT query on **big_cities**. However, when the user tries to run an UPDATE on this table, he or she gets an access denied error from MySQL:

```
C:\>mysql -h megalon -u student -p
Enter password: *********
Welcome to the MySQL monitor.  Commands end with ; or \g.
Your MySQL connection id is 249 to server version: 5.0.1-alpha-nt-max-log

Type 'help;' or '\h' for help. Type '\c' to clear the buffer.

mysql> use world;
Database changed
mysql> SELECT * FROM big_cities ORDER BY Name LIMIT 5;
+------+-------------+-------------+------------------+------------+
| ID   | Name        | CountryCode | District         | Population |
+------+-------------+-------------+------------------+------------+
| 1024 | Bombay      | IND         | Maharashtra      |   10500000 |
| 3357 | Istanbul    | TUR         | Istanbul         |    8787958 |
|  939 | Jakarta     | IDN         | Jakarta Raya     |    9604900 |
| 2822 | Karachi     | PAK         | Sindh            |    9269265 |
| 2515 | Mexico City | MEX         | Distrito Federal |    8591309 |
+------+-------------+-------------+------------------+------------+
5 rows in set (0.02 sec)

mysql> UPDATE big_cities
    -> SET Name = 'Mumbai' WHERE Name = 'Bombay';
ERROR 1142 (42000): update command denied to user 'student'@'GOJIRA' for ta
ble 'big_cities'
mysql>
```

When this user attempts to list all the tables and views in the **world** database, the user sees only those views for which he or she has been granted privileges on, just as with regular tables:

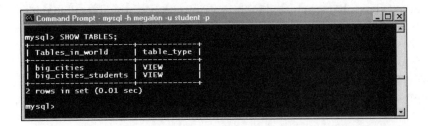

Then there is the question of users accessing information about how views are defined. First of all, you can rest assured that users can't find out what's in base tables upon which they have no privileges by running a SHOW CREATE VIEW, as you can see here:

```
Command Prompt - mysql -h megalon -u student -p
mysql> SHOW CREATE VIEW big_cities;
ERROR 1344 (HY000): EXPLAIN/SHOW can not be issued; lacking privileges for
underlying table
mysql> SHOW CREATE VIEW big_cities_students;
ERROR 1344 (HY000): EXPLAIN/SHOW can not be issued; lacking privileges for
underlying table
mysql>
```

Users also cannot create views without restriction even on views (or tables) on which they have SELECT privileges, as shown here:

```
Command Prompt - mysql -h megalon -u student -p
mysql> CREATE VIEW my_big_cities (city, pop) AS
    -> SELECT Name, Population FROM big_cities;
ERROR 1142 (42000): create view command denied to user 'student'@'GOJIRA' f
or table 'my_big_cities'
mysql>
```

Beginning with MySQL 5.0.1, two new privilege types are introduced: the CREATE VIEW and SHOW CREATE VIEW privileges. Users must have the first of these privileges in order to create views and the second in order to see how existing views were created. In addition, users must have the proper privileges on the tables or views that they wish to use as the basis for new views.

Columns corresponding to these two privileges, named **Create_view_priv** and **Show_view_priv**, are added to the **db**, **host**, and **user** tables of the **mysql** database to accommodate these. Here's the output of a SHOW CREATE TABLE statement showing how these columns are defined in the updated **user** table:

```
Command Prompt - mysql -h megalon -u root -p                          _ □ ×
mysql> SHOW CREATE TABLE user\G
*************************** 1. row ***************************
         Table: user
Create Table: CREATE TABLE `user` (
  `Host` varchar(60) NOT NULL default '',
  `User` varchar(16) NOT NULL default '',
  `password` varchar(45) NOT NULL default '',
  `Select_priv` enum('N','Y') NOT NULL default 'N',
  `Insert_priv` enum('N','Y') NOT NULL default 'N',
  `Update_priv` enum('N','Y') NOT NULL default 'N',
  `Delete_priv` enum('N','Y') NOT NULL default 'N',
  `Create_priv` enum('N','Y') NOT NULL default 'N',
  `Drop_priv` enum('N','Y') NOT NULL default 'N',
  `Reload_priv` enum('N','Y') NOT NULL default 'N',
  `Shutdown_priv` enum('N','Y') NOT NULL default 'N',
  `Process_priv` enum('N','Y') NOT NULL default 'N',
  `File_priv` enum('N','Y') NOT NULL default 'N',
  `Grant_priv` enum('N','Y') NOT NULL default 'N',
  `References_priv` enum('N','Y') NOT NULL default 'N',
  `Index_priv` enum('N','Y') NOT NULL default 'N',
  `Alter_priv` enum('N','Y') NOT NULL default 'N',
  `Show_db_priv` enum('N','Y') NOT NULL default 'N',
  `Super_priv` enum('N','Y') NOT NULL default 'N',
  `Create_tmp_table_priv` enum('N','Y') NOT NULL default 'N',
  `Lock_tables_priv` enum('N','Y') NOT NULL default 'N',
  `Execute_priv` enum('N','Y') NOT NULL default 'N',
  `Repl_slave_priv` enum('N','Y') NOT NULL default 'N',
  `Repl_client_priv` enum('N','Y') NOT NULL default 'N',
  `Create_view_priv` enum('N','Y') NOT NULL default 'N',
  `Show_view_priv` enum('N','Y') NOT NULL default 'N',
  `ssl_type` enum('','ANY','X509','SPECIFIED') NOT NULL default '',
  `ssl_cipher` text NOT NULL,
  `x509_issuer` text NOT NULL,
  `x509_subject` text NOT NULL,
  `max_questions` int(11) NOT NULL default '0',
  `max_updates` int(11) unsigned NOT NULL default '0',
  `max_connections` int(11) unsigned NOT NULL default '0',
  PRIMARY KEY (`Host`,`User`)
) ENGINE=MyISAM DEFAULT CHARSET=latin1 COMMENT='Users and global privileges'
1 row in set (0.00 sec)

mysql>
```

These privileges can be granted and revoked by setting the proper column values in the user, host, or db tables, or (preferably) through the use of one or more of the following:

- GRANT CREATE VIEW

- GRANT SHOW CREATE VIEW

- REVOKE CREATE VIEW

- REVOKE SHOW CREATE VIEW

A full discussion of these is beyond the scope of this chapter; however, if you're familiar at all with the MySQL privilege system, you should not have a great deal of trouble figuring out how these commands ought to be used.

Other Improvements in MySQL 5.0

There are some additional new features in MySQL 5.0 that you may find useful. These are detailed in the next few subsections.

New SELECT INTO Syntax

We've already seen how this can be used with cursors in a stored procedure.
You can also use it to assign values to user variables in a regular SELECT query,
e.g., SELECT name INTO @prodname FROM products WHERE prodid = 327;. Note that
the SELECT must return a single row for this to work. We show an example here:

```
Command Prompt - mysql -h megalon -u root -p                        _ □ ×

mysql> SELECT name INTO @pname FROM products WHERE id = 2;
Query OK, 1 row affected (0.01 sec)

mysql> SELECT @pname;
+----------------------+
| @pname               |
+----------------------+
| Ants Ants Revolution |
+----------------------+
1 row in set (0.01 sec)

mysql> SELECT name, price INTO @pname, @pprice
    -> FROM products WHERE id = 8;
Query OK, 1 row affected (0.00 sec)

mysql> SELECT @pname, @pprice;
+----------------------------+---------+
| @pname                     | @pprice |
+----------------------------+---------+
| INTERCAL Home Study Course | 39.95   |
+----------------------------+---------+
1 row in set (0.00 sec)

mysql> SELECT name INTO @pname FROM products;
ERROR 1172 (42000): Result consisted of more than one row
mysql>
```

New Timestamp Functions

The TIMESTAMPADD() and TIMESTAMPDIFF() functions are introduced in MySQL 5.0.0.
Here are the definitions for each:

TIMESTAMPADD(*interval, expr, datetime*)
TIMESTAMPDIFF(*interval, datetime1, datetime2*)

TIMESTAMPADD() adds *expr interval* intervals to *datetime* and returns the
result, where *expr* is an integer value. TIMESTAMPDIFF() returns the integer difference between *datetime1* and *datetime2* in terms of the unit supplied as *interval*.

In both cases, the *interval* argument may be any one of the values
FRAC_SECOND, SECOND, MINUTE, HOUR, DAY, WEEK, MONTH, QUARTER, or YEAR, and any of
these may optionally be prefixed with SQL_TSI_. The *datetime* expressions may
be any valid DATE or DATETIME values.

A few examples, as shown here, may help to make clear how these functions
are used:

```
Command Prompt - mysql -h megalon -u root -p                        _ |□| x|
mysql> SELECT TIMESTAMPADD(HOUR, 4, '2004-09-01 10:30:30');
+-------------------------------------------------+
| TIMESTAMPADD(HOUR, 4, '2004-09-01 10:30:30') |
+-------------------------------------------------+
| 2004-09-01 14:30:30                          |
+-------------------------------------------------+
1 row in set (0.00 sec)
mysql> SELECT TIMESTAMPADD(DAY, 16, '2004-09-01');
+--------------------------------------+
| TIMESTAMPADD(DAY, 16, '2004-09-01') |
+--------------------------------------+
| 2004-09-17                         |
+--------------------------------------+
1 row in set (0.01 sec)
mysql> SELECT TIMESTAMPADD(MINUTE, 45, NOW());
+----------------------------------+
| TIMESTAMPADD(MINUTE, 45, NOW()) |
+----------------------------------+
| 2004-08-29 15:07:39            |
+----------------------------------+
1 row in set (0.00 sec)
mysql> SELECT TIMESTAMPADD(HOUR, -4, '2004-09-01 10:30:30');
+--------------------------------------------------+
| TIMESTAMPADD(HOUR, -4, '2004-09-01 10:30:30') |
+--------------------------------------------------+
| 2004-09-01 06:30:30                           |
+--------------------------------------------------+
1 row in set (0.01 sec)
mysql> SELECT TIMESTAMPDIFF(HOUR, NOW(), '2004-09-01 12:00:00');
+------------------------------------------------------+
| TIMESTAMPDIFF(HOUR, NOW(), '2004-09-01 12:00:00') |
+------------------------------------------------------+
|                                                 69 |
+------------------------------------------------------+
1 row in set (0.01 sec)
mysql> SELECT TIMESTAMPDIFF(DAY, '2005-01-01', '2004-09-01');
+--------------------------------------------------+
| TIMESTAMPDIFF(DAY, '2005-01-01', '2004-09-01') |
+--------------------------------------------------+
|                                           -122 |
+--------------------------------------------------+
1 row in set (0.01 sec)
mysql>
```

Notice that negative values are possible both for the value of *expr* input to the TIMESTAMPADD() function as well as for the result returned by TIMESTAMPDIFF().

Change in User Variable Behavior

Beginning in MySQL 5.0.0, user variable names are case insensitive. This means that @myvar, @MyVar, and @MYVAR will all be regarded as the same variable, as shown here (using MySQL 5.0.1-alpha):

```
Command Prompt - mysql -h megalon -u root -p                        _ |□| x|
mysql> SET @myvar = 25;
Query OK, 0 rows affected (0.00 sec)

mysql> SET @MyVar = @myvar + 10;
Query OK, 0 rows affected (0.01 sec)

mysql> SET @MYVAR = @MyVar - 5;
Query OK, 0 rows affected (0.00 sec)

mysql> SELECT @myvar;
+--------+
| @myvar |
+--------+
| 30   |
+--------+
1 row in set (0.00 sec)

mysql>
```

If you've been relying on case sensitivity in user variables for any of your MySQL-related work, we recommend highly that you abandon this practice immediately.

New Values for DATE_ADD() and DATE_SUB() Functions

Two new values, WEEK and QUARTER, have been added for use with the DATE_ADD() and DATE_SUB() functions in MySQL 5.0. You can see how these are used and what sorts of results you can expect from them here:

```
Command Prompt - mysql -h megalon -u root -p                           _ □ x

mysql> SELECT DATE_ADD('2004-09-01', INTERVAL 1 WEEK);
+------------------------------------------+
| DATE_ADD('2004-09-01', INTERVAL 1 WEEK)  |
+------------------------------------------+
| 2004-09-08                               |
+------------------------------------------+
1 row in set (0.00 sec)
mysql> SELECT DATE_ADD('2004-09-01', INTERVAL 1 QUARTER);
+---------------------------------------------+
| DATE_ADD('2004-09-01', INTERVAL 1 QUARTER)  |
+---------------------------------------------+
| 2004-12-01                                  |
+---------------------------------------------+
1 row in set (0.00 sec)
mysql> SELECT DATE_SUB('2004-09-01', INTERVAL 1 WEEK);
+------------------------------------------+
| DATE_SUB('2004-09-01', INTERVAL 1 WEEK)  |
+------------------------------------------+
| 2004-08-25                               |
+------------------------------------------+
1 row in set (0.00 sec)
mysql> SELECT DATE_SUB('2004-09-01', INTERVAL 1 QUARTER);
+---------------------------------------------+
| DATE_SUB('2004-09-01', INTERVAL 1 QUARTER)  |
+---------------------------------------------+
| 2004-06-01                                  |
+---------------------------------------------+
1 row in set (0.00 sec)
mysql>
```

Change in the VARCHAR Type

The VARCHAR type is expected to be altered so that it will be possible to store values with more than 255 characters. That hasn't happened yet as of MySQL 5.0.1—if you attempt to define a VARCHAR column with a size of greater than 255 characters, MySQL will simply convert the column to the TEXT datatype. (See Chapter 2 of this book for a discussion of how MySQL "silently" changes column types.) However, we look for a change to take place by the time that MySQL 5.0 appears in a production release.

MySQL 5.1

Looking even further ahead, we expect continued improvements in MySQL 5.1, with the possible addition of another major feature that so far hasn't been implemented yet. This is the implementation of *triggers*. Triggers are almost certain to make an appearance in MySQL 5.1.

We'll give you a conceptual overview of triggers in the following section, and discuss what form we think they're likely to take when they're actually implemented. While it's true that no one can tell for sure what may happen in the future, we do know that MySQL AB say they intend to implement these according to recognized standards, so what we will do is to show you what ANSI SQL says that triggers should be like, and make some observations on how they're implemented in other database management systems.

Triggers

A trigger is a form of stored procedure that executes automatically when a specified event takes place—that is, when an SQL statement modifies data. Triggers are bound to specific types of statements (UPDATE, INSERT, or DELETE) acting on specific tables in much the same way that event handlers or event listeners are bound to particular events occurring on particular interface elements in GUI programming. For instance, a trigger might be associated with an INSERT statement acting on the **products** table which we've been using in our examples, or with an UPDATE statement that affects only the **price** column of that table.

In addition, a trigger is declared in such a way that it acts either before or after the statement to which it's bound takes effect. If the trigger acts before the data-modification statement does, then it cannot "see" any changes caused by that statement; it only "knows" that the statement will affect a given table in a certain manner but not the specifics of that action. A trigger that acts after the triggering statement *does* see any changes caused by the statement and can act upon them.

Some databases (including both SQL Server and Oracle) also support triggers that act in place of the triggering statement using INSTEAD OF rather than BEFORE or AFTER for this purpose. At this time, MySQL is not expected to support this non-standard extension. However, as it certainly supports other non-ANSI additions to SQL, it may be that demand for this feature will be sufficient to prompt its addition in a future release. (As always, don't count on this happening, but don't rule it out, either; and *do* watch for further developments in this area.)

It's also important to understand that triggers operate at the statement level by default. In other words, a trigger normally executes once when a statement of the proper type acts on the proper table, even if that statement affects 3,000 rows. However, the standard does allow for row-level triggers as well. If MySQL supports this in its trigger implementation, then it will be possible for a trigger to execute as many times as there are rows affected by the data-modification statement.

Syntax

Triggers are created using the CREATE TRIGGER command, which in standard SQL has the following syntax:

```
CREATE TRIGGER trigger
{BEFORE | AFTER} {[DELETE] | [INSERT] | [UPDATE] [OF columns]} ON table
[REFERENCING { OLD [ROW] [AS] oldname} | NEW [ROW] [AS] newname }]
FOR EACH {ROW | STATEMENT}
[WHEN conditions]
statement-block
```

Here, trigger is the name of the trigger, and we assume that you'll be able to use any valid MySQL identifier, just as you can now for tables, stored procedures, and so on. The BEFORE or AFTER keyword tells MySQL whether the trigger will fire before or after the operation that modifies data has taken place, and the next clause determines what sort of operation will fire the trigger. Note that it is possible to define multiple operations for a single trigger. For instance, a trigger could be set to fire whenever a query either updates current records or inserts data into a given table, but ignore operations that delete records from that table. It may be possible in MySQL to define triggers on individual table columns as well, but it's not certain at this time whether or not this will be supported, and if so, when.

The FOR EACH clause determines whether the trigger will act at the statement level or the row level, as discussed previously. The WHEN clause may be used to test one or more conditions as part of determining whether or not the trigger should fire. Using the REFERENCING clause, you can assign aliases to the "before" and "after" versions of the table (and columns) with respect to any changes wrought by the data modification statement to which the trigger is bound.

Finally, at the end of this definition comes a block of stored procedure code that is to be executed in the event that the trigger is fired. Here's a brief example of what you might expect to see in the way of a trigger when triggers become available in MySQL. Bear in mind that this must be regarded for now as pseudocode and that the actual triggers implementation may require something slightly different than what you see here:

```
CREATE TRIGGER price_increase
AFTER UPDATE ON products
REFERENCING OLD TABLE AS oldproduct NEW TABLE AS newproduct
WHEN newproduct.price > oldproduct.price
BEGIN
   INSERT INTO price_increases (id, change_date, prodid, oldprice, newprice)
   VALUES ('', NOW(), oldproduct.id, oldproduct.price, newproduct.price);
END
```

This trigger (named **price_increase**) is fired whenever the price of an existing product is increased. When this happens, it inserts the date or date/time when the increase took place, the former price, and the new, higher price into a table named **price_increases**.

The stored procedure code in a trigger should work just like that found in any other stored procedure. We expect that you'll be able to use branching, loops, data definition statements (such as CREATE TABLE and ALTER TABLE), reference other stored procedures and stored functions, and so on.

NOTE   *PostgreSQL doesn't actually support procedural code within a trigger; instead, you must execute a stored procedure that's defined elsewhere. It's conceivable that MySQL could go this route as well, although what information we have available suggests that you'll be able to write a procedure as part of a MySQL trigger when triggers become available, since this capability is part of the SQL standard.*

To delete a trigger once it's no longer needed, the SQL standard provides for a DROP TRIGGER command, whose syntax is simply

```
DROP TRIGGER trigger;
```

where *trigger* is simply the name of the trigger that you wish to drop.

NOTE   *Oracle and Microsoft's SQL Server both support an ALTER TRIGGER command that can be used for changing existing triggers. This command is not currently part of the SQL standard, and PostgreSQL supports triggers quite happily without it. It may not be implemented in MySQL, at least initially, although if there's enough demand for it, it could conceivably be added for compatibility reasons, just as MySQL 5.0.1 supports ALTER VIEW.*

Benefits

Triggers can be used for number of purposes, all of which contribute at least indirectly to making database operations more efficient. These include

- **Auditing and logging**: As shown in the **price_increase** example, we can use a trigger to track certain types of changes in a database by copying or moving data from the table upon which the trigger was set to other tables. It's also conceivable that you could use SELECT INTO OUTFILE or SELECT INTO DUMPFILE in order to create files in delimited formats that are compatible with other applications.

- **Preserving data integrity**: Although it's preferable to use datatypes and foreign key constraints to keep users and applications from inserting invalid data or updating it to "bad" values, there are times when this isn't easy to accomplish. For example, suppose you don't want any products to be listed in the **products** table if their prices exceed one hundred dollars. You might use a trigger to "catch" these before they're inserted and cause them to be inserted into an **expensive_products** table instead.

- **Addressing security concerns**: Triggers can be used to facilitate the segregation of sensitive data into tables or databases for which access can be restricted. Recalling one of the example scenarios we outlined in the "Taking Derived Tables to the Next Level—Views" section earlier in the chapter: Suppose you have an application that obtains membership data for a corporate organization, and you'd like to make some data such as name and e-mail address available to developers working on a public "address book" interface where employees can look up contact information for co-workers. However, you don't want the address book to display private data such as Social Security or taxpayer numbers. To keep this from happening, even by accident, you can use a trigger for INSERT and UPDATE operations on a restricted master **employees** table that copies "public" data such as name, e-mail address, and company telephone extension into an **employees_public** table, and allow the address book developers access to this table only. While we can accomplish the same task using a view, it's good to have an additional choice in implementation, especially in a highly complex system such as the personnel database for a large corporation.

Other Expected Improvements

There are numerous other fixes, enhancements, and additions planned for future versions of MySQL. In this section, we'll take a brief look at some of these, particularly those that are of interest with regard to optimizing database schemas and queries or speeding up general performance.

Full (Outer) Joins

Full joins may be supported in MySQL 5.0 or 5.1. Full joins, which return a NULL for any column in one table that isn't matched in the other, are discussed in Chapter 5.

User Variables

User variables in MySQL 5.0 have already been changed in that the names are no longer case sensitive. Prior to this, @MYVAR and @myvar were treated as separate variables; beginning with version 5.0, they'll be regarded as the same variable.

Another planned change is to allow user variables to be updated in UPDATE statements. For example, if this is done, the following would be possible:

```
UPDATE mytable SET @myvar := col1 + col2;
```

Currently, this can be done only in a SELECT query. It's also likely that user variables will eventually be usable in statements having GROUP BY clauses, like so:

```
SELECT id, @count := COUNT(*) FROM products GROUP BY category_id;
```

SET Functions

Two new functions for working with SET columns are planned. These are ADD_TO_SET() and REMOVE_FROM_SET(). Suppose that we have a **users** table containing a SET column defined as

```
language SET('English,German,Spanish')
```

Were this function to be added, it would then be possible to update the column definition with something like this:

```
ALTER TABLE users
MODIFY language ADD_TO_SET('Portuguese', language);
```

and this:

```
ALTER TABLE users
MODIFY language REMOVE_FROM_SET('German', language);
```

without the need to reiterate all the elements in the set.

Group Functions

The SQL standard provides for three functions that allow you to find out very quickly whether or not any one, some, or all of a set of values is true:

- ANY(): This function returns **TRUE** if one and only one value in the set is true; if no values in the set are true or if more than one value is true, then the function returns **FALSE**.

- SOME(): This function returns **TRUE** if at least one value in a set of values is true.

- EVERY(): This function returns **TRUE** if and only if all values in a set are true.

Here are some examples, noting that the query SELECT price > 100 FROM products; will return a set of 1s and 0s, that is, **TRUE** and **FALSE** values:

```
#  If this query returns 1 (TRUE) then we know only one product has a price
#  greater than 100.00:
SELECT ANY(SELECT (price > 100) FROM products);
#  If there are some products (possibly all of them, but at least one of
#  them) having a price greater than 100.00, then this query will return 1
# (TRUE), otherwise it will return 0 (FALSE):
SELECT SOME(SELECT price > 100 FROM products);
#  If *all* products in the table have prices greater than 100.00, then this
#  query will return 1 (TRUE):
SELECT ALL(SELECT price > 100 FROM products);
```

According to the SQL standard, these functions should work only with sets of Boolean values; however, this could work in MySQL with other types of sets as well, since MySQL interprets 0 as **FALSE** and any other number or string value as **TRUE**.

Summary

We've looked in this chapter at several key new features that are becoming available or are very likely to be over the next few versions of MySQL. All of these features will add significant functionality to MySQL, increasing its power and flexibility in different ways. It seems logical to approach future attractions in a version-by-version fashion, so we started with subqueries and other features implemented in MySQL 4.1, which is almost certain to be available in a production release before the end of 2004. Subqueries, or queries within queries, can often be used to make queries shorter, simpler, and easier to read. In some cases they can even allow us to do in a single SELECT what would otherwise require multiple queries to accomplish without them.

We'd like to remind you at this point that we covered the other major new advance in MySQL 4.1—a new client API—in Chapter 7. These new programming APIs include prepared statements and multiple statements and will make MySQL applications programming much more flexible and efficient.

We also looked at the ability to assign table indexes to separate caches for purposes of fine-tuning key caching, which (beginning in MySQL 4.1.1) can be used to make indexes more efficient.

MySQL 5.0 will provide an implementation of another key SQL concept: that of what are sometimes known as *SQL control statements*. This is another way of expressing the idea of packaging collections of SQL statements so that they can be reused. Databases that do this implement what are known as stored procedures and stored functions, and both of these were already present in the first pre-release version of MySQL 5 (version 5.0.0-alpha) that became available at the end of 2003. While it will likely be sometime in 2005 or 2006 before these are included in a production release, you can download the pre-release from http://dev.mysql.com now, test out the examples we included, and try your hand at writing your own. We also looked at cursors, which provide a way to point at a particular row within a result set and work with its contents.

Beginning with version 5.0.1, MySQL also implements views, which provide a means of defining what are sometimes known as virtual tables, based on queries of existing tables (and sometimes even of other views). Views are extremely powerful, not only because they can provide simplified real-time access to normalized data that would other wise require complicated joins, but also due to the fact that in many cases they can also be used to update the tables on which they're based. In addition, views can help us ensure that read and update access to table data is properly secured.

Looking further ahead, it seems likely that MySQL 5.1 will implement another key SQL feature—triggers. These provide a way to call stored procedures automatically in response to changes made in tables or views. For example, if a query will delete a record from a table, you can (or will be able to) use a trigger to copy data from that record to another table before it's actually deleted.

We saw how stored procedures and views (along with triggers when they're implemented) can make life easier for database designers, developers, and users and can help enhance data security as well. So far as MySQL 5.0 and 5.1 are concerned, we've only scratched the surface here. Complete coverage of stored procedures and views each could easily take up entire chapters—and in future books about MySQL, they very likely will. And while we discussed some other expected future improvements, there will doubtless be new additions that we've either not had space to cover here or haven't been able to foresee. So, as you use MySQL and upgrade to new versions, watch the MySQL web site, and check the documentation for news about new features and changes in existing ones.

Index

Symbols